HANDBOOK OF
English Usage

THE MACMILLAN COMPANY
NEW YORK · BOSTON · CHICAGO
DALLAS · ATLANTA · SAN FRANCISCO

MACMILLAN AND CO., LIMITED
LONDON · BOMBAY · CALCUTTA
MADRAS · MELBOURNE

THE MACMILLAN COMPANY
OF CANADA, LIMITED
TORONTO

HANDBOOK OF
English Usage

HENRY SEIDEL CANBY
JOHN BAKER OPDYCKE

The Macmillan Company
NEW YORK - 1943

PREWORD

This book is for the use of all who need help in speaking and writing, especially in writing. No one should write unless he has something to say. Everyone knows, when he writes, that he should express himself accurately and clearly; everyone hopes that what he has written will be his own expression—his own words composed in his own manner, not a stereotype from a copybook. We all need command of our language; we all hope for style.

Your textbooks in English composition present instruction and exercises in the command of the resources of the language. In this manual the mechanics of language, without a mastery of which you cannot command it, are carefully summarized and arranged for convenient reference. Use this book as you use a dictionary. Much of it is elementary. Only occasionally does it go into technicalities beyond the concern of the everyday writer. Relatively simple as the English language is in its structure and in its modifications, no high-school student, no college student, no professional writer can be sure of saying what he means as he means it, and sure of making it meaningful to others, without frequent reference to the rules for written and spoken English. Keep this book. You will need it all your writing life. You will speak better for having it close at hand for timely help.

But do not believe for a minute that grammar, punctuation, and all the other tools are useful only in attaining mechanical perfection. Your mind is not a machine. When you set to work upon even so ordinary a task as writing a business letter, you are immediately aware of needs other than accuracy. You are communicating with human beings who have emotions, prejudices, hopes, and objectives like your own. In conversation with a man or a woman whose personality or whose thought challenges, you feel something rising within you to meet that challenge. It is your own personality and the activity of your own mind—your own way of feeling and thinking. The problem is to find language flexible enough to move with your feelings and exact enough to present your thoughts clearly and effectively. Such language helps thinking. To be adequate, it must obey its own laws, the laws of the language you are using, whether it be French, Latin, or English. Unless you know those laws, you will fail in communication.

In literature this is the problem of style. Great writers are great because their language flows like molten metal into an intricate mold. There are no impurities in the metal to clog the flowing and no imperfections in the mold to mar the pattern. The result is a writer alive in his writing. The style is the man.

It must be realized that every writer, no matter how unliterary, no matter how little likely to compose stories or poems or essays, meets the problem of style. Style for you, when you are writing letters or reports or anything else, is essentially the complete and accurate expression of yourself. Without language, you cannot express yourself; without command of language, you cannot make it express your thought; without mastery of the mechanics of language, you cannot command it—you cannot achieve your style.

Hence, this manual is not merely a collection of rules to be learned and exercises to be done. It is that, of course; but beyond this prosaic use is its real purpose, and this is to help you acquire a style which is your own, which really communicates, which makes your speech and your writing as much a part of the essential you as the hand with which you write. Grammar, punctuation, and composition are techniques, but their real value lies in their service to you in helping you to express yourself accurately, clearly, characteristically, as an educated man or woman should and must do.

The authors acknowledge their indebtedness to Miss Margaret Gillum and to Miss Olive I. Carter for their valuable contributions and suggestions.

CONTENTS

CONTENTS

CONTENTS

HANDBOOK OF
English Usage

WORDS AND THE DICTIONARY

1. Diction means the choice of words for the intelligible expression of thought. It means also the art and manner of expression, particularly as these are shown in the selection of words.

2. Phraseology denotes the grouping and arrangement of words grammatically in accordance with the laws and customs of language.

3. Style implies the coloring of expression characteristic of a writer or a speaker; the style is the man indeed. Both diction and phraseology are essentially weighed in estimates of style, but they are relatively objective, while style is subjective. You may be able to copy a person's diction and phraseology, but you cannot really copy his style.

4. Usage means the mode and practice of employing words in speaking and writing. *Standard, reputable,* or *literary usage* is that employed, and therefore sanctioned, by the best speakers and writers—the diction and phraseology that are customary in the literature of the day. *Colloquial usage* is that of educated persons in general conversation. It varies with the different English-speaking countries and with different sections of the same country. Expressions characteristic of a section are called *localisms. Idiomatic usage* is that peculiar to a people or to a district. It is akin to *dialect. Vulgar usage* is that employed by uneducated persons who are little touched by literary models. It includes slang and other undesirable modes of expression.

Standard usage is accepted and understood wherever a language is used; vulgar usage is limited to the country or section of a country where it prevails; some colloquial English expressions will be understood in Australia but not in the United States, and vice versa. This means that slang and localism are narrowest in the field of usage, that standard usage is widest, that colloquialism is somewhere between—closer to standard usage than to slang and localism.

THE DICTIONARY

5. The **dictionary** records usage; it does not establish it. You may safely be guided by good dictionaries in regard to the spellings, the meanings, and the uses of words. The authorities may differ, but they will be right nevertheless, for their records simply reflect differences in usage. The leading dictionaries employ different methods in labeling words. Their signs and symbols, which are clearly explained in their introductions, must therefore be studied and understood. Adopt one dictionary as your regular guide and acquaint yourself with the unabridged edition, if for no reason other than to see what a tremendous undertaking it is to record the more than a half million words that constitute the English language. Do not lean on the dictionary exclusively, however. Your first authority should be the language of reputable speakers and writers who will sometimes use pronunciations and meanings not yet recorded in the dictionary. But you may be sure that they soon will be. However, you must consult the dictionary for authority up to the time of its last printing. In the smaller editions of the dictionaries, revisions and additions are made quite frequently.

Here is a list of the services that the dictionary renders for your immediate use. It gives:

    I. Meaning
       1. All uses of a word

   II. Spelling
      1. Syllabication
      2. Compounds—hyphened, solid, separate words
      3. Simplified and conservative forms

  III. Pronunciation
      1. Accents
      2. Sounds

  IV. Derivation

   V. Combinations

VI. Usage
  1. Colloquial
  2. Slang
  3. Vulgarism
  4. Idiom
  5. Dialect
  6. Department (**nautical, military, scientific, and all other special fields**)

VII. Synonyms

VIII. Antonyms

IX. Parts of speech
  1. Plurals
  2. Parts of verbs
  3. Degrees of comparison of adjectives

In addition to all this, even in abridged editions, dictionaries give the names of important persons, events, documents, and places; foreign phrases; abbreviations; spelling and punctuation rules; rhyme vocabulary; tables of weights and measures; signs and symbols used in various fields of activity; rules for preparing copy for the press; and still other information. In the study of the different classifications of diction and usage that follow, it will be necessary for you to make the dictionary your constant companion.

Use right words—

6. A specific word is an exact, precise, or definite word. It is the opposite of a **generic,** or general, word. *Animal* is generic; *dog,* specific; *terrier* and *fox terrier* are still more specific. *Building* is generic; *mansion, house, cottage, hut,* and *hovel* are specific in diminishing degrees. *Tempt* is generic; *allure, attract, bewitch, captivate, charm, decoy, entice, fascinate, lure* are specific equivalents. Specific words are, as a rule, clear, unhackneyed, and emphatic, and in all forms of expression are to be preferred to vague, abstract, or general terms. But generic words, used in relation to specific ones, are important; they correspond to the main divisions in an outline, for instance, as specific words do to the elaborating points. Generic words help to get under way in any form of composition; specific words carry on to the desired end.

EXERCISES

1. Every animal has its particular method of attack. Indicate what it is by supplying the specific verb after each of the following:

1. The bee ? .	6. The elephant ? :
2. The bird ? .	7. The goat ? .
3. The bull ? .	8. The horse ? .
4. The cat ? .	9. The lion ? .
5. The dog ? :	10. The snake ? .

2. Substitute specific terms for generic in the following:

1. The objects on sale were a confused mass.
2. He cut it off quickly with a sharp utensil.
3. The view from the highest point is in all respects phenomenal.
4. The naturalist discovered a plant under the tree.
5. Our host supplied us with many kinds of entertainment.
6. Our detective became mistrustful when he saw the lights.
7. He looked very tired as he entered the room with her.
8. Space was so limited that there was no room for anything else.
9. The moon was out; the girl was there; but where was my tongue?
10. The birds sang in the morning and the sun shone brightly.
11. They were reposing on the most comfortable pieces of furniture.
12. As he strolled away from the place he looked unhappy and sad.
13. Her beauty was an eternal joy, and her behavior was marvelous.
14. The boys had a wonderful time and expressed their pleasure aloud.
15. They thought the many amazing features of the place were very nice.

7. A concrete word is a word that conveys a sense or perception picture to the mind; it denotes materials and things rather than actions, conditions, or qualities. *Rose, sugar, water* are concrete words. It is the opposite of an **abstract word,** which is one that names an idea, condition, characteristic, quality, and the like, such as *motion, sweetness, beauty.* Concrete words are more direct than abstract words because they are more pictorial. Visions, theories, philosophies—all kinds of *isms*—are appropriately expressed by abstract terms; actualities, by concrete terms.

Sometimes the figurative use of a concrete word makes it

4

abstract. If you say *The treasure has been found in a crevice under the rock, treasure* is concrete. If you say *As a friend, Mary has been a treasure, treasure* is abstract. Both concrete and abstract words may be specific or generic; thus, *machine* is a concrete generic word; *mower* is a concrete specific word; and *virtue* is an abstract generic word; *honor,* an abstract specific word.

EXERCISES

1. Compose sentences using each of the following as concrete and as abstract:

avenue	fault	measure	reward
device	incentive	outlet	source
escape	jewel	price	trap

2. Classify the following as generic abstract or generic concrete. Then supply as many specific equivalents of each as you can:

book	cowardice	illness	tact
building	furniture	noise	vehicle
clothing	hope	probity	wrong

3. Classify the following as specific abstract or specific concrete. Then supply a generic word for each:

booby	cleanness	speed	tutor
brook	crop	submission	vigor
cheer	pencil	tenacity	visage

8. Connotation is the meaning suggested or implied by a word or expression over and above its actual meaning. The actual meaning is called **denotation.** The word *home,* for instance, *denotes* a place to live; it *connotes* refuge, comfort, love, congeniality, pleasant memories. It contains overtones and associations that expand it far beyond its literal meaning. Contrast the merely denotative *The man climbed through the barrier* with *The fugitive scrambled through the barbed-wire entanglements.* The latter sentence is associative and pictorial; the former is merely factual. Connotation gives color and vividness to expression. Use connotative or associative words as much as possible in your speaking and writing, but do not sacrifice accuracy. A man sells a *house;* he cannot sell a *home.*

EXERCISES

1. In the following, substitute words of richer connotation:

1. It was the building in which I lived.
2. Offspring comforts old age.
3. They saluted the banner.
4. Optimism constantly rises in the mind.
5. The battered car of an old model went up the hill.
6. The traveler staying in the desert suffers from lack of water.
7. Fondness leads to matrimony.
8. I recollect the pleased expression on my parent's face.
9. Back is the sailor, back from the ocean, and the hunter from the elevated country.
10. Give me freedom of action or give me decease.

2. Supply a denotative term for each of the italicized terms below and tell what is lost thereby:

1. He was *crestfallen* after the examination.
2. It did not take him long to *cow* the *mob*.
3. He sat *dispirited* and *sulking* in his tent.
4. The experience had been a *wet blanket* to his hopes.
5. *Rover* was nowhere more at *home* than in my *den*.
6. The *sister's* gift was a boon to the *ragamuffin*.
7. Sheer *pluck* and *derring-do* had *won the day* for him.
8. His *long face* and his constant *complaining* made him a *pest*.
9. He *struggled* up the *precipice* in *hair-raising jeopardy* of his life.
10. *Step by step* he *sneaked* up on his *victim*, Watson *lurking* behind the *drapes* all the time, ready to *draw*.

9. Euphony means pleasing sound; the effect of words formed **a**nd combined to please the ear. It makes for ease of utterance as well as for agreeableness of hearing. Harsh, hissing, or discordant sounds—*dg, jdg, sm, sn, st, tch, x, z*—used in succession make pronunciation difficult and listening somewhat unpleasant. Likewise, a succession of similar sounds—*probably exceedingly efficiently* and *congregational devotional song*—disturbs the listener because the series becomes monotonous rather than euphonious. Alliteration or rhyme or marked rhythm unexpectedly injected into prose similarly mars euphony, as the sudden change interrupts the natural pace. *Bill's car and mine are first in line* appearing suddenly in a conversation is too pat for genuine euphony. *Bill's car and mine stand in the first row* is preferable. Good speaking and good writing are euphonious, easy to utter, pleasant to hear. Harsh sounds are a part of our language, however, and are essential to good diction. Use them when you wish to convey harshness; do not inject them carelessly into an otherwise smoothly moving expression.

EXERCISE

Make the following more euphonious:

1. The snake sneaked from under the stone and hissed.
2. Near the rear of the bier stood the grenadier.
3. He hates spinach, especially when it is served with shrimps.
4. Cabbages and Brussels sprouts spread over the patch profusely.
5. Furiously he flew into the forefront of the fray to win the day.
6. The commission has conditioned permission upon his submission.
7. His pick struck a stick from which a flick flew into his face.
8. Seventy Sisters of Charity centered attention upon the situation.
9. Gradually gauging the gadget, he adjusted the gauge with genuine genius.
10. Digressing momentarily and interestingly, he spoke reprovingly of the increasingly endangering bickerings that are nationally and internationally disintegrating our thinking.

10. Synonyms are words having the same or nearly the same essential meaning, as *dry, arid; hide, pelt, skin.* There are no perfect synonyms, for no two words are identical in all meanings, uses, and connotations. There are, rather, degrees of closeness in meaning among synonyms. Moreover, two words may mean almost the same in one connection and something quite different in another connection. You speak, for instance, of an *arid waste* and a *dry throat,* but not of an *arid throat;* of an *elephant's hide* and a *sheep's pelt* and a *man's skin,* but not of a *man's pelt.*

The English language is rich in synonyms. The dictionary shows that for almost every noun, adjective, and verb there is at least one other word which is nearly identical in meaning. Yet failure to make the fine distinctions between two such words may lead to serious mistakes and misunderstandings. A study of synonyms will enable you to select and use words with precision.

EXERCISE

For the italicized word in each of the following, supply the correct or the more exact word:

1. That is an *item* in your make-up that I do not like.
2. The climate here is *healthy*, and I shall therefore *stop* longer.
3. I saw a *funny* picture in the *news sheet* today.
4. One important *factor* in that cake is *nice* icing.
5. He is *liable* to win the prize if he continues this *credible* work.
6. In the *matter* of your new dress, I think there should be *less* buttons.
7. Food is an important *thing* in maintaining a *wholesome* constitution.
8. He is under the *delusion* that I *resist* his *visitations* to my daughter.
9. He *presented* his address after the *spectators* had assembled and the doors had been *shut*.
10. My *experience* in visiting the *plant* was an important *part* of an *outing* *distinguished* for its many *unusual elements*.

11. Antonyms are words of opposite meaning, as *black, white; good, bad; right, wrong.* They offer an effective means of attaining emphasis by contrast or balance. In famous orations are found such emphatic antonyms as *half free and half slave; false freedom is license, true freedom is liberty.* In using antonyms it is important to select the best and most accurate opposites. Antonyms should be of the same part of speech and should belong to the same word classifications. *Foolish,* for instance, is a better antonym of *wise* than are *fatuous, fickle,* and *silly,* for these are specific, whereas *wise* and *foolish* are generic. To contrast *worthless* with *pure gold* is to balance a literal term against a figurative one, an adjective against a phrase.

Though often the opposite meaning can be expressed by adding a prefix or a suffix to a word, antonyms cannot always be constructed by using the same suffix or prefix. The prefix *in,* for example, is not always negative; *valuable* and *invaluable* are not antonyms. The prefix *un* is negative in *unworthy* but intensifying in *unloosen.* You say *impossible* in contrast with *possible,* not *unpossible* or *dispossible.* The antonym of the adjective *direct* is *indirect;* of the verb *direct, misdirect.* *Prejudiced* is an antonym of *disinterested,* but *uninteresting* is an antonym of *interesting.* The suffixes *ful* and *less* usually signify antonyms, as *faithful* and *faithless,* but *unfaithful* is also an antonym of *faithful.*

The ways of the language, then, are peculiar here as elsewhere, and the dictionary must be consulted freely. In the dictionary, definitions of generic adjectives, nouns, and verbs are followed by synonyms and antonyms, indicated respectively by *Syn.* and *Ant.* For example:

> *earnest*—**Syn.** grave, serious, sober, solemn; **Ant.** frivolous, insincere, playful, trifling.
> *vexation*—**Syn.** chagrin, mortification; **Ant.** appeasement, gratification, mollification, peace, satisfaction, serenity, tranquillity

EXERCISES

1. Supply the best antonyms for each of the following:

able	comedy	grief	lengthy
agreeable	courage	guilt	manageable
benediction	defeat	ignoble	maximum
blessing	discord	interchangeable	revelation
broad	dull	interest	sorrow
brusque	enemy	just	variation
card	failure	knowledge	wakeful

2. Rewrite each of the following sentences so that the contrasted ideas are uniformly expressed:

1. He is lazy, but he nevertheless works.
2. She thought the glass was transparent, but she could not see through it.
3. Their journey was not hazardous, so they made it in safety.
4. The riders mounted their steeds awkwardly, but they rode with grace.
5. They all thought him selfish, but his contribution proved him otherwise.
6. Everybody thought him guilty, but he was acquitted.
7. He is rated neither as poor nor as one with a great deal of money.
8. The clerk who was ill is now enjoying health again.
9. We thought he was eligible, but he was found not to be.
10. Always be polite to your elders rather than the contrary.

3. Supply the missing antonym in each of the following:

1. The army will either retreat or ? .
2. We shall proceed courageously or ? .

3. We had an easy lesson but a(n) ? teacher.
4. Sobriety is said to be for age, ? for youth.
5. Our discomforts are over at last, and we shall now have ? .
6. Those two elements are not consistent, but, rather, ? .
7. His cunning has done much for him, but he will soon decide that ? is better.
8. Deny it now if you will, you shall one day have to ? it.
9. Whether your fate be happiness or ? , always remain true rather than ? to your friends.

4. By the use of prefixes give the following opposite meanings:

1. It was an attractive sight.
2. The prisoner was identified.
3. The assets of the firm are liquid.
4. He is determined about the problem.
5. Mount your horse when the order is given.
6. He has sufficient funds for starting the journey.
7. Moral practices should be encouraged.
8. Never agree with a colleague unless you are certain.

5. For each italicized verb in the following list, select from the other verbs on the same line the one that is closest in meaning and the one that is most remote in meaning:

apply—ask, canvass, entreat, ignore, request, solicit, use
battle—combat, contend, contest, fight, struggle, submit, yield
bestow—confer, donate, give, grant, present, refrain, withhold
calculate—compute, count, estimate, guess, hazard, reckon, wager
camouflage—cloak, conceal, deceive, disguise, reveal, screen, show
capture—apprehend, arrest, catch, free, liberate, secure, seize
cater—deny, feed, furnish, neglect, provide, purvey, supply
chase—follow, hound, hunt, lead, precede, pursue, seek
close—conclude, end, finish, open, start, stop, terminate
collect—amass, congregate, dissipate, garner, gather, muster, scatter
destroy—annihilate, demolish, efface, kill, protect, raze, save
detach—attach, disconnect, join, loosen, separate, sever, unfasten
detest—abhor, abominate, despise, hate, like, loathe, respect
discount—abate, add, deduct, diminish, increase, lessen, reduce
displease—annoy, disturb, gratify, offend, please, repel, vex
distinguish—befuddle, characterize, confuse, differentiate, discern, judge, perceive
divide—cleave, connect, detach, part, separate, sunder, unify
doubt—believe, challenge, deny, distrust, question, suspect, trust
echo—imitate, repeat, reproduce, resound, reverberate, silence, still

educate—deceive, develop, edify, enlighten, instruct, misguide, train
effect—accomplish, achieve, cease, discharge, execute, fail, perform
effervesce—bead, bubble, fizz, foam, hiss, pacify, quiet
elect—ballot, call, choose, decide, discard, reject, select
end—begin, cease, close, commence, complete, die, discontinue
estimate—appraise, consider, measure, misjudge, reckon, vacillate, value
fascinate—captivate, charm, delight, enchant, estrange, intrigue, repel
fawn—cringe, crouch, defy, flatter, insult, toady, truckle
fetch—bring, carry, depart, get, go, obtain, take
fidget—fret, fuss, repose, rest, shake, squirm, worry
flash—darken, gleam, glisten, glitter, obscure, scintillate, sparkle
forgive—absolve, avenge, excuse, insult, pardon, release, remit
freshen—brighten, cheapen, quicken, refresh, renew, revive, wear out
gather—collect, cull, distribute, glean, pick, pluck, sow
glorify—belittle, distinguish, exalt, honor, inferiorize, praise, transform
growl—cheer, complain, exult, grumble, howl, lament, snarl
hail—accost, affront, call, cheer, greet, salute, snub
head—control, guide, manage, rule, subordinate, supervise, tail
heed—attend, ignore, note, notice, observe, overlook, regard
hint—conceal, indicate, insinuate, intimate, mislead, suggest, whisper
hound—bait, chase, disregard, harass, ignore, persecute, track
ignore—attend, disdain, heed, neglect, omit, overlook, slight
impair—damage, destroy, improve, injure, lessen, restore, weaken
incite—actuate, arouse, instigate, pacify, stir, subdue, urge
jeer—deride, eulogize, gibe, praise, ridicule, scoff, taunt
judge—decide, fluctuate, rule, sentence, try, umpire, waver
keep—hold, own, possess, preserve, relinquish, retain, yield
laugh—chuckle, cry, giggle, guffaw, roar, smile, weep
leave—arrive, come, depart, go, let, quit, withdraw
like—appreciate, disapprove, enjoy, fancy, love, prefer, scorn
litter—adjust, arrange, confuse, derange, disorder, jumble, scatter
loose—attach, bind, detach, free, liberate, release, unfasten
lurch—lean, level, roll, stagger, steady, sway, wobble
march—defile, file, journey, parade, stroll, walk, wander
mask—conceal, cover, disclose, disguise, hide, reveal, veil
mend—better, correct, deteriorate, improve, patch, repair, worsen
mingle—blend, combine, isolate, join, merge, mix, separate
mistake—blunder, err, miscalculate, right, slip, stray, understand
nerve—brace, embolden, imbue, intimidate, invigorate, strengthen, **terrify**
notice—heed, ignore, miss, observe, regard, remark, see
nurse—abuse, aid, attend, cherish, foster, harbor, hurt
object—abet, disapprove, oppose, protest, resent, resist, support
observe—blind, follow, notice, obey, omit, remark, say
obtain—acquire, attain, forfeit, gain, lose, procure, win

offend—anger, befriend, disgust, displease, gratify, pain, wound
pace—amble, journey, lag, retreat, step, tread, walk
pamper—annoy, coddle, favor, hinder, humor, indulge, spoil
pause—cease, continue, hesitate, linger, proceed, stop, wait
perceive—blind, comprehend, discern, feel, know, misunderstand, see
persist—continue, endure, give up, persevere, plod, remain, succumb
plan—design, devise, disarrange, disorganize, muddle, project, scheme
please—delight, disturb, divert, gratify, injure, pain, satisfy
polish—burnish, dull, furbish, gloss, shine, smooth, tarnish
profit—accrue, benefit, gain, improve, lose, make, suffer
prop—brace, loosen, stay, support, truss, uphold, weaken
punish—chasten, chastise, comfort, correct, discipline, hurt, reward
quiet—agitate, calm, distract, gentle, pacify, silence, still
raise—deepen, exalt, heave, heighten, hoist, lift, lower
rap—cuff, hit, knock, pet, punch, stroke, whack
reduce—abbreviate, abridge, enlarge, magnify, minimize, shorten, subtract
repair—damage, impair, mend, remedy, renew, replace, restore
sanction—approve, authorize, condemn, confirm, countenance, ratify, reject
scare—alarm, cow, encourage, frighten, hearten, intimidate, shock
shrink—blench, contract, expand, flinch, quail, recoil, unfold
spite—annoy, benefit, grudge, help, irritate, revolt, vex
squeeze—constrict, crown, crush, extend, hug, press, spread
support—bear, bolster, cheer, depress, discourage, encourage, strengthen
take—accept, carry, give, go, obtain, receive, refuse
teach—delude, guide, impart, inform, instruct, mislead, train
torment—harass, ingratiate, injure, plague, salve, torture, wound
trifle—dally, dawdle, fidget, idle, potter, sober, toil
unite—amalgamate, combine, connect, consolidate, incorporate, separate,
    sever
urge—animate, hinder, impel, incite, instigate, restrain, stimulate
vex—fret, harass, molest, solace, soothe, tantalize, tease
work—drudge, exert, labor, operate, play, relax, toil
worship—adore, blaspheme, glorify, idolize, profane, revere, venerate
wound—break, comfort, cut, heal, hurt, injure, sear
yearn—covet, crave, hanker, long, reject, spurn, wish
yield—bear, bring, concede, give, produce, resist, withhold
yoke—couple, divide, join, link, marry, separate, team
zone—consolidate, fraction, isolate, mark off, partition, segregate, unite

12. Homonyms are words that are alike in pronunciation
but different in meaning and often in spelling, as *bare* (nude),
bear (to carry), *bear* (animal); *read, reed; right, rite, write, wright.*
Inflection frequently develops homonyms, as *attendance, attend-*

ants; clause, claws; mince, mints; pause, paws; praise, prays; prince, prints. Pronounced as independent terms, homonyms cannot be told apart; only their use in context determines their meaning and spelling.

The following list contains some of the most common homonyms. Compose sentences in which the members of each group are correctly used. A homonym bee, similar to the spelling bee, may be conducted by having the members of a group compete in using all the given homonyms of a group in a single well-constructed sentence; thus, *All that I live by is with the awl.* As in Shakespeare's day, homonyms are still used as bases for puns.

HOMONYMS

ail, ale	but, butt
aisle, isle, I'll	buy, by, bye
all, awl	cannon, canon
altar, alter	cant, can't
arc, ark	capital, capitol
ascent, assent	cast, caste
ate, eight	caster, castor
auger, augur	ceiling, sealing
aught, ought	cellar, seller
aye, I	cent, scent, sent
bad, bade	cereal, serial
bail, bale	cession, session
bait, bate	chased, chaste
ball, bawl	choir, quire
baron, barren	chord, cord
beach, beech	cite, sight, site
beer, bier	climb, clime
bell, belle	coarse, corse, course
berth, birth	colonel, kernel
blew, blue	complement, compliment
boar, bore	creak, creek
board, bored	crews, cruise, cruse
borough, burrow	cue, queue
boy, buoy	currant, current
breach, breech	descent, dissent
bread, bred	dew, due
brewed, brood	discreet, discrete
bridal, bridle	doe, dough

HOMONYMS—*Continued*

done, dun	kill, kiln
dual, duel	knave, nave
dyeing, dying	knight, night
earn, urn	knot, not
exercise, exorcise	lain, lane
fain, fane, feign	leach, leech
faint, feint	leaf, lief
fate, fete	lean, lien
faun, fawn	lessen, lesson
feat, feet	loan, lone
fir, fur	made, maid
flair, flare	mail, male
flea, flee	main, mane
flew, flue	maize, maze
flour, flower	mantel, mantle
for, fore, four	marshal, martial
fort, forte	mean, mien
forth, fourth	metal, mettle
foul, fowl	might, mite
franc, frank	miner, minor
freeze, frieze	moan, mown
gait, gate	muscle, mussel
gamble, gambol	mustard, mustered
gilt, guilt	naught, nought
grate, great	nay, née, neigh
groan, grown	O, oh, owe
guessed, guest	oar, ore, o'er
hair, hare	ode, owed
hall, haul	one, won
hart, heart	pail, pale
hear, here	pain, pane
heard, herd	palate, palette, pallet
hide, hied	passed, past
hoard, horde	peace, piece
hoes, hose	peak, peek
hole, whole	peal, peel
holy, wholly	pearl, purl
idle, idol	pedal, peddle
indict, indite	peer, pier
its, it's	plain, plane
jam, jamb	pleas, please
key, quay	plum, plumb

HOMONYMS—*Continued*

pole, poll	soar, sore
pore, pour	stair, stare
pray, prey	stake, steak
pride, pried	steal, steel
profit, prophet	stile, style
quarts, quartz	straight, strait
rain, reign, rein	suite, sweet
rap, wrap	tail, tale
read, red	taper, tapir
real, reel	taught, taut
reek, wreak	tea, tee
rest, wrest	team, teem
ring, wring	tear, tier
roe, row	threw, through
role, roll	throe, throw
root, route	thyme, time
rote, wrote	tide, tied
rough, ruff	to, too, two
rye, wry	toe, tow
sac, sack	told, tolled
sail, sale	troop, troupe
sane, seine	vice, vise
scene, seen	wail, wale
seam, seem	waist, waste
sear, sere	waive, wave
serge, surge	ware, wear
sew, so, sow	way, weigh
shoe, shoo	weak, week
shone, shown	wheal, wheel
sign, sine	whose, who's
slay, sleigh	wood, would
sleight, slight	yoke, yolk
slew, slough, slue	your, you're

EXERCISES

1. For each of the following words there is a corresponding word spelled and pronounced the same but differing in meaning. Write sentences using each word in two senses:

beat	dear	hail	sole
bow	fair	lie	wait

2. For each of the following words there is a corresponding word spelled the same but pronounced differently and having a different meaning. Use each word in both senses. Explain the differences in pronunciation and use:

bass	minute	sow	wind
close	refuse	tear	wound

3. Give two or more homonyms for each of the following:

air	hew	raise	sight
bowl	knows	road	their
caret	meat	seas	vain
heal	pair	shear	veil

Avoid wrong words—

13. An **impropriety** is a word or an expression used in violation of its proper grammatical office. For example, a noun may be improperly used as a verb, as *I suspicioned (suspected) him;* a verb as a noun, as *We have an invite (invitation)*; an adjective as an adverb, as *She is real (really) sorry;* homonyms may be confused, as *They're (There) goes the train;* synonyms may be confused, as *I secured (attained) my goal.* The misuse of words can be avoided only by careful study of synonyms and homonyms, by constant use of the dictionary for both meaning and pronunciation, and by accurate understanding of the rules of grammar.

14. The words in the following list—**Dictional Demons**—are frequently confused with other words that sound like them, have almost the same meaning, or appear to be otherwise related. Study them carefully. Compose sentences to illustrate their correct use.

DICTIONAL DEMONS

ability means power to accomplish, as *He has the ability to build that bridge. Capacity* means power to receive or hold, as *He has the capacity to grow into the presidency.* The former pertains to skill in the exercise of physical or intellectual faculties; the latter, to power to take in knowledge as distinguished from power to express in doing. *Capacity* refers also to physical content, as *The capacity of the tank is one thousand gallons. Ability* is never used in this sense.

accept means to receive; *except*, as a verb, means to exclude. You *accept* a gift; you *except* a name from a list.

admittance is the act of entering or of allowing to enter; *admission* is the right of entrance. The ticket you buy gives you right of *admission;* the ticket-taker grants you *admittance* on your handing him your ticket.

advice is a noun meaning recommendation, instruction, intelligence; *advise* is a verb meaning to recommend or instruct.

affect is a verb (not a noun) meaning to influence, to pretend, to simulate, to tend toward; *effect*, as a verb, means to accomplish, to cause, to bring about, to achieve; as a noun, it means outcome, result. *Prices have been greatly affected by the war* and *He affects not to understand*, and *This device will effect the increased output desired* and *The effect of this new device upon output is already noticeable* illustrate correct usage.

aggravate means to make worse, with particular reference to the physical; *exasperate* means to vex or annoy or to heighten anger, with particular reference to mind or emotion. You *aggravate* a sore by rubbing it; you *exasperate* a person by persisting in doing something he doesn't like. (See *irritate*.)

allusion means indirect reference; *delusion*, false belief or other mental error; *illusion*, mistaken inference or misleading appearance for which one or more of the senses is responsible. You make an *allusion* to a passage in literature; an insane person may be under the *delusion* that he is Napoleon; you may have the *illusion* that the doorbell rang when the steampipes made a ringing sound. *Optical illusion* means deception through the eye; for instance, a small room looks large as result of the placement of large mirrors.

already, one word, is an adverb meaning previously, prior to some past, present, or future time; *all ready*, a two-word phrase, means prepared in every way, or everybody is wholly ready. *I have already spoken to you twice about this* and *We are all ready to go* illustrate correct usage.

alternative refers to two only; *choice*, to two or more. Say *She was given her alternative of the (two) itineraries* and *She has her choice of three different routes*.

altogether is an adverb meaning wholly; *all together* is a phrase meaning all in one place; as *We are altogether dissatisfied* and *We were sitting all together in the car*.

always (see *already* and *altogether*) and *all ways* are illustrated as follows: *She is always tired* and *She is satisfactory in all ways*.

among refers to more than two; *between* refers to two only; for example, *The quarrels among the five children were never very serious* and *The split between the two families appeared to be permanent*.

amount refers to a result brought about by accumulation; that is, aggregate bulk, quantity; *number* refers to countable persons and things; *quantity* refers preferably to bulk and aggregation, but it is correctly used also in reference to bulk that is measurable by units. Say *a certain amount of money* and *a number of bushels* and *a quantity of wheat.*

appraise means to set a price or value upon, to estimate the quality or worth of; *apprise* means to notify, to advise, to inform. *The paintings were appraised at $2500* and *He was immediately apprised of your departure* illustrate correct usage.

apt. See *likely.*

attend and *tend* mean to take care of, to look after. *Attend* is followed by *to; tend* is not followed by *to. I shall attend to that account* and *I shall tend the cashier's desk* illustrate correct usage.

balance denotes the difference between the two sides of any reckoning or account; *remainder* is a more general term used to denote any number or quantity left after something is taken away; *rest* is synonymous with *remainder* in the sense of what is left. Say *I have a satisfactory balance in the bank* and *The remainder of the goods will arrive tomorrow* and *The rest of us went to the party.*

beside is a preposition meaning by the side of; *besides* is both a preposition and an adverb meaning over and above, in addition to. *He sat beside me* and *Besides a trunk she had two suitcases* and *I have two besides* are correct.

between. See *among.*

born is the past participle of the verb *bear* meaning to bring forth, to give birth to. It is used only in the passive voice, as *She was born in Chicago. Borne* is the past participle of the verb *bear* meaning to carry, to support. It is used in both the active and the passive voice, as *She has borne her burdens patiently* and *Heavy burdens were borne by her.*

bring means to come with, that is, motion toward a speaker, as *Bring me that towel; fetch* means to go to, get, and bring, as *Please fetch me a towel from the bathroom; take* means to go with, that is, motion away from a speaker, as *Please take this towel to the bathroom. Carry* is a general, or covering, word used in all three senses.

can indicates power or ability; *may* indicates permission or authorization. Say *May I go out?* not *Can I go out?* The latter sentence would be correct only if there were a question about the physical ability to go out. Be careful to differentiate between *can but* and *cannot but. I can but give him food* means I *can only* give him food—that is all I can do for him. *I cannot but give him food* means I *cannot help* giving him food—his appeal is irresistible.

canvas is a noun meaning a strong, coarsely woven cloth much used for sails and tents; *canvass*, as a verb, means to examine, to inquire, to go about asking for votes, orders, pledges, and the like; as a noun, it means solicitation, inquiry, examination. *The agent canvassed the countryside in his canvas-covered car* illustrates correct usage.

censer is a noun meaning container for burning incense; *censor*, as a noun, means a judge or critic, as of public morals; as a verb, it means to

DICTIONAL DEMONS

14

judge or to put critical value on. *Censure*, as a noun, means blame, disapproval, reproof; as a verb, it means to blame, to condemn. *Censor* is an agent noun; *censure*, an abstract noun. *The censor prohibited the circulation of the book, but he did not censure the author* and *The public censored the novel by refusing to read it* illustrate correct usage.

character is what one is; *reputation* is what one is said or reputed to be. A man's character is reflected in his record; his reputation, in the estimate that others place upon his record.

common means belonging to two or more in joint actions and interests; *mutual* means interchangeable or reciprocal as between two. Say *The democracies are united in a common cause against totalitarianism* and *England and the United States have mutual advantages in standing together. Mutual* is sometimes deliberately used instead of *common* because the latter word may connote cheap or vulgar.

complement, as a noun, means addition, anything that completes; as a verb, it means to make complete, to supply lack in. *Compliment*, as a noun, means praise, congratulation; as a verb, it means to express admiration or show regard. *The objective complement follows the predicate and pertains to the object* and *Our meager stock has now been complemented* and *The teacher complimented him on his work* and *He accepted the compliment gracefully* are correct.

congenial means sympathetic, companionable, having the same tastes and characteristics as another; *genial* means cordial, cheerful, pleasant in manner. *Bill and Harry are congenial classmates* and *A lady with a genial manner entertained us at dinner* illustrate correct usage.

conscience is a noun meaning the inborn faculty that makes for morality; *conscious* is an adjective (the noun is *consciousness*) meaning aware, sensible, able to feel. Spell and pronounce these words correctly. *I am conscious that a great wrong has been done, and my conscience prompts me to correct it* illustrates correct usage.

consul is an official assigned to a foreign port or city to look after his country's business interests and to represent his countrymen when they need aid; *counsel* means advice, opinion, judgment; *council* is an assembly of persons, a meeting, a legislative or other body, a committee. *Consul* and *council* are nouns; *counsel* is both a noun and a verb. The first syllable of *consul* rhymes with *don;* the first syllable of *counsel* and *council*, with *down.*

contemptible means worthy or deserving of disdain or contempt; *contemptuous* means evincing disdain or disgust or contempt. *His behavior was contemptible and we were justified in being contemptuous of him* illustrates correct usage.

continual is an adjective meaning at frequent intervals; *continuous* is an adjective meaning without interruption. *He continually invites me to luncheon* and *We made a continuous run from Burlington to Buffalo. Continued* means taken up again or resumed, as *The continued story is in the latest issue.*

19

credible means worthy of belief or trust, altogether probable; *creditable* means meritorious, deserving of praise; *credulous* means too ready to believe or trust. A *credible* story is a believable story; a *creditable* act is a praiseworthy one; a *credulous* person believes too easily.

delusion. See *allusion*.

desert, as a noun accented on the first syllable, means a barren or forsaken waste, as in *Sahara Desert;* accented on the second syllable, it means anything that is deserved by way of merit or demerit, as in *Imprisonment was a just desert for his crime.* As a verb, *desert* means to forsake, to abandon, to go away. *Dessert* is a noun meaning a sweetmeat served at the end of a meal. *Billy will never desert the dining room until dessert has been served* is correct. The first form above is frequently used as an adjective also, as in *a desert land.*

device is a noun meaning contrivance, plan, scheme, pattern; *devise* is a verb meaning to contrive, to invent, to form ways and means of doing something. *He devised a gadget whereby much time could be saved, but his device did not meet with the favor of the company* illustrates correct usage.

discomfit is a verb meaning to defeat or conquer absolutely; *discomfort*, as a verb, means to pain, trouble, grieve, or dishearten; as a noun, it means uncomfortableness, dismay, disturbance. *We discomfited our opponents by our questions* and *The extreme cold discomforts them* and *The extreme cold caused great discomfort* are correct.

discover means to reveal or to find and bring to the knowledge of others; *invent* means to originate, to devise by ingenuity. Chemical elements and planets are *discovered;* a machine to perform some manufacturing operation is *invented.*

effect. See *affect*.

either. See *neither*.

emigration is the act of going *from* one country to settle in another; *immigration* is the act of coming *into* a country from another for the purpose of settling.

eminent means illustrious, distinguished, famous; *imminent* means threatening, impending. *The eminent statesman said that war is imminent* illustrates correct usage. *Immanent* means remaining within, is present in. This is chiefly a philosophic term, as in *God is immanent in the universe.*

evidence is anything brought forward, as in a court trial, to prove or disprove a claim; *proof* is an item of evidence that helps to prove or disprove a claim. There may be much evidence and very little actual proof. You may say *The evidence against the prisoner covers many pages, but not a single item is to be found in it in proof of his guilt.* Evidence is testimony; proof is arrived at by sifting evidence or testimony.

exasperate. See *aggravate; irritate*.

except. See *accept*.

exceptional means outstanding or unusual; *exceptionable* means objectionable or blamable. You speak of an able secretary as an *exceptional* one; of bad conduct as *exceptionable.*

farther is an adverb only, meaning at or to a greater distance in space or time, as *I have walked farther than you. Further* is an adverb meaning more or additional in degree, as *He said nothing further.* As a verb *further* means to help or promote.

fetch. See *bring.*

few refers to persons or objects that can be counted, as *I have few friends; less,* to amount, quantity, measure, or degree, as *I have less money than you.* Use the correct comparatives and superlatives of these words. They are compared as follows: *few, fewer, fewest; little, less, least.*

flaunt means to show off or make display of, as *The grand lady flaunts her diamonds; flout* means to mock or jeer or to treat contemptuously, as *The kidnaper flouted the authorities.*

flee, meaning to run away or to vanish, becomes *fled* in the past tense and in the past participle. *Flow,* meaning to move or circulate smoothly as a liquid does, is *flowed* in the past tense and in the past participle. *Fly,* to move in or pass through the air as with wings, is *flew* in the past tense and *flown* in the past participle. A fugitive *flees,* a river *flows,* a bird *flies.*

former. See *later.*

formerly is an adverb meaning in time past, heretofore; *formally* is an adverb meaning according to form, precisely, conventionally. *Austria was formerly an independent republic* and *Mr. Smith was formally introduced to the president of the company* illustrate correct usage.

guaranty is used preferably as a noun to mean safety, security, the act of making safe or secure; *guarantee* is used preferably as a verb meaning to secure against loss or damage, to promise the performance of. *He guarantees the heater for a year, and he has given me the guaranty in writing* is correct.

hanged means put to death by hanging; *hung* means suspended from above without support beneath. *They hanged the man at five this morning* and *I hung my hat on the proper hook* illustrate correct usage.

healthful means conducive to health, as *This climate is healthful. Healthy* means having or possessing health, as *This boy is healthy. Wholesome* refers to that which is good for one—drink, food, climate, environment, acquaintances—as, *Wholesome food, wholesome air, wholesome surroundings make the man. Health* is used in the sense of health-giving or health-restoring in such terms as *health resort, health recipe.*

honest means free from fraud, just, true; *honorable* means worthy of honor, noble, illustrious. If a man fails to be *honest,* he may be confronted by the law; if he fails to be *honorable,* he may suffer disgrace and the ill opinion of others but no retaliation by the law. An *honest* act is a just act; an *honorable* act is an act distinguished for its rightness or nobility.

human means pertaining to man or mankind, suitable to man, possessed by man; *humane* means forgiving, kindly, gracious, sympathetic; it also means polite, refined, elegant, as *The humane influences of music are easily provable.*

hygienic means pertaining to the science of the preservation and improvement of personal health. *Sanitary* means concerned with regulations and arrangements that maintain public health. *The daily bath is an important hygienic measure* and *The sanitary conditions of the city are excellent* illustrate correct usage.

illusion. See *allusion.*

import means significance, something implied, meaning, as of a word or a term; *importance* means consequence, weight, value, as in the public mind or esteem. *What is the import of that remark?* means What is the significance of that remark or what is behind that remark? *What importance is there in that sort of art?* means What value is there in that sort of art?

infer means to arrive at a conclusion, to conclude, to deduce; *imply* means to state indirectly, to insinuate, to hint. *I infer from what you say that you think me wrong* and *You imply that I am not acting fairly* are correct usages.

ingenious means clever, possessed of genius; *ingenuous* means frank, candid, naïve. *His solution of the puzzle was ingenious* and *The child's remarks were ingenuous* illustrate correct usage.

invent. See *discover.*

irritate means to excite to momentary anger or impatience. Irritation is intensified exasperation. You may be *irritated* at gossip; you may *exasperate* a hasty temper. (See *aggravate.*)

its, the possessive case of *it,* should never be written with an apostrophe. *It's* is the contraction of *it is,* the apostrophe showing the omission of *i.* *It's clear that the kitten likes its milk* is correct.

later and *latter* are the comparative forms of *late. Later* is used principally in time relationships, as *He came later than I* and *We shall visit you at some later time. Latter* generally refers to order or position and means the second of two, in contrast with *former,* which means the first of two. *Of the two I prefer the latter, but the former is less expensive* and *I shall see you the latter part of the week* are correct. Do not use *latter* in relation to more than two. The superlative forms of *late* are *latest,* meaning most recent, and *last,* meaning final. *The last thing I read yesterday was the latest number of the magazine* is correct.

lay, as a verb, is *laid* in the past tense and in the past participle. It means to place or to put down; it is transitive and thus takes an object. *He laid the book on the table* and *He has laid the book on the table* are correct. *Lie,* as a verb meaning to recline, is *lay* in the past tense and *lain* in the past participle. It is intransitive and does not take an object. *He lay on the couch this morning for two hours* and *He has lain on the couch all evening* are correct. *Lie*, to tell a falsehood, is *lied* in the past tense and in the past participle.

learn means to find out, to acquire knowledge, to study; *teach* means to impart knowledge, to instruct, to make known, to communicate.

leave means to depart or to abandon; *let* means to permit. *You may leave the baby here* and *Please let me take him* illustrate correct usage. If you *leave* someone alone, he is in solitude; if you *let* him alone, you do not interfere with him. *Leave me now, for I must study* and *Let me be* illustrate correct usage.

led is the past tense and the past participle of the verb *lead* (pronounced to rhyme with *deed*). *Lead*, rhyming with *deed*, is also a noun meaning advance position or first. *Lead*, rhyming with *head*, is the name of a metal; it is also a printing term meaning to separate lines of type with pieces of metal called *leads* (rhyming with *heads*).

lend is a verb; *loan* is a noun, preferably not a verb. *Please lend me your pen* and *I should like to make a loan of you* illustrate correct usage. Do not say *Please loan me your pen*. *Loan* is often used as a verb in connection with finance, but such usage is not yet authoritatively sanctioned.

likely is both an adjective and an adverb. As an adjective it means probable; as an adverb, in all probability. *Liable* is an adjective meaning responsible, under obligation; it also connotes likelihood of danger. *Apt*, as applied to persons, means quick to learn, dexterous, or inclined, disposed to; as applied to things, it means suitable, fitting, appropriate. *It is likely to snow* and *As a result of the accident he is liable for damages* and *He is liable to fall if he climbs that tree* and *She is an apt student and her language is therefore likely to be apt* illustrate correct usage.

loose, as an adjective, means free, at liberty; as a verb, to free or untie or unbind; it becomes *loosed* in the past tense and past participle. *Lose* means to part with unintentionally, to miss, to mislay; it becomes *lost* in the past tense and past participle. *Loose* rhymes with *goose; lose* rhymes with *whose*.

loth (*loath*) is an adjective meaning reluctant, averse, unwilling; *loathe* is a verb meaning to hate, to detest. *He was loth to say that he loathed his antagonist* is correct usage.

luxuriant means abundant or profuse in growth; *luxurious*, costly, rich in surroundings. Say *The vegetation is luxuriant* and *The apartment is luxurious*.

majority means more than half of a given number; *plurality* means the larger portion or greater number—the margin by which a candidate outruns his closest competitor. If, in running for office, A receives 1200 votes and B 800 out of a total ballot of 2000, A receives a majority of 400. If A receives 1200 votes, B 450, and C 350, then A receives a plurality of 750, or so many more votes than his nearest competitor.

may. See *can*.

most, as an adjective, is the superlative of *many* and *much*, and means greatest in number or in quantity; as an adverb, it is the superlative of *much* and means in the greatest degree; as a noun, it means the greatest number or amount. *Almost* is an adverb meaning nearly. *Most men smoke* and *Alice is our most popular student* and *Most of the guests have come* are correct. The definitions show that *Most all the girls are going* is illogical and that *Almost all the girls are going* is correct.

much is both an adjective and an adverb. *Much money* and *much interested* are correct. *Very* and *too*, adverbs expressing intensity, are used with adjectives or with other adverbs. *He is very clever; he works very intelligently but too slowly* is correct. Generally speaking, neither *very* nor *too* should be used to modify a past participle directly; *much* is the correct modifier. Say *much admired, very much pleased, too much excited*. Only past participles which are used more like adjectives than like verbs may be modified by *very* or *too*. *He is in a very determined mood* is correct.

mutual. See *common*.

neither (correlative of *nor*) and *either* (correlative of *or*) are preferably used pronominally to refer to one of two, not to one of three or more. *Any, none, one, some*, and other indefinites are used in reference to three or more. Say *I played tennis with Bill and Mary, either* (or *neither*) *of whom could win a championship, I'm sure* and *I saw Tom, Dick, and Harry, none of whom wore a coat*. Do not say *I saw Tom, Dick, and Harry, neither of whom wore a coat*.

As correlative conjunctions, *neither* is followed by *nor* and *either* by *or*, as *Neither John nor Bill is going* and *Either John or Bill is going*.

notable means worthy of note, eminent, distinguished, favorably known; *notorious* means publicly known in an unfavorable way. *He has made a notable record as Secretary of State* and *His mishandling of funds has made his dishonesty notorious* illustrate correct usage.

number. See *amount*.

observance means compliance with law and duty, celebration of customary feasts and holidays; *observation* means the act of seeing or beholding, or an incidental remark in conversation. You speak of the *observance of the Sabbath* and the *observation of the stars*.

personal means relating or pertaining to a person; *personnel* means a group of persons employed. *He gave his personal attention to directing the personnel* is correct.

personalty is a legal term meaning personal property; *personality* is a term in general use meaning individual distinction or quality, a personal being.

practical, in reference to persons, means capable or experienced; in reference to things, useful or valuable. *Practicable* means capable of being put into practice, feasible, usable. *This plan, which has been devised by a practical man with practical knowledge, will prove practicable in every way* illustrates their uses.

precedent means something said or done that serves as an example; *precedence* means a going before, a preceding, priority as of rank or time. The first word is accented on the first syllable; the second, on the second. Thus, the plural of *precedent, precedents*, is not a homonym of *precedence*.

principal is both a noun and an adjective. As a noun, it means the head of an institution, as a school; a leading part; a chief; an employer; one who acts as agent; and a sum of money on which interest accrues. As an adjective, it means leading, first in rank, quality, or importance, as *Honesty is the principal thing*. *Principle* is a noun meaning rule, general truth, law, essence, righteousness, honor, as *An important principle of conduct has been violated* and *He is a man of high principle*.

proof. See *evidence*.

propose means to set before or to offer for consideration; *purpose* means to intend, to resolve, to plan. The former is a verb only; the latter is both a noun and a verb. *I purpose to exhibit working models of what I propose* illustrates good usage.

proposition means that which is proposed or suggested or a formal statement, as in argument and mathematics. It should not be used in the sense of product, undertaking, or person. Say *He is a strange person*, not *He is a queer proposition*. Do not use *proposition* as a verb; *He propositioned me yesterday* is a vulgarism.

provided is a conjunction meaning if, on condition; *providing* is the present participle of *provide*, meaning to furnish. In *He will go provided it does not rain*, the word *provided* is a conjunction of condition and has nothing to do with the verb *provide*. *He will go providing it does not rain* does not make sense.

quantity. See *amount*.

quiet (two syllables), used as an adjective, a noun, or a verb, expresses calmness or silence; *quite* (one syllable) is an adverb meaning entirely, altogether, totally. *The atmosphere was quite restful, for the room was very quiet* is correct.

raise is a transitive verb; *rise* is an intransitive verb. *He raised the window* and *A young man rises when he is introduced to an older person* are correct. *Rise* is used also as a noun, as *the rise in prices* and *the rise of the young statesman*. *Raise* is preferably not used as a noun; it is sheer colloquialism for increase in *He wants a raise in salary*.

recipe means a direction or formula for making something, especially a prescription or a cookery procedure; *receipt* means acknowledgment of having received something, usually money in payment. Though these words come from the same Latin root and formerly had the same meaning, today the above distinction must be observed.

relatives, as a noun, is preferably used to indicate kinfolk; *relations*, to indicate general connections or associations of both things and persons. This distinction is not always observed, but it should be made to avoid using the latter word ambiguously. If you say *He has relations in Chicago,* you may mean either business connections or family connections, whereas if you say *He has relatives in Chicago,* you can mean only the latter.

remainder. See *balance.*

reputation. See *character.*

respectfully is an adverb meaning with respect; *respectively* is an adverb meaning severally, each to each, each in order. *He respectfully gave the lady his chair* and *John and Harry are respectively the secretary and the treasurer of the club.* In the complimentary close of a letter *respectfully* is the correct word.

rest. See *balance.*

set is a transitive verb meaning to place or put; *sit* is an intransitive verb. *I shall set the books here so that we may sit on the windowsill* illustrates correct usage. You *set* a hen on her eggs; she is then really a *sitting* hen but is colloquially referred to as a *setting* hen; she *sits* on eggs, the eggs themselves being called a *set!*

stationary means fixed in position; it implies *at*ness of location, and the word has *a*'s in it; *stationery* means writing paper, and the word has *e* in it, as have *paper* and *letter.* The former is generally an adjective, the latter a noun.

statue is a modeled or sculptured figure; *stature* refers to height or build or size, and is used both literally and figuratively; *statute* is a code or a law. Study the spellings and definitions carefully.

take. See *bring.*

tend. See *attend.*

therefor means for that, for it, and is accented on the second syllable; *therefore* means for that reason, because of that, consequently, and is accented on the first syllable. *I bought it and agreed to pay fifty dollars therefor* and *I like it and I shall therefore buy it* illustrate correct usage.

too. See *much.*

transpire means to leak out, to become known; *happen* means to occur, to take place. Say *The fire happened* (or *occurred) while we were away* and *Since the secret has now been revealed, it transpires that the guilty man has been known from the beginning.*

very. See *much.*

vocation means regular occupation, calling, or trade upon which living depends; *avocation* means subordinate occupation pursued for recreation and pleasure rather than for income. Do not use *avocation* as a general term for all pursuits or activities.

who's is the contraction of *who is; whose* is the possessive case of the pronoun *who. Who's in the room?* and *Whose book is that?* illustrate correct usage.

without is a preposition; *unless* is a conjunction. Use the preposition *without* to introduce a phrase and the conjunction *unless* to introduce a clause.

26

I am not going without you and *I am not going unless you go* are correct. Don't say *I am not going without you go.*

worse is the comparative of *bad*, the superlative of which is *worst. He is going from bad to worse* and *He is going from worse to worst* are correct. *He is going from worst to worst* is impossible.

your is the possessive case of the personal pronoun *you; you're* is the contraction of *you are. Your car is ready, but you're not* is correct. Be sure to place the apostrophe correctly in the contracted form; it stands for *a* in *are*.

15. The words and terms that follow—**Dictional Don'ts**—are illiterate, slang, or colloquial misusages that persist principally in conversation but to a degree also in writing. They represent error, not so much as result of confusion with other words and terms, but rather as result of carelessness or indifference, or both, in regard to usage. When you are confronted with the "pause of doubt" in expressing yourself, consult this list.

DICTIONAL DON'TS

a means one. If *one* cannot logically be substituted for *a* in an expression, *a* is incorrect. *I should a gone* and *I had a work* are illiterate for *I should have gone* and *I had to work.* Say *I like this kind of story*, not *I like this kind of a story.*

after is unnecessary before the perfect participle, as in *After having washed the car I rested.* Say, rather, *Having washed the car I rested* or *After washing the car I rested.*

ain't is an illiterate form. Don't use it for *am not, are not, is not, has not, have not.*

all right. See page 59.

all-round is a colloquial expression. *All-around* is incorrect.

all the, used before comparatives, means by so much, to just that extent. It is not the equivalent of the correlatives *as . . . as* or *so . . . as.* Say *This is as fast as the machine will run*, not *This is all the faster the machine will run.* Similarly, say *We shall accomplish all the more (so much more) for that bit of exercise.*

and should not be used before *etc.* The abbreviation means and others; *and* is therefore unnecessary.

any place, every place, no place, some place should always be written as two separate words and preceded by the preposition *in* when used in the sense of anywhere, everywhere, nowhere, somewhere. Say *I have looked in every place*, not *I have looked everyplace.*

anywhere, everywhere, nowhere, somewhere should be written as single words and should not be spelled with final *s*. *Anywheres, everywheres, nowheres, somewheres* are illiterate forms.

appreciate means to place high value or esteem upon. It is unnecessary to use with it such modifiers as *extremely, greatly, highly, very much.*

as must not be used in the sense of *that* or *whether.* Say *I don't know that* (or *whether*) *he is going,* not *I don't know as he is going. As . . . as* are correlatives in affirmative comparisons; *so . . . as* in negative comparisons. *He is not so well as he was* and *He is just as strong as ever* illustrate correct usage.

attack is dissyllabic in the past tense and in the past participle. Say *at-tacked.* There is no such word as *at-tack-ted.*

awful. See *wonderful.*

badly must not be used as an attribute complement after a linking verb. Say *I feel bad,* not *I feel badly.* The latter would be correct only provided actual feeling were intended, as *I feel badly with my fingers, for they are numb.*

   Badly is colloquial in the sense of so much, very much, greatly. Say, preferably, *He wanted very much to go to the circus,* not *He wanted badly to go to the circus.*

because. See page 183.

bought is the past-tense and the past-participle form of the verb *buy.* There is no such form as *boughten.* Say *I have bought three pencils* and *This is a bought dress,* not *I have boughten three pencils* and *This is a boughten dress.*

broadcast, as a verb, is the same in all parts; *broadcasted* as a past-tense or past-participle form is incorrect.

brought is the past-tense and the past-participle form of the verb *bring.* There is no such form as *broughten.* Say *I have brought the medicine,* not *I have broughten the medicine.*

burst is the same in all forms; *bursted* is incorrect; *bust* is slang.

but that and *but what* should not be used for *that* after *doubt.* Say *I do not doubt that he will come,* not *I do not doubt but that* (or *but what*) *he will come.*

can't hardly (*barely, rarely, scarcely*) constitutes almost a double negative. Do not use *not* with these adverbs, for they themselves imply negation. Say *I can hardly* or *barely* or *rarely* or *scarcely see,* not *I can't hardly* or *barely* or *rarely* or *scarcely see.*

claim means to ask or demand as right; it is used only colloquially in the sense of assert, declare, insist. Say *I claim that watch as my property* and *I insist that he is wrong.* Don't say *I claim that he is in the wrong.*

contact is used preferably as a noun, but it may be used as a verb in the sense of touch or come together, as of things. Do not use it in the sense of see, meet, consult, confer, or interview. Say *I talked with Mr. Brown yesterday,* not *I contacted Mr. Brown yesterday.*

could of. See *of.*

couple, like *pair* and *set,* is singular in form. Say *couple is, pair is, set is* and *couples are, pairs are, sets are.* The expressions *Three couple have arrived* and *Four pair are needed* are unrecommended colloquialisms.

criticism means the making of a comment or the expression of a judgment. The comment may be favorable or unfavorable. Don't use this noun (or the verb *criticize*) in the sense of unfavorable only.

cute. See *wonderful.*

data is a plural noun. Use a plural verb with it. Say *Data are.*

deal of refers to quantity; *many*, to number. Say *We have a great deal of sugar and many apples.*

different implies separation or disagreement, not comparison. It should therefore be followed by the preposition *from*, which implies separation, not by the conjunction *than*, which is used in comparisons. Say *Jack's program is different from mine*, not *Jack's program is different than mine.*

disremember is a dialectic and colloquial term. Don't use it in the sense of forget.

dive is preferably *dived* in the past tense and past participle. The past form *dove* is colloquial and should be avoided.

done used for *did*, the past of *do*, is illiterate. Say *I did it yesterday*, not *I done it yesterday. Done* is illiterate also used in emphatic modification of another verb in the sense of already or actually, as *She has done got the measles. Done* is colloquial in the sense of finished, completed, as *My job is done* and *My dress is done.*

drown is monosyllabic in the past tense and the past participle. Say *drowned.* There is no such word as *drown-ded.*

due to is not a prepositional phrase and should not be used as a substitute for because of or on account of. *The train was late due to the storm* is incorrect. *Due* is an adjective and should modify a noun either directly or as an attribute. *His tardiness was due to the storm* is correct.

else takes the sign of possession in such expressions as *anybody else's coat* and *somebody else's hat.* Don't say *nobody's else skates.*

Don't use *else* superfluously, as in *He has nothing else but money.* In this sentence *but* and *else* both mean besides. *He has nothing but money* is correct.

etc. means and others. Do not use *and* with this abbreviation.

every place. See *any place.*

everywhere. See *anywhere.*

extra is preferably not used in the sense of exceptionally or unusually. Say *That is an exceptionally* or *unusually large car*, not *That is an extra large car.*

favor is not a synonym of *letter.* Say *I have received your letter*, not *I have received your favor.*

fine is an adjective meaning excellent, delicate, refined, of superior quality. Do not use it as an adverb, as in *I enjoyed myself fine.* But it is used colloquially in the sense of good, beautiful, or approved, as *a fine girl, a fine day, a fine car.* These are correct: *He has a fine sense of humor, We shall show you some fine carving, We ground the wheat fine.* In *I feel fine, fine* is a predicate adjective.

first and *firstly* are both adverbs. The shorter form is generally preferred.

fix, as a noun, is too colloquially used for predicament, plight, situation; as a verb, for make right, repair. Say *I found myself in a sorry predicament,* not *I found myself in a bad fix.* Say *The desk has been repaired,* not *The desk has been fixed.*

for should not be used superfluously with *to.* Say *She was willing to play,* not *She was willing for to play.* Say *He wanted her to go,* not *He wanted for her to go* or *He wanted her for to go.*

funny means laughable, humorous. Do not use it in the sense of odd, strange, peculiar, unusual. You may hear a *funny story* and see a *funny picture,* but you do not experience *funny weather* or drive along a *funny road.*

get should not be loosely used in the sense of achieve, acquire, catch, come, gain, have, learn, meet, obtain, receive, secure, suffer, and still other verbs. Such expressions as *get well, get sick, get pneumonia, get on, get ready, get to work, get a seat, get good wages* are colloquial. Do not use *get* after *do* or *did,* or *got* after *have* except for particular emphasis. *I got the money* is preferable to *I did get the money; I have the money,* to *I have got the money.*

gorgeous. See *wonderful.*

gotten is the archaic past participle of *get.* Use *got* instead of *gotten. Gotten* survives in adjective uses, as in *ill-gotten gain,* but *ill-got gain* is quite as good form.

grand. See *wonderful.*

had should not be followed by *of* or by *ought.* If *I had of known* and *I had ought to go* are illiterate expressions for *If I had known* and *I ought to go.* Don't say *had a* for *had to.*

home should not be used for *house.* It is used as an adverb after verbs of motion, as in *He is going home* and *He will come home.* It should be preceded by *at* after verbs of state, as *He is at home.* Do not say *I am home* or *I stay home.*

in is superfluous after such verbs as *add, dive, divide, enter, start, take.* Say *Add six to four, Enter at either door, I take paying guests,* not *Add six in to four, Enter in at either door, I take in paying guests.*

in back of is circumlocution for *behind.* Say *I found it behind the piano,* not *I found it in back of the piano.*

irregardless. There is no such word. See *regardless.*

kind of and *sort of* should not be used in the sense of rather or somewhat. Say *rather tired* and *somewhat bored,* not *kind of tired* and *sort of bored.* These phrases, consisting of a noun and a preposition, are not adverbs and thus do not modify adjectives, adverbs, and verbs.

like is not a conjunction and must not be used in the sense of as if or as though. Say *I feel as if I had been hit* and *It looks as though it were going to rain*, for here *as if* and *as though* are conjunctions connecting subordinate clauses with principal clauses. *I feel like a prince*, in which the preposition *like* is properly followed by *prince* as object, is correct.

line should not be used too loosely. Say *What sort of work is John doing now?* not *What line of work is John doing now?* Say *What kinds of shoes have you?* not *What have you got in the line of shoes?* Say *What do you do?* not *What's your line?* Say *We do not sell carpets*, not *We do not sell anything in the carpet line.*

listen, at the beginning of a statement, is superfluous. Used excessively, it constitutes a vulgarism.

load or *loads* used after *thanks* is incorrect. Say *Thank you* or *Thank you very much*, not *Thanks a load* or *Thank you loads.*

locate is preferably used as a transitive verb. Do not use it in the sense of settle, meaning to take residence. Say *We have settled in the city*, not *We have located in the city. We have located our offices in the city* is correct. Used for find, *locate* is high-sounding. Say *I cannot find my keys anywhere*, not *I cannot locate my keys anywhere.*

lot of (*lots of*) is a commercial term for quantity, size, or number. Used to mean many or much, as *a lot of clothes* and *lots of money*, it is colloquial. *Thank you* and *Thank you very much* are better than *Thank you a lot* or *Thanks lots.*

may of. See *of*.

might of. See *of*.

muchly. See p. 136.

must of. See *of*.

news is plural in form but singular in meaning and use. Use a singular verb. Say *News is*, not *News are.*

nice actually means precise, exact, keen, delicately drawn or made. Used in the sense of pleasant, beautiful, agreeable, it is colloquial. Say *He displayed nice judgment in making that stroke*, not *He is a nice tennis player.*

no good should not be used as a single adjective in the sense of worthless or valueless. The expressions *He's no good* and *That's no good* are sheer colloquialism or slang.

no place. See *any place*.

nowhere is an adverb of place, not of degree. Do not use it, therefore, to modify *like* or *near*. *Nowhere like* and *nowhere near* are illiterate expressions used to mean, respectively, quite unlike and not nearly. *He nowhere near finished the job* is incorrect. Say *He did not nearly finish the job. Anything, anywhere, nothing, something, somewhere* follow the same rule. They should not be used in direct modification of *like* or *near*, inasmuch as they are not adverbs of degree.

of must not be used for *have* after *can, could, may, might, must, shall, will, should, would, ought to;* it must not be used superfluously after *had.*

Must of gone, had of known, ought to of seen, and so forth, are illiterate forms.

But *of* must not be omitted after *kind, manner, sort, style, type* in such expressions as *What style of pen is that?* and *What type of car have you?* These words are nouns, not adjectives. *What type bread do you like?* is an impropriety.

off should not be followed by *of.* Say *Keep off the grass,* not *Keep off of the grass.* Say *It fell off the ledge,* not *It fell off of the ledge.*

on is superfluous after such verbs as *add, blame, plan, take.* Say *They blame me, We plan to see you, We take boarders,* not *They blame it on me, We plan on seeing you, We take on boarders.*

on account of is a phrasal preposition meaning because of. Don't use it as a conjunction. Say *He is going away because he is ill,* not *He is going away on account of he is ill.* It is correct to say *He is going away on account of illness* and *He is going away because of illness.*

only should be used sparingly as a conjunction meaning but or except that. Say *I intended to go, but I was detained by illness* and *I should have gone except that I was called away,* in preference to *I intended to go, only I was detained by illness* and *I should have gone, only I was called away.*

Place *only* as close as possible to the word it modifies. Say *I have only one* and *We walked only a short distance,* not *I only have one* and *We only walked a short distance.*

ought should not be preceded by *had.* Say *I ought to have gone,* not *I had ought to have gone.* See *of.*

out is superfluous after such words as *deal, die, end, lose, open, start, win.* Say *He won,* not *He won out; He started yesterday,* not *He started out yesterday.*

Out should not be used in the sense of gone. Say *There is no more pie,* not *The pie is out.*

pair. See *couple.*

party should not be used to denote an individual person; *party* refers to more than one. Say *I wrote to that person,* not *I wrote to that party.* In legal expressions, however, *party,* as in *party of the first part* and *party of the second part,* correctly denotes an individual.

per is a Latin word meaning through, by, by means of. It should be used only before Latin words now accepted as part of English diction, as *per capita, per cent, per diem, per se.* Its use before English words, as *per day, per month, per year,* is permissible in bookkeeping and statistical expression but not in composition.

phenomena is plural; *phenomenon* is singular. Say *Phenomena are* and *Phenomenon is.* There is no such word as *phenomenas.*

plead is preferably *pleaded* in the past tense and past participle. Colloquially the past is frequently seen and heard as *pled.* Say *He pleaded eloquently,* not *He pled eloquently.*

plenty is properly a noun meaning a great amount or an abundance. Used as an adjective or an adverb in such expressions as *He has plenty courage* and *I am plenty tired*, it is a barbarism. The term *a plenty* is an American colloquialism, as *He has money a plenty* (sometimes written as one word—*aplenty*). The adjective form is *plentiful*.

portion means share or allotment. When a whole is divided into parts, the part assigned or allotted to some person or purpose is called a portion. Such share may not be a proportionate part. You may cut an apple into equal parts but you may give to Bill a larger portion of the apple than you keep for yourself.

posted, especially in the phrase *well posted*, is used colloquially to mean informed (well informed). *I shall keep you informed* is preferable to *I shall keep you posted*.

pretty is an adjective and should modify a noun. The adverbial usage in the sense of very or very much, as in *pretty tired, pretty often, pretty worried*, is considered colloquial.

proved is the past tense and the past participle of *prove*. The past-participle form *proven* is rapidly falling out of use except as an adjective, as in *proven resources* and *proven facts*. But *proved resources* and *proved facts* are likewise correct.

quite is an adverb of degree meaning wholly, surely, really, as in *quite right* and *quite absent-minded*. Its use as a synonym for very, somewhat, rather is colloquial. Say *very tired, somewhat disappointed, rather tall*.

quite a few, quite a little, quite some are colloquial expressions meaning considerable. Say *many books, a great deal of rain*, not *quite a few books, quite a little money, quite some rain*.

rarely means not often and is correctly used with *if ever* and *or never*—*rarely if ever* and *rarely or never*. The expressions *rarely ever* and *rarely or ever* are contradictory. Don't use *rarely* with negative forms, such as *don't, doesn't*. (See *can't hardly*.) These are correct usages: *We rarely if ever go there, We rarely or never go there, We rarely go there, We hardly ever go there*. (See *seldom*.)

real is an adjective meaning actual, genuine, authentic. It should not be used for the adverbs *very* and *really*. Say *She is very beautiful* and *I am really shocked*, not *She is real beautiful* and *I am real shocked*.

regardless means without regard. There is no such word as *irregardless*. The prefix *ir*, meaning without, is unnecessary because the suffix *less* also means without.

right is not an adverb of degree and must not be used for *very* or *so*. Don't say *right clever* or *right quick*. Instead of *right away*, say *at once, immediately, instantly,* or *directly*.

same should not be used as a substitute for *it* or *they*. Say *I have examined the car (cars) and find it (them) in good condition*, not *I find same in good condition*.

say, used at the beginning of a remark, is superfluous. Used excessively, it constitutes a vulgarism.

see, used at the conclusion of a statement, is superfluous. Used excessively, it constitutes a vulgarism.

seldom means not often and is correctly used with *if ever* and *or never*. The expressions *seldom ever*, *seldom or ever*, and *seldom or rarely ever* are contradictory (see *rarely*). Don't use *seldom* with negative forms, such as *don't*, *doesn't*, *haven't*, *won't*. Say *We seldom go*, not *We don't seldom go*. These are correct usages: *We seldom or never go to the games*, *We seldom if ever go to the games*, *We seldom go to the games*.

series, like *species*, is the same in the singular and the plural. Use a singular or a plural verb as the sense requires. Say *Two series of articles were published; one series was long. There are several species of lily; one species is the tiger lily*. There is no such word as *serie*. *Specie* is not the singular of *species;* it means coin.

set. See *couple*.

should of. See *of*.

sight of, used in the sense of much or a great deal, is dialectic and colloquial. Don't say *We raised a sight of corn last year* for *We raised a great deal of corn last year*.

size is a noun, not an adjective. Say *A large-sized coat is required* or *A coat of large size is required*, not *A large-size coat is required*.

so, as an adverb of degree, is usually weak and general rather than intensive, as it is usually meant to be. Say *I was greatly shocked*, not *I was so shocked*. It should be followed by *that* as a connective in purpose or result clauses. Say *I studied Friday night so that I might be free on Saturday*, not *I studied Friday night so I might be free on Saturday*.

sold is the past tense and the past participle of *sell*. Do not use it in the sense of convinced or persuaded or won over. Say *I am in favor of his idea*, not *I am sold on his idea*.

some is an impropriety when it is used as an adverb, as in *He played some*. Say, rather, *He played a little* or *to some extent*. Say *I am somewhat tired*, not *I am some tired*.

    Some is slang in such expressions as *some car* and *some goal*, meaning respectively *a fine car* and *a phenomenal goal*.

some place. See *any place*.

somewhere. See *anywhere*.

sort of. See *kind of*.

species. See *series*.

strata is plural; *stratum* is singular. Say *Strata are* and *Stratum is*.

such, explained by a relative clause, is preferably followed by the relative pronoun *as*, not *that*. Say *We shall abide by such regulations as may be made*, not *We shall abide by such regulations that may be made*.

sure, used for surely, is slang. Say *Surely I am going with you* and *Will you go with me? Surely,* not *Sure I am going with you* and *Will you go with me? Sure.*

suspicion is a noun, not a verb. Don't use it for *suspect.* Say *I suspect him,* not *I suspicion him.*

swell. See *wonderful.*

take and is colloquial in expressions such as *Take and beat the eggs.* Say simply *Beat the eggs.*

televise is *televised* in the past tense and past participle. Don't say *televisioned.*

than should be used only in comparative expressions, as *No sooner had I entered than the curtain went up.* Don't use *than* for when, till, or until. Say *I had hardly reached the house when it began to rain* and *She scarcely noticed him until he began to shout,* not *I had hardly reached the house than it began to rain* and *She scarcely noticed him than he began to shout.*

that and *this* should not be used as adverbs of degree meaning so. Say *so big, so large,* not *this big, that large.* The use of these demonstrative adjectives as adverbs is colloquial, to say the least.

through is colloquial in the sense of finished. Say *I have finished the book* preferably to *I am through with the book.*

try is usually followed by *to,* not by *and.* Say *Try to come,* not *Try and come.* When the second verb is co-ordinate with *try, and* is correct, as in *If I try and fail, I shall be heartbroken.*

Use *try* sparingly as a noun in the sense of attempt.

United States is preferably preceded by *the* and used as singular, as *The United States is the greatest country in the world.* When used to mean a collection of states rather than a unified whole, the name may be preceded by *these* and followed by a plural verb, as *These United States are certain to stand together as one nation.*

up is superfluous after such verbs as *amount, close, connect, cripple, divide, end, finish, open, rest, scratch, settle, wind, yield.*

use, as a noun, should not be preceded by *no* or *some* or *what* without a preceding preposition. Say *This is of no use, This is of some use, Of what use is this?* not *This is no use, This is some use, What use is this?*

used to could is an illiterate expression sometimes used to convey the meaning once could or was once able to. Don't say *My father used to could play tennis.* Say *My father could once play tennis* or *My father used to be able to play tennis.*

ways must not be used for singular *way* in such expressions as *a short way, a little way, Walk a little way with me.*

when should not be used for *than* after a comparative expression. Say *I had no sooner come in than you telephoned,* not *I had no sooner come in when you telephoned.*

where and *wherever* should not be followed by *at* in such expressions as *Where is he?* and *Wherever can he be?* The idea of *at* is contained in *where.*

Don't use *where* for *that* in such expressions as *I see in the paper where John is drafted.* Say, rather, *I see in the paper that John is drafted. Where* pertains only to place.

with is primarily a preposition. Used as a verb or a part-verb, it is a collo- quialism (see *through*). Say *The party is over*, not *The party is over with; I agree with you*, not *I'm with you; That's done*, not *That's over* or *done with*.

wonderful, like *awful, cute, gorgeous, grand, lovely, mad, marvelous, mean, swell*, and other similar adjectives, should not be used extravagantly and indiscriminately. Angel cake is *delicious*, not *wonderful*; a character may be *lovely* (inspiring love), but not *gorgeous*. Make adjectives and adverbs suit logically the words they modify.

woods is plural. Do not say *a woods*. The singular collective noun *wood* is preferable to *woods*. Say *There are many oak trees in this wood*.

would of. See *of*.

16. A **barbarism** is a new term, a distorted term, or a term that has not yet been accepted as standard. Though unacceptable as good diction, it is not necessarily unintelligible. Barbarism sometimes results from doing violence to good words, as in *youthify, burglarize;* that is, adding *fy* or *ize* to form verbs. It results also from clipping, or back-formation, as *to auto, to burgle, to jell, to taxi.* But most barbarisms result from the careless or ignorant use of words, as *complected* and *irregard- less* emphatically prove. In its lowest form, barbarism is called **vulgarism,** which is an expression not necessarily coarse but below the level of what is ordinarily regarded as barbarism. *Ain't, gents, theirn, yourn* are vulgarisms.

EXERCISE

Express the following in standard English, retaining the idea contained in each barbarism:

1. He suicided, to the surprise of everyone.
2. I disremember where he told me to auto the goods.
3. He orated so well that the audience enthused.
4. As a speechifier he undoubtably proved himself tops.
5. He went out gangstering but could find nowheres to burgle.
6. As a preventative try tonicking up your system.
7. The trapezer at the circus out-attracted all the animals;
8. She is a piano concertess whose box-office make is plenty.
9. Hern is bigger than ourn, but it ain't powerfyin' like yourn.
10. You want to jellify that juice for bread spreading when we picnickize.

17. Pomposity, as applied to expression, means showy or long words or fine-sounding terms, such as *emporium* for *store, tonsorialist* for *barber, obsequies* for *funeral, ratiocinate* for *think, sumptuous collation* for *good dinner.* It is simple, direct, and natural to call a spade a spade; it is awkward, pompous, and affected to call it "a metallic implement for individual excavating by means of pedal pressure." Foreign terms such as *chef d'oeuvre* for *masterpiece, savoir faire* for *tact, de trop* for *unwanted,* and such British expressions as *lift* for *elevator, box* for *trunk, braces* for *suspenders* generally sound pompous when used by Americans. Short, simple, unpretentious language is preferred by persons of good taste.

EXERCISE

Express each of the following in much simpler language (you will have to consult the dictionary):

1. In the field of psychological research he was little more than an ostentatious tyro.
2. He pirouetted with such astounding velocity that his nether limbs and pedal extremities were indiscernible.
3. Reclining languidly in his sybaritic *robe de chambre,* he gave but negligent ear to their eleemosynary appeals.
4. The unfathomable hebetude of the unpredictable yokel made him emphatically *persona non grata* in exclusive circles.
5. His execution of the symphonic masterpiece was indubitably the *pièce de résistance* of the phenomenal musicale.
6. The ancestral escutcheon has been indelibly corrupted by this detestable adolescent scion of our illustrious house.
7. After the terpsichorean activities of the swains and debutantes had terminated and the sumptuous repast had been consumed, the *bal masque* was reluctantly adjourned.
8. Accept my gratitude for your appreciated favor of even date, and permit me to state that I shall take pleasure in conferring with the personnel of the corporation and participating in their deliberations on the calendar date you specify.

18. Slang, says Partridge, is "low, illiterate language; the special vocabulary of low, illiterate, or disreputable persons." This is a very sweeping statement, but slang is sometimes uncouth and vulgar, as well as grotesque and novel, spicy, vigorous, and picturesque. Most slang is deservedly short-lived. A little of it persists and even moves upward through colloquialism into standard usage; *mob, prig, buncombe, coax, fun* were once slang words.

There are many different classifications of slang. Every human pursuit tends to develop words and phrases, inelegant perhaps, but nevertheless meaningful, that are intimate in the speech of workers. Slang that is intelligible to the initiated only is sometimes called **cant** or **jargon**. (The latter word is also used to mean any wordy or roundabout expression.) The jargon of thieves is called **argot**. A slovenly mixture of foreign tongues heard originally and still frequently along waterfronts and in shipping centers is called **lingo**. These and other kinds of slang are popular but unauthorized forms that combine the qualities of oddness, smartness, and catchiness in their expression.

Rare indeed are the persons who can use slang or let it alone, for it tends to victimize its users until they depend on it, often involuntarily, for the expression of their most earnest thoughts. When you use slang, make sure you have in reserve a better equivalent which you can immediately substitute for it.

EXERCISE

Express the following in better English, being sure to retain the ideas intended:

1. The bookie gave me a wrong tip.
2. It griped me to think of how close I came to passing that test.
3. That speech didn't get across, because it was a put-up job.
4. He swiped my lunch and then had the nerve to tell me it was swell.
5. She tried to put one over on the committee, but she didn't get away with it.
6. The jitterbugs at the World's Fair of 1940 were right there!
7. Cut it out or I'll slap your ears down.
8. I told my father that not having a car cramped my style.
9. I had a hunch he would spill the beans.
10. I gave him a good answer, but he flunked me anyway.

19. A **trite** term is one that has become stale from overuse. Trite words are sometimes called *hackneyed* (commonplace) or *stereotyped* (unoriginal) words. *Along these lines* and *look into the situation* are trite business expressions; *holy bonds of matrimony* and *sumptuous repast* are worn-out newspaper expressions; *wended their way* and *deem it advisable* are stale conversational phrases; *Life is real, life is earnest* and *Breathes there the man with soul so dead* are overworked literary quotations; *feline ferocity* and *ancestral domicile* are trite epithets.

Other trite phrases to be avoided, if you wish to achieve a fresh and interesting style, are:

come what may	too numerous to mention	fits and starts
under the knife	be that as it may	a long-felt want
pleased to meet you	conspicuous by his absence	more easily said than done
make a beeline	better late than never	too full for utterance
steal a march	as I was saying	rendered a selection

You will be able to extend this list from what you hear (and perhaps you yourself say) in a single day.

EXERCISE

Supply a better expression for each trite one below:

1. The scene beggars description.
2. We heard a dull thud.
3. He sets people by the ears.
4. He said he had a mind to complain.
5. We're going to rack and ruin.
6. He did it all at one fell swoop.
7. They regard him as a budding genius.
8. What I say is, it stands to reason.
9. His supreme effort was nipped in the bud.
10. By hook or crook he has become monarch of all he surveys.

20. Wordiness means excessive or too many words, words that are superfluous and tend to obscure meaning. It is sometimes called **redundancy** and has many different forms. One is **circumlocution;** that is, talking around a subject without really getting at the heart of it. Another is **tautology,** which means

needless repetition, such as *refer back, repeat again, first begin-
nings, endorse on the back, complete monopoly, round in shape,
small detail, fellow classmates, free gratis.* Still other synonyms
for redundancy may be found in the dictionary. Make it a point
to use only as many words as are necessary to convey your meaning, no fewer and *no more.*

EXERCISE

The following sentences illustrate wordiness. Restate each more succinctly:

1. He is aged about ten years old.
2. We met up with them just after supper time.
3. The width of the room is about ten feet wide.
4. Throughout the entire school there was universal approval.
5. The teacher he asked me to repeat again what I had only just said.
6. Connect that pipe up with this one here in my hand.
7. From John's standpoint of view I ought to return back.
8. The end of that dead-end road terminates about a mile down.
9. Please let me have the one that is round in form, not the square-shaped one.
10. From whence he came, to whither he is going, I know not at all.
11. It is undeniably true that he endorsed the check on the back.
12. According to my point of view, I think he did it as best as he could under the conditions and circumstances he had to cope with.
13. In my behalf they did that favor for me without my so much as even mentioning or suggesting that they do such a thing.
14. As far as I am concerned, in case you care to know, I do not think his autobiography written by himself is anything like so good as the biography of the life of Lincoln that he wrote.
15. What I always say is that in the end a body always has to pay for the free liberties he hadn't ought take while he is driving on the road in his automobile.

Adapt special words and phrases to proper uses—

21. An archaism is a word or a term that is old-fashioned and therefore no longer generally used, such as:

albeit	certes	howbeit	wight
anent	choler	meseems	wot
belike	doth	methinks	yclept
betwixt	eftsoons	prithee	ye (you)
bounden	haply	quoth	ye (the)
burthen	holpen	wert	y^t (that)

The old *e* ending—*olde, shoppe*—is a characteristic of archaic forms.

22. An **obsolete** term is one that is even more old-fashioned than an archaic one, such as *bene* for prayer, *consecute* for follow, *homespun* for rustic. An **obsolescent** term is a word that is on its way to becoming obsolete, such as *buggy* for light horse-drawn vehicle.

Archaic, obsolete, and obsolescent words are found in poetical and religious writings, and occasionally in advertisements, where they supply atmosphere. Use them in your own expression only when you wish to create the atmosphere of a past period.

EXERCISE

For each archaic word in the following sentences substitute one in good standing:

1. Now wherefore stopst thou me?
2. Ye call me chief and ye do well.
3. Certes, 'tis his bounden duty to bestead thee.
4. Nary a wight liveth, methinks, who can save the day.
5. Ah, lackaday, I prithee be not wroth with me.
6. And he spake unto them and said, Verily, Verily.
7. Thou mayst go an thou wilt, but thou needst not return.
8. He departed forsooth with the bene of every homespun in the riding.
9. Anent thy burthens, God wot, mine own be not so light.
10. Eftsoons he had gotten help, and it was then proven that he was unworthy.

23. Colloquialism means informal or conversational expression. There are varying degrees or qualities of colloquial language. You will probably be more particular about your conversation when you are applying for a position than when you are talking to your family and friends. *That's the boy I spoke to you about this morning* is colloquial for *That is the boy about whom I spoke to you this morning.* Such contracted forms as *aren't, we'll, they're, I've* are colloquial. Do not use colloquialisms so constantly that your expression becomes generally loose. If, on the other hand, you avoid them altogether, your speech and writing will be stiff and artificial.

EXERCISE

Rewrite the following colloquial expressions in literary form:

1. We'll meet you halfway in price if you'll promise prompt payment.
2. We've decided to go in for sport just as you've done year after year.
3. They're not particularly interested unless there's big profit.
4. It's been a cold winter, but we've had little snow.
5. He's told us over and over again that we're to be there.
6. Who'd've believed that he could've been so foolish!
7. She's going in for acting but she's getting no encouragement from me.
8. Well, let me see, we shan't need the books I told you about after all.
9. He'd never even heard of it, and wasn't he surprised!
10. Oh, say, I'll get there by and by if you'll have patience.

24. An **idiom** is an expression that has become fixed in a peculiar groove of meaning as the result of persistent usage. The phrase *in clover,* for example, once meant literally standing or sitting in clover. It may still be used in that sense, but long ago it began to be used to mean in prosperity or in pleasant circumstances, and now it is used more frequently with this idiomatic meaning than with the literal one. Similarly, *in hot water* generally means in trouble rather than really in hot water.

Careless persons commit impropriety by using phrases not recognized as idioms, as *different than* for *different from, staying by John's* for *staying at John's, off of the grass* for *off the grass, alongside of the wharf* for *alongside the wharf, inside of a room* for *inside a room, a sale on ties* for *a sale of ties, as best as I can* for *as best I can, nowhere like as good* for *not so good as, I want in* for *I want to go in.*

Idioms are often a stumbling block to the student of a foreign language, for, as has been pointed out, words and phrases used idiomatically cannot be taken at their face value in any language. Even in English, idioms differ as between American and British usage. The Britisher asks *to be put down at the bottom of the street;* the American, *to be let off at the end of the street.*

In clover is a pictorial or figurative idiom; *at John's* (rather than *by John's*) is a grammatical or technical idiom. Use the former type only when it is fitting to your expression and will be understood. Do not mix idioms in a sentence so that one suggests a picture out of harmony with another. Observe usage, especially of prepositions, so that you may thus be helped to use technical idioms correctly.

EXERCISES

1. Explain in your own words the meaning of each figurative or pictorial idiom below:

at bay	mince matters
at cross purposes	nick of time
at large	nip and tuck
at loggerheads	on a high horse
at odds	on margin
by and large	on the rocks
cap the climax	play ball
crossing bridges	play second fiddle
do oneself proud	prick up one's ears
far and away	pull one's leg
get the upper hand	put one's foot in it
get wind of	rise to the occasion
hard and fast	run the gantlet
have a chip on one's shoulder	run to earth
have a mind to	show the white feather
have an ax to grind	stand up for
hue and cry	stands to reason
in bad odor	stick to one's guns
in the same boat	straight from the shoulder
kith and kin	through thick and thin
lion's share	to a turn
make free	to be taken in
make something of	to call a spade a spade
make up to	to come a cropper
might and main	with flying colors

2. Use each of the following technical or grammatical idioms in a sentence

accede *to*	admit *of* (permission)
accommodate *to* (conform)	admit *to* or *into* (location)
accommodate *with* (supply)	agree *in* (together in)
accompany *by* (persons)	agree *to* (a proposition)
accompany *with* (things)	agree *with* (a person)
acquiesce *in*	angry *at* (something)
adept *in*	angry *with* (a person)
adequate *for* (a purpose)	center *in* or *at* or *upon*
adequate *to* (a demand)	coincident *with*

43

compare *to* (example)
compare *with* (valuation)
consist *in* or *of*
contend *for* (to champion)
contend *with* (to quarrel)
convenient *for* (use or purpose)
convenient *to* (near)
correspond *to* or *with* (objects)
correspond *with* (write)
desirous *of* (success)
desirous *to* (succeed)
devoid *of*
differ *from* (in characteristics)
differ *with* (in opinion)
disagree *about* (something)
disagree *in* (views)
disagree *with* (someone or opinion)
dissent *from*
identical *with*
independent *of*
liable *for* (damages)
liable *to* (someone)
meddle *in* (affairs)
meddle *with* (machine)
monopoly *of*

need *of* or *for*
oblivious *of*
part *from* (person)
part *with* (object)
prefer *to*
preparatory *to*
prerequisite *to*
prodigal *of*
reconcile *to* (circumstances)
reconcile *with* (one idea with another)
rely *on* or *upon*
resemblance *between* or *to*
responsible *for* (action)
responsible *to* (authority)
sensible *of* (one's faults)
sensible *to* (troubles of another)
subscribe *for* (a publication)
subscribe *to* (a cause)
treat *of*
unequal *in* (merit)
unequal *to* (a task)
vest *in* (heirs)
vest *with* (authority)
wait *for* (someone)
wait *on* (serve)

3. In each of the following, the English idiom has been violated. Write it as it should be:

1. We are going to stay to home.
2. We shall entertain to dinner.
3. He wants I should go along.
4. This is different than that.
5. He twice knocked and wanted in.
6. I don't remember of the lesson.
7. He talked like he understood.
8. We came up with the elevator.
9. Bring this note to the office.
10. The house is convenient with the garage.
11. He took my homework on me.
12. I have around a dollar in my pocket.
13. Please excuse my son from being absent.
14. She has had experience of running a car.
15. We are going on a wedding next week.
16. He did it on his own accord.

17. This is equally as bad and nowhere near enough.
18. Let's go over by my grandmother's.
19. Try and say it out loud.
20. You cannot help but find it if you look everyplace.

25. **A localism** is a word or an expression peculiar to a certain section or province of a country. It is sometimes called a **provincialism.** The following are localisms or provincialisms: *you-all (you), tote (carry), chunk (piece), plumb (completely), reckon (think), calculate (think), right smart (considerable), turn out the coffee (pour the coffee), redd up (to tidy), out of kilter (out of order)*. Localisms provide an effective means of creating local color and, in dialogue, of delineating character. They are neither reputable nor standard, however, and should be used with discrimination, for the localisms of one community may not be understood in another.

EXERCISE

In the following, substitute a standard term for each localism:

1. Silas Brown has a bad crick in his back.
2. Please don't chuck the corn on the wheat.
3. I never heard tell of such a contraption.
4. I calculate that stoop is a little too high.
5. Soon as I heard how he was held I went right off.
6. That's a right smart chunk of a boy you've got there, Abner.
7. He went plumb out of his mind soon as he heerd about it.
8. I been totin' that gun now for nigh on three year.
9. We walked a piece down the lane till we heard the barn door chirkin'.
10. She says she reckons as how there must be fairies at the bottom of the garden.

26. **A technical word** is a word that is specific or peculiar to some business, trade, or profession. *Factor* is a technical business word meaning agent; *lobscourse,* a technical nautical word for a stew made of meat, vegetables, and biscuit; *chiaroscuro,* a technical art word meaning a particular process for reproducing light and shade in painting; *sit-down,* a technical industrial term for a strike in which employes remain idle, or "sit down," at their places of regular work. Highly technical words should be addressed only to a limited audience. For instance, to a fellow practitioner a doctor speaks of a *troublesome varix;* to the patient he speaks of the *permanent enlargement of a vein.*

EXERCISE

Rewrite each of the following so that it may be understood by the average person:

1. Make that upper maintopsail taut.
2. Here is a large silo beside the barn.
3. He shouted "Fore" at the top of his voice.
4. This is her second love set.
5. That play was distinctly off side.
6. The torque on the crankshaft doesn't function.
7. The radio can't be used because the antennae are broken.
8. One of the pontoons on his amphibian has come off.
9. Please push the tormentor back to the right of the proscenium.
10. After putting the litmus in, he held the pipette up to the light.

REVIEW EXERCISE

The following sentences contain faulty diction—barbarism, slang, mixed idioms, and the like. Most of them contain more than one fault. Rewrite them more acceptably in accordance with the foregoing instruction in the use of words:

1. He was carrying an odd variety of packages.
2. We're going chryslering the length and breadth of the land.
3. The old boy with one foot in the grave is now in an awful rut.
4. Wasn't it too marvelously wonderful and stunning for words!
5. Be that as it may, I shall never again be at a loss to answer him.
6. Lady Follyblond wore a whacky rag and a screwball feather at the track.
7. At ye little olde knittinge shoppe ye will find virtus, bibelots, and whatnots.
8. Acquaintances and patrioteers, I come to inter Caesar, not to laud him.
9. A botanical specimen by any other cognomen would be as saccharine.
10. After the hobo had adjusted his monocle he proceeded on his way.
11. Never repeat to me again the narration of that awful story.
12. After we had gotten our luggage collected together we started out.
13. I shall precede you so that I may see where your footsteps lead.

14. I'll be goldurned if that old mare hain't kicked over the traces again.
15. He's a rolling stone that don't let his right hand know what his left is doing.
16. To function or not to function, that is the interrogation.
17. They decided to beard the lion in his den and put their cards on the table.
18. He accused me of having fish to fry, whereas I simply had the cart before the horse.
19. We recently visited one of the greatest American manufacturing centers.
20. I was invited to visit a theatrical presentation, and it was wonderful.
21. I once had an acquaintance of mine who possessed prodigious knowledge.
22. There were many different types of groups among the spectators at the play.
23. By and large, in the long run, there's no accounting for personal tastes.
24. What I mean to say is, the man saw an unusual bird, if you know what I mean.
25. The difference between the top rung and the lowest is an unappreciable one.
26. The little man was inferiorized by the big rough fellow who came in.
27. On the anniversary of the date of my birth I shall have a party of friends.
28. The antediluvian relative bequeathed his dough to my dissimulating cousin.
29. He was sadly mistaken but he still and all thought himself the goods.
30. I have read farther in the book than you have, and I like it fine.
31. We had lots of fun; there was a lot of people there; we played lots of games.
32. You are liable to fall if you drive in that kind of a way.
33. I never heard an audience enthuse as that one did at the ball game.
34. Lord and Lady Billionblood are cruising on their galleon in the Mediterranean.
35. Between the lot of them they have decided to stick around and laze.
36. When I propositioned him about the job, he became awfully suave and vacillating.
37. When they were already to go, I contacted the guide about rates and etc.
38. While she is universally loved by all she ain't no saint of a female.
39. I talked to him aplenty about the notable scrape he had gotten into.
40. It has never been proven that I tried to alibi you the other p.m.
41. As I say, a body never knows what's goin' to happen of a social evenin'.

42. He edged himself to the edge of the seat in order to pass more specific judgment.
43. Miss Comely played exceedingly beautifully and wonderfully efficiently.
44. Please put that in black on paper of the color of pure snow.
45. Looking up or below, forward or behind, you have an excruciatingly lovely view.
46. In reply to your letter of the fifteenth inst. beg to be permitted to say.
47. Hoping to see you soon and with all my best wishes, I remain yours, etc.
48. He New York Centraled to Chicago, and from there he gassed it to St. Louis.
49. What I say is, be sure you're right, and then look before you leap across bridges.
50. I except your apology and wish to state I am much effected by your kind words.
51. His observance of the stars has enabled him to write the most incredulous stories about them.
52. There is no precedence in the law to justify a man's selling his personality in this manner.
53. When I propositioned him about buying his property, I could see that he was very much aggravated at my low offer.
54. He had gotten plenty sore, and irregardless of anything I could say, he closed up the deal.
55. I disremember the date on which I broadcasted, but no sooner had I finished when the night raid occurred.

SPELLING, SYLLABICATION, PRONUNCIATION

SPELLING

27. English **spelling** is difficult because words are not always spelled as they are pronounced. When you are in doubt as to the spelling of a word, you instinctively pause. This is your cue to look up the word immediately. No matter how difficult spelling is for you, by practice and perseverance you can learn to spell correctly. How? As follows:

1. By owning *and using* conscientiously a pocket dictionary.
2. By visualizing a word; that is, by looking at it intently and thereby establishing in your mind the relative positions of the letters in it. This prevents mistaking *angel* for *angle*, *American* for *Armenian*, *correspondent* for *corespondent*, *dairy* for *diary*, *fiction* for *friction*, and the like.
3. By syllabizing a word; that is, by learning to write and to pronounce it according to the syllables of which it is composed, and clinching initial and final letters of each syllable.
4. By pronouncing accurately and with slow, precise repetition.
5. By writing and rewriting and re-rewriting correctly the words you have difficulty with.
6. By tracing out words correctly letter by letter in the air.
7. By finding a "fixing device" for a troublesome letter, as *SEPAAAAAARATE* or *sepArate* or *priv(eye)lege* or *priv(myself)lege* or *station(lEttEr)ry* and *station(At)ry*.
8. By making a hobby of a troublesome word until you *own* it.
9. By comparing a troublesome word with words similar to it.
10. By keeping "pet" lists of your spelling troubles.
11. By keeping a word notebook in which you classify words for study and reference—a Scott list, a Stevenson list, a geography list, a community list, a baseball list, etc.
12. By discussing your spelling troubles with your school friends.
13. By studying word derivation; that is, roots, prefixes, and suffixes in an unabridged dictionary. Knowledge of a foreign language, especially Latin, is a great help in learning to spell correctly.
14. By fixing in your mind the principles of the best spelling rules. Though all of them have exceptions, by studying the rules you will at least be brought "close up" to some commonly misspelled words, and with practice you should be able to spell them correctly.

28. In order to understand the most common rules in English spelling you must know the following terms:

Monosyllable—a word of one syllable, as *for*.

Dissyllable—a word of two syllables, as *fortune*.

Trisyllable—a word of three syllables, as *fortunate*.

Quadrisyllable—a word of four syllables, as *fortunately*.

Polysyllable—a word of five or more syllables, as *unfortunately*.

Root—the main, original part of a word, to which additions are made, both before and after: *for(t)s* is the Latin root in the word *fortune*. **Stem** and **base** are other names for *root*.

Prefix—a group of letters added to the beginning of a word, as *un*fortunately.

Suffix—a group of letters added to the end of a word, as fortun*ate*.

Silent letters—letters not heard when a word is pronounced, as fortun*e*.

Diphthong—a combination of two vowels with the sound of one, as in *ei*ght and h*ea*t.

Digraph—a combination of two vowels or of two consonants pronounced as one sound, as *ou*t and *th*in.

Macron (ˉ)—the long mark over a vowel that indicates that it is pronounced long, as in bē.

Breve (˘)—the short mark over a vowel that indicates that it is pronounced short, as in yĕt.

The **acute accent** (′) indicates that a syllable should be stressed. In the *Webster Dictionary* the bold-face acute accent indicates primary stress and the light-face acute accent indicates secondary stress, as *con′den sa′tion*. In the *Standard Dictionary* one acute accent indicates primary stress and two acute accents indicate secondary stress, as *con″den sa′tion*. In the *Concise Oxford Dictionary* primary accent is indicated by a period placed after the accented vowel, as *con den sa · tion*.

For other diacritical marks see Webster's *New International Dictionary* and Funk & Wagnalls' *Standard Dictionary of the English Language*.

29. Final e

1. Final silent *e* preceded by a consonant is usually dropped before a suffix beginning with a vowel, as:

desire	— e	+	able	=	desirable
love	— e	+	able	=	lovable
owe	— e	+	ing	=	owing
place	— e	+	ing	=	placing
plane	— e	+	ing	=	planing
televise	— e	+	ing	=	televising
time	— e	+	ed	=	timed
write	— e	+	ing	=	writing

2. Words ending in *e* preceded by soft *c* or *g* retain the *e* before suffixes beginning with *a* or *o* in order to keep the *c* or *g* soft, but drop the *e* before suffixes beginning with *e* or *i*. (Generally, in words derived from the Latin or the Greek, *c* and *g* are soft before *e, i,* and *y,* as in *cellar, circle, policy, general, engine, gyrate.* Before *a, o,* and *u,* they are usually hard, as in *call, cold, cube, gallant, good, gullible.*)

					But
advantage	+	ous	=	advantageous	
change	+	able	=	changeable	changing
courage	+	ous	=	courageous	encouraging
enforce	+	able	=	enforceable	forcing, forcible
manage	+	able	=	manageable	managing
venge	+	ance	=	vengeance	revenging

A few words ending in *ge* retain the *e* before *ing* to prevent confusion, as *singe, singeing* (to prevent confusion with *singing*). The word *dye* retains the *e* in *dyeing* to prevent confusion with *dying,* the present participle of *die.*

3. Words ending in silent *e* preceded by *i* drop the *e* and change the *i* to *y* before a suffix beginning with *i*. This prevents the doubling of *i*. Observe the equation:

$$die - e = di$$
$$\text{substituting } y \text{ for } i = dy$$
$$\text{adding } ing = dying$$

When the suffix does not begin with *i,* the change to *y* is unnecessary, as:

		But
hie	hied	hying
tie	tied	tying
vie	vied	vying

51

4. Words ending in *oe* usually retain both vowels before *ing,* as:

		But
canoe	canoeing	canoed
hoe	hoeing	hoed
toe	toeing	toed

5. Words ending in silent *e* preceded by *u* drop the *e* before a suffix beginning with a vowel, as:

argue	— e	+ able	= arguable
blue	— e	+ ed	= blued
blue	— e	+ ish	= bluish
glue	— e	+ ing	= gluing
true	— e	+ ism	= truism

6. Sometimes final *e* must be retained in order to keep a word trisyllabic, as in *a cre age* (not *ac rage*) and in *lin e age* (meaning race or family descent). Both *linage* and *lineage,* pronounced *lĭn'ĭj* and meaning alignment of lines of type or writing, are correct. The *e* is retained, too, in *lineal—lin e al—*in order to show three syllables. The present participle of the verb *eye* is spelled either *eying* or *eyeing.*

7. In words ending in the diphthong *ee* both *e*'s are retained before a suffix, as *agreeable, seeing.* Two *e*'s are sufficient, of course, when the suffix begins with *e,* as *freest, overseer, treed.*

8. Before suffixes beginning with a consonant, such as *dom, ful, ling, ly, ment, ness—dukedom, hopeful, changeling, lovely, movement, fickleness—*final silent *e* is usually retained. But there are some exceptions, as *acknowledgment, argument, awful, duly, judgment, truly.* Both *woeful* and *woful* are correct.

9. When *ly* is suffixed to an adjective ending in *le* preceded by a vowel, the adjective form usually remains intact, as *futile, futilely; sole, solely.* But note that *whole* becomes *wholly.* Adjectives ending in *le* preceded by a consonant, however, usually change the *le* to *ly* to form the adverb, *feeble, feebly; idle, idly; possible, possibly.*

EXERCISE

The following words are correctly spelled. Explain the spelling of each in accordance with the foregoing exposition.

adviser	creator	fricasseeing	pursuer
agilely	declaration	fusible	reducible
announcement	desirable	hateful	refereed
arguable	desirous	hireling	rudeness
arrival	endurance	hoping	safety
believable	erasure	likely	sincerely
breezy	exercised	lovable	sincerity
ceasing	fleecy	noticeable	troublesome
changeableness	freely	paging	vengeance
confidence	freedom	probably	virtual

30. Final consonant

1. Monosyllables ending in a single consonant preceded by a single vowel double that consonant before a suffix beginning with a vowel. Observe the equations:

$$\text{bag} + \text{g} + \begin{cases} \text{age} = \text{baggage} \\ \text{ed} = \text{bagged} \\ \text{ing} = \text{bagging} \end{cases}$$

$$\text{beg} + \text{g} + \begin{cases} \text{ar} = \text{beggar} \\ \text{ed} = \text{begged} \\ \text{ing} = \text{begging} \end{cases}$$

$$\text{blur} + \text{r} + \begin{cases} \text{ed} = \text{blurred} \\ \text{ing} = \text{blurring} \\ \text{y} = \text{blurry} \end{cases}$$

$$\text{hop} + \text{p} + \begin{cases} \text{ed} = \text{hopped} \\ \text{er} = \text{hopper} \\ \text{ing} = \text{hopping} \end{cases}$$

$$\text{plan} + \text{n} + \begin{cases} \text{ed} = \text{planned} \\ \text{er} = \text{planner} \\ \text{ing} = \text{planning} \end{cases}$$

$$\text{thin} + \text{n} + \begin{cases} \text{ed} = \text{thinned} \\ \text{er} = \text{thinner} \\ \text{est} = \text{thinnest} \\ \text{ing} = \text{thinning} \end{cases}$$

$$\text{wet} + \text{t} + \begin{cases} \text{ed} = \text{wetted} \\ \text{er} = \text{wetter} \\ \text{est} = \text{wettest} \\ \text{ing} = \text{wetting} \end{cases}$$

Gas follows the rule in *gassed, gassing, gassy,* but departs from it in *gaseous, gases, gasiform, gasify, gasometer.*

2. Words of two or more syllables ending in a single consonant preceded by a single vowel and accented on the last syllable, double that consonant before a suffix beginning with a vowel, as:

acquit′	acquitted	acquitting		
allot′	allotted	allotting	allottable	
commit′	committed	committing	committal	committee
control′	controlled	controlling	controllable	controller
equip′	equipped	equipping		
*infer′	inferred	inferring	inferrible	
intermit′	intermitted	intermitting	intermittence	intermittent
*prefer′	preferred	preferring		
rebel′	rebelled	rebelling	rebellion	rebellious
*refer′	referred	referring	referrible	
*transfer′	transferred	transferring	transferrer	

* In these words the final *r* is not doubled before *able,* as *infer′able, pref′erable, ref′erable, transfer′able.* (*Infer* and *refer* have two adjective forms.) Note also the exceptions *transference, transferor* (legal), *transferee.*

The words *acquit* and *equip* fall under this rule because *qu* is pronounced like the consonants *kw* and the *i* is therefore really a single vowel in an accented syllable. The letter *x* is never doubled; thus, *perplex, perplexed, perplexing. Excel* follows the rule in doubling the *l* in the past tense and in the present participle—*excelled* and *excelling.* It doubles the *l* also in *excellence* and *excellent,* even though they are not accented on the last syllable.

3. When in words of two or more syllables the accent falls on a syllable other than the last, or when it is shifted because of the suffix, the final consonant is not doubled, as:

al′ter	altered	altering	alterable
*appar′el	appareled	appareling	
ban′quet	banqueted	banqueting	banqueter
ben′efit	benefited	benefiting	benefiter

*bi'as	biased	biasing	
broad'en	broadened	broadening	
*car'buret	carbureted	carbureting	carburetor(er)
devel'op	developed	developing	developer
*e'qual	equaled	equaling	
*kid'nap	kidnaped	kidnaping	kidnaper
mer'it	merited	meriting	meriter
par'allel	paralleled	paralleling	
*quar'rel	quarreled	quarreling	quarreler
*trav'el	traveled	traveling	traveler
*wor'ship	worshiped	worshiping	worshiper

* In these words the final consonant is doubled sometimes in this country, always in England. The shorter forms are preferred in the United States.

The words derived from *equal* come under this rule because *qu* is pronounced like the consonants *kw* and the *a* is really a single vowel in an unaccented syllable, but *equality* and *equalize* are never spelled with two *l*'s.

4. The greatest variations in spelling occur in words ending in *l*. Note that *cancellation* still doubles the *l*. Both *councilor* and *councillor* are permissible forms. *Chancellor* and *chancellery*, *crystalline* and *crystallize* are spelled with double *l*. *Tranquil* is preferably spelled with one *l* in derived forms, as *tranquilize, tranquilization; tranquillity*, however, is usually spelled with two *l*'s, although one *l* is also correct. *Humbugged, humbugging* and *zigzagged, zigzagging* are other exceptions to the rule.

5. The forward shift of accent prevents the doubling of the final consonant in *conference, deference, preferable, preference,* but in *conferred, deferred, preferred* the accent is not shifted and the consonant is therefore doubled.

6. A final consonant preceded by two vowels—a diphthong or a digraph—is not doubled, regardless of accent, as:

appear	appeared	appearing		appearance
applaud	applauded	applauding	applauder	
avoid	avoided	avoiding	avoider	avoidance
brief	briefed	briefing	briefer	briefest

55

conceal	concealed	concealing	concealable	
devour	devoured	devouring	devourer	devourable
entreat	entreated	entreating	entreaty	
feel		feeling	feeler	
join	joined	joining	joiner	
retain	retained	retaining	retainer	retainable
seal	sealed	sealing	sealer	
wear		wearing	wearer	wearable

7. There are sometimes two reasons for not doubling a final consonant. For instance, in words ending in *ion,* as *occasion,* the final consonant *n* is preceded by two vowels and the accent is not on the last syllable. The *n* is not doubled, therefore, in *occasional, occasioned,* and similar words.

8. A word ending in two consonants never doubles the final consonant before a suffix, as *amend, amendable, amended, amending, amendment; collect, collected, collectible, collecting, collection.* Note:

afford	afforded	king	kingdom
arm	armful	learn	learner
bind	bindery	object	objection
calm	calmness	resist	resistance
digest	digestible	trust	trusty
help	helpless	whirl	whirling

9. A single final consonant preceded by a vowel is not doubled before a suffix beginning with a consonant; thus, *development, fitful, winsome.*

10. The letter *c* has the sound of *k* before *a, o,* and *u,* as in *can, cow, cut;* it often has the sound of *s* before *e, i,* and *y,* as in *cement, civil, cycle.* To retain the hard sound, words ending in *c* add *k* before a suffix beginning with *e, i,* or *y,* as:

colic				colicky
frolic	frolicked	frolicking	frolicker	frolicky
mimic	mimicked	mimicking	mimicker	
panic	panicked	panicking		panicky
picnic	picnicked	picnicking	picnicker	picnicky
shellac	shellacked	shellacking	shellacker	
traffic	trafficked	trafficking	trafficker	

31. Ei and ie

1. When a word contains *ei* or *ie* pronounced *ee*, as in *bee*, the *i* usually precedes the *e* except after *c*. Note the following:

believe	piece	ceiling
chief	siege	conceit
grieve	wield	deceive
niece	yield	receive

See exceptions to 3 below.

2. The rhyme rule for these troublesome diphthongs runs as follows:

I before *e*
Except after *c*,
Or when sounded like *a*,
As in *neighbor* and *weigh*.

Note the following in which the pronunciation of the diphthong is not *ee*, but *a:*

deign	neigh	veil
eight	rein	vein
freight	their	weight

3. Another statement of the rule is that *e* follows *c*, and *i* follows all other letters. The words *friend, mischief, handkerchief,* and *sieve* come under this rule. Exceptions include *either, leisure, neither, seize, weird, financier.*

4. When the diphthong is sounded as short *i* or as long *i* the spelling is generally *ei:*

Short i		*Long i*
counterfeit	eiderdown	kaleidoscope
forfeit	gneiss	seismic
sovereign	height	sleight

See exceptions to 3 above.

32. Final y

1. See page 78 for plurals of words ending in *y.*
2. A word ending in *y* preceded by a vowel generally retains the *y* before a suffix, as:

annoy	annoyed	annoying	annoyer	annoyance
array	arrayed	arraying		
buy		buying	buyer	buyable
convey	conveyed	conveying	conveyance	
*gay	gayer	gayest	gayness	
*lay		laying	layer	
*pay	payee	paying	payer	payable
*say		saying	sayer	
*slay		slaying	slayer	
stay	stayed	staying	stayer	

* These are exceptions in regard to certain forms. *Gaily* and *gaiety* are now preferable to *gayly* and *gayety*, though the latter spellings are not incorrect. *Lay, pay, say* are *laid, paid, said* in the past tense and the past participle. *Payed* is the spelling of the past tense of *pay* only when it means to pass out, as a rope. The principal parts of the irregular verb *slay* are *slay, slew, slain.*

3. A word ending in *y* preceded by a consonant changes the *y* to *i* before a suffix. When the suffix begins with *i,* however, the *y* is retained to prevent the doubling of *i.* Note the following:

				But
accompany	accompanied	accompaniment		accompanying
busy	busily	busied	busier	busying
copy	copied	copier		copying, copyist
defy	defiant	defied	defiance	defying
easy	easier	easiest	easily	
glory	gloried	glorious	glorify	glorying
pity	pitiless	pitied	pitiful	pitying
woolly	woollier	woolliest	woolliness	

4. When a suffix beginning with a vowel (except *i*) is added to a monosyllable ending in *y* preceded by a consonant, *y* is generally changed to *i,* as *drier, flier, shiest.* This is true of nouns as well as of the comparative and superlative forms of adjectives. The forms *dryer, flyer, shyest* are not incorrect, however.

5. When a suffix beginning with a consonant is added to a monosyllable ending in *y* preceded by a consonant, the *y* is usually retained, as *dryly, shyness.* The form *drily* is permissible, but the *y* must be retained before the suffix *ness,* as *dryness.*

33. Prefixes and suffixes

1. When a prefix ends with the same letter as that with which the root begins, both letters are retained:

co	+	operation	= co-operation (or coöperation)*
dis	+	satisfy	= dissatisfy
in	+	numerable	= innumerable
mis	+	spell	= misspell
non	+	negotiable	= nonnegotiable
over	+	rule	= overrule
pre	+	eminent	= pre-eminent (or preëminent)
re	+	enter	= re-enter (or reënter)
un	+	natural	= unnatural

* When the same vowel appears at the end of the prefix and at the beginning of the root, either a hyphen should be used between the vowels or a dieresis should be placed on the second one to tell the eye that there are two syllables—that the vowels do not form a diphthong. The hyphened form is preferable.

Remember that the prefixes *dis* and *mis* have only one *s*. Do not double the *s* in such words as *disappoint* and *misapprehend*, which have the double letter in the root, not in the prefix.

2. When a suffix begins with the same letter as that with which the root ends, both letters must be retained:

accidental	+	ly	= accidentally
soul	+	less	= soulless
sudden	+	ness	= suddenness

3. When *all, full,* or *well* is combined with another word to make one new word, one *l* is usually dropped:

all	+	most	= almost	all + ways	= always
all	+	ready	= already	full + fill	= fulfill (or fulfil)
all	+	though	= although	help + full	= helpful
all	+	together	= altogether	well + come	= welcome

The words *all right* have not yet been combined.

4. When a suffix beginning with a consonant is added to a word ending in two *l*'s, the second *l* may be retained, as *dull, dullness; fulfill, fulfillment; skill, skillful;* but *dulness, fulfilment,* and *skilful* are permissible spellings.

Some **words** **may** be spelled with two *l*'s or with **one** *l*, as *enroll, enrol; instill, instil.* With suffixes beginning with a consonant these words may therefore be spelled *enrollment* or *enrolment; instillment* or *instilment. Installment* and *instalment* are both correct, but *instal* is not. When the suffix begins with a vowel, the two *l*'s must be used, as *duller, enrolling, fulfilled, installation, skilled.*

5. The suffix *or* is used with nouns only; the suffixes *ar* and *er* with both adjectives and nouns, as *beggar, polar, owner, larger.* The noun suffixes *er* and *or* both denote agent (doer of an act), and some words may be spelled with either ending. There is a difference in meaning, however. The ending *er* is used for the general sense, as *adviser* for anyone who advises and *promiser* for anyone who promises; the ending *or* is used in law to distinguish the doer of an act from the receiver of an act, as *promisor,* the one who makes the promise, in contrast with *promisee,* the one to whom the promise is made. Other legal terms ending in *or* and *ee* are *advisor, advisee; assignor, assignee; devisor, devisee; donor, donee; grantor, grantee; lessor, lessee; obligor, obligee; vendor, vendee.*

6. There are no hard-and-fast rules for learning to spell troublesome suffixes, but a few suggestions may help:

Inform yourself by means of the dictionary about such pairs of trouble-makers as *depositary* and *depository, intension* and *intention, mandatary* and *mandatory, passable* and *passible, persuadable* and *persuasible, sanatorium* and *sanitarium. Shakspere* may be spelled either with nine letters or with eleven, *Shakespeare.* The adjective forms are *Shaksperian, Shaksperean, Shakespearian,* and *Shakespearean.* The winter-sport word *ski* is *skied* in the past tense and *skiing* in the present participle.

If you have a knowledge of Latin, you will note that the suffixes *able, ance,* and *ant* are usually found in English words derived from Latin verbs whose infinitives end in *are,* as *portable, importance, expectant.* The suffixes *ence, ent, ible* are found in words derived from verbs of other conjugations, as *permanence, confident, credible.*

Grouping words according to the endings they have in common will enable you to learn several words at the same time. You learn the ending of one word and associate with that word all the words like it; for example: *ceed* words—*exceed, proceed, succeed; cede* words—*accede, concede, precede, recede, secede; re* words—*acre, chancre, massacre, mediocre, ogre.* Long lists can be formed of words ending in *able* and *ible, ant* and *ent, ance* and *ence, sion* and *tion,* and other suffixes.

34. Not all spelling troubles are connected with the endings of words. You sometimes misspell because you omit letters or syllables in pronunciation. These words are stumbling blocks:

accidentally	February	incalculably	peculiarly
actually	generally	interest	popular
arctic	government	laboratory	quiet
carrying	history	library	recognize
courteous	illustrious	originally	studying
enthusiastically	immediately	particularly	temporarily

Sometimes the opposite kind of error occurs. Words mispronounced with too many syllables are misspelled accordingly. Here are examples:

athletics	Elizabethan	mischievous	similar
cruelty	finally	possibly	stupendous
desirous	grievous	probably	tremendous

TROUBLESOME SPELLINGS

abscess	asparagus	biscuit	cantaloupe
accidentally	athletic	boundary	(cantaloup)
accommodate	auxiliary	Britannica	capacity
acknowledgment	axle	broccoli	captain
advertise		bungalow	carburetor
allege	bachelor	buoyant	(carbureter)
amateur	banister	burglar	ceiling
analysis	battalion	business	cemetery
answer	beggar		centenary
apparent	beneficent	calendar	centennial
arctic	benefited	cancellation	chaise longue
article	bindery	candidate	changeable

61

chauffeur
chautauqua
coconut
coincidentally
colander
collectible
colonel
column
committee
concede
connoisseur
conqueror
conscientious
consensus
consistent
contagious
convenience
coolly
counterfeit
courageous
courtesy
crackajack
crystallize
cushion
cylinder

daguerreotype
deity
desiccated
despair
desperate
develop
diarrhea
    (diarrhoea)
dietitian
    (dietician)
dilapidated
dilettante
diphtheria
disappear
disappoint
disastrous
discernible

dissatisfy
duffel
duly

ecstasy
eighth
ellipse
embarrass
equalize
erysipelas
escalator
exaggerate
exceed
excel
excellent
exhilarate
existence
exorbitant
extraordinary

familiar
fascinating
faucet
February
fiery
Filipino
forbear
forego
forehead
foreign
friend
fuchsia
fuselage
fusillade

gabardine
gauge (gage)
gazetteer
government
grammar
grandeur
grateful
grievous

guardian
guerrilla
    (guerilla)

handkerchief
harass
height
hemorrhage
hindrance
hosiery
hygiene
hypocrisy
hypocrite

idiosyncrasy
impostor
incidentally
indictment
indispensable
infinitesimal
inflammation
innocuous
innuendo
inoculate
insistence
interest
iridescent
irrelevant
irresistible
isosceles
isthmus
itinerary

jeopardy
jewelry
judgment

khaki
kimono
knowledge
kohlrabi

laboratory
ladle

larynx
lavender
liar
library
liniment
liquefy
loathsome

mackerel
magnificent
maintenance
maneuver
    (manoeuvre)
mantelpiece
marriage
marshmallow
medieval
merchandise
millennium
millionaire
mineralogy
miniature
mischievous
mortgage
mucilage
muskmelon

naphtha
necessary
nickel
nineteen
ninety
ninth
noticeable

obstacle
occasion
occurred
occurrence
omitted
outrageous

pageant	psalm	rhubarb	surprise
pantomime	psychology	rhythm	
parallel	pumpkin		tariff
paralysis	punctilious	sacrilegious	terrific
parishioner		sanatorium	tragedy
parliamentary	quandary	sandwich	tranquillity
pavilion	quay	sanitarium	transcendent
peaceable	questionnaire	sarsaparilla	transferred
penitent	queue	Saturday	trousseau
percolate	rarefy	saxophone	tyrannical
perseverance	rarity	schedule	Tuesday
persistence	recede	scissors	
perspiration	receipt	seize	vegetable
Philippines	recognize	separate	vengeance
picnicked	recommend	sergeant	vermilion
plausible	reconnaissance	shepherd	vertical
plebeian	reference	siege	veterinary
pneumonia	referred	similar	vilify
poignant	Renaissance	sincerely	villain
precede	rendezvous	solemn	
preference	repentance	sophomore	Wednesday
preferred	repetition	stratagem	weird
prejudice	reservoir	strategy	woolen
privilege	resistance	superintendent	woolly
probably	restaurant	supersede	worsted
prodigy	reveille	superstitious	
pronunciation	rheumatism	surgeon	yacht

SYLLABICATION

35. The best rule for the **division of words** at the ends of lines is to divide as rarely as possible. But if part of a word must be carried to a second line, division should be made between syllables. **Syllabication** is determined generally by pronunciation but sometimes by word derivation. If a group of letters cannot be pronounced naturally and easily as a syllable, it should not be written separately; *sch-edu-le* is incorrectly divided. Nor can a one-syllable word be divided, regardless of its length, as *baked, chance, laughed, thought*.

As there are no infallible rules for dividing words, the dic-

63

tionary must be consulted frequently. A few general principles, however, should be followed:

1. Divide after an accented syllable, as *catas'-trophe, collab'-orate,* or near the middle of a word, as *occu-pation, immor-tality.*

2. Divide after an unaccented prefix, as *pre-fer, re-sent, de-spair.* If the prefix is accented, divide according to pronunciation, as *pref-erence, des-perate, rec-ompense.*

3. Divide before a suffix, as *child-ish, acknowledg-ment, read-able.* This rule applies when a root (especially of a verb) ends in a double consonant pronounced as one, as *add-ed, bluff-er, call-ing, stiff-ly* (see 6, 10 below). Do not divide the consonants. Do not divide the following suffixes which are pronounced as one syllable:

cion — suspi-cion	*cial* — ra-cial	*ceous* — herba-ceous
gion — le-gion	*sial* — controver-sial	*cious* — vi-cious
sion — occa-sion	*tial* — par-tial	*geous* — coura-geous
tion — rela-tion	*tious* — cau-tious	*gious* — reli-gious

Though the suffixes *able* and *ible* have two syllables, these syllables should preferably not be divided, as *laud-able* (not *lauda-ble*), *ed-ible* (not *edi-ble*).

4. Divide compound words only between their natural parts, as *heart-broken* (not *heartbro-ken*), *note-worthy* (not *notewor-thy*), *silver-ware* (not *sil-verware*). If an expression is always written with a hyphen, do not divide it further, as *co-operation* (not *co-oper-ation*), *self-control* (not *self-con-trol*).

5. A single consonant between two vowels belongs in the second of the two syllables concerned unless the first of the syllables is accented; *me-lo-dious, co-lo-nial, fu-tile* and *mel-ody, col-ony, futil-ity* are correctly divided.

6. Divide between double consonants separate by derivation (see 3 above), as *com-mis-sion, sud-den, oc-cur-rence.* This rule applies when the final consonant of a verb is doubled before adding *ing,* as *run-ning, control-ling.*

7. Divide between two consonants not pronounced as a single sound, as *diges-tion, struc-ture, trum-pet, sig-nal.*

8. Do not divide digraphs, such as *ch, ck, gh, gn, ng, ph, sh, th,* which are pronounced as a single sound. Write *ca-thedral* (not *cat-hedral*), *dash-ing* (not *das-hing*), *re-scind* (not *res-cind*), *di-a-phragm* (not *diap-hragm*).

9. The ending *le* should be joined to the letter which precedes it, as *nim-ble, hur-dle, ri-fle, jin-gle, crin-kle, am-ple, lit-tle.* The digraph *ck,* however, must not be divided; *buck-les* and *trick-les* are correct divisions.

10. Do not divide a word so that a single letter stands on a separate line, as *a-way, i-rony, storm-y, loon-y.* It is preferable not to divide a word so that only the last two letters appear on the second line, as *attend-ed, promot-er, honest-ly, proper-ty.*

11. It is preferable not to divide words of fewer than six letters, such as *any, even, only, after, never, often, water, woman.*

12. Write the following complete on one line: names of persons, as *Roosevelt;* initials of a person's name, as *H. G.* (Wells); abbreviations, as *A.M., Ph.D., Y.M.C.A.;* figures and the symbols that accompany them, as *$1,247.72, 7:15 p.m.;* street addresses, as *224 Fulton Avenue;* dates, as *November 25, 1865.*

EXERCISE

Explain at what points, if any, the following words should be divided at the end of a line:

accommodate	dubious	jingle
action	embarrass	jingling
angle	environment	knotty
bugle	essential	lackey
burned	ethical	lovely
calcium	frantically	marriageable
candidate	freckles	maximum
can't	frenzied	megaphone
comparatively	frolicsome	photographic
costume	grandeur	recognition
customarily	hiatus	satisfactorily
doesn't	idiot	tactical

PRONUNCIATION

36. The two major difficulties in **pronunciation** are the distribution of accent and the adjustment of vowel sounds.

1. Initial, internal, and terminal slurring of syllables must be avoided, as *fraid* for *afraid; rithmetic* for *arithmetic; dikshnri* for *dictionary; libry* for *library; fif* for *fifth; beggin* for *begging.* Equally objectionable are the addition of a syllable to a word, as *atheletics* for *athletics* and *probabably* for *probably,* and the accenting of the wrong syllable, as *orches′tra* for *or′chestra* and *positive′ly* for *pos′itively* and *superflu′ous* for *super′fluous.*

2. One vowel should not be carelessly pronounced for another, as *cendy* for *candy; Amurican* for *American; detectuve* for *detective; dooty* for *duty.* This kind of mispronunciation is even worse in diphthong combinations such as *toime* for *time; oil* for *earl; joinal* for *journal.*

3. Final silent *e* tends to make a preceding vowel long: *plane* rhymes with *main,* and *hope* rhymes with *soap;* whereas *plan* rhymes with *man* and *hop* rhymes with *top,* the *a* and *o* being short vowels. Doubling a final consonant before a suffix makes the preceding vowel short. The first syllable of *planning* rhymes with *Anne,* but *planing* rhymes with *raining.*

4. As for consonants and consonant combinations, be careful not to say *colletch* for *college; jairman* for *chairman; pidy* for *pity; air* for *hair; singger* for *singer; wed* for *red; idear* for *idea; childern* for *children; modren* for *modern; queshun* for *question; taught* for *thought; wat* for *what; wite* for *white; lugshoori* for *luxury.*

The foregoing represent only a few samples or types of common mispronunciations. You will find it interesting to make lists of frequently mispronounced words of each type; for example, lists of words in which voiced *th* is wrongly used for voiceless *th, ch* is sounded like *j, r* is pronounced like *w.*

All dictionaries give the correct pronunciation (or pronunciations) of every word they contain. In each dictionary there is a key to the symbols used. This key should be thoroughly mastered by every student who does not wish to be handicapped or considered illiterate because his pronunciation is incorrect or careless.

The following list includes those words in everyday use that are most frequently puzzling to the young speaker. Use it for both study and reference. The pronunciations given are those found in *Webster's New International Dictionary*.

abdomen (ăb·dō'měn; ăb'dŏ·měn)
absolutely (ăb'sŏ·lūt·lĭ)
absurd (ăb·sûrd')
acclimate (ă·klī'mĭt; ăk'lĭ·māt)
accompanist (ă·kŭm'pà·nĭst)
across (à·krŏs')
acumen (ă·kū'měn)
address (ă·drĕs')
adept (ăd'ĕpt; ă·dĕpt')
admirable (ăd'mĭ·rà·b'l)
adult (à·dŭlt'; ăd'ŭlt)
alias (ā'lĭ·ăs)
alloy (ă·loi'; ăl'oi)
ally (ă·lī')
alma mater (ăl'mà mā'tēr; äl'mà mä'tēr)
altimeter (ăl·tĭm'ĕ·tēr)
amenable (à·mē'nà·b'l; à·měn'à·b'l)
Amherst (ăm'ērst)
amortization (à·môr'tĭ·zā'shŭn)
amortize (à·môr'tīz)
apparatus (ăp'à·rā'tŭs; ăp'à·răt'ŭs)
applicable (ăp'lĭ·kà·b'l)
archipelago (är'kĭ·pĕl'à·gō)
architect (är'kĭ·tĕkt)
arctic (ärk'tĭk)
Arkansas (är'kăn·sŏ; är·kăn'zăs)
arraign (à·rān')
asparagus (ăs·păr'à·gŭs)
athlete (ăth'lēt)
attacked (à·tăkt')
autopsy (ô'tŏp·sĭ)
auxiliary (ôg·zĭl'yà·rĭ)
Avon (ā'vŭn)

bade (băd)
banquet (băng'kwĕt)
Barbados (bär·bà'dōz)
barbarous (bär'bà·rŭs)
beneficent (bĕ·nĕf'ĭ·sĕnt)
berserk (bûr'sûrk)
bestial (bĕst'yăl; bĕs'chăl)
blatant (blā'tănt)
boundary (boun'dà·rĭ)
bouquet (boō·kā'; bō·kā')
Bowdoin (bō'd'n)
breeches (brĭch'ĕz)
bronchial (brŏng'kĭ·ăl)
brooch (brōch; brooch)
bureaucracy (bū·rŏk'rà·sĭ; bū·rō'krà·sĭ)

calliope (kă·lī'ŏ·pě)
candidate (kăn'dĭ·dāt)
Caribbean (kăr'ĭ·bē'ăn; kă·rĭb'ē·ăn)
cello (chĕl'ō)
cerebral (sĕr'ĕ·brăl)
chameleon (kà·mē'lĕ·ŭn)
champion (chăm'pĭ·ŭn)
chasm (kăz'm)
chastisement (chăs'tĭz·měnt)
Chicago (shĭ·kô'gō)
chiropodist (kī·rŏp'ŏ·dĭst)
chocolate (chŏk'ŏ·lĭt)
choleric (kŏl'ēr·ĭk)
cigarette (sĭg·à·rĕt')
clematis (klĕm'à·tĭs)
Cleopatra (klē'ŏ·pā'trà; klē'ŏ·pä'trà; klē'ŏ·păt'rà)

67

clique (klēk)
column (cŏl′ŭm)
combatant (kŏm′bà·tănt)
comparable (kŏm′pà·rà·b′l)
compromise (kŏm′prŏ·mīz)
comptroller (kŏn·trōl′ēr)
condolence (kŏn·dō′lĕns)
conduit (kŏn′dĭt; kŏn′dŏō·ĭt)
conspiracy (kŏn·spĭr′à·sĭ)
contrary (kŏn′trēr·ĭ)
conversant (kŏn′vēr·sănt)
corps (kōr; *plural,* kōrz)
coupé (kōō′pā′)
coupon (kōō′pŏn)
creek (krēk)
crept (krĕpt)
culinary (kū′lĭ·nĕr′ĭ)

dachshund (däks′hŏōnt′;
     dăks′hŏōnd′; dăsh′hund′)
daguerreotype (dà·gĕr′ŏ·tīp;
     dà·gĕr′ĕ·ŏ·tīp)
data (dā′tà; dä′tà)
deaf (dĕf)
debris (dĕ·brē′; dĕb′rē)
decade (dĕk′ād)
decorous (dĕk′ŏ·rŭs; dĕ·kō′rŭs)
deference (dĕf′ēr·ĕns)
deficit (dĕf′ĭ·sĭt)
de luxe (dĕ lŏōks′; dĕ lŭks′)
demise (dĕ·mīz′)
despicable (dĕs′pĭ·kà·b′l)
detail (dĕ·tāl′; dē′tāl)
diaeresis (dī·ĕr′ĕ·sĭs)
dirigible (dīr′ĭ·jĭ·b′l)
disastrous (dĭ·zàs′trŭs)
discretion (dĭs·krĕsh′ŭn)
dishevel (dĭ·shĕv′ĕl)
divan (dī′văn; dĭ·văn′)
docile (dŏs′ĭl)
dolorous (dŏl′ēr·ŭs; dō′lēr·ŭs)
dramatis personae (drăm′à·tĭs
     pēr·sō′nē)

drowned (dround)

eczema (ĕk′zĕ·mà)
Edinburgh (ĕd′ĭn·bŭ·rŭ)
electoral (ĕ·lĕk′tēr·ăl)
English (ĭng′glĭsh)
epitome (ĕ·pĭt′ŏ·mē)
epoch (ĕp′ŏk; ē′pŏk)
equitable (ĕk′wĭ·tà·b′l)
err (ûr)
errata (ĕ·rā′tà)
escalator (ĕs′kà·lā′tēr)
espionage (ĕs′pĭ·ŏ·nĭj;
     ĕs′pĭ·ŏ·näzh′; ĕs·pĭ′ŏ·nĭj)
explicable (ĕks′plĭ·kà·b′l)
exquisite (ĕks′kwĭ·zĭt)
extant (ĕks′tănt; ĕk·stănt′)
extraordinary (ĕks·trôr′dĭ·nĕr′ĭ)

faucet (fô′sĕt)
February (fĕb′rŏō·ĕr′ĭ)
finale (fĕ·nä′lå)
finance (fĭ·nàns′)
financial (fĭ·năn′shăl)
finis (fī′nĭs)
flaccid (flăk′sĭd)
Foch (fŏsh)
forbade (fŏr·băd′)
forehead (fŏr′ĕd)
formerly (fôr′mēr·lĭ)
formidable (fôr′mĭ·dà·b′l)
fragile (frăj′ĭl)

gala (gā′là)
garage (gà·räzh′)
garrulous (găr′ù·lŭs; găr′ōō·lŭs)
genealogy (jĕn′ĕ·ăl′ŏ·jĭ)
genuine (jĕn′ù·ĭn)
Geoffrey (jĕf′rĭ)
gesture (jĕs′tùr)
gigantic (jī·găn′tĭk)
gladiolus (glăd′ĭ·ō′lŭs;
     glà·dĭ′ŏ·lŭs)

Gloucester (glŏs'tẽr)
Goethe (gû'tĕ)
gondola (gŏn'dŏ·là)
government (gŭv'ẽrn·mĕnt)
granary (grăn'à·rĭ)
gratis (grā'tĭs)
Greenwich (grĭn'ĭj; grēn'wĭch;
    grĭn'wĭch; grĕn'wĭch)
grievous (grēv'ŭs)
grimace (grĭ·mās')
gunwale (gŭn'ĕl)

handkerchief (hăng'kẽr·chĭf)
hangar (hăng'ẽr; hăng'gär)
harass (hăr'às)
height (hīt)
heinous (hā'nŭs)
herculean (hûr·kū'lĕ·ăn)
history (hĭs'tŏ·rĭ)
homogeneous (hō'mō·jē'nĕ·ŭs)
horizon (hŏ·rī'z'n)
hospitable (hŏs'pĭ·tà·b'l)
hypocrisy (hĭ·pŏk'rĭ·sĭ)

ignoramus (ĭg'nŏ·rā'mŭs)
illustrate (ĭl'ŭs·trāt; ĭ·lŭs'trāt)
impious (ĭm'pĭ·ŭs)
implacable (ĭm·plā'kà·b'l;
    ĭm·plăk'àb'l)
impotent (ĭm'pŏ·tĕnt)
incognito (ĭn·kŏg'nĭ·tō)
incomparable (ĭn·cŏm'pá·rà·b'l)
indict (ĭn·dīt')
inevitable (ĭn·ĕv'ĭ·tà·b'l)
inexorable (ĭn·ĕk'sŏ·rà·b'l)
inextricable (ĭn·ĕks'trĭ·kà·b'l)
infamous (ĭn'fà·mŭs)
influence (ĭn'flōō·ĕns)
inquiry (ĭn·kwīr'ĭ; ĭn'kwĭ·rĭ)
integral (ĭn'tĕ·grăl)
interesting (ĭn'tẽr·ĕs·tĭng)
intricate (ĭn'trĭ·kĭt)
Iowa (ī'ŏ·wà)
irrelevant (ĭr·rĕl'ĕ·vănt)

irreparable (ĭ·rĕp'à·rà·b'l)
irrevocable (ĭ·rĕv'ŏ·kà·b'l)
isolate (ī'sŏ·lāt; ĭs'ŏ·lāt)
Italian (ĭ·tăl'yăn)
italic (ĭ·tăl'ĭk)

jugular (jŭg'ŭ·lẽr; jōō'gŭ·lẽr)
just (jŭst)

kept (kĕpt)
khaki (kä'kĭ)

laboratory (lăb'ŏ·rà·tō'rĭ)
lamentable (lăm'ĕn·tà·b'l)
larynx (lăr'ĭngks)
leisure (lē'zhẽr; lĕzh'ẽr)
length (lĕngth)
library (lī'brĕr·ĭ)
licorice (lĭk'ŏ·rĭs)
longevity (lŏn·jĕv'ĭ·tĭ)
lyceum (lī·sē'ŭm)

machination (măk'ĭ·nā'shŭn)
medieval (mē'dĭ·ē'văl)
mineralogy (mĭn'ẽr·ăl'ŏ·jĭ)
miniature (mĭn'ĭ·à·tu̇r)
mirage (mĭ·räzh')
mischievous (mĭs'chĭ·vŭs)
Moscow (mŏs'kō)
municipal (mṳ·nĭs'ĭ·păl)
muskmelon (mŭsk'mĕl'ŭn)
mustache (mŭs·tàsh'; mŭs'tàsh)

naïve (nä·ēv')
nape (nāp; năp)

often (ŏf'ĕn)
orchestra (ôr'kĕs·trà)
ordeal (ôr·dē'ăl; ôr'dē·ăl)
orgy (ôr'jĭ)

parliament (pär'lĭ·mĕnt)
particular (pẽr·tĭk'ṳ·lẽr)
penalize (pē'năl·īz)
Penelope (pĕ·nĕl'ŏ·pĕ)

percolate (pûr′cŏ·lāt)
peremptory (pẽr·ĕmp′tŏ·rĭ;
   pẽr′ĕmp·tŏ′rĭ)
perhaps (pẽr·hăps′)
perseverance (pûr·sĕ·vẽr′ăns)
perspiration (pûr·spĭ·rā′shŭn)
pharmaceutical (fär′ma·sū′tĭ·kăl)
phraseology (frā′zē·ŏl′ŏ·jĭ)
pianist (pĭ·ăn′ĭst; pē′a·nĭst)
poem (pō′ĕm)
pogrom (pŏ·grŏm′)
poignant (poin′yănt)
poinsettia (poin·sĕt′ĭ·a)
positively (pŏz′ĭ·tĭv·lĭ)
posthumous (pŏs′tu̇·mŭs)
precedence (prē·cē′dĕns)
precedent (prĕs′ĕ·dĕnt)
preferable (prĕf′ẽr·a·b′l)
premature (prē′ma·tūr′)
pretense (prē·tĕns′)
pretty (prĭt′ĭ)
primarily (prī′mẽr·ĭ·lĭ)
probably (prŏb′a·blĭ)
promulgate (prŏ·mŭl′gāt)
pronunciation (prŏ·nŭn′sĭ·ā′shŭn)
propaganda (prŏp′a·găn′da)
pumpkin (pŭmp′kĭn)
puttee (pŭt′ĭ)

quantity (kwŏn′tĭ·tĭ)
quay (kē)
quietus (kwī·ē′tŭs)

radiator (rā′dĭ·ā′tẽr)
radio (rā′dĭ·ō)
recipe (rĕs′ĭ·pē)
recognize (rĕk′ŏg·nīz)
recuperate (rē·kū′pẽr·āt)
referable (rĕf′ẽr·a·b′l)
regime (ra·zhēm′)
regular (rĕg′u̇·lẽr)
reputable (rĕp′u̇·ta·b′l)
respiratory (rē·spīr′a·tŏ′rĭ;
   rĕs′pĭ·ra·tō′rĭ)

revocable (rĕv′ŏ·ka·b′l)
robust (rŏ·bŭst′)
rodeo (rō′dĕ·ō; rŏ·dā′ō)
romance (rŏ·măns′)
roof (ro͞of)
room (ro͞om)
Roosevelt (rōz′vĕlt)
route (ro͞ot)
ruse (ro͞oz)

sacrilegious (săk′rĭ·lē′jŭs)
salmon (săm′ŭn)
salve (säv; săv)
sarsaparilla (sär′sa·pa·rĭl′a)
saucy (sô′sĭ)
scenario (sē·nä′rĭ·ō; sē·när′ĭ·ō)
schism (sĭz′m)
scion (sī′ŭn)
secretive (sē·krē′tiv)
sinecure (sī′nĕ·kūr; sĭn′ĕ·kūr)
sleek (slēk)
solemnity (sŏ·lĕm′nĭ·tĭ)
sonorous (sŏ·nō′rŭs)
sophomore (sŏf′ŏ·mōr)
Spokane (spŏ·kăn′)
spontaneity (spŏn′ta·nē′ĭ·tĭ)
status (stā′tŭs)
strata (strā′ta; străt′a)
strength (strĕngth)
strictly (strĭkt′lĭ)
suicidal (sū·ĭ·sī′dăl)
suite (swēt)
superfluous (su̇·pẽr′flo͝o·ŭs)
surprise (sẽr·prīz′)

temperament (tĕm′pẽr·a·mĕnt)
tepid (tĕp′ĭd)
Terpsichore (tûrp·sĭk′ŏ·rē)
theater (thē′a·tẽr)
tomato (tŏ·mä′tō; tō·mä′tō)
toward (tō′ẽrd; tōrd)
tragedy (trăj′ĕ·dĭ)
traverse (trăv′ẽrs)

tribune (trĭb′ūn)
tsetse (tsĕt′sĕ)

ultimatum (ŭl·tĭ·mā′tŭm)

vagary (vȧ·gâr′ĭ)
vaudeville (vōd′vĭl; vô′dĕ·vĭl)
vehement (vē′ĕ·mĕnt)
verbatim (vûr·bā′tĭm)

vice versa (vī′sĕ vûr′sȧ)
virulent (vĭr′ů·lĕnt; vĭr′ōō·lĕnt)

Wednesday (wĕnz′dĭ)
Worcester (wōōs′tēr)
worsted (wōōs′tĕd)

Yosemite (yŏ·sĕm′ĭ·tĕ)

zoology (zŏ·ŏl′ŏ·jĭ)

BRIEF REVIEW OF GRAMMAR

THE PARTS OF SPEECH

37. The words of every language are classified, according to their function, meaning, and use in expression, into eight broad divisions called **parts of speech:** noun, verb, pronoun, adjective, adverb, preposition, conjunction, interjection. They are listed here in the order of their importance. Nouns and verbs are the essential parts of speech. There can be no complete and satisfactory expression in a sentence without a noun and a verb, though sometimes one or the other is implied rather than expressed. Of the more than half a million words in English, every one may be placed in one of the eight groups. Some words belong to more than one group, depending upon their use in a sentence. The noun, the pronoun, and the adjective are grouped together for grammatical treatment, since they are generally associated in use. The verb and the adverb "operate" together, as a rule, in sentence practice. The preposition and the conjunction are "subject to call" in any and all grammatical relationships. The interjection is the one independent, or detached, part of speech and is usually accorded last treatment.

In this sentence—*But, alas, ill fortune descended upon him later*—the eight parts of speech are seen at work. *But* is a conjunction joining and contrasting this expression with a preceding one. *Alas* is an interjection expressing emotion. *Ill* is an adjective limiting the meaning of *fortune. Fortune* is a noun. *Descended* is a verb stating an action in relation to its subject *fortune. Upon* is a preposition showing the relation between *descended* and *him. Him* is a pronoun standing in place of a noun. *Later* is an adverb of time modifying the verb *descended.* Though this is a short sentence, it nevertheless contains all the parts of speech and illustrates each part in its customary functioning.

38. Inflection is a change or a modification made in the form of some of the parts of speech in order to express ideas more accurately. Conjunctions, prepositions, and interjections undergo no inflection. Nouns are inflected for number, case, and sometimes for gender; pronouns, for gender, person, number, case; verbs, for person, number, tense, voice, mode; most adjectives and most adverbs, for degrees of quality, quantity, or relation. A list, table, or paradigm of inflections for nouns and pronouns is called **declension;** for verbs, **conjugation;** for adjectives and adverbs, **degrees of comparison.**

English is not a highly inflected language. One part of speech may therefore be used for another. This versatility of the parts of speech makes for free communication. But unless you use accurately the few inflections there are, you may be misunderstood or judged illiterate. The following pages will point out the rules of inflectional usage of the parts of speech as isolated units and in relation to each other.

Some inflections are discernible in a word at sight. *Tom,* as it stands, for instance, is a proper noun, singular number, masculine gender. But its person and case cannot be known until it is expressed in relation to other words in a sentence. Look at the word *fell* separate and apart from other words, and you cannot even tell what part of speech it is. Relate it to other parts of speech and you are able to understand both its classifications and its inflections, as *I fell down* and *We shall fell that tree* and *This is a smooth fell* and *He made a fell thrust.*

When you **parse** a word, you should give its exact and extended classification. When you give the **syntax,** or **construction,** of a part of speech, you should explain its relationship to other words in the sentence company that it keeps (see pages 147–148). In the sentence *But, alas, ill fortune fell upon him later,* for instance, *fortune* is parsed as follows: common noun, neuter gender, third person, singular number; its syntax, or construction, is nominative case, subject of the verb *fell.*

Nouns

39. A **noun** is the name of anything—a place, a person, an animal, an object, a material, a condition, or a quality. It is also called a **substantive**. Nouns are divided into two general classes: common and proper.

1. A **common noun** denotes a general group or an indefinite member of that group; a **proper noun** is the name given to a particular individual in a group. In *Harry is a boy, Harry* is a proper noun; *boy,* a common noun. A proper noun should always begin with a capital letter. Sometimes a common noun is made from the name of a person or a country, as *china, macadam, mackintosh.* Common nouns are not capitalized. But when a proper noun is used to denote that a person has the characteristics possessed by the individual to whom the name originally belonged, it retains the capital, as *He was a very Judas.*

2. A **concrete noun** is the name of any material object, as *ball, desk, shirt, stone.* An **abstract noun** is the name of an idea, quality, or characteristic, as *beauty, fear, knowledge, perfection.*

3. Some common nouns are used to denote a group of things constituting a unit. These are classified as **collective nouns.** *Audience, class, army, team, herd* are examples. (See page 80.)

EXERCISES

1. Classify the following nouns:

boycott	Japan	peace	strength
character	japan	school	tree
corps	machinery	soul	umbrella
fleet	navy	Soviet	Washington
generosity	Niagara Falls	star	Monument

2. Give the abstract noun derived from each of the following adjectives, nouns, and verbs:

abstemious	friend	long	sober
acknowledge	grow	major	temperate
apt	hate	short	wise
decent	hero	slave	woman
five	hinder	slow	young

3. Give a common noun associated with each of the following:

Caspian	Hudson	Mexico	San Francisco
Colorado	India	Panama	Seattle
Etna	Madagascar	Sahara	Sierra Nevada

4. Give a proper noun as an example of each of the following:

continent	game	ocean	race
document	motor car	park	steamship
flower	mountain	peninsula	street

5. Identify each of the following proper nouns and use each as a common noun in your own composition:

| Ampere | Burgundy | Pompadour | Utopia |
| Boycott | Iris | Tartar | Watt |

6. In what respect is each capitalized noun below both special and general?

He is a modern Caesar.   She is the Venus of the beach.
Mathematics is my Waterloo.   Don't carry coals to Newcastle.
There is a Judas in our club.   He is a Daniel come to judgment.
I am a doubting Thomas.   He thinks he is another Shakespeare.

7. Give the plural of a concrete noun represented by each of the following collective nouns:

apiary	covey	family	pack
audience	crew	fleet	school
chorus	crowd	flock	team
class	drove	league	union

8. Give the collective noun which may be used in place of each of the following:

animals	horsemen	robbers	stars
birds	islands	rooms	states
books	outlaws	senators	teachers
fish	performers	soldiers	togs

9. Use in sentences each of the following nouns, first as concrete and then as abstract (see page 4):

award	glass	pearl	story
badge	harbor	price	treat
character	industry	ship	trophy
cup	name	smile	youth

75

Nouns have various qualities which influence their meaning and form. These are gender, person, number, and case.

40. Gender is that distinction made among nouns and pronouns which indicates whether they signify male sex, female sex, either sex, or neither sex. Nouns indicating male sex are called **masculine,** as *man, Bill;* those indicating female sex, **feminine,** as *lady, mare;* those indicating either sex, **common,** as *citizen, child;* and those indicating neither sex, **neuter,** as *table, tree.*

Nouns are inflected in three ways for gender:

1. Sometimes an entirely different word is used to distinguish masculine from feminine, as:

Masculine	Feminine
boy	girl
drake	duck
father	mother
king	queen
master	mistress
rajah	ranee

2. Gender is sometimes indicated by a suffix, such as *a, ess, ina, ine, trix,* which in some instances is accompanied by a change in the root form. Some examples are:

Masculine	Feminine
administrator	administratrix
baron	baroness
czar	czarina
hero	heroine
sultan	sultana

3. Gender is sometimes indicated by prefixing or compounding, as:

Masculine	Feminine
bull-calf	cow-calf
cock-sparrow	hen-sparrow
he-goat	she-goat
landlord	landlady

76

Differentiations in gender have tended to disappear. Words like *author, chairman, executor,* and *horse* denote either gender.

Right: Thomas Marshall made his daughter his *executor.*
Right: Margaret Mitchell is the *author* of *Gone with the Wind.*
Right: Kitty is a beautiful bay *horse.*

41. Person is the term used to indicate whether a noun or a pronoun represents the person speaking (**first person**), the person spoken to (**second person**), or the person spoken of (**third person**). A noun is in the first person only when it is used in apposition with the first person of the personal pronoun: *I, John Jones, do make this my last will and testament* or *We girls had a very good time.* The second person is found only in direct address, as *Bill, please close the door.* Most nouns are used in the third person.

42. Number is that property of nouns and pronouns which signifies whether only one person or thing or more than one is meant. Number is either **singular** or **plural**.

The **plural** of nouns is formed in the following ways:

1. The most common formation is the addition of *s* to the singular, as *chair, chairs.* Singulars ending in *s, x, z, ch* (soft), *sh* add *es,* as *gas, gases; fox, foxes; buzz, buzzes; church, churches; bush, bushes.*

2. Nouns ending in *f* or *fe* preceded by a long vowel or by *l* usually change the *f* or *fe* to *v* and add *es* to form the plural, as *calf, calves; wife, wives.* Exceptions are words containing *oo,* as *hoof, roof,* which add *s.* Other words ending in *f* and *fe* form their plurals regularly, as *bluff, bluffs; giraffe, giraffes; relief, reliefs.* A few nouns use both methods, as *beef, beefs* or *beeves; scarf, scarves* or *scarfs.*

3. Nouns ending in *o* preceded by a consonant form their plurals by adding *es;* some nouns ending in *o* preceded by a vowel add *s.* A few may be made plural in either way. There are many exceptions to the final-*o* rule, and the dictionary must be consulted. Note the following:

cargo—cargoes	studio—studios
tomato—tomatoes	halo—halos or haloes
cameo—cameos	volcano—volcanoes or volcanos

4. Nouns ending in *y* preceded by a consonant change *y* to *i* and add *es* to form the plural, as *ally, allies; lady, ladies.* Nouns ending in *y* preceded by a vowel generally add *s*, as *alley, alleys; money, moneys.* In words that end in *quy, qu* is pronounced as *kw*, a consonant sound. Hence the *y* is changed to *i* and *es* is added to form the plural, as *colloquy, colloquies.*

5. A few plurals end in *en*, as *ox, oxen; child, children; brother, brethren* (or *brothers*).

6. Some nouns form their plurals irregularly, as *tooth, teeth; mouse, mice; woman, women.*

7. Foreign nouns, especially scientific terms, upon first adoption into English tend to retain their foreign plurals. Gradually, however, they come to use *s* or *es* to form the plural. When retained, the foreign plurals usually follow these principles: Many Latin nouns ending in *us* change *us* to *i;* some change *us* to *era.* Latin nouns ending in *um* and Greek nouns ending in *on* change the ending to *a;* Latin nouns ending in *a* change to *ae;* Greek nouns in *a* add *ta.* Nouns ending in *ex* or *ix* change to *ices;* French nouns in *eau* add *x;* nouns in *is* change to *es* or *ides.* Below is a brief list of common foreign nouns with their plurals.

Singular	Foreign Plural	English Plural
alumnus (masc.)	alumni	alumni*
alumna (fem.)	alumnae	alumnae
appendix	appendices	appendixes
automaton	automata	automatons
beau	beaux	beaux, beaus
datum	data	data
focus	foci	focuses
formula	formulae	formulas
genus	genera	genera, genuses
hiatus	hiatus	hiatuses, hiatus
index	indices	indexes, indices
memorandum	memoranda	memorandums
stigma	stigmata	stigmata, stigmas
thesis	theses	theses
vertebra	vertebrae	vertebrae

* This form is increasingly used as of common gender.

Be careful not to use a singular verb with a foreign noun that is singular in appearance but plural in meaning, as *data, memoranda.*

Right: These data are conclusive.
Wrong: This data is conclusive.

8. Hyphened compounds usually form the plural on the principal part, as *rubber-stamp, rubber-stamps; mother-in-law, mothers-in-law; hanger-on, hangers-on; knight-errant, knights-errant.* A few hyphened compounds pluralize both parts, as *knight-templar, knights-templars.* Most solid compounds are pluralized regularly, as *bookcase, bookcases; classroom, classrooms; handful, handfuls.* The plural of *manservant* is *menservants.*

9. Proper nouns are pluralized by means of *s* and *es,* as *Ednas, Jameses, Leos;* those ending in *y* simply add *s,* as *Marys.* A word referred to as a word merely, regardless of meaning, formerly took the apostrophe and *s* to form the plural. The preference today is to add only the *s,* as *Capitalize your Johns and make your pros and cons clear.*

Preferable: There are too many *ands* in this composition.
Less used: There are too many *and's* in this composition.

10. The titles preceding proper names, rather than the names themselves, are usually pluralized. Say *the Misses Ferguson, Drs. Albert and Horace Munson, Fathers Breen and McQuillan, Sisters Althea and Rosaria.* The one exception is *Mrs.,* which would be awkward and confusing if put into the plural form. Say *Mrs. Browns* to indicate two married women named Brown.

11. Letters, figures, signs, symbols, and other characters are pluralized by adding an apostrophe and *s,* as *Mind your p's and q's. There are two s's in "harass."*

12. In stock quotations the apostrophe is omitted: *5s, 4s, 3s, 1945s, 3½s.*

Right: The Bonded Mining Company is calling in some of its bonds; I have notice to send in my *1945s.*
Wrong: I have notice to send in my *1945's.*

13. Several nouns, especially the names of animals, grains, and materials, are the same in the singular and the plural. Examples are *barley, deer, granite, iron, salmon, sheep, trout.* But used to refer to species of different kinds, such terms may be pluralized regularly, as *the trouts of Colorado* and *the wheats of Canada.*

14. Some nouns are plural in appearance but singular in use and meaning. Words in *ics* predominate in this group, as *acoustics, athletics, economics, mathematics, measles, news, politics.*

15. A collective noun is singular or plural in number according to its meaning in a sentence. *Committee* is a collective noun. *The committee meets today* shows that the committee is a unit. *The committee go to their homes* shows that the members of the committee are acting, not as a unit, but as individuals.

16. With a few nouns the plural has a different meaning from the singular. One plural of *compass,* for instance, means measuring instruments rather than guides or limits. *Good* indicates a moral force, and *goods* merchandise. *Spectacle* means a display, but *spectacles* means eyeglasses as well as displays. Note also:

> brothers (blood relation); brethren (members of a society)
> cloths (kinds); clothes (garments)
> dies (stamps); dice (gambling cubes)
> fish (collective); fishes (distributive)
> geniuses (men); genii (spirits)
> shot (collective); shots (distributive)

17. Nouns indicating pairs are usually construed as plural, as *pincers, scissors, trousers, tweezers.* The plural forms *alms, bellows, eaves, riches* are now regarded as having no singular.

18. Some nouns denoting measure, quantity, and weight are commonly used in the singular after a numeral that signifies plural, such as *brace, couple, dozen, gross, head, pair, score, yoke,* as *The farmer bought three yoke of oxen.* The modern tendency, however, is to make the numeral and the noun agree, as *She possessed six pairs of shoes.*

EXERCISES

1. Give the opposite gender form of each of the following:

abbess	empress	marquis	peacock
baron	fox	mayor	ram
bride	giant	milkman	roe
bull-calf	heifer	murderer	stag
czar	hind	nun	sultan
doe-rabbit	lass	ogre	traitor

2. Reread each of the following sentences in a different person, making whatever changes may be required:

1. We fellows are going to the circus.
2. Harry brought me his new book.
3. O God, have mercy upon me!
4. Clara, will you accompany me?
5. Stay, John, until the storm passes.
6. I, Sol Tone, am the man you want.
7. The child is father of the man.
8. Come unto Me, ye weary and heavy laden.
9. To each of you is bequeathed a fortune.
10. We, the members, declare this out of order.

3. Write the plural of each of the following:

aide-de-camp	mantrap	sergeant at arms
beau idéal	mother-of-pearl	table d'hôte
billet-doux	notary public	valet de chambre
brigadier general	poet laureate	vice-president
commander in chief	postmaster general	will-o'-the-wisp
man-eater	post office	wrongdoer

4. Write the plural of each of the following:

arithmetic	elk	maid of all work	physic
axis	envoy extraordinary	minister plenipotentiary	portmanteau
butterfly	fife	Miss Williams	quarto
camel driver	four-in-hand	Mrs. Williams	rhetoric
castaway	genus	oasis	rhinoceros
caucus	jay	octavo	roof
crocus	journey	octopus	runaway
cuckoo	lady director	onlooker	series
debutante	looker-on	pailful	shelf
dilettante	madam	passer-by	spendthrift

5. Each of the following plurals may have a different meaning from its corresponding singular. Compose sentences that will show this difference.

advices	heavens	pains	senses
airs	honors	parts	silks
ashes	humors	physics	skies
attentions	letters	powers	spirits
bearings	lights	premises	troubles
bitters	looks	pretensions	vapors
colors	loves	quarters	vespers
confidences	morals	regards	waters
damages	numbers	returns	wits
decencies	orders	sands	works
graces	organs	scenes	writings

6. Explain the meaning of each italicized word below:

1. That was an excellent roast of *beef*.
2. The *beeves* were herded in the runway.
3. The *content* of the essay is not clear.
4. We looked through the *contents* of the room.
5. It is the *custom* of the group to sit in silence for an hour every day.
6. We got through the *customs* with no difficulty.
7. The old Spanish *customs* were peculiar.
8. The medicine had strange *effects* upon him.
9. All personal *effects* were sold at the auction.
10. There are weird *forces* at work upon us.
11. The office *forces* are on strike.
12. What *manner* of man is he?
13. Always use good *manners*.
14. He likes the novel of *manners*.
15. He hasn't enough *iron* in his make-up.
16. The criminal was placed in *irons*.
17. These *irons* are not hot.
18. The man isn't worth his *salt*.
19. Ye are the *salt* of the earth.
20. He takes *salts* for his rheumatism.
21. Mother has lost her *spectacles* again.
22. We saw several thrilling *spectacles* at the fair.
23. In what *respects* are they different?
24. We shall pay our *respects* to the nominee.

7. Correct all sentences below that are incorrect because of wrongly used number. (Consult the dictionary when you are in doubt.)

1. All possible means was taken.
2. That data is insufficient.

3. This oats are moldy.
4. That poultry look healthy.
5. The banns has been pronounced.
6. I caught ten trouts this morning.
7. Thanks is due the committee.
8. This little pistol is a great firearms.
9. The summons were delivered by the officer.
10. We saw two rhinoceri at the zoo.
11. What a strange phenomena this is!
12. What are the news today?
13. A broad strata of ore has been found.
14. How many specieses have you there?
15. This tongs are made of wrought iron.
16. That two innings was exciting.
17. Those gallows has been torn down.
18. That barracks accommodate one thousand.
19. Civics are a most interesting study.
20. The Misses Smiths are coming to dinner.

43. **Case** means the relation of nouns and pronouns to certain other words in a sentence. There are three cases in English: nominative, possessive, and objective.

44. The **nominative case** is used—

1. When a noun is the subject of a sentence or of a finite verb: *Falcons were formerly trained to hunt.*

2. When a noun is used as a predicate complement following a copulative, or linking, verb: *Lincoln was a great president.*

3. When a noun is used in direct address: *Bill, please close the door.*

4. When a noun stands with a participle in an independent construction connected, however, by thought with the rest of a sentence: *The rain having stopped, we prepared for the journey.*

5. When a noun is in apposition with a noun in the nominative case: *The man is Tony, the gardener* and *George, my brother, has just come from Europe.*

The position of a noun in a sentence does not affect its case. Note the position of the underscored nominative in each of the following: *Attend to that, John. Has Harry come yet? There is a lady in the car. Were Bill here, I'd tell him. I shall not go; neither will John. "That," said Tom, "is what I mean." Doomed is our Daniel!*

45. The **possessive case** is used when a noun denotes possession, origin, or source.

1. The possessive case is the only inflected case. It is shown by the apostrophe followed by *s* or by the apostrophe alone. The possessive singular is usually formed by *'s*, as *boy's prize, day's work.* When the noun ends in *s* or in another hissing sound, only the apostrophe is used, as *Dickens' novels,* although some writers prefer the apostrophe and *s* with names of one syllable, as in *Jones's.* When the plural of a noun ends in *s*, the possessive plural is formed by adding an apostrophe only, as *dolls' dresses, scouts' possessions.* When the plural does not end in *s*, the possessive plural is formed by adding an apostrophe and *s*, as *children's hats, women's activities.*

2. Compound nouns take the sign of the possessive at the end, as *mother-in-law's cake, mothers-in-law's cakes; man-of-war's appearance, men-of-war's appearance.*

3. If two or more names are used to denote joint possession, the sign of ownership is placed only with the last, as *Beaumont and Fletcher's plays, Germany and Italy's alliance.* If two or more names are used to denote individual ownership, the sign of possession should appear with each, as *John's and Bill's hats, Sarah's, Mary's, and Helen's chances.*

4. A plural possessive may be used with a singular noun, as *ladies' lounge,* and a singular possessive with a plural noun, as *man's feet.*

5. In possessive terms denoting no actual ownership the apostrophe is frequently omitted, especially if such terms are proper, as *Teachers College, All Souls Church, Actors Equity, Farmers Trust Company.*

6. Usually the possessive case of a noun has the same meaning as the possessive phrase beginning with the preposition *of. The inventions of Thomas Edison* and *Thomas Edison's inventions*

mean the same. The use of the phrase instead of 's is preferred to awkward wording.

Right: Mr. Burton gave a report upon *the work of the Association for Improving the Condition of the Poor.*

Awkward: Mr. Burton gave a report upon *the Association for Improving the Condition of the Poor's work.*

The use of a phrase instead of 's is preferred when a series of possessives makes a bungled and confusing sequence.

Right: My traveling companion proved to be *the sister of the wife of Bill's friend.*

Awkward: My traveling companion proved to be *Bill's friend's wife's sister*

Sometimes the single preposition makes the meaning ambiguous. If you say *the persecutions of the Saracens,* you may mean the persecutions they suffered or the persecutions they inflicted upon others. Clarify the meaning by a modifying phrase.

Right: The persecutions of the Crusaders by the Saracens did not daunt the spirit of the Christian armies.

Ambiguous: The persecutions of the Saracens did not daunt the spirit of the Christian armies.

7. The possessive case of a noun or a pronoun is usually required before a gerund, or verbal noun, as *Harry's coming, the boy's playing.*

Take care to distinguish between the gerund, or verbal noun, and the participle which modifies a noun. If the action is the thing talked about—that about which the assertion is made—the verb form is used as a noun.

Right: Harry's coming was anxiously awaited by his mother. (gerund)

Right: Harry, *coming* home for the first time in three years, was anxiously awaited by his mother. (participle used as modifier)

Wrong: Harry coming was anxiously awaited by his mother.

8. The inflected possessive—the 's form—should be confined to the names of living beings or personified objects and to idiomatic expressions denoting time, space, or measure.

Right: The *ship's deck* was crowded with passengers. (*Ship* is usually per-
  sonified.)
Right: The *horse's manger* was quite empty.
Right: The *king's son* traveled a *day's journey.*
Wrong: Get some hay from the *barn's mow.*
Wrong: What is the *room's size?*

9. By a double possessive is meant the idiomatic expression
in which both the inflected possessive and the *of* possessive are
used, as *a novel of Eliot's* or *a play of O'Neill's.* What is really
meant is *a novel of Eliot's novels* or *a play of O'Neill's plays.*
The expressions *a novel of Eliot* and *a play of O'Neill* are correct, but they sound strange because they are not idiomatic.

Right: A play of O'Neill's was chosen for one high-school dramatic production.
Unidiomatic: A play of O'Neill was chosen for one high-school dramatic production.

10. In appositive expressions in which there is no comma
because the meaning is restrictive (see page 247), the sign of
possession is used with the noun nearest the thing possessed, as
*my brother John's car, Alfred the Great's reign, Mary Queen of
Scots' death.*

46. The **objective case** is used—

1. When a noun is the object of a verb, of a participle, or of an
infinitive, as *Mary did her work* (*work* is the direct object of
the verb *did*); *Mary, doing her work, became ill* (*work* is the
object of the participle *doing*); and *Mary tried to do her work*
(*work* is the object of the infinitive *to do*).

2. When a noun is used as cognate object of a verb; that is,
when it repeats the meaning of an otherwise intransitive verb,
as *She lived a sad life* and *They fought a good fight.* The cognate object should always have a modifier; else there is no point
in repeating the term.

Right: She *lived a most unhappy life.*
Wrong: She *lived a life.*

3. When a noun is used as an objective complement; that is, when it means the same thing as the direct object or explains or describes it. In *They made Carol captain,* the word *captain* explains what they made Carol, and the sentence is incomplete without it. The objective complement must not be confused with a noun in apposition. Such verbs as *appoint, call, choose, constitute, elect, find, make, name, ordain, think* take objective complements denoting rank, office, position, name, and the like.

Right: They made Bill *manager.*
Right: The Conferates elected Jefferson Davis *president.*

4. When a noun is used as a retained object after a passive verb. In *We gave the position to Bill, position* is the direct object of active *gave.* In *Bill was given the position, position* is retained as object of passive *was given* (see page 129).

5. When a noun is the indirect object of a verb, as *I gave Mr. Jones my report* and *Get your mother the book. Mr. Jones* and *mother* are the objects, respectively, of the prepositions *to* and *for* understood after the verbs.

6. When a noun is used as the object of a preposition, as *Look on the table* and *Go into the house.*

7. When a noun is used like an adverb, as *I studied an hour* and *It is worth ten dollars.* This construction is called the adverbial objective.

8. When a noun is in apposition with a noun or a pronoun in the objective case, as *I talked with Henry, the teller at the bank* and *I saw him, the president of the senate, yesterday.*

EXERCISES

1. Write the possessive plural feminine of each of the following:

czar	god	man	shepherd
duck	governor	monk	stag
duke	hero	negro	waiter
earl	host	nephew	widower
executor	ianitor	prophet	wizard

2. Write and pronounce the possessive singular and the possessive plural of the following:

Aaron	Edwards	Harts	Queen Mary
Aarons	Field	Jeffreys	The Prime Minister of England
Adam	Fields	Mark	The Prince of Wales
Adams	German	Marks	Thucydides
Boyes	Gross	Matthew	Willet
Bridge	Hargreave	Matthews	Willets
Bridges	Hargreaves	Max	William
Chinese	Harris	Norman	Williams
Edward	Hart	Portuguese	Zwingli

3. Express the following possessives less awkwardly:

1. The Columbia Plate Glass Company's building.
2. The Committee on Public Information's report.
3. The Society for the Prevention of Cruelty to Animal's policy.
4. The Chairman of the Committee for the Propagation of the Faith's speech.
5. The Colorado Interscholastic Athletic League's rules and regulations.

4. What two or more meanings has each of the following? Express each so that it means one thing only.

1. Atkinson's murder.
2. The major's praises.
3. The culprit's persecution.
4. The brother's reward.
5. Elizabeth's picture.
6. Harrison's statue.
7. Coxey's invasion.
8. Parkinson's novel.
9. Harry's desertion.
10. Parents' love.
11. Bradford's defeat.
12. My boy's interest.

5. Give the case of each noun in the following passage, and explain it construction in the sentence:

I had expected to find Sicily lovely, and it exceeded all my hopes. The boat drew into the harbor of Palermo on a bright, sunny afternoon. My friends, who had left their home in Messina very early in the day to meet my boat, were soon aboard to help me through the customs. What a lot of noise! One of the inspectors objected to a large package of newspapers I had brought from New York, but after some discussion he promised that we might have them if I came again the next day. By that time he had received instructions from his superiors to let me have them. I felt free to enjoy the sunshine, the beautiful and fragrant spring flowers, the magnificent buildings with their carvings and mosaics, and all the wonderful relics of ancient and medieval days.

Pronouns

47. A **pronoun** is a word used in place of a noun to avoid awkward or monotonous repetition. *John brought his mother the book that she sent him to get* is much more graceful than *John brought John's mother the book that John's mother sent John to get.* But sometimes the noun must be repeated.

Ambiguous: John's father says that he thinks he will return to college.
Clear: John's father says that John thinks he will return to college.
Clear: John's father says that he thinks John will return to college.

48. The word to which a pronoun refers is called the **ante-cedent** (from the Latin words *ante* and *cedo,* meaning go before). A pronoun agrees with its antecedent in person, number, and gender, but its case depends upon its construction in a sentence. With few exceptions (explained below) a pronoun must have a definite noun or other pronoun as antecedent.

1. In statements like *It rains often, It is cold, It is said* there is no antecedent for *it.* In this usage *it* is called an **expletive.** The pronoun *it* sometimes introduces the logical subject of the sentence, as in *It was generally believed that the man was innocent.* Here the clause *that the man was innocent* is in apposition with *It,* and the clause is the logical subject.

2. Such pronouns as *whoever, whichever,* and *whatever* usually have antecedents that are implied rather than definitely expressed, as *Whoever broke the case should pay for it;* that is, *the person who(ever) broke the case should pay for it.*

3. A pronoun should not have as an antecedent a noun in the possessive case.

Wrong: Mary's home, *who* won the tennis tournament, is a pretty little Cape Cod cottage.
Right: Mary, who won the tennis tournament, lives in a pretty little Cape Cod cottage.

49. Pronouns are divided into the following classes: personal, relative, interrogative, demonstrative, indefinite, and ~~adjective.~~

50. Personal pronouns. A personal pronoun is one that shows by its form whether it denotes the person speaking, the person spoken to, or the person or thing spoken about. No other English part of speech has so many inflections; by its structure it shows person, number, gender, and case. The following paradigm presents all the personal pronouns in all their forms:

PARADIGM

	Nominative Case	*Possessive Case*	*Objective Case*
Singular			
First person	I	my or mine	me
Second person	you (thou)	your or yours (thy or thine)	you (thee)
Third person			
Masculine	he	his	him
Feminine	she	her or hers	her
Neuter	it	its	it
Plural			
First person	we	our or ours	us
Second person	you (ye)	your or yours	you (ye)
Third person	they	their or theirs	them

1. Personal pronouns have the following compound **intensive** and **reflexive** forms: *myself, thyself, yourself, himself, herself, itself, ourselves, yourselves,* and *themselves.* These forms are used to intensify and to emphasize, as *I saw the man himself;* and to serve as object in the reflexive, or "turning-back," pronominal use, as *I hurt myself* and *She praised herself.* Do not use these compound forms alone as subjects. (*Ourself* is used with *we* to refer to a single person in formal or regal style.)

Right: A friend and *I* have rented a summer cabin.
Wrong: A friend and *myself* have rented a summer cabin.

The use of the simple personal pronoun as an intensive or a reflexive is provincial and should be avoided.

Right: I bought *myself* a new car.
Wrong: I bought *me* a new car.

The reflexive suffix must not be added to *his, me, their; hisself, meself, theirself* are illiterate forms.

Do not use *own* with *self* in order to intensify further a term already intensive, as *my own self, your own selves. Own* may correctly be used as an intensifying adjective pronoun after a possessive adjective, as *I shall use my own (pen)* and *This is my own (book).*

2. A personal pronoun in the nominative case should not be added to a noun, thus forming a double subject.

Right: Mary went to the picnic.
Wrong: Mary she went to the picnic.

3. Used co-ordinately with a series of nouns and pronouns, both *I* and *we* should be given the last position.

Right: He, Tom, Harry, and I are going.
Wrong: I, he, Tom, and Harry are going.
Right: The Shelleys, the Breens, and we have tickets together.
Wrong: We, the Shelleys, and the Breens have tickets together.

This is sometimes called the *courtesy construction.* If the predicate of such a series denotes guilt or disgrace of any sort, it is sometimes ruled that the first-person pronouns should come first, as *I and Bill were arrested for speeding.*

4. The personal pronoun *he* and its inflected forms are often used in a general sense to denote either masculine or feminine gender or to avoid the repetition of *one.*

Right: Everybody must do *his* work.
Unnecessary: Everybody must do *his* and *her* work.
Right: If any man or woman wants credit, *he* must come early.
Unnecessary: If any man or woman wants credit, *he* or *she* must come early.
Wrong: If any man or woman wants credit, *they* must come early.
Right: One needs to have *his* wits about *him* in an emergency.
Awkward: One needs to have *one's* wits about *one* in an emergency.

5. Singular nouns following the words *each, every, no* and the correlatives *either . . . or* and *neither . . . nor* are referred to by singular pronouns. The pronoun is singular when two or more singular antecedents connected by *and* are modified by *each, every,* or *no.*

Right: *Each member* of the orchestra provided *his* own instrument.
Wrong: *Each member* of the orchestra provided *their* own instruments.
Right: *Every student* and *every teacher* carried *his* emblem.
Wrong: *Every student* and *every teacher* carried *their* emblem.
Right: Neither the *man* nor the *boy* will identify *himself.*
Wrong: Neither the *man* nor the *boy* will identify *themselves.*

6. If a change of gender occurs in singular subjects connected by the correlatives *either . . . or* or *neither . . . nor,* the pronouns should be repeated or, better still, the construction changed.

Awkward: Either *John* or *Mabel* will take *his* or *her* car.
Preferable: Either *John* will take *his car* or *Mabel* will take *hers.*
Or: Either John or Mabel will take a car.

If a change of number occurs in the subjects, the plural antecedent should be placed last in the series and the pronoun should agree with it, or each statement should be completed independently.

Right: Neither the *dog* nor the *cats* have eaten all *their* food.
Wrong: Neither the *cats* nor the *dog* have eaten all *their* food.
Wrong: Neither the *cats* nor the *dog* has eaten all *its* food.

7. A singular or a plural pronoun may refer to a collective noun. If the noun represents a single unit, the singular form is correct. If it represents individuals acting independently within the unit, the plural form should be used.

Right: The jury has rendered *its* decision.
Right: The jury are divided in *their* opinions.

8. A pronoun is preferably not used to refer to only one part of a compound antecedent.

Not recommended: Mr. and Mrs. Harold Nugent are visiting *her* parents.
Right: Mr. and Mrs. Harold Nugent are visiting *Mrs. Nugent's* parents.
Right: Mr. and Mrs. Harold Nugent are visiting *their* daughter.

9. When a noun in apposition is added to a pronoun, the case form of the pronoun is determined by its use in the sentence.

Right: *We* girls are going to the party.
Wrong: *Us* girls are going to the party.
Right: Give *us* fellows a chance.
Wrong: Give *we* fellows a chance.
Right: A group of *us* students attended court.
Wrong: A group of *we* students attended court.

10. The objective case of the pronoun follows a verb or a preposition. When there is more than one object, the second pronoun as well as the first must be in the objective case.

Right: Mother called Mary and *me*.
Wrong: Mother called Mary and *I*.
Right: Clara is going with you and *me*.
Wrong: Clara is going with you and *I*.

11. In comparative expressions after *as* and *than* the case of the pronoun is determined by its relation to the verb understood in the completed statement.

Right: He is taller than *I* (am tall).
Wrong: He is taller than *me*.
Right: We have as many trophies as *they* (have).
Wrong: We have as many trophies as *them*.
Right: I like him as well as (I like) *her*.
Right: She knows my sister better than (she knows) *me*.

The case form of the pronoun in such constructions as these clarifies meaning. In *He likes Jane better than me,* for instance, the objective case *me* makes clear that the full sentence is *He likes Jane better than he likes me.* Similarly, in *He likes Jane better than I,* the nominative *I* makes clear that the full sentence is *He likes Jane better than I like her.* (See also page 193.)

12. The objective case is correct when, in an infinitive clause, the pronoun follows the verb *to be*. In that construction it agrees with the subject of the infinitive, which is usually in the objective case.

Right: They believed the winner to be *him*.
Right: They believed *him* to be the winner.
Wrong: They believed the winner to be *he*.

13. The **possessive** forms *mine, thine, his, hers, ours, yours, theirs,* and occasionally *its,* are called **independent possessives** because they may stand alone and not modify nouns. When they are used as subjects, their number depends upon the number of the noun understood.

Right: Theirs (automobile) *has* arrived, but *mine has* not.
Right: Theirs (tickets) *have* arrived, but *mine have* not.

The possessives *my, thy, his, her, its, our, your, their* modify nouns and are sometimes classified as **possessive adjectives** to distinguish them from the independent possessives.

14. Never use an apostrophe with a possessive personal pronoun (except *one's*). The apostrophe in such contractions as *I'm, he's, it's, you're, they've* stands for omitted letters in the verbs.

Right: This book is *hers.*
Wrong: This book is *her's.*
Right: Its corner was broken.
Wrong: It's corner was broken.

15. Before a gerund, or verbal noun, use the possessive form of the pronoun except when the emphasis is on the person or thing acting rather than on the action itself.

Right: Mother eagerly awaited *our* coming.
Wrong: Mother eagerly awaited *us* coming.
Right: Mother saw *me* thinking.
Wrong: Mother saw *my* thinking.

16. For the sake of clarity and smoothness the pronouns within one sentence should be kept in the same person. This practice is called **pronominal sequence.**

Right: We never know what the new day may bring *us.*
Wrong: We never know what the new day may bring *you.*
Right: If *you* would have a friend, *you* must be a friend.
Wrong: If *we* would have a friend, *you* must be a friend.
Right: If *a fellow* would have a friend, *he* must be a friend.

17. Though there is a tendency to use colloquially such expressions as *It is me* and *It is her,* good speakers and writers prefer the nominative case after the verb *to be.*

Right: It is *I* (he, she, we, they).
Wrong: It is *me* (him, her, us, them).

18. The objective form should not be used as the subject of a sentence.

Right: *He and I* did the work.
Wrong: *Him and me* did the work.
Wrong: *Him and I* did the work.

19. The objective form *them* must not be substituted for a demonstrative adjective.

Right: Have you read any of *those* books?
Wrong: Have you read any of *them* books?

20. Personal pronouns should not be omitted from key constructions. This is a somewhat common but none the less deplorable tendency in business expression (see page 327).

Right: We have your order of the twelfth.
Wrong: Have your order of the twelfth.
Right: I shall see Mary tomorrow.
Wrong: Shall see Mary tomorrow.

EXERCISES

1. Supply the missing pronouns in the following:

1. Request that goods be forwarded immediately.
2. Am thirty years of age and should like the position.
3. Solicit your attention to these extraordinary values.
4. Shall take the matter up with the proper authorities.
5. Give best to Clara and tell to write soon.
6. Trust to have the privilege of meeting soon.
7. Will certainly follow advice so kindly given.
8. Put foot on pedal, press down, and then forge ahead.
9. Charles Hepson and wife have just departed.
10. Received books, thank you, and greatly indebted to you.

2. Insert *its* and *it's* as required in the following:

1. The kitten has lost   ?   ribbon.
2. I think   ?   going to rain because   ?   cloudy.
3. I like   ?   soft fur but fancy   ?   going to shed.
4.   ?   a long lane that has no turning.
5.   ?   a pity that dog has lost   ?   collar.
6.   ?   windy and the tree shakes   ?   limbs.
7. When   ?   rainy   ?   wheels are likely to skid.
8. When   ?   summertime in Lombardy,   ?   summer in my heart.
9. He said   ?   interesting to see a bud open   ?   petals.
10. "   ?   no use," said he, "   ?   flavor is gone and   ?   too late to restore it."

3. Explain the type of error in each of the following sentences, and correct the sentence:

1. Mother told Betsy that she might go skating after dinner.
2. Bob explained to Fred why he was not on the team.
3. This is Jim's ticket, who is fourth in line.
4. I am wearing Mother's ring, who received it as a gift on her eighteenth birthday.
5. The man explained to Allen that he was using the wrong entrance.
6. Everybody brought their own lunch.
7. Somebody has forgotten their hat.
8. Each of the girls are enthusiastic about their club.
9. Neither my parents nor my sister have lived on a farm.
10. Have you seen Janet's purse, who left it here on the table?

51. Relative pronouns. A relative pronoun refers to a noun or a pronoun in a principal clause and serves also as a connective element between a principal clause and a subordinate clause. Its case depends upon its use in the sentence.

The relative pronouns are *who, which, what, that,* and, rarely, *as* and *but.* In addition there are the compounds *whoever, whichever, whatever,* and their variants. *Who* refers to persons or to personified things; *which* refers to lower animals and to things; *that* refers to persons, animals, or things:

> We met a man *who* directed us.
> He likes tennis, *which* is an excellent exercise.
> Here is a boy *that* will help.
> This is the car *that* I want.

When you are in doubt whether to use *who* or *which,* you may safely fall back upon *that.* Use *that* also to avoid unnecessary repetition, as *He said that the boy who* (not *that*) *was wanted had left that bouquet for the teacher.*

Right: The family *that* I helped was appreciative.
Right: He told me of great men and great sights *that* he had seen.

What and the compound relatives contain their own antecedents:

> I know *what* (that which) you mean.
> *Whoever* (the one who) wants to go may have a ticket.
> I'll do *whatever* (the thing which) is expected.

As used as a relative follows *such* and *same; but* used as a relative occurs in negative expressions and has the meaning *who does not:*

> He gave me such books *as* would help.
> There is no one *but* believes him innocent.

1. *Who* is the only relative that has complete case forms, **as:**

Nominative	who
Possessive	whose
Objective	whom

Whose is frequently used also as the possessive of *which,* as in *The undiscover'd country from whose bourn no traveller returns.* It is often substituted for the possessive forms *of whom* and *of which* because it is shorter and less awkward. Though *whose* is preferably not used for lower animals and for inanimate things, the best writers and speakers admit exceptions to this rule.

Right: I selected a book the title *of which* had attracted me.
Right: I selected a book *whose* title had attracted me.

2. Use *whom, whomever,* and *whomsoever* correctly in objective-case constructions.

Right: The man *whom* I spoke to is my uncle.
Right: The man to *whom* I spoke is my uncle.
Wrong: The man *who* I spoke to is my uncle.
Right: Invite *whomever* you wish. (him, her, the one)
Wrong: Invite *whoever* you wish.

To determine whether to use *who* or *whom,* substitute the personal pronoun for which it stands in the subordinate clause; for example, *Mary is a girl who (she,* not *her) has great ability.* Use the same case for the relative pronoun as you would use for the personal pronoun.

3. Parenthetical expressions do not affect the case of relative pronouns in a subordinate clause.

Right: He is the boy *who,* I believe, deserves the award.
Wrong: He is the boy *whom,* I believe, deserves the award.
Right: She is a person *whom,* I understand, people trust.
Wrong: She is a person *who,* I understand, people trust.

4. Place a relative pronoun as close as possible to its antecedent in order to avoid ambiguity of reference.

Right: He that is without pity is a monster.
Wrong: He is a monster *that* is without pity.

5. The relative pronoun is often omitted when the meaning is clear without it. Such practice is colloquial rather than literary.

Right: This is the man (whom) I gave it to.
Right: This is the book (which) I spoke of.
Right: She is a woman (whom) I have met.

The relative should not be omitted, however, if its omission makes the sentence awkward.

Right: They are still in the predicament in *which* you found them.
Awkward: They are still in the predicament you found them in.

When the relative is the object of a preposition, the preposition may conclude the sentence, but it must not be repeated.

Right: This is the book *to which* I referred.
Colloquial: This is the book *which* I referred *to.*
Wrong: This is the book *to which* I referred *to.*

6. In colloquial usage a relative pronoun may refer to a group of words—a phrase or a clause—as an antecedent. A single adjective, however, must not be used as an antecedent.

Right: He said that the man was destitute, a statement which I refused to believe.

Colloquial: He said that the man was destitute, which I refused to believe.

Right: Be courteous, for without courtesy no one will like you.

Wrong: Be courteous, without which no one will like you.

7. The co-ordinate conjunctions *and* and *but* should not be used before a relative pronoun unless another relative in a similar construction precedes.

Right: The carpenter *who* won the prize *and who* built my house has been swamped with contracts.

Wrong: The carpenter winning the prize *and who* built my house has been swamped with contracts.

Right: He is a man *who* is always kind *and who* places the interests of others above his own.

Wrong: He is a kind man *and who* always places the interests of others above his own.

8. Relative clauses are never written as complete sentences.

Right: This is the house plan which we have selected.

Wrong: This is the house plan. Which we have selected.

9. Different relative pronouns should not be used to refer to the same antecedent in a single construction.

Right: The woman who spoke and who made such a fine impression is my first cousin.

Wrong: The woman that spoke and who made such a fine impression is my first cousin.

10. The relative *that* should, as a rule, be used in preference to *who* or *which* to introduce a restrictive clause. In *My brother that is in Africa is ill,* I am restricting my statement to one of my brothers, the one in Africa. In *My brother, who is in Africa, is ill,* I am making a statement about the illness of my only brother and am incidentally adding the information that he is in Africa. (See page 158.)

EXERCISES

1. Insert in each of the following sentences the missing relative pronoun:

1. Here is the boy you want to see.
2. The car we met was speeding.

3. There is a house I like very much.
4. The suit he wore was made in London.
5. Where is the fruit I brought you?
6. The horse I put my money on will win.
7. Here is the person I gave it to.
8. Everything he touches turns to gold.
9. The college I wish to attend is in Illinois.
10. She is the one I intend to marry.

2. Simplify each of the following by means of a relative pronoun:

1. We like the man. He motored us to the station.
2. The child was playing in the yard. The child was bitten by the dog.
3. There goes the popular student. He participates in all sports.
4. The car has run fifty thousand miles. We bought it from Timothy.
5. We saw that big sheep dog. His leg was broken by the speeding car.
6. I have read two novels. These novels were written by Edna Ferber.
7. That man robbed our school building. He has been caught at last.
8. The picture of Washington hangs in the schoolroom. The picture has fallen to the floor.
9. The young man is not going to the party. We met him at the soda fountain yesterday.
10. I met the movie actor at the preview. He is the one you told me about when I saw you in Hollywood.

3. For each italicized phrase below, substitute a clause beginning with a relative pronoun:

1. He gave the card to a child *in ragged clothes.*
2. My teacher sent a note home *complaining about my conduct.*
3. The old lady is a person *of most extraordinary habits.*
4. The steed, *rearing and agitated,* was white with sweat.
5. He has bought a new car *with all kinds of improvements.*
6. I could not understand the man *with the pronounced lisp.*
7. I did not see the picture *with the extraordinary coloring.*
8. We shall admit no one *without a card of identification.*
9. That beautiful house *located on the lake* has been burned.
10. They arrived in a car *covered with mud* and in clothing *creased and dirty.*

4. In each of the following sentences use the correct form of *who* or *whoever.*

1. He is a man   ?   , I feel sure, will succeed.
2. Appoint as editor   ?   you think is best qualified.
3.   ?   did you meet on your trip?
4. The man   ?   was given the position began his work yesterday.

5.   ?   do you think took the money?
6.   ?   did they consider responsible for the accident?
7. Jim was the one   ?   I recognized first.
8. My father,   ?   you have met, is a civil engineer.
9. Please return   ?   book you have borrowed.
10. In their enthusiasm they spoke to   ?   they met.
11. Sell tickets to   ?   will buy them.
12.   ?   the gods would destroy they first make mad.
13. He is a man   ?   everybody hates and fears.
14. She is the friend with   ?   I spend my vacations.
15. She is not the person   ?   I wanted   ?   help me.

5. Point out the error in each of the following sentences and write each sentence correctly:

1. The agent that I met and who represents the singer has arrived.
2. They are unfit to work with others who cannot comply with rules.
3. Beliefs which prevail are those of greatest worth.
4. There is the same woman as we saw at the museum yesterday.
5. We think we had better do the same that he does.
6. That man is a boor who does not give a lady his seat.
7. He is still in the same position in which you placed him in.
8. He is the truant boy and whom is obliged to bring his parents.
9. Who who has seen him can tell who he looks like.
10. He is said to be very clever which makes him conceited.

52. Interrogative pronouns.

52. Interrogative pronouns. An interrogative pronoun is one that is used to ask a question, either direct or indirect. The interrogatives are *who, which,* and *what.* For the most part, they are similar to the relative pronouns. There is one difference, however, in the use of *who* and *which. Who* is general or universal; *which* is limited or selective, asking for any one out of a given group or number.

Right: Who answered the telephone?
Right: Which of you answered the telephone?

Although the colloquial use of the interrogative *who* for *whom* is less objectionable perhaps than the same mistake in the use of the relatives *who* and *whom,* care should nevertheless be exercised to use the objective case correctly.

Right: Whom are you going to the game with?
Wrong: Who are you going to the game with?

Right: *Whom* did you call?
Wrong: *Who* did you call?
Right: She asked me *whom* I saw.
Wrong: She asked me *who* I saw.

Inasmuch as the subject of an infinitive is usually in the objective case, an interrogative or a relative pronoun, in an infinitive clause, that refers to the subject of the infinitive should also be in the objective case.

Right: *Whom* do you believe *him* to be?
Wrong: *Who* do you believe *him* to be?

EXERCISE

In each blank space below insert the correct relative or interrogative:

1. ? is the man ? owns the car ? won the race?
2. Do you consider him one of the greatest men ? ever lived?
3. ? did you dance with at the party, and ? did you wear?
4. ? do you take the woman to be, and ? is she with?
5. She is the girl ? took the prize ? was offered by the club.
6. This is the actor of ? I spoke when you asked ? I went with.
7. ? the boy is, he is not one ? I should care to vouch for.
8. ? shall I write to in regard to the book of ? you spoke?
9. ? do you think I met while I was out walking with the man?
10. You should be careful ? you associate with.

53. Demonstrative pronouns. A demonstrative pronoun is one that points out. The demonstratives are *this* and *that* with their plurals *these* and *those,* as *This is the day* and *These are the books I want.*

54. Indefinite pronouns. An indefinite pronoun is one that is general in its reference. The indefinites most frequently used are:

all	each	many	one
another	either	neither	other
any	everybody	nobody	several
anybody	everyone	no one	some
anyone	few	none	somebody
both	little	nothing	someone

1. Indefinite pronouns may be used as adjectives. Some grammarians call them adjective pronouns or pronominal adjectives, according to their principal use in a sentence. In *Several men have arrived, several* is an adjective. In *There were several at the dinner, several* is a pronominal adjective or an indefinite pronoun.

2. Observe that *each* is singular. A pronoun referring to it as antecedent must be singular.

Right: Each of the girls brought *her* skates.
Wrong: Each of the girls brought *their* skates.

3. Similarly, *anybody, everybody, nobody, somebody,* and other compounds of this type are singular. Pronouns referring to them must therefore be singular. If the gender is not definite or is common, the masculine form of the pronoun is used.

Right: Everybody did *his* best.
Wrong: Everybody did *their* best.
Right: No one forgot *his* ticket.
Wrong: No one forgot *their* ticket.

4. *None* is a contraction of *no one* and is therefore logically singular. Colloquially, however, it is commonly used as a plural. The antecedent will help you determine whether a plural or a singular verb should be used.

Right: How many *boys have* come? *None have* come.
Right: Which *book is* for sale? *None is* for sale.
Right: Which *books are* for sale? *None are* for sale.

It is sometimes ruled that *none,* together with *number, remainder, rest,* is singular when it refers to a whole as a unit and that it is plural when it refers to individuals in a group severally. Preceded by *a* the word *number* is regarded as plural; preceded by *the,* as singular.

5. Whether *either* and *neither* should be regarded as singular or plural depends upon their antecedents (see page 24).

Right: Are *boys* or *girls* to be appointed? *Either are.*
Right: Is *John* or *Alice* going? *Neither is.*

6. Careful writers use the expression *each other* of two only; the expression *one another,* of more than two.

Right: The mother and her child love *each other.*
Right: All the neighbors envy *one another.*

7. *Little, less, least* refer to quantity; *few, fewer, fewest,* to number.

Right: She has had *fewer* (opportunities) than we.
Right: He has *less* (money) than his friend.

8. When *else* is used in conjunction with another word, such as *anybody, anyone, no one,* or *somebody,* to show possession, it takes the sign of possession, *'s.*

Right: No one else's responsibility; *everybody else's* time.
Wrong: Somebody's else book; *no one's else* fault.

9. The emphatic or reflexive form of the indefinite pronoun *one* is either *oneself* or *one's self.* The two forms are used interchangeably, as a rule, but the former may be regarded as the true reflexive and the latter as the emphatic indefinite to be used in direct reference to one's own personality; thus, you say *One is expected to help oneself* (himself) and *One must do nothing to damage one's self* (respectability).

REVIEW EXERCISES

1. Explain every pronoun in the sentences below—define; classify; name the antecedent; give the gender, person, number, and case; tell what special significance, if any, it has:

1. The busy sylphs surround their darling care,
   These set the head and those divide the hair.
2. Whoso eats thereof forthwith attains wisdom.
3. I consider myself beholden to whoever lends a hand.
4. Whosoever hath Christ for his friend shall be sure of counsel.
5. Whosesoever sins ye remit they are remitted unto them.
6. With whomsoever thou findest thy gods, let him not live.
7. I will do whatsoever thou sayest unto me.
8. Here is the tyrant again, him that I told you of.
9. Certain there are who may be depended upon.
10. Naught's had, all's spent
    Where our desire is got without content.

2. Read or write each of the following correctly and explain your correction:

1. None but the studious deserves to pass.
2. This coat is nobody's else but mine.
3. Neither of them are doing what they were told to do.
4. Every one of the boys have forgotten their papers.
5. Somebody has placed their coat on the wrong peg.
6. Please give them papers to the clerk.
7. The girl's dress who was now performing looked expensive.
8. Neither Bill nor I can do their examples.
9. Everybody on the fields ask to have their picture taken.
10. The wife and husband love one another.
11. The members of the team all like each other.
12. Anyone may have their word disputed by whomever wishes to disagree.

3. Compose sentences in which each of the following pronouns is used as the subject or the object of a verb in the third person, present indicative:

all	each	less	one another
another	each other	many	other
any	either	neither	several
anybody	everybody	nobody	some
anyone	everyone	no one	somebody
anything	everything	none	someone
both	few	one	such

4. Rewrite each of the following so that the word *one* appears but once:

1. One should always try hard, no matter what one is doing.
2. One can never tell what may happen to one.
3. One often finds it difficult to decide what is one's duty.
4. One must do one's best if one hopes to succeed in one's career.
5. One becomes very nervous about one's driving when one gets involved in traffic.

5. Rewrite the following sentences, omitting all superfluous pronouns:

1. The new boy he went to the store.
2. The children they all talked at once.
3. The paper it tells about the new building.
4. Their hats and their shoes and their coats are wet.
5. He himself and I myself will join you yourself.

6. This catalog it tells the price of the seeds.
7. We entered that contest that John might have that assistance that he needed.
8. Mary she insisted that they must stop that kind of teasing that made her so nervous.
9. The warrior bold he'd storm and scold, and half of his men to death he's sold.
10. John B. Harrison says, says he, that he won't vote for Governor B—; not much, says he.

6. Correct the following sentences so that there will be no pronouns without definite antecedents:

1. I like print shops and therefore choose it as may profession.
2. We entered World War I to make it safe for democracy.
3. He is a highly educated person and he makes good use of it.
4. The boy's father said that he thought he ought to work harder.
5. They signed on the dotted line and it gave them great privileges.
6. When you hit the line hard, it makes you feel like a man.
7. He is highly talented, but it has not turned his head.
8. That lad is very conceited, and it makes everyone dislike him.
9. He stayed in the water too long, and it made him sick and taught him a good lesson.
10. He has always been a most kindly person and has always been well liked for it.

7. Reword the following so that in each sentence all the pronouns are in the same person.

1. One cannot be too careful about your conduct.
2. As you enter the room one sees the large painting.
3. When we go to the theater, you are always in suspense.
4. If you want a good record, a fellow must do his very best.
5. One never knows what you are able to do till he is put to the test.
6. He reminded the students that we are just where your forefathers were.
7. If one lives in a glass house, we must not throw stones.
8. If a body meet her comin' through the rye; if a fellow kiss us, need you cry?
9. As you take the seat, a person immediately notices how nicely they have adjusted it for driving.
10. When we arrived, everybody in our party was happy but tired, and they began to change our clothes and make themselves clean and tidy.

8. Rewrite each of the following sentences so that each pronoun will agree with its antecedent in number.

1. One must keep their mind on their work if they would succeed.
2. Everybody should be careful about their health.
3. A person has a right to know their legislative representatives.
4. England expects every man to do their duty.
5. Nobody should attempt to avoid their duty as citizens.
6. Anybody should be informed as to what to do when they are in a fire.
7. All in the class were eager to sign his name to the petition.
8. Everyone in the class was eager to sign their name to the petition.
9. No man has the right to evade their duty as an American voter.
10. Loading and unloading all day takes its toll of sweat and strength.

9. Insert *them, these, those* correctly in the blanks below:

1. The boys will take ? to the field with ? .
2. They will find ? pictures in the book we gave ? .
3. ? coats are too large and ? are too small.
4. Take ? and give ? to ? students.
5. May I have ? , please, instead of ? .
6. Please tell ? that we want ? papers.
7. I want ? there by ? boxes.
8. Give ?   ? chairs in the attic.
9. I like ? but ? are better than ? .
10. He gave ? to me yesterday, but I returned ? to him.

10. Correct the misused pronouns in each of the following:

1. Me and him are ready to go.
2. Nobody except he and I is allowed to attend.
3. All them that have finished may leave the room.
4. Who did he say he is going to vote for?
5. The best seats should be given to we alumni.
6. Who did you nod to as me and Bill were talking?
7. He works harder than me but fails oftener than me.
8. She said that neither you nor me are allowed to leave.
9. It is us who the special privileges are to be given to.
10. Us fellows want you to give the medal to whomever deserves it.
11. I shall never forget them dancing on the snow-covered lawn.
12. It is them whom the teachers think deserve the punishment.
13. Him having been administered a scolding, us classmates were glum.
14. Beside Jim and I sat a person who nobody paid any attention to.
15. Please tell me whose going to the village with ourselves.

Adjectives

55. An **adjective** is a word used to describe or limit the meaning of a noun or a pronoun. Adjectives are divided into two general classes: descriptive and limiting.

A **descriptive adjective** is one that pictures or describes, as *rough edge* and *large boat*. A **limiting adjective** is one that limits, bounds, or specifies, as *certain people* and *double strength*. A limiting adjective that denotes number is called a **numeral adjective.** If a numeral adjective answers the question "How many?" it is a **cardinal,** as *three boys;* if it answers the question "In what order or position?" it is an **ordinal,** as *tenth place.* The adjectives *this, that, these,* and *those* are often called **demonstrative adjectives.** Be sure to use *this* and *that* to modify singular nouns, as *this kind* and *that sort; these* and *those* to modify plural nouns, as *those kinds* and *these sorts.*

There are minor classifications of adjectives. An adjective formed from a proper noun is called a **proper adjective,** as *American industry* and *British navy;* an adjective formed from a verb is called a **participial adjective,** as *deciding factor* and *known facts;* an adjective used as a noun is called a **substantive adjective,** as *the pure in heart.* If a substantive adjective refers to a quality, it is called an **abstract adjective;** if to persons or things, a **concrete adjective.** The substantive *pure* above is abstract. In *The poor you have always with you, poor* is concrete, *people* being understood after it. A pronoun used as an adjective is called a **pronominal adjective.**

56. An adjective that stands directly before the noun or pronoun it modifies is called an **attributive adjective,** as *an intelligent student.* An adjective that stands after a copulative, or linking, verb and qualifies the subject of that verb is called a **predicate adjective,** as *She looks bad* and *The sugar is brown.* Such verbs as *appear, be, become, feel, look, seem, smell, sound, taste* are usually followed by a predicate adjective. Do not use an adverb in such constructions:

Right: I feel *bad.* It smells *sweet.* It sounds *beautiful.*
Wrong: I feel *badly.* It smells *sweetly.* It sounds *beautifully.*

ADJECTIVES

In all the correct forms the predicate adjective describes or explains the subject and completes the predicate. If the word following the verb modifies or pertains to the verb only, it is an adverb; thus, *She looks badly* means that the looking is done in a bad manner.

57. An adjective that describes or explains an object and at the same time completes a verb is called an **objective adjective** or an adjective used as **objective complement,** as *They made the place respectable.* In this sentence *respectable* describes *place* and completes *made.*

58. *A, an,* and *the* are limiting adjectives. They are sometimes called **articles.** *A* and *an* are the **indefinite articles;** *the* is the **definite article.** *A* is used before words beginning with a consonant sound, no matter what the first letter of such words; *an* is used before words beginning with a vowel sound, no matter what the first letter of such words; thus, *a man, a dog; an appetite, an entrance.* Note that words like *heir, honor,* and *hour,* though they begin with the consonant *h,* are pronounced as if they began with a vowel; and *union, unit,* and *university,* though they begin with a vowel, are pronounced as if they began with the consonant *y.*

Right: An heir, an honor, an hour.
Wrong: A heir, a honor, a hour.
Right: A union, a unit, a university.
Wrong: An union, an unit, an university.

In England, and sometimes in the United States, when the first syllable of a word beginning with *h* or with *u* pronounced like *y* is unaccented, the article *an* is used, as *an hotel, an historian, an unique performance.*

As *a* and *an* mean or imply *one,* they are incorrect after such phrases as *fashion of, kind of, manner of, sort of, type of,* which imply more than one:

Right: What *manner of man* is he?
Wrong: What *manner of a man* is he?
Right: What *sort of book* is that?
Wrong: What *sort of a book* is that?

59. Comparison. Most adjectives are inflected to denote degrees of qualifying or intensifying. These are called **degrees of comparison.** There are three such degrees: the **positive,** denoting merely that quality exists; the **comparative,** denoting that quality exists to a greater or less degree; and the **superlative,** denoting that it exists to the greatest or least degree.

1. Adjectives of one syllable and many adjectives of two syllables form the comparative degree by suffixing *er*, and the superlative degree by suffixing *est*. Some adjectives of two syllables and most adjectives of more than two syllables form the comparative by inserting the word *more* before the positive for increasing, or ascending, comparison and the word *less* for decreasing, or descending, comparison. They form the superlatives by inserting the word *most* or *least* respectively, thus:

Positive	Comparative	Superlative
grand	grander	grandest
noble	nobler	noblest
fertile	less fertile	least fertile
beautiful	more beautiful	most beautiful
wonderful	less wonderful	least wonderful

2. Some adjectives may be compared in two ways, as *common, commoner, commonest,* or *common, more* or *less common, most* or *least common.* For ascending comparison, as has been seen, the suffixes *er* and *est* are used. For descending comparison there are no suffixes; *less* and *least* must be used, as *less grand* and *least grand.* Do not use double comparative or superlative forms, that is, both *more* and the suffix *er* or *most* and the suffix *est,* with the same term.

Right: Lovelier, smoothest.
Wrong: More lovelier, most smoothest.

3. Some adjectives have no comparative degree but form a superlative by adding *most* as a suffix, as *end* and *endmost, top* and *topmost.* And some adjectives are compared irregularly, as follows:

Positive	Comparative	Superlative
bad evil ill	worse	worst
far	farther	farthest
fore	former	foremost or first
forth	further	furthest or furthermost
good	better	best
hind	hinder	hindmost or hindermost
(no positive)	hither	hithermost
in	inner	inmost or innermost
late	latter or later	last or latest
little	less or lesser	least
low	lower	lowest or lowermost
many much	more	most
near	nearer	nearest or next
(no positive)	nether	nethermost
nigh	nigher	nighest or next
old	older or elder	oldest or eldest
out	outer	outmost or outermost utmost or uttermost
(no positive)	thither	thithermost (rare)
(no positive)	under	undermost
up	upper	uppermost or upmost

The positive forms of several of the adjectives above are used also as adverbs, as *forth, in, out, up.*

4. Adjectives that in themselves denote an absolute quality or quantity are generally regarded as impossible of comparison; for example:

absolute	final	perpendicular	total
boundless	horizontal	preferable	triangular
circular	illimitable	round	unique
complete	inevitable	square	universal
empty	mutual	sufficient	vacant
eternal	perfect	supreme	vertical

Comparison is correctly stated in such expressions as *more nearly square* (not *more square*), and *most nearly round* (not *roundest*). But expressions such as *more perfect* and *most supreme* are found in literature from the time of Shakespeare to the present.

5. The **comparative degree** is used to refer to two; the superlative, to more than two.

Right: John is the *better of the two*.
Right: Bill is the *best of the three*.
Wrong: Which do you like the *better—apples, pears, or peaches?*
Wrong: Of these *two*, which do you like *best?*

6. The **superlative degree** is sometimes used to denote a very high order without any idea of comparison, as *my dearest boy, my most devoted friend*. The comparative, likewise, may be used in an absolute sense to emphasize degree of quality rather than to denote specific comparison, as *at the better shops everywhere* and *the higher criticism*.

The adjective is a much abused part of speech. Avoid using inappropriately such extravagant adjectives as *awful, wonderful, colossal, marvelous, grand, extraordinary, stupendous*.

Right: That was a *very good* picture.
Wrong: That was a *most stupendously and colossally absorbing* picture.

EXERCISES

1. Write the adjective form of each of the following. Consult the dictionary for those about which you are uncertain:

Africa	China	Ireland	Shaw
Algiers	Colombia	Italy	Siam
Austria	Cuba	Naples	Sweden
Belgium	Denmark	Norway	Switzerland
Brazil	France	Paris	Turkey
California	Greece	Scotland	Venice
Chile	Holland	Shakespeare	Vienna

2. Explain why *a* or *an* should be used before each of the following:

ax	hand	Irishman	uniform
cry	herb	orange	usurper
ear	historical	pear	X-ray
European	hue	umbrella	yacht
ewe	invalid	umpire	yew

3. In each blank supply a correct comparative or superlative:

1. This is a(n) ? problem than that.
2. Her hair is ? than her sister's.
3. This is the ? trouble she has ever known.

4. Hers is the ? case the doctor has ever had.
5. This one may be ? than hers; indeed, it may be the ? .
6. His speech was ? than I expected, but by no means the ? .
7. They have just rounded up the ? criminal in the community.
8. She drives the ? car in the neighborhood, but Jane's is ? , I think, and even my own is ? .

4. Complete the following comparisons to Harry's advantage or disadvantage:

1. I am happy but Harry is ? .
2. I am good but Harry is ? .
3. I am naughty but Harry is ? .
4. I am fantastic but Harry is ? .
5. I am usually lonely but Harry is ? .
6. I am short and stocky but Harry is ? and ? .
7. I am frequently incorrigible but Harry is ? .
8. I am considered difficult but Harry is ? .
9. I am very eccentric but Harry is ? .
10. I am dull and stupid but Harry is ? .

5. Use an adjective in place of each italicized expression below:

1. He is *very fond of himself*.
2. She is a woman *of very strange habits*.
3. Turner is *always ready for a fight*.
4. His home is *located just beyond the town*.
5. Their story is *entirely beyond belief*.
6. James is *possessed of plenty of this world's goods*.
7. He is always *evincing the most courteous attitude*.
8. Don't be *inclined to exaggerate trivial matters*.
9. She is *never known to tire of hearing her own voice*.
10. He was born *with a silver spoon in his mouth* in a country *flowing with milk and honey*.

6. Write the following correctly:

1. I am tiderer than I have ever been before.
2. He is the hardheartedest man in the world.
3. I like this the better of the three.
4. He has the most worriedest look.
5. Which of those two delicacies is the sweetest?
6. This slice of beef is the donedest there is.
7. I think you go from worst to worst.
8. Her stockings are sheerer than mine.
9. We had a most absolutely excruciating time.
10. Her work was pronounced more perfect than mine.

11. I think this is more preferable to that.
12. He stands in a most supreme position.
13. That was the appetizingest melon I ever ate.
14. These sort of people never get very far.
15. A man with a earned income can retain his self-respect.

Verbs

60. A **verb** is a word that expresses action, state, or condition.

61. In regard to *form,* verbs may be classified as follows:

1. A **regular,** or **weak, verb** is one to which *ed* (or *d*) is added to denote past time, as *walk, walked; provoke, provoked.* An **irregular,** or **strong, verb** is one that undergoes some internal change in order to denote past time, as *run, ran; sing, sang.*

2. A **principal,** or **notional, verb** is that member of a verb phrase that contains the main idea of the phrase. It is the last verb in such a phrase; thus, in *have seen* and *has been tried, seen* and *tried* are the principal verbs. *Have* in the first example and *has been* in the second example are **auxiliary,** or **helping, verbs.**

3. A **defective verb** is one that lacks some of the parts that most verbs have. The verbs *must, can, may,* and *shall* lack, for instance, the participles—they have no form corresponding to *having* or *spoken.*

4. A **redundant verb** is one that has more than one form for the past tense or for the past participle; the verb *light,* for example, may be either *lit* or *lighted* in the past tense; the verb *mow* may be *mowed* or *mown* in the past participle.

5. A **causative verb** is one that expresses agency or cause and is derived, as a rule, from another word, as *darken* from *dark; frighten* from *fright.*

Of all these classifications the most troublesome one in everyday usage is probably that of strong and weak verbs. Following are the principal parts—the present indicative, the past, or imperfect, indicative, and the past participle—of the most troublesome irregular verbs in English. The present participle is sometimes included in the parts of the verb. It is invariably formed by adding *ing* to the present indicative.

IRREGULAR VERBS

Present	Past or Imperfect	Past Participle	Present	Past or Imperfect	Past Participle
awake	awoke (awaked)	awaked (awoke)	lead	led	led
be	was	been	let	let	let
bear	bore (bare)	born (borne)	lie	lay	lain
beat	beat	beaten	lose	lost	lost
become	became	become	pay	paid	paid
begin	began	begun	plead	pleaded (plead, pled)	pleaded
bend	bent	bent	put	put	put
beseech	besought	besought	rid	rid	rid
bid	bade (bid)	bidden (bid)	ride	rode	ridden
bite	bit	bitten	ring	rang	rung
blow	blew	blown	rise	rose	risen
break	broke	broken	run	ran	run
bring	brought	brought	see	saw	seen
broadcast	broadcast	broadcast	set	set	set
burst	burst	burst	shake	shook	shaken
buy	bought	bought	shine	shone	shone
choose	chose	chosen	shoe	shod	shod
cling	clung	clung	shrink	shrank	shrunk
come	came	come	shut	shut	shut
cost	cost	cost	sing	sang	sung
dive	dived (dove)	dived	sink	sank	sunk
do	did	done	sit	sat	sat
draw	drew	drawn	slay	slew	slain
drink	drank	drunk	slink	slunk	slunk
drive	drove	driven	speak	spoke	spoken
eat	ate	eaten	spit	spat	spat
fall	fell	fallen	spring	sprang	sprung
fight	fought	fought	steal	stole	stolen
flee	fled	fled	stride	strode	stridden
fling	flung	flung	string	strung	strung
fly	flew	flown	strive	strove	striven
forbid	forbade	forbidden	swear	swore	sworn
forget	forgot	forgotten	swim	swam	swum
freeze	froze	frozen	swing	swung	swung
get	got	got	take	took	taken
give	gave	given	teach	taught	taught
go	went	gone	tear	tore	torn
grow	grew	grown	think	thought	thought
hang	hung (hanged)	hung (hanged)	throw	threw	thrown
			wake	woke (waked)	waked
hear	heard	heard	wear	wore	worn
hit	hit	hit	weep	wept	wept
hurt	hurt	hurt	wet	wet	wet
knit	knit (knitted)	knit	wring	wrung	wrung
lay	laid	laid	write	wrote	written

62. In regard to their *relationships* to other parts of speech in a sentence, verbs are classified as follows:

1. A **transitive verb** is one the action of which passes over to a receiver, as in *John threw the ball; ball* receives the action of *threw.* When the subject is the doer of the act, the verb is in the **active voice,** as *threw.* When the subject is acted upon, the verb is in the **passive voice,** as in *The ball was thrown by John.*

2. An **intransitive verb** is one the action of which does not pass over to a receiver, as *John dances.*

3. A **copulative,** or **linking, verb** is one that merely connects a preceding word or idea with a following one, as *He looks weak.* The word that follows such a verb is usually the predicate adjective (see page 154). The most commonly used copulative verbs are *appear, be, become, come, feel, get, go, grow, keep, lie* (to *recline*), *look, remain, sit, seem, sound, stay.*

4. An **impersonal verb** is one that is indefinite in regard to subject and thus in regard to source of action, as *It rains* and *It snows.*

5. A **cognate verb** is one followed by an object that repeats its idea, as *He slept a peaceful sleep;* such an object should be modified by an adjective (see page 86).

6. A **verb of incomplete predication** is one that means nothing unless it is followed by a complement, as *The stone feels* and *The horse became;* supply *cold* after *feels* and *obstreperous* after *horse,* and predication is completed.

EXERCISES

1. Express each of the italicized expressions by means of a single verb:

1. The woman *lost consciousness.*
2. At last we *went aboard* the good ship.
3. They were permitted *to continue on their way.*
4. We *turned back* to the introduction.
5. The crew *got off the ship* when we reached port.
6. Tired and weary, they *fell by the wayside.*
7. The old car was *restored to good condition.*
8. The once valuable documents were *consigned to flames.*
9. At last his strenuous tasks were *brought to a termination.*
10. She was told to *do* her music lesson *over again.*

2. Which of the following verbs are transitive and which are intransitive?

1. The coat wore well.
2. He wore a gray coat.
3. The canoe floats.
4. They floated the canoe.
5. He read intently.
6. He read a good book.
7. Don't burn your finger.
8. The wood burns brightly.
9. They rejoiced at your success.
10. The news rejoices them.
11. Let your horses walk.
12. Walk your horses.
13. Drive slowly.
14. Please drive me home.
15. The wind blew a gale.
16. The wind blew my hat off.
17. The wind blew fiercely.
18. We dined out.
19. We dined them.
20. They dined us sumptuously.

3. Compose a sentence using each of the verbs below as a transitive verb:

1. He ran.
2. He flew.
3. He cried.
4. He recovered.
5. He rested.
6. He pushed.
7. He puffed.
8. He squeezed.
9. He tripped.
10. He pressed.
11. He moved out in the spring.
12. He tried harder than ever.
13. He received at five o'clock.
14. He dined in grand style.
15. He drove in a leisurely way.
16. He smokes at regular intervals.
17. He nevertheless meant well.
18. He changes naturally with the times.
19. He never eats in the diner.
20. How he stormed at the intruder.

4. In each of the following, an incorrect past tense or past participle is used. Make the necessary corrections.

1. We done our work.
2. The house has fell.
3. I have swam two miles.
4. He has threw the ball.
5. She has wore the new dress.
6. He strided into the room.
7. He set on the little stool.
8. The teacher ringed the bell.
9. The blacksmith shoed the horse.
10. He blowed it at the wrong end.
11. He slinked across the broad lawn.
12. He has foughten a good fight.
13. St. George slayed the dragon.
14. I have ate four large apples.
15. The bag was bursted at once.
16. She may never have saw me.

17. I thought he had went.
18. These stockings have shrank.
19. The package has came at last.
20. They hung him at five this morning.

63. The **conjugation** of a verb is the orderly statement of all its persons and tenses in both voices and numbers, in all modes. The **synopsis** of a verb is the orderly statement of one person and number in all tenses and modes and both voices, or in a certain designated mode and voice.

In conjugating a verb six tenses are given in the indicative and subjunctive modes. The imperative mode has only the present tense. The potential mode, when given, has four tenses— present, past, present perfect, and past perfect. The infinitive has present and perfect tenses; the participle has present, past, and perfect.

1. There are three conjugations of the verb, the **simple,** the **emphatic,** and the **progressive.** The simple conjugation of most verbs can be given in all forms in both voices. The passive voice is formed by adding the past participle of a verb to every form of the verb *to be.*

CONJUGATION OF THE VERB *BE*

INDICATIVE MODE

PRESENT TENSE

Singular	*Plural*
I am	We are
You are (Thou art)	You are
He is [1]	They are

PAST TENSE

I was	We were
You were (Thou wert)	You were
He was	They were

[1] Or *she* or *it* throughout.

FUTURE TENSE

I shall be

You will be (Thou wilt be)

He will be

We shall be

You will be

They will be

PRESENT PERFECT TENSE

I have been

You have been (Thou hast been)

He has been

We have been

You have been

They have been

PAST PERFECT TENSE

I had been

You had been (Thou hadst been)

He had been

We had been

You had been

They had been

FUTURE PERFECT TENSE

I shall have been

You will have been

  (Thou wilt have been)

He will have been

We shall have been

You will have been

They will have been

SUBJUNCTIVE MODE

PRESENT TENSE

I be [1]

You be (Thou be)

He be

We be

You be

They be

PAST TENSE

I were

You were (Thou were)

He were

We were

You were

They were

FUTURE TENSE

I should [2] be

You would be (Thou would be)

He would be

We should be

You would be

They would be

PRESENT PERFECT TENSE

I have been

You have been (Thou have been)

He have been

We have been

You have been

They have been

[1] Preceded by *if, lest, that, though, till* or *unless* throughout.

[2] The future forms may be *shall, will, should,* or *would be* in all persons.

PAST PERFECT TENSE

The same in form as in the indicative mode.

FUTURE PERFECT TENSE

I should have been	We should have been
You would have been	
(Thou would have been)	You would have been
He would have been	They would have been

POTENTIAL MODE

PRESENT TENSE

I may be [1]	We may be
You may be (Thou mayst be)	You may be
He may be	They may be

PAST TENSE

I might be	We might be
You might be (Thou mightst be)	You might be
He might be	They might be

PRESENT PERFECT TENSE

I may have been	We may have been
You may have been (Thou mayst have been)	You may have been
He may have been	They may have been

PAST PERFECT TENSE

I might have been	We might have been
You might have been (Thou mightst have been)	You might have been
He might have been	They might have been

IMPERATIVE MODE

PRESENT TENSE

Singular	*Plural*
Be (you or thou)	Be (you or ye)

INFINITIVES

PRESENT	PERFECT
To be	To have been

PARTICIPLES

PRESENT	PAST	PERFECT
Being	Been	Having been

[1] Other potential auxiliaries are *can* (*could*) and *must*.

THE VERB *LOVE*

INDICATIVE MODE

PRESENT TENSE

ACTIVE   PASSIVE

Singular

I love   I am loved
You[1] love   You are loved
He loves   He is loved

Plural

We love   We are loved
You love   You are loved
They love   They are loved

PAST TENSE

Singular

I loved   I was loved
You loved   You were loved
He loved   He was loved

Plural

We loved   We were loved
You loved   You were loved
They loved   They were loved

FUTURE TENSE

Singular

I shall love   I shall be loved
You will love   You will be loved
He will love   He will be loved

Plural

We shall love   We shall be loved
You will love   You will be loved
They will love   They will be loved

[1] The plain form *Thou*, with the corresponding *t*, *st*, or *est* suffix of the verb, may be substituted throughout in the second person singular number.

PRESENT PERFECT TENSE

Singular

I have loved	I have been loved
You have loved	You have been loved
He has loved	He has been loved

Plural

We have loved	We have been loved
You have loved	You have been loved
They have loved	They have been loved

PAST PERFECT TENSE

Singular

I had loved	I had been loved
You had loved	You had been loved
He had loved	He had been loved

Plural

We had loved	We had been loved
You had loved	You had been loved
They had loved	They had been loved

FUTURE PERFECT TENSE

Singular

I shall have loved	I shall have been loved
You will have loved	You will have been loved
He will have loved	He will have been loved

Plural

We shall have loved	We shall have been loved
You will have loved	You will have been loved
They will have loved	They will have been loved

SUBJUNCTIVE MODE

With the exception of the third singular present active and the third singular present perfect active—(*If*) *he love* and (*If*) *he have loved* respectively—the subjunctive is the same as the indicative.

POTENTIAL MODE

PRESENT TENSE

Singular

I can love	I can be loved
You can love	You can be loved
He can love	He can be loved

Plural

We can love	We can be loved
You can love	You can be loved
They can love	They can be loved

PAST TENSE

Singular

> I could love
> You could love
> He could love

> We could be loved
> You could be loved
> He could be loved

Plural

> We could love
> You could love
> They could love

> We could be loved
> You could be loved
> They could be loved

PRESENT PERFECT TENSE [1]

Singular

> I can have loved
> You can have loved
> He can have loved

> I can have been loved
> You can have been loved
> He can have been loved

Plural

> We can have loved
> You can have loved
> They can have loved

> We can have been loved
> You can have been loved
> They can have been loved

PAST PERFECT TENSE

Singular

> I could have loved
> You could have loved
> He could have loved

> I could have been loved
> You could have been loved
> He could have been loved

Plural

> We could have loved
> You could have loved
> They could have loved

> We could have been loved
> You could have been loved
> They could have been loved

IMPERATIVE MODE

PRESENT TENSE

Singular

Love (you or thou)

Plural

Be loved (you or ye)

[1] Some of the potential forms with the auxiliary *can* are technical merely, and would rarely if ever be used.

INFINITIVES

PRESENT

To love	To be loved

PERFECT

To have loved	To have been loved

PARTICIPLES

PRESENT

Loving	Being loved

PAST

Loved	Been loved [1]

PERFECT

Having loved	Having been loved

2. The **emphatic conjugation** of the verb is formed by using *do* as an auxiliary in the present tense, and *did* in the past tense. This form of the verb occurs only in these tenses, active voice, indicative and subjunctive modes, and in the present imperative.

INDICATIVE AND SUBJUNCTIVE MODES

PRESENT

I do go	We do go
You do go	You do go
He does go	They do go

PAST

I did go	We did go
You did go	You did go
He did go	They did go

IMPERATIVE MODE

PRESENT
Do go

3. The progressive form of the verb or the **progressive conjugation** denotes action as continuing. It is formed in the active voice by adding the present participle to every form of the verb *to be;* in the passive voice, by adding the past participle to the progressive form of the verb *to be*. The passive-voice progressive form of many verbs is not used, though it can be formed. Fol-

[1] This is a technical form merely.

lowing is a synopsis in the first singular progressive indicative
of the verb *to love:*

	Active	Passive
Present	I am loving	I am being loved
Past	I was loving	I was being loved
Future	I shall be loving	I shall be being loved
Present Perfect	I have been loving	I have been being loved
Past Perfect	I had been loving	I had been being loved
Future Perfect	I shall have been loving	I shall have been being loved

It will be noted from this that some of the passive progressive
forms are so unusual and awkward as to be called into use but
seldom, if at all. The commonest use of the progressive forms
of the verb occur in the present and past indicative and in the
two tenses of the infinitive.

> He is building a house.
> The house is being built.
> He ought to be playing.
> You ought to have been playing.

64. With the exception of the verb *be,* English verbs undergo
changes for **person** and **number** only in the third person singular present and present perfect indicative, as *he loves* and *he has
loved.* In the ancient style (also called plain, religious, poetical, or
elevated style) are found special inflections in the second person
singular and occasionally in the third person singular, such as
thou art, thou shalt, thou canst, thou mayst, he hath, he saith.
The endings *st* and *th* are shortened forms of *est* and *eth* respectively.

1. Terms such as *besides, with, along with, together with, as
well as, accompanied by, in addition to,* added to a singular subject, do not affect the number of the subject. The predicate
must be singular to agree with the singular subject.

Right: Alice, together with Mary and Jane, *is* going to the party.
Wrong: Alice, together with Mary and Jane, *are* going to the party.

2. Predicates agree with collective-noun subjects according to
the meaning of such subjects. If the subject denotes a group
regarded as a whole or as a unit, the predicate must be singular;

if it denotes separate individuals or fractional parts, it must be plural.

Right: The herd *was frightened.*
Right: The herd *were attacking* one another.
Wrong: The herd *were frightened.*
Wrong: The herd *was attacking* one another.

3. The number of the verb used with a relative pronoun agrees with that of the antecedent of that relative pronoun. Do not mistake the antecedent.

Right: This is one of the most interesting books that *have* ever been published.
Wrong: This is one of the most interesting books that *has* ever been published.

In this sentence the antecedent of *that* is *books,* which is plural, not *one.* The verb must therefore be plural.

4. Singular nouns and pronouns used as subject and connected by *either . . . or* or *neither . . . nor* or *whether . . . or* require singular predicates.

Right: Neither John nor Bill *is* here.
Wrong: Neither John nor Bill *are* here.

5. *Don't,* a contraction of *do not,* must not be used with *he, she, it,* or with a singular noun as subject; *doesn't,* a contraction of *does not,* is the correct form. *I don't (do not)* and *you don't (do not)* are correct.

Right: He *doesn't* care, she *doesn't* like it, it *doesn't* match, and the family therefore *doesn't* want it.
Wrong: He *don't* care, she *don't* like it, it *don't* match, and the family therefore *don't* want it.

65. Tense is that inflection of a verb which denotes action in relation to time, as present, past, future, or perfect. It is important to distinguish between the past tense and the perfect tenses. **Past tense** denotes action as of past time but not necessarily completed or definite action. *I saw,* the **past tense,** denotes any time in the past; *I have seen,* the **present perfect tense,**

denotes action completed at the present time. *I had seen (him before I called you)*, the **past perfect tense,** denotes that the action had been completed before a specific time or happening in the past. The present perfect and past perfect tenses are indicated respectively by the auxiliaries *have* and *had,* the latter being the past tense of the former.

The tense partitions are not always sharply defined. The present tense may, for instance, denote future time, as *On the tenth I go to Albany.* The present tense may be used also for the past in order to bring to life a past action, as *Columbus reaches America, not the Indies.* This is sometimes called the **historical present.**

66. The **future tenses** are formed by using *shall* and *will* as auxiliaries.

1. Use *shall* with the first person and *will* with the second and third persons to express simple future time.

> I shall be eighteen tomorrow.
> You will be eighteen tomorrow.
> He will be eighteen tomorrow.

2. Use *will* with the first person and *shall* with the second and third persons to express determination:

> I will assist her.
> You shall assist her.
> He shall assist her.

3. In asking a question always use *shall* with the first person:

> Shall I help?
> Shall I go?

4. In asking a question use *shall* with the second and the third person if *shall* is expected in the answer; use *will* if *will* is expected in the answer.

> *Question:* How old shall you be on your next birthday?
> *Answer:* I shall be eighteen.
> *Question:* Will you go with me tomorrow?
> *Answer:* I will.

5. In indirect discourse *shall* or *will* is used according as the one or the other would be used if the sentences were expressed in direct discourse.

> *Indirect:* He says he shall be late.
> *Direct:* He said, "I shall be late."
> *Indirect:* She said that she should be twenty tomorrow.
> *Direct:* She said, "I shall be twenty tomorrow."
> *Indirect:* He said he would go in spite of all opposition.
> *Direct:* He said, "I will go in spite of all opposition."

6. *Should* and *would* follow the above rules for *shall* and *will*. *Should* is also used in the sense of *ought*. *Would* is sometimes used in the sense of habitual or customary action:

> You should be studious.
> She would cry at the least annoyance.

67. The term **sequence of tenses** means the logical relationship of time as expressed by two or more predicates in the same expression. When the predicate in the independent clause is present or future, the predicate in the dependent clause may be in any tense. When the predicate in the independent clause is in the past tense, the predicate in the dependent clause must denote past time.

> *Right:* He *says* he *wants* to go.
> *Right:* He *says* he *wanted* to go.
> *Right:* He *says* he *shall* go.
> *Right:* He *said* he *had* won.
> *Right:* He *said* he *should* go.

1. If, however, a dependent clause expresses a general truth —something that is true regardless of the meaning of the independent clause—the present tense must be used in the dependent clause.

> *Right:* He *said* that Washington *is* the capital of the United States.
> *Wrong:* He *said* that Washington *was* the capital of the United States.

2. The present infinitive may indicate the same time as the principal verb, as *They want to go.* However, if the principal

verb refers to the past, and, in that past, action was taken, then the infinitive must be in the present, even though the principal verb is past, present perfect, past perfect, or future perfect.

Right: They *had resolved to kill* him, and did so.
Wrong: They *had resolved to have killed* him, and did so.
Right: We *have* long *been expecting to go.*
Wrong: We *have* long *been expecting to have gone.*

68. Voice is usually changed from active to passive by using the object of the active verb as the subject of the passive; that is, the active-voice expression *John hit Bill* becomes in the passive voice *Bill was hit by John.* If a sentence has an active verb followed by both direct object and indirect object, it may be changed into the passive form in two ways:

Active: Mr. Jones gave me a book.
Passive: I was given a book by Mr. Jones.
Passive: A book was given me by Mr. Jones.

In the first passive form, *book* is the **retained object;** in the second, *me* is the **retained indirect object.** Of the two passive forms, the latter is simpler and more logical than the former and is thus preferable (see page 87).

69. Mode means the manner in which an action or a state is expressed.

1. An expression that denotes action as happening or having happened, or the opposite, or one that asks a question, is said to be in the **indicative mode.** *He bought a book* is **declarative indicative;** *He did not buy a book* is **negative indicative;** *Did he buy a book?* is **interrogative indicative.**

2. An expression that denotes wish or prayer, likelihood, condition contrary to fact, doubt, supposition, concession, command, purpose, or fear, is said to be in the **subjunctive mode.** This mode is used mostly in subordinate expressions, that is, in dependent clauses. But in the first two illustrations below it is used in independent expressions:

Wish or *prayer:* Thy will *be done.*
Likelihood: I *had gone* but for you.
Condition contrary to fact: If he *had taken* my advice, he would have
  passed.
Doubt or *uncertainty:* Whether he *be* honest or not, I do not know.
Supposition: Suppose it *were* to fall.
Concession: Though he *kill* me, yet will I do it.
After words of command: He commands that there *be* no quitters.
Purpose: Answer briefly, that you *be* not *misunderstood.*
Fear: They are frightened lest something terrible *occur.*

In expressions of doubt the indicative mode is often used instead of the subjunctive.

3. Expressions denoting action or state as possible, probable, or necessary, and expressions in the form of an entreaty or a wish are said to be in the **potential mode.** This is expressed by using the auxiliaries *can, could, may, might, must, would, should.* It has no future or future perfect tense. Since the potential mode is sometimes regarded as another form of the subjunctive, the word *potential* is not mentioned in all grammars.

4. An expression that denotes command, wish, or permission is said to be in the **imperative mode,** as *Leave the room* and *Bless my soul* and *Go if you wish.*

70. The **infinitive** is not a mode. It does not assert action; it names action. It therefore has the qualities of both noun and verb. *To* is called the **sign of the infinitive** and usually appears with it. But it is omitted, as a rule, after *bid, dare, feel, hear, help, let, make, mark, observe, please, see, watch,* and a few other verbs, and the infinitive is then called *elliptical.*

Right: I saw him *go.*
Wrong: I saw him *to go.*
Right: I made him *hurry.*

1. The infinitive has voice and tense (present and perfect) but no person and number. It is modified as finite verbs are. It may take an object, an objective complement, or a predicate nominative, and may have a subject.

2. The **present infinitive,** as pointed out above, may be used

after any tense, as *I want to see, I wanted to see, I shall want to see, I have wanted to see, I had wanted to see, I shall have wanted to see.*

3. The **perfect infinitive** indicates action completed at the time of the principal verb. It must not be permitted to repeat the time of the principal verb that it follows, as in *She had hoped to have seen him* for *She had hoped to see him.* And its influence of meaning upon a preceding predicate must be carefully weighed. *I was to have come yesterday* means that I did not come; *He ought to have done it* means that he did not do it.

71. The **participle** is not a mode. Like the infinitive, it names action rather than asserts it. Like the infinitive, too, it has the qualities of both noun and verb, and it may similarly be used as a modifier, adjective as a rule.

In the structure of the verb (see conjugations on pages 118–125) there are three participles—present, past, perfect. These all function as verbs, that is, as action words. They also function as adjectives, as: (1) **present participle**—*Hurting himself on the stairs, John called a doctor;* (2) **past participle**—*Hurt by his fall, John called a doctor;* (3) **perfect participle**—*Having hurt himself, John called a doctor.* In all three of these sentences the participle is used adjectively to modify the subject *John.* Participles so used have the nature of adjectives as well as of verbs. Like adjectives, they modify nouns and pronouns; like verbs, they have tense and voice, may be modified by adverbs, and may take objects, as *Dressed smartly in her best gown, Alice looked attractive* and *Having heard the whistle, they stopped work.*

72. Used as a noun the participial form of the verb is called a **gerund** or **verbal noun.** It names action and therefore has the nature of both a noun and a verb. As a noun it has case, and it is often modified by an adjective. As a verb it has tense and voice; it may take an object, an objective complement, or a predicate nominative; and it may be modified by an adverb. Verbal nouns which have lost nearly all their verbal nature and thus become almost pure nouns are modified only by adjectives and do not take an object.

Close distinctions are sometimes drawn between the gerund and the verbal noun in their grammatical uses. For all practical purposes, however, they may be regarded as so nearly alike as to be the same. It is sufficient to remember that the gerund is somewhat more of a verb than of a noun, and that the verbal noun is somewhat more of a noun than of a verb.

Gerund—Driving a car recklessly may cause an accident.
*Verbal noun—*Reckless *driving* is dangerous.

Infinitives, participles, and gerunds are sometimes grouped together under the name **verbals**.

EXERCISES

1. Rewrite each of the following active verbs as passive, retaining, of course, the meaning of each expression:

1. I mailed him a present.
2. I offered him my car.
3. She told me a story.
4. We gave her a prize.
5. She granted me permission to go.
6. They presented him with a book.
7. I bought him a new boat.
8. I found him a new route.
9. He gave them a special performance.
10. We presented the bride and groom with a house and lot.

2. Substitute the past tense wherever needed in the following:

1. I have won a medal last night.
2. He has seen many novelties while visiting the fair last week.
3. Have you ever missed a day while you were a senior?
4. I have motored eighty miles yesterday.
5. He has not shown any ambition all last year.
6. It has been three months since I have lost my ring.
7. I have lost my gloves the other night.
8. I have learned many lessons when I worked for you.
9. When I have arrived at Niagara I was awe-stricken.
10. When they have received their trunks, they dressed to go out.

3. Substitute the present perfect tense wherever needed in the following:

1. Did you do your work yet?
2. He is working here now for a long time.
3. I traveled thousands of miles since I last wrote you.
4. He is a good boy ever since I knew him.
5. We are living in Boston for several years.
6. He is very industrious since he is with us.
7. Did you receive your bonus yet?
8. Ever since he was demoted he didn't show any interest.
9. For the last year he is never without funds.
10. We are residing here ever since we left you.

4. Substitute the past perfect tense wherever needed in the following:

1. He was afraid he took the wrong road.
2. The old car looked as if it was used for trucking.
3. He was larger than any elephant I ever saw.
4. You could have found it if you looked in the house.
5. The water was higher than I ever before saw it.
6. I was disturbed that you did not write me before.
7. They permitted me to leave, for I was there before.
8. When we saw what he did, we were extremely sorry.
9. He could not have come if you did not help him get ready.
10. She was more gracious than any other hostess I ever met.

5. Insert *shall* or *will* as required in each of the following:

1. ? I give you this paper?
2. ? you go to the party with me?
3. He ? comply with your request.
4. She ? be sorry to hear about that.
5. When ? we go to the library?
6. I ? starve unless you feed me.
7. You ? do what I tell you to do.
8. He ? go to jail for this offense.
9. We ? wear our new snow togs.
10. He ? win the medal as the result of hard work.
11. You ? do as the boss commands.
12. They ? go to the circus in spite of him.
13. You ? not starve, for I ? feed you.
14. I ? choke; no one ? pound my back.
15. ? we stroll toward the armory?
16. I ? call for you at one if you ? be ready.
17. You ? find that he ? do what he promises.
18. I hope that you ? be able to come to the affair.

133

19. Say that you ? come or I ? be disappointed.
20. You ? succeed if you try again and again.

6. Substitute another word or other words for *will* or *shall* in each sentence, making sure to retain the meaning:

1. I will not be followed.
2. Thou shalt not steal.
3. You shall do as I say.
4. Will you go with me?
5. You shall speak more considerately.
6. I think you will be detained.
7. You will be detained.
8. He said that they will come.
9. He shall be sorry for this.
10. We shall eat more slowly hereafter.

7. Rewrite each of the following, correcting the sequence of verbs:

1. While the birds were scattering, the gun fails to go off.
2. She is in the middle of her speech when she forgot the words.
3. The tragedy occurred at noon, and we know it before one o'clock.
4. After the train has left, the people sadly walked home.
5. You have written me and ask how I was getting along.
6. He told us that Denver was the capital of Colorado.
7. They were really shocked when he comes dancing in.
8. When I call the office the nurse says the doctor has been out.
9. He is consumed with curiosity and he was satisfied.
10. She goes downtown, got herself a new dress, and has worn it home.

8. Explain what is wrong with the following sentences and write them correctly:

1. Anna, together with Sara, are going to the theater.
2. It don't fit in with my plans.
3. The committee is unable to agree.
4. We were hurt to learn he had run away instead of faced the music.
5. We had expected to have seen the bride at the church door.
6. She is one of the most accomplished women that has addressed us.
7. The boy accompanied by his parents are going to the fair.
8. Either Edith or Tom are going to write to me.

9. Explain what is wrong with the following sentences and write them correctly:

1. To lie and to steal is disgusting.
2. To lie or to steal are disgusting.

3. Time and tide waits for no man.
4. This one works more easily, don't it?
5. My three weeks' visit were very beneficial.
6. One of the three boys have been missing since last Monday.
7. This is one of the best books that has ever been written.
8. That you have wronged me do appear in this.
9. If I had have thought, I'd not have done it.
10. Near the entrance stands a statue and a large vase.
11. I will drown; no one shall save me.
12. Mr. Blaine, to say nothing of Mr. Coe, were in great spirits.
13. I would have brought you some apples, had I not have forgotten.
14. Did he tell you his story, and entreated you to contribute?
15. The convention are going to adjourn into a committee of the whole.
16. A complete unit consist of a thousand men.
17. A thousand men constitute a complete unit.
18. He don't think he should have been pleased to have met you.
19. There is sometimes more than one man to a counter.
20. If you had chewed your food instead of gulping it, you would feel better.

Adverbs

73. An **adverb** is a word or a group of words used to modify or intensify the meaning of a verb, an adjective, or another adverb.

1. Adverbs are classified as to form and as to use or meaning. In form, they may be **simple**, as *now, here, there, frankly;* **compound** or **derived**, as *elsewhere, hereto, thereupon, wherever;* phrasal, as *arm in arm, at once, between times, here and there.*

2. According to use or meaning, adverbs may express:

Affirmation: certainly, truly, yes
Cause or *reason:* consequently, hence, therefore, thus
Degree: much, partly, quite, rather, very
Direction: back, forward, onward, yonder
Doubt: perhaps, possibly, probably
Interrogation: whence, where, whither, why
Manner: foolishly, how, namely, quickly
Negation: no, not, nowise
Number: first, secondly, tenthly
Place or *location:* behind, there, topmost, within

Relation: when, where, while (see adverbial conjunctions and relative
  adverbs, page 143)
Responsive: certainly, no, surely, yes
Time: daily, hitherto, recently, since, today, tomorrow
Verbal: out (*They went out*), within (*He remained within*). (Such adverbs
  are so closely linked with verbs as to be really a part of a verb
  phrase.)

In all such classifications there is necessarily some overlapping
of function.

3. Although many adverbs are formed by adding *ly* to adjectives, as *certainly, sincerely, clearly,* not all words ending with
ly are adverbs. Many such words are adjectives, as *costly, cow-
ardly, deadly, likely, lovely.* Nor should *ly* be added carelessly
to words supposedly to form adverbs; there are, for example,
no such forms as *fastly, muchly, thusly.*

4. Do not use inappropriate and extravagant adverbs:

Right: You are wearing a *very* pretty hat.
Wrong: You are wearing the *most intriguingly* beautiful hat.

74. Like adjectives, adverbs are compared to denote degrees
of qualifying or intensifying, as *soon, sooner, soonest; happily,
more* or *less happily, most* or *least happily.*

1. There are several irregular comparisons:

Positive	Comparative	Superlative
badly or ill	worse	worst
far (distance)	farther	farthest
forth (progress)	further	furthest
late	later	latest or last
little	less	least
much	more	most
near	nearer	nearest or next
nearly	more nearly	most nearly
well	better	best

Several of these forms, it will be noted, may be used also as
adjectives.

2. Adverbs which denote absolute or independent quality in
and of themselves, such as *completely, horizontally, immortally,*

infinitely, perfectly, perpendicularly, squarely, totally, uniquely, universally, are generally regarded as impossible of comparison.

3. Do not use double comparative forms of adverbs:

Right: This will be delivered *sooner* than that.
Wrong: This will be delivered *more sooner* than that.

EXERCISES

1. Use another modifier for *somewhat* in each of the following:

1. I am somewhat disappointed.
2. She hesitated somewhat.
3. He is somewhat ill.
4. They are somewhat upset.
5. Mine is somewhat like this.
6. His attitude is somewhat awkward.
7. I am somewhat suspicious of her.
8. Make it somewhat thicker.
9. They have had a somewhat hard time.
10. He will be somewhat surprised to see them.

2. Insert an adverb of degree at some correct place in each of the following:

1. He inexcusably left the room.
2. They were disappointed on their return.
3. Your attitude toward me is absurd.
4. The black clouds approached threateningly.
5. They behaved impolitely and inconsiderately.
6. He spoke fluently and interestingly.
7. I am sorry he failed disastrously.
8. We think him lazy but clever.
9. She is better now but she must be careful.
10. I was ill and could not attend your charming party.

3. For each italicized expression use a single adverb that conveys the same idea:

1. She tripped *without intending to.*
2. He left *of his own free will and accord.*
3. He sputtered *in a highly comical manner.*
4. He contributed *with free and open heart.*
5. *Beyond peradventure* that young man will go far.
6. *From time to time* they take a motor trip.
7. She entered the room *with the utmost confidence.*

8. The announcement was made *with great emphasis*.
9. *By great good luck* we came through the gulch unharmed.
10. We were received by the officer *with great cordiality*.

4. Rewrite each of the following more economically by substituting a single adverb for certain words and phrases. Other slight changes may be required to make the proper adjustment.

1. He made two attempts.
2. She was given two trials.
3. He had a heavy fall.
4. He suffered serious injury.
5. Her work was a dismal failure.
6. They made a diligent search.
7. He reads everything and never tires.
8. He shows great eloquence in speaking.
9. The team put up a brave fight.
10. She has proved a great disappointment.

5. Explain the exact meaning of each of the following:

1. She went alone.
   She alone went.
2. She is an only girl.
   She is only a girl
3. He merely won second place.
   He won merely second place.
4. He hardly gave me a whole one.
   He gave me hardly a whole one.
5. He kindly introduced me to the senator.
   He introduced me to the kindly senator.

6. In each blank space supply an adverb that carries out pictorially the idea of the preceding verb:

1. The rooster crowed   ?   every morning.
2. The waves roared   ?   during the storm.
3. The rain pattered   ?   on the tin roof.
4. The shutter rattled   ?   on its hinges.
5. The car whizzed   ?   through the town.
6. The wind howled   ?   during the night.
7. The elephant lumbered   ?   along.
8. The eagles shrieked   ?   in fright.
9. The chicks chirped ? in their baskets.

10. The dogs barked   ?   at the strangers.
11. Kitty curved her back   ?   and hissed   ?   .
12. He trudged   ?   up the hill and then sat down   ?   to rest.

7. Write the following correctly:

1. I am astoundingly interested.
2. This stands more perpendicularly than that.
3. He drove wildlier than he should have driven.
4. She undoubtedly did it cleverlier than the others.
5. He drove too fastly through the town.
6. He was just too appallingly stubborn for words.
7. We had a gorgeously wonderful time.
8. I have read farther than John has.
9. He goes from worst to worst.
10. He behaved mannerly.

Prepositions

75. A **preposition** is a word or a group of words used to show relation between a word or words following it and a word or words preceding it.

Prepositions are classified as follows:

Simple: at, by, but, for, from, in, of, with
Compound: beneath, beside, into, throughout, upon, within, without
Phrasal: according to, because of, in regard to, in spite of, instead of, on account of
Participial: concerning, notwithstanding, pending, regarding

76. The preposition generally introduces an adjective or an adverbial phrase. If such a phrase modifies a noun or a pronoun, it is called an **adjective phrase,** and it may either describe or limit; thus, *a person of great charm* and *a period of six years.* If such a phrase modifies a verb, an adjective, or an adverb, it is called an **adverbial phrase,** and it may be used to express various relationships, such as:

Accompaniment: I am going *with John.*
Agency: It was done *by Bill.*
Appeal: Tell me *by all* that is dear to you.
Cause: He came *for treatment.*

Condition: We are *in a predicament.*
Degree: He passed higher *by ten points.*
Destination: She is going *to Mexico.*
Direction: He went *toward the station.*
Instrument: Hang the goose up *by the feet.*
Manner: This was done *by hand.*
Measure: We sell it *by the quart.*
Place or *situation:* He lives *in Concord.*
Purpose: He begged *for the refugee.*
Source: He came *from Brazil.*
Time: She died *in the autumn.*

77. Such prepositional phrases as *in the main, on the whole, in truth, for example, in a word, in any case* usually have no close grammatical relationship with other parts of the sentence.

78. The object of the preposition must be in the objective case (see page 93):

Right: He divided it between Mary and *me.*
Wrong: He divided it between Mary and *I.*

EXERCISES

1. Tell what relationship is expressed by each prepositional phrase in the following:

1. I shall attend with my brother.
2. This house was built by Clark & Simpson.
3. Swear on your honor never to reveal this.
4. We are going down to the sea for refreshment.
5. He got us all into a sorry mess.
6. We went over the lesson by leaps and bounds.
7. He will go to St. Louis tomorrow.
8. Hold this steadily by the handle.
9. He reached the peak by toeing into the rock.
10. We shall drop in toward evening.

2. Explain what part of speech each italicized word is in the following:

1. We motored *along* the river.
2. Won't you come *along?*
3. He has gone to the Great *Beyond.*
4. *Beyond* the Alps lies Italy.
5. The place you seek lies far *beyond.*

6. After much confusion, they were finally *off*.
7. Please take your coat *off* the chair.
8. That play was *off* side.
9. We are taking the *down* route today.
10. John has gone *down* the river.
11. Put that *down*, please.

3. Explain the shades of difference in the uses of *on*, *by*, and *after* below:

1. *On* that issue I beg to differ.
2. Washington is *on* the Potomac River.
3. *On* my soul, I never heard of such a thing!
4. He has heavy responsibilities *on* his shoulders.
5. She fainted *on* hearing the news.
6. Please have this done *by* Thursday.
7. You have done magnificently *by* me.
8. We shall travel north *by* east.
9. These *by*-products are sold everywhere.
10. *After* the rain we went for a drive.
11. We thought we heard the report of the *after* gun.

4. Explain the difference in meaning between the parallel expressions below:

1. He works day by day.
   He works by day.
2. He works at all times.
   He works at times.
3. He ran in the house.
   He ran into the house.
4. He is listening to the music.
   He is listening for the signal.
5. Sit here and look on.
   Please look after him.
6. Look to your behavior, young man.
   Look around the place.
7. You are answerable to the police.
   You are answerable for reckless driving.
8. I differ with you about that.
   This differs from that in color.
9. He is anxious about her health.
   He was made anxious by the threat.
10. He seems anxious to please.
    He is anxious for promotion.

5. Insert the proper preposition in each blank:

1. He borrowed money ? me.
2. I was accompanied ? her yesterday.
3. She fell ? the balcony ? the ground.
4. The tank is filled ? snow.
5. I shall go only ? your permission.
6. Come ? my office immediately.
7. The decision lies ? you and your colleagues.
8. This, ? two or three others, will be mounted.
9. She is very angry ? me.
10. They are sitting ? the window.
11. Send it ? me ? the above address.
12. They are going to California ? air.
13. They sneaked ? the house ? midnight.
14. We have been almost killed ? kindness.
15. We were struck ? astonishment.

Conjunctions

79. A **conjunction** is a word or a group of words that connects words, phrases, clauses, or sentences, and at the same time establishes relationship between the elements thus connected. Unlike prepositions, conjunctions do not influence case.

80. Conjunctions are classified according to form as follows:

Simple: and, but, so, though
Compound or *derived:* however, indeed, nevertheless, inasmuch
Phrasal: on the one hand, on the other hand, in conclusion

81. According to use there are two general classes of conjunctions: co-ordinate and subordinate. A **co-ordinate conjunction** connects elements of equal rank. A **subordinate conjunction** connects dependent or minor elements with independent or major ones.

Co-ordinate conjunctions are classified as follows:

Additive or *copulative:* also, and, besides, likewise, moreover, then
Adversative or *contrasting:* but, however, nevertheless, notwithstanding, still, yet
Disjunctive or *separative:* but, either . . . or, neither . . . nor, else, otherwise
Illative or *final:* consequently, hence, so, thus, therefore, as a consequence, as a result, so that

Such adverbs.as *also, besides, consequently, hence, however, likewise, moreover, nevertheless, otherwise, so, still, then, therefore, thus,* serving both as adverbs and as connectives between clauses, are by some authorities called **conjunctive adverbs.**

Subordinate conjunctions are classified as follows:

> *Cause* or *reason:* as, because, for, inasmuch as, since, whereas, wherefore
> *Comparison* or *degree:* as, otherwise, rather, than, as much as
> *Concession:* although, provided, save, though, inasmuch
> *Condition:* if, provided, since, unless
> *Manner:* as, how
> *Place:* whence, where, whereat, wherever, whither
> *Purpose* or *result:* lest, that, so that, in order that
> *Time:* after, before, ere, till, until, when, whenever, while
> *Introductory to noun clauses:* how, that, whether
> *Introductory to adjective clauses* (sometimes called relative conjunctions): as, that, which, who

Subordinate conjunctions which introduce adverbial clauses are called **adverbial conjunctions.** Such adverbs as *after, as, before, how,. since, till, until, when, whence, whenever, where, wherever, whether, while,* serving both as adverbs and as connecting words, are sometimes called **relative adverbs.**

82. Correlative conjunctions are co-ordinate and subordinate conjunctions that are used in pairs. The co-ordinate correlative conjunctions are:

> *both . . . and: Both* he *and* I are ill.
> *either . . . or:* He is *either* afraid *or* bewildered.
> *neither . . . nor:* He was *neither* afraid *nor* bewildered.
> *whether . . . or:* He does not know *whether* to go *or* to stay.
> *not only . . . but also:* He is *not only* learned *but also* wise.

The subordinate correlative conjunctions are:

> *as . . . so: As* five is to three, *so* ten is to six. (proportion by verbs)
> *as . . . as:* Try to be *as* gracious *as* she. (proportion by adjective or adverb)
> *if . . . then: If* he'd do a thing like that, *then* we must repair to our homes. (condition or consequence)
> *though (although) . . . yet: Though* he despise me, *yet* will I do it. (concession)
> *whereas . . . therefore: Whereas* we have been thus oppressed, we *therefore* now demand redress. (consequence or result)

In expressions like *so . . . as, so . . . that, such . . . as,* and *such . . . that, so* is usually an adverb and *such* may be either an adjective or an adverb, but they function as correlatives of the conjunctions *as* and *that.*

such . . . as: Such books *as* we have are yours. (classification)

such . . . that: His work is of *such* poor quality *that* he cannot pass. (consequence)

so . . . as: His reply was *so* curt *as* to embarrass us. (consequence or result)

so . . . that: She was *so* badly hurt *that* she could not walk. (consequence or result)

1. Be sure to use conjunctions logically.

Right: He fell and was seriously hurt.
Wrong: He fell but was seriously hurt.

2. Be sure that correlatives are correctly paired:

Right: Neither John *nor* Bill is going.
Wrong: Neither John *or* Bill is going.

3. Correlatives should stand as close as possible to the terms they connect; that is, before the same parts of speech:

Right: He is *not only* ill *but also* penniless. (*ill* and *penniless* are adjectives)
Wrong: Not only is he ill *but also* penniless.

EXERCISES

1. By using conjunctions make each of the following groups read as one well-connected sentence:

1. We should like to stay longer. We are leaving today. Tom is ill.
2. The spectators cheered. He was exhausted. He ran from the field.
3. He had never seen the circus. He went this year. He was thrilled.
4. The car was damaged. The chauffeur was hurt. We escaped injury.
5. It was a beautiful morning. The foliage concealed the bird. We heard its merry song.
6. He is ten years old. His parents died long ago. He now lives with his grandparents.
7. The wind blew at a terrible gale. Trees were uprooted. Many persons were injured.

CONJUNCTIONS 82

8. The hard-fought game lasted two hours. There was no touchdown. The crowd was disappointed.

9. He was seriously ill. He insisted upon playing. He may die of the injuries.

10. I am always punctual. You should know this after all these years. How could you go without me?

2. The sentence parts below are not logically connected. Correct them by supplying different conjunctions:

1. He lost control of the engine, and he was therefore unconcerned.
2. She is an expert player, but she nevertheless wins many games.
3. Not only shall I be glad to come, and I shall bring Jim along.
4. Ask but it shall be given unto you; seek though you shall find.
5. Although it is snowing heavily, he is not going to the office.
6. He made very high marks in all subjects, but he expects to pass.
7. It was not that I loved Caesar less, and I loved Rome more.
8. Though you obey orders strictly, it is not unlikely that you will be promoted.
9. They have attained their highest ambitions, yet they appear to be contented.
10. It is a newly paved and little used road, but I shall therefore take it.

3. Place the conjunctions correctly in the following:

1. He neither claims to be a success nor a failure.
2. One was either tired of the road or the other was.
3. Not only are they coming early, but they are staying late.
4. To get there on time he both traveled by plane and automobile.
5. We shall either read *Ivanhoe* or one of the modern stories.
6. Both Charles went to the city and his brother also.
7. Not only did he use dangling participles but as well wrong connectives.
8. He hopes both in regard to swimming and running also to take the coveted prize.
9. Whether he was kept late at school as has been reported or when he heard the band Billy Larson prevailed upon him to go to the circus, I cannot say.
10. Not only will he not do the lesson, but as well he refuses to do his regular chores.

4. Insert the proper conjunction in each of the following:

1. Walk ? I do.
2. Walk ? you wanted to.
3. Do not go ? you really care to.

145

4. Do not turn off the ignition   ?   the car is in motion.
5.   ?   you start at once, you will miss the train.
6. Do   ?   you are told, and choose   ?   this   ?   that.
7. It looks   ?   it would snow,   ?   I shall go   ?   or no.
8.   ?   you do that,   ?   I am done with you.
9.   ?   you hate me for it, I must   ?   do it.
10. He worked   ?   hard   ?   he undermined his health.

5. Rewrite the following sentences so that the co-ordinate elements are placed in uniform construction:

1. They began to pull and struggling at the oars.
2. We are going with Bill, and with Tom and Harry.
3. We wash, paint, grease, repair cars and also simonize them.
4. These fruits are clean, fresh, without taint of any sort.
5. It was a small car and having but one seat and very powerful.
6. They could not go farther, for the road was under repair and also because a tire was punctured.
7. She promised him to go at once if he would promise bringing her home promptly.
8. She loved to dance into the wee small hours and then taking a moonlight stroll.

Interjections

83. An **interjection** is a word or a group of words that expresses strong or sudden emotion; as a rule it has no grammatical relation to other elements in a sentence.

1. Interjections are usually classified according to the kind of feeling they express or to the kind of impulse that evokes them, such as aversion, exultation, interrogation, joy, pain, praise, sorrow, surprise. Some of the most commonly used word and phrase interjections are:

ah	hello	ugh	never again
alas	indeed	well	not on your life
aye	pshaw	whoa	well done
bravo	tch	yea	well I never
ha	tut	I say	you don't say

2. Probably the two most frequently used interjections are *O* and *oh.* Note the differences in their meaning and use. *O* is used in direct address; it is always capitalized and is not followed by any mark of punctuation, as *O Almighty God. Oh* is used to express such emotions as sorrow, pain, hope, longing, surprise, and is followed usually by a comma, sometimes by an exclamation mark, and occasionally by no mark at all; it is capitalized only at the beginning of a sentence, as *Oh, why doesn't she come?* Some writers use these words interchangeably, but it is more satisfactory to differentiate between them.

EXERCISE

Tell what emotion is expressed by the interjection in each expression below:

1. Behold, the bridegroom cometh!
2. Hip, hip, hurrah!
3. Fie upon you, Algernon!
4. Ship ahoy! Ship ahoy!
5. Ugh, how he offends me!
6. Welcome, stranger, to these parts!
7. Oh, dear, what is it now!
8. Halt! who goes there?
9. Hush, my lad, don't cry!
10. Well, of all things!
11. Heigh-ho! Here he is again.
12. Whoa there, Buddy!
13. And, oh, the difference to me!
14. Oh, boy, was I disappointed!
15. Well done, thou good and faithful servant!

PARSING AND SYNTAX

84. Parsing means explaining a word by giving its classification as a part of speech and its form or inflection. **Syntax, or construction,** means the explanation of grammatical relationships among the words in a sentence. For example, to parse *John* in the sentence *John runs,* say: noun, proper, third, singular, masculine; to give the syntax of *John* say: nominative, subject of *runs.* The words *person, number, gender,* etc., need not be given, as they are clearly understood.

In parsing give the following information:

1. For **nouns** and **pronouns**—name, classification, person, number, gender, case, use. For a pronoun give also agreement with the antecedent.
2. For a **finite verb**—regular or irregular, transitive or intransitive, principal or auxiliary, tense, voice, mode, agreement with subject in person and number, use in the sentence.
3. For **infinitives** and **participles**—same as for finite verbs except person, number, mode.
4. For **adjectives** and **adverbs**—kind, degree, use.
5. For a **preposition**—kind, kind of phrase in which used, words between which relation is shown.
6. For a **conjunction**—kind, use.
7. For an **interjection**—kind.

Observe the parsing of the underlined words in the following sentence:

Turning abruptly to his right, he saw the beautiful and imposing sunset.

Turning—verb; regular; intransitive; principal (notional); present; active; participle; modifies the subject *he*.

abruptly—adverb; manner; positive; modifies *turning*.

to—preposition; simple; used in adverbial phrase *to his right*, modifying *turning*, shows relation between *turning* and *right*.

right—noun; common; third; singular; neuter; objective, object of the preposition *to*.

he—pronoun; personal; agrees with an antecedent (understood) in third; singular; masculine; nominative, subject of the verb *saw*.

saw—verb; irregular; transitive; principal; past; active; indicative; agrees with its subject *he* in third singular; predicate of the sentence.

beautiful—adjective; descriptive; positive; modifies the object of the verb, *sunset*.

and—conjunction; co-ordinate; connects the two adjectives *beautiful* and *imposing*.

It may be well to review briefly here the following rules:

1. Subjects of finite verbs are in the nominative case.
2. Predicate nominatives are in the same case as the words to which they refer.

3. Objects of verbs and of prepositions, indirect objects, and objective complements are in the objective case.
4. The subject of the infinitive is in the objective case.
5. A pronoun agrees with its antecedent in person, number, and gender, but its case depends upon its construction in the clause in which it stands.
6. Finite verbs agree with their subjects in person and number.
7. An appositive agrees in case with the word it explains; it usually agrees in person, number, and gender also, and is usually of the same part of speech.
8. Nouns and pronouns in the construction of nominative absolute and nominative by direct address are in the nominative case.

EXERCISE

Parse each word in the following passage:

If our flattery is sincere, it is done without the use of wax. The etymology of *sincere* is doubtful, but it is supposed to come from *sine*, without, and *cera*, wax. The etymology is explained as referring originally to vessels free from the wax used in making metal-work, ornaments, and the like. People were as apt then as they are now to do deceptive work by filling hidden parts with baser metal and material, somewhat, perhaps, like the metal-work done in dishonestly constructed buildings. It finally became necessary for an honest workman in ancient times to mark his ware as pure, unmixed, genuine, without wax. It is thus used by Browning in *The Ring and the Book:*

"Wood is cheap
And wine *sincere* outside the city gate."

Such is seemingly the historical etymology and definition of the word. One might venture to say, however, that probably not one person in a thousand is aware of the fact that when he ends his letter with the complimentary close "Sincerely yours," he is virtually writing "Yours without wax."

—E. Shultz-Gerhard in *American Education*

SENTENCES, PHRASES, CLAUSES

The parts of speech are important only as they are combined in related and intelligible groups as phrases, clauses, and sentences. Let us study them in those expressional relationships. Some repetition here of their usage as individual language units will help to fix and emphasize correct usage.

SIMPLE SENTENCES

85. A **sentence** is a group of words which expresses a complete thought. If it states, asserts, or affirms, it is called **declarative,** as *Lincoln freed the slaves.* If it questions, it is called **interrogative,** as *Do you believe in democracy?* If it commands or forbids, it is called **imperative,** as *Leave the room* and *Do not enter;* requests, entreaties, and prayers are usually expressed in this form, as *Please hand this to him* and *Spare my child* and *Have mercy upon us, O Lord.* If it exclaims, or expresses thought with emotion, it is called **exclamatory,** as *What fools these mortals be!* and *Oh, what a tragedy has been enacted!* The exclamatory sentence may or may not contain an interjection.

The sentences defined and illustrated above may be expressed in negative form by the use of negative words such as *none, nothing, no, not, neither, nor, never,* or by the use of words bearing negative prefixes, such as *non, in, un, im, il.* Thus, *He did not attend the show* is negative declarative; *Will he not attend the show?* is negative interrogative; *Do not attend the show* is negative imperative; *What, not attend the show!* is negative exclamatory. It is a mistake to use only *not* to make negative expressions. *Nothing, none, never* are more emphatic, as a rule, than simply *not. I ask nothing* and *I will give him none* are stronger, for instance, than *I do not want anything* and *I will not give him anything.*

86. The **subject** of a sentence is that about which something is stated, asked, ordered, or exclaimed by the use of a finite verb. The **predicate** of a sentence is that which states, asks, orders, or exclaims something about the subject by the use of a finite verb. The word **finite** is most important, for it means limited or restricted or bound by number, person, and time. Infinitives and participles are not thus bound; hence, they cannot be used as predicates. Only such verbs as have number, person, tense, and mode may be predicates. *The boy receiving good marks,* therefore, is not a sentence. It has a subject *boy,* but nothing is stated, asked, ordered, or exclaimed about *boy.* Action or state is merely named, not asserted or affirmed. In *The boy received good marks* the verb is finite; there is a subject and a predicate; the expression is therefore a sentence. The subject is usually omitted before verbs expressing command or wish, as *Go!* and *Would he were here* for *You go* and *I would he were here.* The subject of a principal clause is sometimes understood when it is the antecedent of a relative pronoun, as *Who dances must pay the fiddler* for *He who dances must pay the fiddler.*

87. Usually the subject of a simple sentence is a noun or a pronoun, as *The rains came* and *He is the prize winner;* but it may also be one of the following: an adjective used as a noun, as *The good die young;* an infinitive used as a noun, as *To study is to progress;* a gerund, or verbal noun, as *Walking is good exercise;* a prepositional phrase, as *In the beginning is the first phrase in the Bible.* The subject of a complex sentence may be a clause (see page 157). The subject may, indeed, be any part of speech used as a noun or in place of a noun; as *Merely* (adverb) *has an interesting history; But* (conjunction) *turns many a surprise; If* (conjunctive adverb) *is a mighty word; Oh* (interjection) *is too carelessly used.* The word standing as subject in these cases should be underlined in copy, italicized in print.

88. *It, they, you,* and *one* are sometimes used as so-called **impersonal subjects** when they do not refer to a particular person but are used in a generalizing sense (see page 167).

89. A sentence may consist of only one word, as *Go!* But most sentences consist of more than one word, as *Go away* or *Sam dances.* Both subject and predicate are usually modified, as *The beautiful new car runs with ease.* Here the word *car* is the grammatical subject, and with its three adjective modifiers it is the complete or logical subject. Similarly, *runs* is the grammatical predicate, and with its modifying phrase it is the complete or logical predicate. The names are important only in explaining grammatical relationships. Note, for instance, that in *No one among all the pupils is more popular and studious* the grammatical subject *one* and the grammatical predicate *is* are not the important words. *Among all the pupils* is more important than *one,* and *more popular and studious* is more important than *is,* but without *one* and *is* there would be no sentence. The word nearest the verb—*pupils* in this instance—is likely, through the ear, to influence its number, but the grammatical subject is singular, so we say *One of the pupils is* rather than *One of the pupils are* (see page 125).

90. In normal order the subject of a sentence precedes the predicate and stands as close to it as possible, but to avoid monotony of expression it is frequently desirable to depart from the normal order. Successive sentences should not all begin with the subject or with the same word. Order and wording should be varied. In aiming at variety of construction, however, do not permit unusual placement of a subject to cause violation of the rules of agreement. In *There are a lady and a gentleman waiting, lady* and *gentleman* are subjects, though they follow the predicate. In *That woman, besides the two standing there, is to be taken by the police,* the grammatical subject *woman* is far removed from the predicate *is* by elements of the complete subject; yet, as explained and illustrated above, it must be found in order to determine the correct agreement of the predicate.

91. A simple sentence contains but one subject and one predicate, either or both of which may be compound, as *Joe and Tom run* and *Joe runs and jumps* and *Joe and Tom run and jump.* The single members in such compounds as well as the compound group as a unit may be modified by elements making up complete subjects and complete predicates, as *The boys of Groton and those of Exeter are in the best of training and will meet tomorrow.* Here *boys* and *those* are the grammatical subject, the former modified by *of Groton* and the latter by *of Exeter; are* and *will meet* are the grammatical predicate, the former modified by *in the best of training* and the latter by *tomorrow.*

It has been seen above that subjects are modified by adjectives, possessive adjectives, adjective phrases, expressions in apposition, and predicate nominatives; that predicates are modified by adverbs and by adverbial phrases, and are finished, or completed, by complements. In other words, complete subjects consist of everything pertaining to the grammatical subject, and complete predicates consist of everything pertaining to the grammatical predicate.

92. A **complement** is a word or a group of words used to complete the meaning of certain verbs. There are four kinds of complements: the direct object, the indirect object (sometimes called dative), the predicate nominative or subjective complement (also called predicate attribute, attribute complement, predicate noun, predicate nominative), and the objective complement.

1. The **direct object** of a verb, sometimes called **object complement,** completes the meaning of the verb and therefore receives the action of the verb. It may be a noun, a pronoun, a phrase, a gerund, or a clause, as:

> He promoted *Harry.*
> I love *him.*
> He tried *to swim.*
> He replied, "*Not to my knowledge.*"
> I like *walking.*
> They said *that they would come.*

2. The **indirect object** receives the action of the verb only in a removed or secondary degree indicated by the preposition *to* or *for* understood. It is sometimes regarded as an elliptical prepositional phrase. It is used mostly after verbs like *give, lend,*

hand, offer, grant. The indirect object may be a noun, a pronoun, a verbal noun, or a clause, as:

> I gave *John* the book.
> I gave *him* a book.
> He gave *studying* but little time.
> Give *whoever is in want* food, clothing, and shelter.

3. The **predicate nominative** completes the predicate and means the same as the subject. It usually follows a copulative, or linking, verb. It may be a noun, a pronoun, a phrase, a gerund, or a clause. An adjective so used is called the **predicate adjective**; it modifies the subject as well as completes the verb, as:

> He is a *student.*
> This is *he.*
> The terror in his eyes was *beyond description.*
> His job is *to keep you busy.*
> Reading is not necessarily *studying.*
> The fact is *that you are wrong.*
> He is *good.*

4. The **objective complement** completes the meaning of the verb and explains or modifies the direct object of the verb. It may be a noun, a pronoun, an adjective, a phrase, a gerund, or a clause, as:

> They elected John *captain.*
> They thought John *me.*
> He painted the fence *red.*
> He made them *of the same color.*
> She made him *understand.*
> They pronounced the patient *improving.*
> Reading made him *what he is.*

PHRASES

93. A **phrase,** in the grammatical sense of the word, is a group of two or more related or associated words having no subject and predicate. The word *phrase* is used principally to mean a prepositional phrase, an infinitive phrase, or a participial phrase, as, respectively, *in the winter, to try hard, seeing the end*. But *as well as* and *beautiful snow* and *according to* and *generally speaking* and *for the sake of* are also phrases, as is any other dependent or subordinate group of words without subject and predicate.

94. **Prepositional** and **infinitive phrases** may be used as nouns, as adjectives, and as adverbs. Any phrase used as a noun may be called a **substantive phrase**. A **participial phrase** may be used only as an adjective.

Noun phrases:

Gerund: Running at full speed caused him to fall.
Prepositional: In the gloaming is a poetic phrase.
Infinitive: To suffer in silence is the hardest test.

Adjective phrases:

Participial: Running at full speed he fell.
Prepositional: The boy *in the fifth seat* recited.
Infinitive: She gave him some fruit *to eat*.

Adverbial phrases:

Prepositional: He went *with his father*.
Infinitive: They ran *to overtake us*.

Phrases may be compound, as:

Running fast and breathing hard, he went past like the wind.
We shall move *in the spring or in the fall*.
Learn *to labor and to wait*.

95. According to use, phrases are classified as noun, adjective, and adverbial.

A **noun phrase** is a phrase used as a noun:

Subject: In excess means overweight.
Object: She whispered, *"On the tenth page."*
Object of preposition: He came from *beyond the lines*.
Objective complement: He made them all *of the same material*.
Subjective complement: His behaviour is *beyond reproach*.

An **adjective phrase** is a phrase used as an adjective:

Descriptive: He is a man *of courage.*
Limiting: He is the oldest *of four.*
Predicate adjective: They seemed *in dire distress.*
Appositive: The city *of New Orleans* is probably the most interesting city
  in the United States.

An **adverbial phrase** is a phrase used as an adverb. The most
common uses of adverbial phrases are the following; for additional relationships see pages 135–136.

Place: He went *to school.*
Time: They left *in the evening.*
Manner: He plays *with skill.*
Cause: He was absent *on account of illness.*
Purpose: She begged *for the cause.*
Degree: He passed higher than I *by ten per cent.*
Instrument: The bridge was destroyed *by dynamite.*
Agency: I was struck *by Jim.*
Accompaniment: He went *with the guides.*

The **nominative-absolute phrase** is really adverbial in nature.
It indicates time, cause, reason, or condition.

John having gone, I entered.
The shower having passed, we started.
The sun having set, we left.
Deliveries being delayed, the sale was postponed.

96. Phrases are sometimes extravagant, sometimes economical.
A single word or two words may often serve as an adequate substitute for a phrase. In *The car runs with ease,* the adverbial
phrase may be reduced to *easily.* In *She is a girl of great charm,*
the adjective phrase may be condensed to *very charming,* as *She is
a very charming girl.* Note, too, that a phrase may often be substituted for a clause, as *She hopes to win the medal* instead of
She hopes that she may win the medal; and that the appositive
may sometimes do the same for a phrase, as *Thompson, my best
man, arrived last night* instead of *Thompson, who is my best
man, arrived last night* (see page 187).

97. A phrase must not be mistaken for a complete sentence;

it is always a **fragment**, never a unit of complete expression. *Seeing someone in the distance* conveys an idea only, not a complete thought. Built into relationship with subject and predicate, this participial phrase may constitute an important part of a complete statement, as *Seeing someone in the distance, John decided to turn back* (see page 190).

CLAUSES

98. A **clause** is a part of a sentence which differs from a phrase in that it has a subject and a predicate. It is therefore a simple sentence which is combined with some other sentence or sentences to form a compound or a complex sentence. A **compound sentence** consists of two or more clauses that are independent of one another and are connected by expressed or understood co-ordinate conjunctions, as *The sun is high and the birds are a-wing*. A **complex sentence** consists of one principal, or independent, clause and one or more subordinate, or dependent, clauses, as *We went to their aid because they are our friends*. A **compound-complex sentence** consists of two or more independent clauses and one or more dependent clauses, as *I do not know how you regard this action, but I do know how I regard it*. A **complex-complex sentence** is a complex sentence in which a dependent clause is subordinate to another dependent clause, as *I was pleased when I heard that he was successful*, in which the noun clause *that he was successful* is the object of the predicate of the adverbial clause *when I heard*.

There are three kinds of clauses: noun, adjective, and adverbial.

99. **Noun clauses** are used as nouns are used:

> *Subject:* *That you have wronged me* doth appear in this.
> *Object:* I say *that you have wronged me.*
> *Appositive:* It now appears *that you have wronged me.*
> *Predicate nominative:* The fact is *that you have wronged me.*
> *Objective complement:* His education made him *what he is today.*
> *Object of a preposition:* I am not sure of *what he intended to do.*

Any clause used as a noun may be called a **substantive clause.**

1. The preposition *of,* expressed or understood, followed by a noun clause, is a common construction after the adjectives *sure* and *certain. Of the fact* may sometimes be understood after these words, thus making the clause that follows appositive, as:

> I am sure that he will go.
> I am sure of the fact that he will go.

2. Noun clauses are usually introduced by the conjunction *that.* They may be introduced by other words, however, as:

> He said *that* he was going.
> He asked *when* the train went.
> I don't know *why* you did it.
> I don't know *how* he came.
> I asked *whether* you were there.
> I can't see *where* he went.

3. The infinitive with its subject in the objective case is sometimes used as a noun and classed as a noun clause, called an **infinitive clause.**

> We consider *her to be the best in the class.*

100. Adjective clauses modify nouns or pronouns. They are usually introduced by the relative pronouns *who, which,* and *that,* and are thus sometimes called **relative clauses** (see page 96).

> He *who would succeed* must work.
> The parcel *which was sent yesterday* had been opened by the censor.
> They gave a medal to the boy *that won.*

1. A relative clause may be restrictive or nonrestrictive. A **restrictive clause** is one that cannot be omitted without changing the meaning of the independent clause, as *The man that made the attack has been arrested.* A **nonrestrictive clause** is one that is merely descriptive or explanatory and thus may be omitted without affecting the meaning of the independent clause, as *Woodrow Wilson, who was a great reader, was an eminent war president.* A nonrestrictive clause is set off by commas; a restrictive clause is not so set off. In a restrictive clause *that* should generally be used in preference to *who* or

which, as *The pupil that* (not *who*) *works the hardest wins the medal* and *The book that* (not *which*) *you sent me is interesting.*

2. Adjective clauses may be introduced also by words other than relative pronouns, as:

> The reason *why* he failed is easy to understand.
> This is the house *where* he lives.
> This is the day *when* he is expected.
> Such *as* we had we gave them.
> There is not a boy *but* will pass.

101. Adverbial clauses are used as adverbs are used. They are italicized below:

> *Cause:* I went *because I was ordered to go.*
> *Comparison:* That young man is taller *than this one* (*is*).
> *Concession: Though it is raining,* I shall not take my umbrella.
> *Condition: If we are going to the circus,* please bring my coat.
> *Manner:* He plays the game *as the rules direct.*
> *Place:* She does her Christmas shopping *wherever she happens to be.*
> *Purpose:* I shall advise him *in order that he may do better next time.*
> *Result:* The meeting took place Monday *so that he was able to attend* before he left for Boston Tuesday morning.
> *Time:* I shall leave *when the clock strikes ten.*

102. Every independent clause has a *sound of completeness;* every dependent one, a *sound of incompleteness.* Listen for these notes of completeness and incompleteness. Independent clauses make sense on their own; dependent clauses do not. If you write *He gave me a pencil. Which was not sharpened,* you betray bad ear. The clause *Which was not sharpened* sounds incomplete. It is a dependent fragment of a complex sentence which should read *He gave me a pencil which was not sharpened.* This kind of fragmentary expression in clauses parallels the incomplete phrases explained on pages 156–157. A dependent clause, like a phrase, is a suspended part and must be contained in the expression to which it is related, not separated as an independent element.

103. Do not use the compound sentence unless you can secure more complete unity of thought than is attainable by simple sentences. In *The sun is high and the birds are a-wing, the sun* *is high* may quite properly be an independent simple sentence, and *the birds are a-wing* another simple sentence. But the two together in a single compound sentence convey a more unified "spirit of meaning." In *John goes to school, and Bill goes to college, and Mary is at work,* the compounding is carried too far; unrelated ideas are strung together unnecessarily, resulting in a choppy construction that lacks unity and coherence. *And, but,* and *so* are usually the offending connecting words in such stringy constructions. In *He came to the conference late, and we had begun the discussion, but his tardiness disturbed us, so we had to begin again,* for instance, the "stretched-out" co-ordinate clauses are loose and detached. They are not equally important, though the co-ordination implies that they are.

104. Members of a compound sentence are usually connected by co-ordinate conjunctions, such as *and, but, for, or, so, while, yet.* A comma is placed before the conjunction if there is danger that one clause may run into another and cause confusion; otherwise no comma is required. If there is no connecting conjunction, the clauses are separated by a semicolon. Observe *I went down with Mary and Bill, and Harry met us at the station* and *The old gentleman lived in Columbus for many years; toward the end of his life he moved to Denver.*

105. A "stringy" effect is produced also by the tandem-clause construction. By **tandem clauses** is meant a succession of modifying clauses. This construction is sometimes called the house-that-Jack-built construction, as *This is the cat that caught the rat that lived in the house that Jack built* and *I gave the book to the chap who went to college with my brother who left when the war broke out.* Expressions containing both clauses and phrases linked together in this manner are confusing, as *This is the kind of outing for young people of the community in which I have lived ever since I was married.* In other words, any expression that piles one construction upon another in a monotonous, tacked-on series is to be avoided.

106. The appositive and the infinitive may be substituted for the clause as well as for the phrase (see page 156). In *There goes*

Jameson, who was elected president, the idea is simple, but the construction is complex. Say instead *There goes Jameson, president-elect* or *Jameson, the newly elected president.* Again, in *That is the truck that will do your work,* the complex construction may be avoided by using the infinitive, as in *That is the truck to do your work.*

SENTENCE ANALYSIS

107. Analysis is the resolution, or breaking-up, of a sentence into its word, phrasal, and clausal parts, and the explanation of the relationship of these parts.

In analyzing a simple sentence state:

1. Kind of sentence	5. Simple predicate
2. Complete subject	6. Complements
3. Simple subject	7. Phrases, with use
4. Complete predicate	8. Word modifiers

In analyzing a complex or a compound or a compound-complex sentence state:

1. Kind of sentence
2. Independent clauses
3. Dependent clauses

    (*a*) Kind of each
    (*b*) Relation of each to independent clause
    (*c*) Modification of each
    (*d*) Connection of each

4. Complete and simple subject of each independent clause
5. Complete and simple predicate of each independent clause
6. Complements in each independent clause
7. Phrases, with use, in each independent clause
8. Word modifiers of each independent clause
9. Subjects, predicates, complements, phrases, word modifiers of each dependent clause

Observe the analysis of following sentence:

When he turned abruptly to his right, he saw the beautiful and imposing sunset.

1. This is a complex declarative sentence, consisting of one independent clause and one dependent clause.

2. The independent clause is *he saw the beautiful and imposing sunset*.
3. The dependent clause is *When he turned abruptly to his right*. This is an adverbial clause of time, modifying the verb *saw* in the independent clause. *When* is a relative conjunction connecting the dependent with the independent clause.
4. The complete subject of the independent clause is *he*. *He* is also the simple subject.
5. The complete predicate of the independent clause is *saw the beautiful and imposing sunset*. *Saw* is the simple predicate.
6. *Sunset* is the direct object of the verb *saw*.
7. *Beautiful* and *imposing* are adjectives modifying *sunset*. *And* is a conjunction connecting *beautiful* and *imposing*.
8. *He* is both the simple and the complete subject of the dependent clause.
9. The complete predicate is *turned abruptly to his right*. *Turned* is the simple predicate.
10. *Abruptly* is an adverb modifying *turned*.
11. *To his right* is an adverbial phrase modifying *turned*.

In writing the analysis of a sentence make it as clear as possible by using short paragraphs and by numbering the parts. Underline words quoted from the sentence so that they will stand out clearly and not be read as part of your explanation.

EXERCISES

(Occasional sentences in these exercises should be assigned for analysis according to the above instruction.)

1. Re-express the following as interrogative sentences and as negative sentences:

1. The story is a very interesting one.
2. Merchandise is selling very cheap now.
3. The title gives you a clear idea of the contents.
4. The movie is filled with high adventure and romance.
5. He met with an untimely and tragic death in the air.
6. That invention made him a millionaire overnight.
7. Write a novel, sell it to the movies, and take me to see the picture.
8. Oh, how that latest screen story of his thrilled me!
9. His latest story is about a well-known political figure.
10. Try to come over to our house tonight.

2. Reduce each of the following phrases to a single word:

   1. without thinking
   2. in a frivolous manner
   3. by a circuitous route
   4. with a heart all aflutter
   5. without meaning to
   6. by the skin of his teeth
   7. in an unbecoming way
   8. with his tongue in his cheek
   9. in close association
   10. without any system whatever

3. Express each italicized group below by means of a single word:

   1. He went for the officer *with speed.*
   2. He is a young man *of great talent.*
   3. They expressed themselves *with sympathy.*
   4. Sister left the room *with a smile on her face.*
   5. The banker has contributed *with generosity.*
   6. The water supply has been pronounced *in a sanitary condition.*
   7. The site of the lodge was on *a peak of the mountains.*
   8. He keeps all appointments *on the dot.*
   9. The critics say he is a poet *of exceptional talent.*
   10. He supported me with his mind, with his heart, and with his spirit.

4. Give a phrase that is the opposite of each of the following:

   1. weeping and wailing
   2. weary with traveling
   3. a brilliant young student
   4. a quiet and shady drive
   5. helter-skelter
   6. a distant poor relative
   7. in a heterogeneous mass
   8. with all his might and main
   9. with his heart in his mouth
   10. over and above

5. Explain the difference in meaning between the two complex sentences in each group below. Then write each as a simple sentence.

   1. You who are always so studious must help Harry.
      You must help Harry who is always so studious.
   2. Andrew, who is wearing shorts, is the brother of Tom.
      Andrew is the brother of Tom who is wearing shorts.

3. The garage is alongside the house which is painted red.
   The garage, which is painted red, is alongside the house.

4. The vessel which foundered was aided by the plane.
   The vessel aided the plane which foundered.

5. Mabel who was driving with Bill was thrown from the car.
   Bill who was driving with Mabel was thrown from the car.

6. In sentences of your own composition use the following noun clauses as subjects:

1. That you were right	6. Whatever you do
2. Whether he will go	7. That he was wronged
3. How it happened	8. Where they are now
4. Whatever he may say	9. What it was about
5. What the chief said	10. That the sun shone

7. In sentences of your own composition use the following noun clauses as objects:

1. where he went	6. whatever happened to me
2. what he said	7. that might is right
3. that he would go	8. what you have said
4. whether I could go	9. that he will survive
5. how he did it	10. whether they are coming

8. Make each of the following a simple sentence by substituting an infinitive for a dependent clause:

1. He ordered that I go at once.
2. They expected that it would rain.
3. They went to the city in order that they might buy goods.
4. There was nothing else that I could do.
5. The officer ordered that the prisoner be executed at once.
6. We had no food that we could send to the sufferers.
7. They had nothing that they could substitute for the lampshade.
8. He went to night school that he might qualify for a certificate.
9. Bill went to the party that he might again see his sweetheart.
10. The principal told the graduates that they must be prepared to fight.

9. Make each of the following a simple sentence by substituting an appositive for a dependent clause:

1. This is Chicago, which is the city in which I was born.
2. I have come to see Blankton, who is an old college friend.
3. We shall very soon arrive in London, which is the capital of England.
4. The prize went to my two nephews, who are named Edward and Harris.

5. At the entrance are two grand old elms, which are the largest in the town.
6. That statue of Lincoln, which is the finest in the world, is worthily placed.
7. I listened to the speech over the radio, which is the most intrusive and the most irresistible of all modern inventions.
8. At the very peak of the mountain is the large hotel, which has become the most popular and the most expensive in the county.
9. We drove the new car, which is a Buick, over the recently finished boulevard, which has been named Excelsior Parkway.
10. I took my guest, who is my dear old Uncle George, to hear the concert given in the musical capital of the United States, which is New York City.

10. Combine each fragment below with some expression of your own composition to form a good complex sentence:

1. since this is so
2. as someone remarked
3. that the rumor is true
4. as well as it can be done
5. so well as it can be done
6. whose sad heart is breaking
7. wherever you may be
8. though much may be said for him
9. because I missed the train
10. whenever the day comes
11. as I have many times been told
12. of whom we were speaking
13. whichever way you consider it
14. however that may be
15. though he wrote as well as he could

QUALITIES OF EXPRESSION

108. The terms following are those most commonly used in connection with composition:

1. **Coherence**—the holding or "sticking" together of parts; that is, the relating and connecting of sentence elements as they should stand grammatically.

2. **Compactness**—conciseness, brevity, economy, and solidity in sentence structure; that is, the packing of sentence elements closely together without waste of words.

3. **Completeness**—inclusion in a sentence of all words and phrases necessary to the adequate expression of its thought.

4. **Consistency**—harmony and accord and appropriateness of sentence elements; that is, the arrangement of sentence parts so that they logically agree in form and idea.

5. **Emphasis**—stress or prominence given to certain words and phrases in order to make them more impressive than others.

6. **Unity**—singleness, or oneness, of sentence thought; that is, concentration upon a single main idea or point of view in a sentence to the exclusion of everything else.

7. **Variety**—avoidance of sameness, monotony, or repetition among sentence parts; that is, the diversifying of sentence expression so that it is not dull or tiring.

It is obvious that these definitions overlap somewhat. If a sentence is compact, it is very likely also to be unified and coherent; if it is emphatic, it is very likely also to be consistent and varied. But these principles are best studied by concentrating on one at a time.

COHERENCE

Relate sentence parts coherently—

109. Make a pronoun refer to a definite word rather than to a general idea. In each of the following sentences the pronoun refers to a general idea, and its reference is thus said to be **broad.**

1. If you balance yourself on your left foot, it will help you.
2. The weather finally cleared, which pleased them immensely.
3. They offered to promote him without examination, and that cheered him.

The pronoun *it* in the first sentence, *which* in the second, *that* in the third, all refer to a preceding statement or clause as a whole rather than to a single word. As a matter of fact, the major part of the reference in each case is to the idea expressed in the verb in the preceding clause. Pronouns should refer to nouns and other pronouns, rarely to any other part of speech. These are correct readings of the above:

1. If you balance yourself on your left foot, this act (or device or precaution) will help you *or* Balancing yourself on your left foot will help you.
2. The weather finally cleared, and they were pleased immensely *or* The clearing of the weather pleased them immensely.
3. They offered to promote him without examination, and the offer cheered him *or* He was cheered by their offer to promote him without examination.

1. The use of *that* and *which* in such broad references as those above cannot be entirely condemned, as it abounds in literature. Therefore, when these pronouns convey an unmistakably single idea, they may be regarded as convenient and economical.

2. The pronouns *it, they, you* and *one* are frequently used with indefinite reference, as *It rains* and *They're putting up a new building on that site* and *You never know* and *One can never tell.* These are idiomatic and therefore acceptable forms. But used broadly or loosely as in *It says that it's going to rain* for *The paper prophesies rain; You're put into prison for acts of that sort* for *Acts of that sort are punishable by imprisonment; They'll never get out alive* for *The victims will never get out alive; One has to take one's chances on one's way through life* for *One has to take his chances on his way through life,* these pronouns may lead to confusion and misunderstanding.

3. *There* is sometimes wrongly used for indefinite or impersonal *it,* as in *There is no disgrace to lose once.* This should, of course, read *There is no disgrace in losing once* or *It is no disgrace to lose once.*

EXERCISE

Correct the broad pronominal reference in each of the following:

1. He put in an appearance at last, which gave her great comfort.
2. If you place a cushion behind you, it will be easier to drive.
3. It says in this book that close shaving is dangerous to the skin.
4. You know you're likely to be locked up for doing such a thing.
5. They said they would play on the fifteenth, and that suited us.
6. When the sexton tolls the bell it means a funeral in the church.
7. He was assured that he might go free if he would sign on the dotted line, but he wouldn't do that.
8. If you will read these instructions about playing the game, it will be very helpful.
9. You can't tell what they're likely to do when it dawns upon them that the funds have run out.
10. There is no distinction to be singled out as a high-standing pupil, though it is generally so regarded.

110. Make a pronoun refer to an important, or major, word in an expression rather than to a subordinate one, such as a possessive form, a parenthetical term, or an understood word. In each of the following sentences the pronoun refers to some minor or subordinate term. Such pronominal reference is called **weak.**

1. The porter's duties are trying, and they leave him exhausted when night comes.
2. In Venice, the city of canals, they take the place of streets.
3. John has always admired writers, and he is going to make that his lifework.
4. The gun-toter said, "Don't worry; it isn't loaded."

In the first sentence *him* refers to possessive *porter's;* in the second, *they* refers to doubly subordinate *canals*—object of *of* in an appositive phrase; in the third, *that* refers to *writing* understood, not to *writers;* in the fourth, *it* refers to *gun,* which is only

misplace
dangling
participle } — *Pronouns* —
modifiers
connectives

COHERENCE

broad
weak or no } *divided ref.*

111

half the antecedent. In the following revisions weak reference is
avoided by change of construction: *wrong*

1. As his duties are trying, the porter finds himself exhausted when
   night comes.
2. Canals in Venice, the city of canals, take the place of streets.
3. John has always admired writers, and he is going to make writing
   his lifework.
4. The gun-toter said, "Don't worry; the gun isn't loaded."

EXERCISE

Correct the weak pronominal reference in each of the following:

1. Billy was assigned to the apple-paring machine, and when he had
   finished, he cut them in halves.
2. Although Tommy's share of the profits amounted to very little, he
   proved himself a good sport.
3. In Chicago, sometimes called the windy city, they not infrequently
   blow a gale of sixty miles an hour.
4. My mother-in-law said that she had it on her side and was going to
   prosecute to its full extent.
5. In Brooklyn, the city of churches, they sometimes have steeples and
   sometimes Gothic towers.
6. My son associates with artists a great deal, and is going to make it
   his profession.
7. When we had completed our visit to the pineapple plantation, the
   proprietor presented each of us with a dozen of them.
8. The old horse-and-buggy days are over, and it has now become an
   antique. *＋ possible antecedent*

**111. Leave no doubt in the construction of your sentences
as to the antecedent of a pronoun.** Omit a pronoun altogether
and substitute a noun for it if you cannot make its antecedent
quite clear. Vague, ambiguous, or ridiculous meaning results
from the violation of this rule.

In each of the following sentences the pronoun may refer to
one of two or more words. So misused, it is said to have **divided**
reference.

1. The policeman pursued the robber to the corner, where he went into
   a cellar.
2. John said his father thought he ought to buy a new car.
3. He ran the car into the gutter that he was driving.

The first sentence is ambiguous—*he* may refer to either *robber* or *policeman*. In the second sentence, the antecedent of *he* is in doubt. In the third, *that* seems absurdly to refer to *gutter*.

To correct divided pronominal reference it may be necessary to reconstruct a sentence, to use direct discourse, or to substitute a noun for the vague pronoun even though the close repetition of the noun may not be euphonious. The above sentences are here written coherently:

1. The policeman pursued the robber to the corner and saw him go into a cellar *or* The robber was pursued to the corner by a policeman, who went into a cellar.
2. John said, "Father thinks I ought to buy a new car" *or* John said, "Father thinks he ought to buy a new car."
3. He ran into the gutter the car that he was driving.

EXERCISE

Correct the divided pronominal reference in each of the following:

1. Alice told Mary that she danced better than Jane.
2. Billy ran after the culprit, but he stubbed his toe.
3. When the beggar rang Anderson's doorbell, he was scared.
4. When a candidate for office approached him, he was always polite.
5. He patiently pushed the lawn mower over the lawn which was very dull.
6. She gathered up from the dresser all the articles which had an ample mirror.
7. The odor of new-mown hay was pleasing to the sense of smell which had been cut and left to dry.
8. I had been working all day at my old typewriter attached to my desk which had two keys missing.
9. Patting old Dobbin on the nose as he leaned over the fence, my uncle fastened a bag to it and I watched him while he enjoyed his dinner.

112. Place words, phrases, and clauses as close as possible to the elements they logically modify. *Almost, ever, hardly, merely, only, rarely, scarcely* are the most commonly misplaced words. In the following sentences the modifiers are wrongly placed:

1. I only have three.
2. The horn sounded as we went down the road in warning.
3. The accident had occurred the day before which upset her

In the first example, the adverb *only* logically modifies *three*, not *have;* in the second, the phrase *in warning* modifies *sounded;* in the third, the clause *which upset her* modifies *accident.* These elements—word, phrase, clause—should therefore be placed as follows:

1. I have only three.
2. The horn sounded in warning as we went down the road.
3. The accident which upset her occurred the day before.

EXERCISE

Rewrite the following so that modifying words, phrases, and clauses stand close to the elements they modify:

1. He merely asked for a glass of water.
2. We drove up along the river and around the falls laughing and singing.
3. They took us out to the fort which was located on the point in the car.
4. He said it was the most beautiful picture he had almost ever seen.
5. The affair took place at midnight which led to his surprising arrest.
6. Paint a notice on the billboard in which you warn against trespassing.
7. He wrote the account of yesterday's outing on the typewriter.
8. The brawl took place just one hour before which led to the murder.
9. They went to the museum which is located on that beautiful knoll in the park having the world-famous painting in it.
10. She has just bought herself a tract of land in the southern part of the island which is now being made ready for her new house.

113. Avoid so-called split, or wedge, constructions; that is, do not insert words, phrases, or clauses between closely related parts of a sentence. The following are not good:

1. Please without any more fuss do as you are told.
2. You could if you really wanted to do that for me.
3. Bill during his three weeks' absence missed much work.
4. I ask you to as quickly as you possibly can return with that report.

In the first sentence, a four-word phrase falls between the predicate and its object; in the second, a five-word clause splits, or wedges, a verb phrase; in the third, a five-word phrase separates subject from predicate; in the fourth, the infinitive *to return* is split by a six-word clause.

The split, or cleft, infinitive should be avoided when it makes an expression awkward and incoherent. When it makes the phrase compact and emphatic, as in *to thoroughly understand* and *to emphatically denounce,* there is no valid objection to it. It is generally considered better, however, to regard as inseparable the sign of the infinitive, *to,* and the verb which goes with it.

Here are the foregoing sentences stated more coherently:

1. Please do as you are told without any more fuss.
2. You could do that for me if you really wanted to.
3. During his three weeks' absence Bill missed much work.
4. I ask you to return with that report as quickly as you can.

A modifier placed between the parts of a sentence so that it may be understood to relate either to something preceding or to something following is called a **squinting modifier** or a **squinting construction.** Thus, in *The boy who tries in nine cases out of ten wins,* the phrase *in nine cases out of ten* may modify either *tries* or *wins;* it "squints" at both, and the meaning is therefore ambiguous. To be coherent the sentence must read *The boy who tries, wins in nine cases out of ten* or *The boy who in nine cases out of ten tries, wins.* The latter sentence is not so good as the former because of the wide separation of the subject *who* from the predicate *tries.* But if the latter expresses the meaning, the sentence should be reconstructed as follows: *If, in nine cases out of ten, a boy tries, he wins.*

EXERCISE

Correct the split and squinting constructions in the following:

1. Every man in the pursuit of happiness must needs be free.
2. I want you to in every possible manner assist my brother.
3. When the car skidded for an instant I thought we were lost.
4. I expect you without coaxing or insistence to play when asked.
5. He assured me when the bell rang he would put it into effect.
6. I don't want you, please, to even so much as ever again mention his name.

7. What good would be in the event you were to do this thing accomplished?
8. Finding myself in a speedboat for the first time in my life I felt seasick.
9. Inasmuch as the car can make eighty miles an hour on good roads it should be run with great care.
10. The pupil who a dozen times a week copies his homework from someone else's paper comes to realize sooner or later the error of his ways.

114. Avoid dangling, hanging, or suspended constructions; that is, be sure that the word logically modified by a participle or an infinitive is actually expressed. Such elements standing at the beginning of a sentence should generally be made to modify the subject. The following are wrong:

1. Arriving late, it was too dark to see the flowers.
2. In turning the wheel the handle came loose and hit me.
3. To get the most out of the treatment a week should be spent here.

The initial phrase in each of these sentences dangles—it is left hanging or suspended—because there is no word supplied for it logically to modify. To correct this incoherence a different subject must be supplied, one to which the initial phrase may be grammatically attached; or the sentence must be reconstructed. These are correct:

1. Arriving late, we found it too dark to see the flowers *or* Owing to our late arrival it was too dark to see the flowers *or* When we arrived it was too dark to see the flowers.
2. In turning the wheel I was hit by the handle, which came loose *or* While I was turning the wheel the handle came loose and hit me *or* The handle of the wheel came loose and hit me while I was turning it.
3. To get the most out of the treatment you should spend a week here *or* You should spend a week here in order to get the most out of the treatment.

Such dangling phrases may also make trouble when used at the end of a sentence, as:

1. She had become very nervous, resulting from the accident.
2. Your car must be in first-class condition to enjoy a motor trip.

These are correct:

1. She had become very nervous as result of the accident *or* Her nervousness, resulting from the accident, had become very serious.
2. To enjoy a motor trip you must have your car in first-class condition *or* Your car must be in first-class condition if you would enjoy a motor trip.

When, however, an initial or a concluding phrase pertains to the expression as a whole rather than to any specific word or construction, the foregoing rule does not apply. The following, for instance, are correct:

1. Generally speaking, this is a very satisfactory car.
2. This is a most shocking situation, to say the least.

EXERCISE

Correct the dangling phrases in the following:

1. After filling up the gasoline tank, the journey was soon ended.
2. Having received the refund, a new purchase was made.
3. To understand the game thoroughly this pamphlet must be read.
4. In talking to the supervisor the policy was clearly explained to me.
5. The car had only one light, caused by a collision with a truck.
6. Perfect study facilities are imperative to do your lessons well.
7. On opening the window, the cool mountain air came in refreshingly.
8. The oration of the day was made impressive by quoting freely from history.
9. After eating six green apples, the doctor was called in to prescribe.
10. Having received two complimentary tickets, the entertainment was attended.

115. Avoid elliptical clauses. An elliptical clause is one in which the subject and the predicate (or a part of the predicate) must be understood from what precedes. Unless the understood parts fit in logically with the rest of the sentence, the clause dangles and causes ambiguity, absurdity, or vagueness. The following are wrong:

1. While driving along the river road the axle broke.
2. My heart always palpitates while running.
3. Do not eat the frankfurter until nicely roasted.

The elliptical clause in the first sentence should read *While I was driving* (any subject may be supplied); in the second, *while I am running* or *when I run;* in the third, *until it is nicely roasted.*

EXERCISE

Correct the dangling elliptical clauses in the following:

1. When twenty-one years old, his inheritance was paid to him.
2. While going to market this morning, the traffic lights were off.
3. Do not think of drinking that water until thoroughly boiled.
4. When old, the world will cast you aside without so much as a shrug.
5. While eating and drinking on deck, the actors gave us a good show.
6. My bag came open and all the books fell out while hurrying to the office.
7. While battling the furious rattler, his stick broke and he had to run.
8. Hundreds of books were read in our old home library when a boy.
9. When ten years of age my mother died; when twelve, my father.
10. Unless perfectly cooked, do not eat early garden vegetables.

Connect sentence parts coherently—

116. Use connectives that accurately and logically express the connection desired (see conjunctions, pages 142–143). Do not use a conjunction of time for one of concession or condition; do not use *without* and *like* as conjunctions in place of *unless* and *as if;* do not overuse *and, but, so, then, where,* and *while* as connectives. The following expressions are not well connected:

1. While he is ignorant of farming, he has raised excellent crops.
2. When you wish to win a prize, you must be willing to make sacrifices.
3. He says he will not go to the party without we go with him.
4. He is going to run on the side of the field like his opponent did.
5. He came in and sat down and took off his hat and read.
6. He went but he didn't want to, but he got along all right.
7. He had been soaked by the heavy rain, so he changed his clothes.
8. If you find yourself in an accident, then you must notify the police.
9. I see where the officials are going to change those old traffic rules.

Here the connection in each is made more coherent:

1. Though he is ignorant of farming, he has raised excellent crops.
2. If you wish to win a prize, you must be willing to make sacrifices.
3. He says he will not go to the party unless we go with him.

4. He is going to run on the side of the field as his opponent did.
5. He came in, took off his hat, sat down, and read.
6. He went, though he didn't want to, and he got along all right.
7. Inasmuch as he had been soaked by the heavy rain, he changed his clothes.
8. If you find yourself in an accident, you must notify the police.
9. I see that the officials are going to change those old traffic rules.

A nice use of conjunctions within sentences and between sentences reflects logical thinking. If you use *while* in both *While I was away the house burned* and *While he is seriously ill, he never loses courage,* you forget to make the finer distinctions in expression. Similarly, *I see where the paper says rain* for *I see that the paper says rain; She was suffering keenly and she played the part* for *She was suffering keenly but she played the part* or *Though she was suffering keenly, she played the part; He couldn't see the sign, he was so enraged; so I went to his assistance* for *He was so enraged that he couldn't see the sign; I therefore went to his assistance,* reveal dulled or blunted understanding of the association of ideas.

While means during the time that. *When* means at the time that. The former has the idea of duration in it; the latter, the idea of staled or "stationary" time. Say *While I was ill* (that is, during my illness) *I read three books* and *When I returned from the office* (that is, at the time of my return) *I found Mary here.* (For *only* used as a conjunction see page 32.)

EXERCISE

Rewrite each of the following, making the connection in each more coherent and logical:

1. The car runs like it needs servicing.
2. Without you buy tickets in advance, you will not be admitted.
3. When a man desires to make money, then he must be willing to work.
4. I accepted the invitation, so she said come early, so I did.
5. Snakes are abroad at night as well, and you should be careful then too.
6. While I do not think that point very important, I accept it.
7. Tommy put the assignment on the board while the pupils copied it.

8. It had been very hot, so everybody had been suffering, and so I bought ice cream for the whole party.
9. She is rarely seen to take a moment's rest, only when she is forced to or where she realizes how tired she is.
10. Here in America we go in for sport too much as an end rather than as a means; and in England it is a means rather than an end; and France is more likely to take the American attitude.

117. Confine the conjunctions *and* **and** *but* **to strictly co-ordinate uses.** These conjunctions should connect grammatical elements—words, phrases, or clauses—that are similar in construction. They should not connect a clause with a phrase, a word with a clause or a phrase. The following are incorrect:

1. They began to cheer and waving.
2. This is a handmade shoe and which will give you excellent service.
3. Alice was bright, cheery, and surrounded by friends.
4. In the afternoon I met many of the contestants whom I had formerly taught but could not recall their names.
5. I like to drive a good car—one that has a powerful engine and driving seems like floating in the air.

In the first sentence, *and* connects the infinitive *to cheer* and the verbal noun *waving,* which are not similar forms; in the second, *and* connects the preceding independent clause with the following dependent (adjective) clause; in the third, *and* connects the two adjectives with the participle *surrounded;* in the fourth, *but* connects a relative clause with an independent clause; in the fifth, *and* connects a relative clause with an independent clause. These readings are correct:

1. They began to cheer and (to) wave their hats *or* They began cheering and waving.
2. This is a handmade shoe which will give you excellent service.
3. Alice was bright and cheery, and she was surrounded by friends.
4. In the afternoon I met many of the contestants whom I had formerly taught but whose names I could not recall.
5. I like to drive a good car—one that has a powerful engine and that makes motoring seem like floating in the air.

As a rule, do not use *and that, and which, and who* (or *but* in each instance) in a sentence unless there is a preceding *that* or *which* or *who* with which *and* (or *but*) makes co-ordinate connection, as *He is the boy who won the prize and who is to be promoted.* Here both relatives refer to *boy,* and their connection by *and* is good. In *He is the boy and who is to be promoted* the conjunction *and* has no co-ordinate relative before it to connect with *who* following, and the sentence is thus incorrect. In the following sentence, however, observe that *but* connects two independent clauses, and *that* modifies *story: He told me he had swum the Hellespont but that story I could not believe.*

Note that in *She wrote of jewels and medals and tokens* and *He has integrity and industry and ambition,* the connected nouns are of a kind—concrete in the first sentence, abstract in the second. But in *We heard of the distinction and medal he won,* the two nouns connected by *and* are in widely different categories. When this is the case, it is better to set apart by extended phrasing the terms that are not co-ordinate in idea though co-ordinate grammatically, as *We heard of the distinction and of the medal he won.*

EXERCISE

Rewrite each of the following with more coherent connection:

1. He came out first and with flying colors.
2. She ran out of the room and leaving her papers flying.
3. They found him sullen, morose, and in no frame of mind to satisfy them.
4. She met many old friends but none of whom she knew at college and could therefore not place.
5. Here is the head boy of the school and who is going to college next year.
6. He likes to swim in a big pool and having lots of room to splash about.
7. They brought a trout home with them and which was the biggest I ever saw.
8. We knew about his courage and ultimate success and both of which aroused our admiration.
9. The greatest obstacle he has had is discouragement but which he is at last overcoming.
10. Don't forget that you must make the best of this defeat and to turn it ultimately into success.

**118. Place correlative conjunctions as close as possible to con-
nected terms;** that is, the members of such correlative pairs as
*either . . . or, neither . . . nor, not only . . . but also, both . . .
and, whether . . . or* should stand directly before the nouns,
adjectives, verbs, phrases, or other elements that they connect.
The following are wrong:

1. Mary neither likes Sally nor Sam.
2. He was not only kind to the children but also to the grown-ups.
3. Both the father was hurt and the mother also.

In the first sentence, the correlatives *neither . . . nor* logically
connect *Sally* and *Sam,* not *likes* and *Sam;* in the second, the
correlatives *not only . . . but also* connect the two phrases *to the
children* and *to the grown-ups;* in the third, the correlatives *both
. . . and* connect *father* and *mother.* These are correct:

1. Mary likes neither Sally nor Sam.
2. He was kind not only to the children but also to the grown-ups.
3. Both the father and the mother were hurt.

The misuse of *whether . . . or* as correlatives results, as a rule,
from lack of parallelism (see page 197); thus, *Whether he intends
coming here or to go there no one knows* is corrected by paralleling rather than by replacing the connected elements. The sentence should read *Whether he intends to come here or to go
there no one knows* or *Whether he intends coming here or going
there no one knows. He intends* is understood before *to go* in
the one, and before *going* in the other.

Such conjunctions of contrast as *however, nevertheless, yet,
still, notwithstanding* should be placed as close as possible to the
actual point of contrast. They should rarely be placed at the
beginning or at the end of an expression, because these positions
are properly reserved for emphasis (see page 210). *He must nevertheless do as he is directed* is better than *He must do as he is
directed nevertheless; You cannot expect him, however, to take
such advice to heart* is preferable to *You cannot expect him to
take such advice to heart, however.*

EXERCISE

Rewrite each of the following for better placement of correlatives:

1. He traveled both by plane and automobile.
2. Not only is he hurt but he is also bitter.
3. They went either to see a ball game or a play.
4. Whether it is more comfortable to sit there or standing I cannot say.
5. They not only took me into their secrets but my friend also.
6. He hopes both in regard to work and play that you will be benefited.
7. He cannot be either expected to accomplish much or lose much, however.
8. That sort of remark is uncalled for both on the part of pupils and teachers.
9. Not only did he use dangling participles but also faultily placed correlatives.
10. I shall approach him and make my request, his gruff appearance notwithstanding.

119. Omit no necessary words after connectives of parallel expressions. Such omissions may easily lead to confused grammatical construction and thus to serious misunderstanding (see page 195). The following are wrong:

1. You may force him to study but not think.
2. You may put a bridle on a horse but not an automobile.
3. You will find him disliked by all who know him, and particularly those who work with him.
4. He told us that he could not come, he wouldn't if he could, and he hated the whole idea of the club.

In the first of these sentences, *to* should be repeated before *think;* in the second, *on* must be repeated before *an automobile;* in the third, *by* must be repeated before *those;* in the fourth, *that* should be repeated before the last two noun clauses. These are correct:

1. You may force him to study but not to think.
2. You may put a bridle on a horse but not on an automobile.
3. You will find him disliked by all who know him, and particularly by those who work with him.
4. He told us that he could not come, that he wouldn't if he could, and that he hated the whole idea of the club.

Great inconsistency is found in the use of *that* introducing noun clauses (example 4 above). Be careful not to use *that* before one noun clause and omit it before another in parallel construction. Note the following:

Right: I hope that you arrive on time and that all goes well. (Both *thats* expressed.)

Right: I hope you arrive on time and all goes well. (Both *thats* omitted.)

Not recommended: I hope you arrive on time and that all goes well. (One *that* omitted and one *that* expressed.)

EXERCISE

Improve the coherence of the following by supplying the omission in each:

1. They like to collect old handmade furniture and prepare it for sale.
2. He admits that he made the noise and, as we all surmised, threw the eraser, but did not steal Rosie's sandwich.
3. She is a very popular young woman among her friends in the school, and her many relatives, and especially her co-workers.
4. Inasmuch as he had failed several times, though he had not been entirely to blame, and had become sullen and morose, they decided to give him a special program.
5. You can lead a horse to water but not make him drink; you can lead a dolt to study but not make him think.
6. Our greatest desire is to co-operate with those pupils who are promoting the honor system, and stop cheating in examinations.
7. If John will come and bring his banjo (though he always insists he is out of practice) and Billy will come and bring his guitar, we shall have a jolly outing.

120. Subordinate ideas properly by using accurate connectives. Some ideas require subordination through the agency of adjective clauses; some, through the agency of adverbial clauses; some, through the agency of noun clauses. The following sentences have illogical connectives, for the ideas in each are unequal, not co-ordinate as the conjunction indicates:

1. I shall be glad to introduce you to Mrs. Wilmerding and she is staying with us now.
2. He came up to my desk and demanded money but I was engaged in an important telephone conversation.
3. The reason for her going with that boy is a mystery and everyone says so.

Here the ideas are coherently connected through proper subordination:

1. I shall be glad to introduce you to Mrs. Wilmerding, who is staying with us now.
2. While I was engaged in an important telephone conversation, he came up to my desk and demanded money.
3. Everyone says that the reason for her going with that boy is a mystery.

EXERCISE

Write each of the following as a complex sentence with the proper subordination of parts:

1. He is returning from the West tomorrow. I read so in the paper.
2. That old mill by the river is picturesque and it seems to be falling down bit by bit.
3. The Hawaiian Islands are populated by Japanese, Chinese, Portuguese, and native Hawaiians, and they live together quietly and peacefully.
4. They will meet us on the field at three o'clock but bad weather may prevent their doing so.
5. He believes in his ability to pass all of his subjects this term, but he may be disappointed.
6. Then we came suddenly upon the famed Blue Hill. This is the highest mountain in the state.
7. That boy will be our next captain. You saw him at lunch yesterday. He is now head pupil in scholarship.
8. She has eaten nothing for three whole days and she is probably not feeling well.
9. They may be able to come to our party tonight but they are not sure.
10. He brought down two German planes from a great height. I read this in the official report.
11. Harris Ogden was elected almost unanimously. He once vowed never to run for office.
12. They have been absent a long time. This is the reason for their not knowing some of the work.

121. Avoid using unnecessary and illogical connectives. Such repetition of connectives as these sentences contain is monotonous and incoherent (see page 175):

1. We were very much disappointed, for we hadn't expected this accident to happen, for we had, indeed, made every effort to prevent it.

2. He had made the team but he wasn't satisfied even yet, but determined to gain the other goals for which he had set out, but many thought he would get no further honors.
3. Please tell me who that girl is who impressed us all by the address which she delivered at commencement last evening.

Such words as *as, and, for, since, that, which, who, though* are the commonest offenders under this rule. It has been pointed out on page 180 that in parallel constructions their repetition is correct and desirable. But in expressions in which there is no parallelism they are bewildering. Correction is possible, as a rule, only by reconstruction, as:

1. In spite of our efforts to prevent it, the accident happened, and we were very much disappointed.
2. He had made the team but he wasn't satisfied even yet. He had set his mind on other goals and was determined to win them. Many thought, however, that he could get no further honors.
3. Who is the girl that impressed us all with her commencement speech last evening?

The connection in *The reason I didn't go is because I was ill* is both repetitious and illogical. *Reason* and *because* convey the same meaning. *Because* introduces adverbial clauses only. In such sentences as this it is wrongly used to introduce a noun clause that stands as an attribute complement explanatory of the noun *reason*. All such clauses are properly introduced by *that;* thus, *The reason I didn't go is that I was ill* is correct. But by omitting *reason is* and the required attribute element, the sentence may be correctly read *I didn't go because I was ill; because* now properly introduces an adverbial clause. This misuse of *because* occurs quite as frequently at the beginning of a sentence as at the end, as *Because he is old is no guaranty of his wisdom.* This should read *That he is old* or (better) *His being old is no guaranty of his wisdom.*

Do not use *or* for *and* in expressions indicating choice or selection. *You must choose between this and that* or *You must choose either this or that* is correct. *You must choose between this or that* and *You must choose either this and that* are absurd, for *or* cannot be correlative with *between* in the one, *and* cannot be correlative with *either* in the other.

But is used superfluously in *I cannot help but try*. Say, rather, *I cannot help trying* (meaning *I can do nothing except try*), or *I can but try* (meaning *I can only try*). In the latter sentence *but* is an adverb meaning only.

Do not repeat *that* in introducing a noun clause. Say *I assure you that, provided I recover, I shall be at the meeting*, not *I assure you that, provided I recover, that I shall be at the meeting*. In the latter, incorrect, form the intervening phrase *provided I recover* tends to make the writer or speaker forget that the noun clause has already been properly introduced. The preferred position of introductory *that* in such constructions as this is before rather than after thrown-in material.

EXERCISE

Rewrite the following, making connections economical and logical:

1. One of the reasons why I didn't know my lesson is because we had company last night.
2. They were told that his selection wavers between Bill or Harry.
3. Because he drives that old car is no argument that he cannot afford a better one.
4. Though he had not been well, we did not expect this serious turn, though the doctor did not seem surprised.
5. As I entered, Mary was coming out looking as though something had happened—as something probably had.
6. Because he has failed this time doesn't mean, I hope, that he cannot help but put forth greater effort next time.
7. He at first thought that he couldn't accept, but when he learned that everybody had contributed, he decided that it might be said that he was too proud.
8. The proof of his being indifferent is because he never accepts any of her invitations.
9. His answer depends upon whether I go and whether Mary arrives.
10. No one doubts that, conditions being what they are, that it has been hard for him to make a choice between staying here or going West.

122. Avoid using *when* **and** *where* **to introduce noun clauses, especially in definitions.** *That* and *whether* are the most commonly used words in introducing noun clauses. Define a word by a synonym whenever the synonym is shorter or more familiar than the word defined. Define it, that is, by a word of the same part of speech. But if this cannot be done, your definition should begin with some such term as *act of* or *form of* or *phase of.* Do not use any form of the word defined in your definition. Do not begin a definition with *when* or *where* unless these words are part of the meaning.

In defining a term state, first, the class to which it belongs; second, the element or quality that distinguishes it from other members in the class; thus, *A chair is a piece of furniture* (classification or genus) *on which to sit* (distinction or differentiation). These are wrong:

1. Sprinting is when you run at top speed for short distances.
2. Handball is where players in a walled court use the hands in striking a ball.

The use of *when* in the first sentence suggests that sprinting is a time; of *where* in the second, that handball is a place. These are better:

1. Sprinting is running at top speed for short distances.
2. Handball is a game played in a walled court by players who use their hands in striking a ball.

It is better to say *Noon is midday or twelve o'clock* than *Noon is when the clock strikes twelve,* even though time is a major element in the definition. In the same way *The horizon is the apparent meeting place of earth and sky* is somewhat better than *The horizon is where earth and sky seem to meet.*

EXERCISE

Write the following definitions in better form:

1. A square is where a figure has equal angles and equal sides.
2. A holiday is when people in general do no work.
3. Suicide is when somebody purposely kills himself.

4. Description is describing what something looks like.
5. The cash-and-carry system is where you pay cash and take merchandise with you.
6. A partition is where you build a separation wall between two rooms or other apartments.
7. Stupidity means stolid or where a person has dullness of wit and understanding.
8. An automobile is something to ride in when you are out in the open air.
9. When you have a period of time assigned to you for rest and recreation, that is a vacation.
10. Football is where eleven players on each side of a white line try to push a large ball backward and forward until a goal is reached by one side or the other.

COMPACTNESS

Make your sentences compact—

123. Use a word to do the work of a phrase when possible without loss to the idea intended. The sentences

1. She ran down the corridor in haste.
2. They hailed the new teacher with enthusiasm.
3. We are studying the history of ancient times.

may without the slightest loss of meaning be more economically stated thus:

1. She ran down the corridor hastily.
2. They hailed the new teacher enthusiastically.
3. We are studying ancient history.

But this does not mean that you must try to reduce all phrases to words. In the first place, such reduction cannot always be made, as in *We took a walk in the cool of the evening* and *A word to the wise is sufficient.* In the second place, it is not always desirable, for a phrase may give a sentence a smoothness and rhythm that a word cannot achieve, as in *A thing of beauty is a joy for ever* and *A bird in the hand is worth two in the bush.*

EXERCISE

Reduce every phrase in the following to a word or two:

1. Her talk was delivered in a monotonous way.
2. I shall do that job with promptness.
3. There were six officers of the staff.
4. They met the situation with discretion.
5. At long last I may speak with freedom.
6. This is a car with durability.
7. He kept his room in a neat condition.
8. The boy of the senior class is wearing a hat of straw.
9. A day of pleasure was spent on the sands of the sea.
10. By the day, by the week, by the month, by the year, they deliver merchandise to us.

124. Use a word or a phrase to do the work of a clause when possible without loss to the idea intended. The sentences

1. The game was finished just as the sun was setting.
2. That woman who is very intelligent should have known better.
3. That car has run one hundred thousand miles and it has never been out of repair.

may without loss of meaning be more economically stated thus:

1. The game was finished at sunset.
2. That very intelligent woman should have known better.
3. That car has run one hundred thousand miles without being out of repair.

EXERCISE

Make the following more compact by reducing clauses to words or phrases:

1. Who will look after the costume that belongs to my sister?
2. We drove straight to the field and we made it in record time.
3. That is the kind of book that one finds interesting.
4. There is a car that impresses people.
5. While she was visiting in India she bought much beautiful ivory.
6. I hurt my hand seriously and I therefore hurried to the doctor.
7. That young prince who is very handsome is going to visit America when summer comes.
8. The setting sun bathed the world in gold as it sank grandly below the mountain tops.

9. The boy who entered from Boston in December made a record like that of the boy who entered from Denver in March.
10. Bill has a fine new boat which he calls *Bluster Point* and which is painted a flaming scarlet.
11. An unusually interesting schedule has been devised by which every student in the college is privileged to take part in at least one public game.
12. The sharp wind that whistled through every chink of our rough cabin was too much for the boy who lay shivering in the corner.

125. Use an infinitive or an infinitive phrase, or a participle or a participial phrase, or a gerund or a gerund phrase to do the work of a clause when possible without loss to the idea intended. Note that the following:

1. While I was sitting in the park I was approached by a beggar.
2. When we learned of the outbreak of war, we were greatly shocked.
3. They fully expected that he would win the coveted award.
4. They could find nothing that they could substitute for the table.

may without the slightest loss be more economically stated thus:

1. Sitting in the park I was approached by a beggar.
2. On learning of the outbreak of war we were greatly shocked.
3. They fully expected to win the coveted award.
4. They could find nothing to substitute for the table.

EXERCISE

Reduce every clause in the following to an infinitive or a participial or a gerund phrase:

1. When I talked to John about it, I was informed that I had better mind my own business.
2. While it was making the hairpin curve yesterday the *Mercury Express* took a tumble down the mountain.
3. In order that his constituents might be informed of the new policy he addressed a public meeting.
4. As I was leaving the house this morning I was startled by a stranger who was sitting on the doorstep.
5. She had no pie that she could give to the beggar; she had no regrets that she had to disappoint him.
6. We arrived early so that we might have as much time as possible with our boys and girls.

7. She went to college at night so that she might qualify to take the bar examinations in the fall.
8. There was no other course that they could follow, no other company that they might go with.
9. When she arrived at the Administration Building she was told that she should sign the visitors' register.
10. He taught me how to play the difficult classic on the violin.

126. **Use an appositive word or phrase instead of a clause when possible without loss to the idea intended.** The sentences

1. This is Baton Rouge, which is the place where I was born.
2. The old lady who seemed to be ill asked me to help her cross the street.
3. They decided to give a coming-out party for their nieces, who are named Alice, Clara, and June.

may without the slightest loss be more economically stated thus:

1. This is Baton Rouge, my birthplace.
2. The old lady, apparently ill, asked me to help her cross the street.
3. They decided to give a coming-out party for their nieces Alice, Clara, and June.

EXERCISE

Reduce every clause in the following to an appositive:

1. We are going to search for Robert who is our long-lost cousin.
2. They are paying a long visit to Ankara, which is the capital of Turkey.
3. At the very top of the mountain is So High, which is a famous recreation park.
4. Rolling sullenly about a mile from shore could be seen the *Electonia*, which was a large tramp ship.
5. At the entrance are two large statuesque gateposts which are Egyptian sculptures of Cleopatra's reign.
6. She plays tennis a great deal, which is probably the very best all-round exercise game.
7. She took her friend Horace, who is already a famous pianist, to Paris, which is one of the musical centers of the world.
8. Billy took her out in his new car, which is a twelve-cylinder Packard, over the highway, which is called Merritt Parkway.
9. That portrait over the mantelpiece, which is the best he has ever done, has been bought by Tompkins, who is a college classmate of his.

10. He has three large sheep dogs which are called Blunder and Donder and Blitzen, and they protect him against all vicious invaders who might come to rob or commit nuisance or set fire to buildings.

COMPLETENESS

Make your sentences complete—

127. Use phrases and dependent clauses as parts of sentences rather than as independent fragments. These are wrong:

1. Passing through at sunrise. We saw the mountain gorgeously colored.
2. Early in the evening. Supper was served on the terrace.
3. He insisted upon walking. Although the car was waiting.
4. Whoever he was. He wasn't very popular.
5. You ought to answer. To tell him the truth. To invite him here.
6. He liked his graduation present. A brand-new Buick.

In the first two examples a participial phrase and a prepositional phrase stand alone as independent units, but each is really a part of the independent clause which follows. In the third and fourth, dependent clauses are wrongly separated as if they were independent; in the fifth, a series of infinitive phrases, and in the last, an appositive phrase, are detached.

These are correct:

1. Passing through at sunrise, we saw the mountain gorgeously colored.
2. Early in the evening supper was served on the terrace.
3. He insisted upon walking, although the car was waiting.
4. Whoever he was, he wasn't very popular.
5. You ought to answer, to tell him the truth, to invite him here.
6. He liked his graduation present—a brand-new Buick.

Exclamatory and interrogative words, phrases, and clauses may sometimes be used as fragments, but never without close and well-understood connection with context. They are usually conversational or, if used in writing, are a device for emphasis. *"What about it?" "Not at all." "Never again!" "Now, for that game!" "She looked up, her eyes and dimples smiling at me. And flirting with me!"* are a few illustrations of allowable incomplete expressions. Use such expressions cautiously in writing.

EXERCISE

Rewrite each of the following as a complete sentence:

1. She started the motor. When they had finished their conversation.
2. Having it out with his teacher. He admitted he lost his temper.
3. Climbing down the hill slowly. There it was. The snake we had killed.
4. While she was playing tennis. Her car was stolen. From the garage.
5. He was driving an old Ford T Model. One of the early horseless buggies.
6. He declared that he wouldn't go. That he hated them all. That he was tired of this constant run-around.
7. In that cavern by the upper mountain. They found many curious remnants of previous occupancy.
8. They were exhausted. When they reached us. After that difficult and perilous way up the mountain.
9. Having seen him but once. When he was only a child. She hardly knew him now. Tall and mature. As he was.
10. They came suddenly upon the iron cross. Which stood in the middle of the road. Where they were supposed to turn right.

128. Bring every sentence to a logical and grammatical conclusion; do not leave the latter part of it "hanging in mid-air." The following are wrong:

1. He told us how, as a young man who had come to America without a penny in his pockets
2. The mere suggestion that I was not able to carry all the work I had planned for the term
3. Do you recall that in the museum at Madrid where we spent so many delightful hours?

These sentences begin correctly but are not completed. What was *told* in the first, what effect the *mere suggestion* had in the second, what you are asked to *recall* in the third are not revealed, yet these are the very things that the sentences were calculated to tell. Here they are complete:

1. He told us how, as a young man who had come to America without a penny in his pockets, he made his way to fame and fortune.
2. The mere suggestion that I was not able to carry all the work I had planned for the term, discouraged me very much.
3. Do you recall that in the museum at Madrid, where we spent so many delightful hours, we saw the Titian now being so much discussed in the papers?

EXERCISE

Complete the construction of each of the following:

1. There is a young man who, unless he is helped with his lessons
2. You remember that in his announcement in which he spoke of the game
3. As far as my being to blame, please remember that this is my first accident
4. The fact that I had never driven a car with automatic gears, being at a loss how to start
5. Though he has had a great deal of experience, owing to his long service at the factory
6. Inasmuch as John had to be at the college all day presiding at conferences, and kept away from his lessons
7. Sitting comfortably in a car as it goes along one always sees with the greatest possible delight
8. The mere thought of his having to go to war again and fight—perhaps lose his life—
9. As for her losing her diploma and Bill's forgetting his speech, disappointing as it all is
10. Please do not worry as far as my driving, for I wear an honor token for safety on my license plate

129. Include every word necessary to a clear and definite comparison. In expressing the *comparative degree,* the thing or person compared must be *ex*cluded from the class or group of comparison. Either *else* or *other* is used, as a rule, to make this exclusion. In expressing the *superlative degree* the thing or person compared must be *in*cluded in the class or group of comparison. These are wrong:

1. He is shorter than all the pupils.
2. He is the shortest of all other pupils.
3. New York City is larger than any city in the United States.
4. New York City is the largest of all other cities in the United States.

These are correct:

1. He is shorter than any other pupil *or* than anyone else in the class *or* than all the other pupils.
2. He is the shortest of all the pupils *or* the shortest pupil.
3. New York City is larger than any other city in the United States.
4. New York City is the largest of all the cities in the United States *or* is the largest city in the United States.

Compare one thing with another thing; do not compare a thing with a quality or an abstraction or a part. *The power of this car is equal to a steam engine* is wrong, for abstract *power* is compared with concrete *steam engine. The power of this car is equal to that (power) of a steam engine* is correct.

In comparative statements *as . . . as* or *so . . . as* are correlatives before and after positive-degree forms; neither may be omitted. In comparative statements expressed by the suffix *er* or by the words *more* or *less, than* must be used as correlative except at the end of an expression; thus, *He is as shrewd as, if not shrewder than, Eliot* and *He is as shrewd as Eliot, if not shrewder* are correct. *He is as shrewd, if not shrewder, than Eliot* is wrong.

Ambiguity may occur in the use of a noun after *than* in a comparative statement (see page 195). *He likes Jane better than Mary* may mean either that he likes Jane better than he likes Mary or that he likes Jane better than Mary likes Jane. In such comparison as this the dependent clause must therefore be completed unless context otherwise clarifies meaning.

EXERCISE

Write the following incomplete comparisons as they should be:
1. In this instance my opinion is as good, if not better, than his.
2. These are healthier, though not so good-looking, as the others.
3. This country imports more copper than all countries in the world.
4. She has the worst disposition of anyone I know.
5. This is softer in texture but just as durable as the other.
6. There goes the most interesting pupil of all others in our class.
7. The wool in my suit is not silky like John's suit.
8. This is the highest building of any in the world.
9. Bill has the meanest dog of any other man in the countryside.
10. Mrs. Elwell insists that she drives the family car better than her husband.

130. Omit no part of a paired expression that is necessary to correct grammatical construction. If the form of the word understood in paired expressions is not the same as the corresponding form expressed, the right form must be supplied.

1. *I am attached and interested in Howard* is wrong because

of the omission of *to* after *attached*. The sentence should read *I am attached to and interested in Howard*. But if the prepositions required after such paired verbs are the same, no repetition is required; thus, *I have been scolded and punished by my teacher* is correct, *by* being understood after *scolded*.

2. *I never have and I never will do it* is wrong because of the omission of *done* after *have*. The sentence should read *I never have done it and I never will do it*. If, however, the forms of the principal verb are the same after such paired auxiliaries, no repetition is required; thus, *I cannot and will not see him* is correct, *see* being understood after *cannot*.

3. *This is one of the most beautiful, if not the most beautiful, scenes I have ever witnessed* is wrong because of the omission of *scenes* after the first *beautiful*. The sentence should read *This is one of the most beautiful scenes, if not the most beautiful scene, I have ever witnessed*. The following reading is also correct and is generally preferred: *This is one of the most beautiful scenes I have ever witnessed, if not the most beautiful*. In expressing this sort of comparison aloud the speaker usually accents the second *the*.

EXERCISE

Supply the omission in each of the following:

1. He has always been fond and attentive to her.
2. She is neither afraid nor agreeable to the proposition.
3. She is one of the cleverest, if not the cleverest, girl in the class.
4. I have never seen, and now I never shall, the beautiful Niagara.
5. He has been a competitor and a winner of many medals in the school.
6. He never has and he never will go to any of those political meetings.
7. The plan appealed but was not approved by the committee.
8. They were overcome at what was one of the greatest sights, if not the greatest, they had ever seen.
9. She admitted that she never had and never could swim the Channel, and that her promoters never did and never could have told such a falsehood.
10. Though Miss Angel was interested and liked by the boy, she found him by no means the best, or even among the best pupils, in her class.

131. Include every word, phrase, and clause necessary to logical expression and accurate understanding. The omission of a part of speech usually results in ambiguity and gives the impression of haste or ignorance. Avoid:

1. Yours received *for* Your note is received. (noun and verb omitted)
2. Am seventeen years old *for* I am seventeen years old. (pronoun omitted)
3. She is happier than any girl *for* She is happier than any other girl. (adjective omitted)
4. I like Sally better than Jane *for* I like Sally better than I like Jane *or* better than Jane does. (pronoun and verb omitted) (See page 93.)
5. She was very impressed *for* She was very much impressed. (adverb omitted)
6. What use is that? *for* Of what use is that? (preposition omitted)
7. This is as good if not better than that *for* This is as good as, if not better than, that. (conjunction omitted)

Now note how incompleteness causes vagueness or ambiguity in the following expressions:

1. *They accused the secretary and the treasurer* means that two persons were accused. *They accused the secretary and treasurer* means that one person holding two offices was accused. If the former is meant and the latter expressed, the incomplete form may make trouble.

2. *Gravel will go through that sieve as well as sand* is ambiguous because it is incomplete. The meaning probably is that gravel will go through the sieve as well as sand *will,* but the expression might be taken to mean that gravel will go through the sieve as well as through sand.

3. *Standing before him were children whom he could not tell whether they were qualified or not* is vague and "muddled" because of the omission of *about* or *regarding* before *whom—Standing before him were children regarding whom he could not tell whether they were qualified or not* or (simpler) *Standing before him were children whose qualifications he did not know.*

4. *They liked him so well that they promoted him to manager* is absurd, for *manager* denotes a person, whereas promotion

denotes a position. The intended expression is *They liked him so well that they promoted him to the position of manager* or *to a managership* or *that they made him manager.*

5. *He was always absorbed in cards, such as pinochle* is absurd, for *cards* does not parallel *pinochle,* the one indicating the agency by which the other—the game called pinochle—is played. *He was always absorbed in some card game, such as pinochle* is correct.

6. *He sold more tickets than seats* is absurd, for *tickets* and *seats* are not logically the parallel terms. The correct reading is *He sold more tickets than there were seats.*

7. *Of the names listed only two were accepted as speakers* is absurd, for *two* refers to *names* and names are not speakers. The sentence should read *Of the pupils listed only two were accepted as speakers.* Now *two* refers to the noun *pupils.*

8. *The novel* A Tale of Two Cities *takes place in London and Paris* is absurd, for novels do not take place. What is meant is *The action of the novel* A Tale of Two Cities *takes place in London and Paris.*

9. *An interesting case of what a good record should be occurred yesterday* is absurd, for a case does not occur. Say rather *An interesting case of what a good record should be was presented yesterday* or *was brought to our attention yesterday.*

10. Make certain that the terms listed in a sentence as parallel are indeed parallel. *He had knives, guns, rackets, wearing apparel, trophies, and various other utensils, thrown higgledy-piggledy around his room* is illogical, for wearing apparel and trophies cannot be listed as utensils. Substitute *objects* for *utensils* to make the sentence correct.

EXERCISE

Make each of the following complete:

1. This room is fifteen feet diameter.
2. He understands every phase of the chauffeur.
3. He asked what altitude they were flying.
4. He went into the living room to read Dante and smoke.

5. They have always been interested in cars, especially racing.
6. He said he didn't know what purpose that was.
7. The whole affair is unworthy your attention.
8. They walked eight or nine miles distance.
9. She is fond of studying architectural plans, as houses.
10. The secretary and the manager brought his suitcase.
11. Of all the names presented, this one will do the best work.
12. Yours at hand. In reply would say am twenty years of age.
13. The cabin is fifteen feet width and twenty-five length.
14. She was very embarrassed for a moment but soon recovered her composure.
15. The president and vice-president were very late at the meeting.
16. The fruit juice poured through the strainer as well as the sirup.
17. He now understands every operation of the telegrapher.
18. Everywhere in the room were people whom he could not tell whether they were friends or foes.
19. Though he supplied more uniforms than soldiers, the captain and secretary were patient with him.
20. He never has and he never will go there again, though he regards the place as one of the most healthful, if not the most healthful resort, in the world.

CONSISTENCY

Make your sentences consistent—

132. Keep similar ideas in similar constructions. The following are not good:

1. Striving, though you fail, is better than to idle.
2. He won a prize of great value and having great usefulness.
3. He is a member of the dramatic club, of the speakers club, and he is also a member of the rifle club.
4. The man was lean and lanky, and he had a strong inclination to pick a quarrel with everybody.
5. When you enter that school you are required to have fine recommendations, presenting a certificate of health; they also require tuition in advance.

The first parallels a gerund with an infinitive; the second, a prepositional phrase with a participial phrase; the third, two phrases with a clause; the fourth, a compound attribute complement with a clause; the fifth, an infinitive phrase, a participial phrase, and an independent clause. There are other kinds of out-of-balance expressions, but these are typical. Note the improvement as a result of parallel constructions for similar ideas:

1. To strive, though you fail, is better than to idle, *or* Striving, though you fail, is better than idling.
2. He won a prize of great value and usefulness.
3. He is a member of the dramatic club, of the speakers club, and of the rifle club, *or* He is a member of the dramatic, speakers, and rifle clubs.
4. The man was lean and lanky and pugnacious.
5. When you enter that school you are required to have fine recommendations, to present a certificate of health, and to pay tuition in advance.

But do not make the mistake of balancing ideas that are fundamentally dissimilar. In *Gossiping is damaging* and *To see is to believe* and *"In the red" means out of pocket* there is the uniformity of construction demanded by the ideas themselves. In such expressions as the following, however, there is clearly no such demand:

1. She was angry, excited, and upset, and required sympathy and attention.
2. The speaker was very happy in his remarks on patriotism and in the manner of his delivery, and in these respects he is worthy of applause.

The last idea in each of these is different from the preceding ones and should not therefore be similarly connected. The following are correct:

1. She was angry, excited, and upset; she required sympathy and attention.
2. The speaker was very happy in his remarks on patriotism and in the manner of his delivery; for these he is worthy of applause.

EXERCISE

Improve each of the following by paralleling constructions as much as possible:

1. She dropped her bag in the corridor, and her book was lost in the yard.
2. Those sweaters are made of silk and having mother-of-pearl buttons.

3. To know when to stop is having what is known as tact.
4. Your job is to receive at the door, saying a kind word, and you must smile.
5. Keen eyesight, having steady nerves, and a person of alertness are essentials for safe driving.
6. Everybody liked him because he was genial and because he was accommodating, and because of these qualities he will get on.
7. He approached in a haste that frightened us and informed us in a halting and hesitant manner.
8. When you have finished washing the dishes, and then after making the beds, you may come to me for further orders.
9. We have two reasons for wanting to go: to see the sights, and in the second place, wanting to hear the speeches.
10. Billy liked his teacher for her kindness, for her knowledge, and for her sprightly manner, and for these qualities all of the pupils, as well as their parents, liked her too.

133. Keep tense and voice uniform. Note the inconsistent change of tense in:

1. As soon as the alarm was given he runs to the hydrant.
2. She says she will go if she didn't have to work.

The past form *was given* is inconsistent with the present form *runs* in the first sentence; *says* and *will go* are inconsistent with *did* in the second. These are correct:

1. As soon as the alarm is given he runs to the hydrant *or* As soon as the alarm was given he ran to the hydrant.
2. She says she will go if she doesn't have to work *or* She said she would go if she didn't have to work.

The tenses are now uniform—all present or all past. It is pointed out on page 127 that the historical present may be used to vivify and emphasize expression—to give to past events a present or living quality, as *Washington now risks the hazardous crossing.* But the historical present should be used guardedly, never unexpectedly or abruptly in the midst of other verbs not in the present tense, and never in connection with unimportant or trivial happenings. And note also that a clause expressing a present truth requires a present-tense verb, no matter what the tense of the verb is in a related clause, as:

He replied that Sacramento is the capital of California.
We were reminded that honesty is the best policy.

Here the past tense in the one clause and the present tense in the other are logical (see page 128).

Note the inconsistent change of voice in:

1. She was studious, and a diploma was therefore given her.
2. You may walk for miles in this air and fatigue will never be felt.

This inconsistency is likely to occur in compound and complex sentences in which a change of subject is made unnecessarily (see page 221). Note these improvements:

1. She was studious and she therefore received a diploma *or* She has been studious and has therefore been given a diploma *or* She was studious and therefore received a diploma.
2. You may walk for miles in this air and you will never feel fatigued *or* You may walk for miles in this air without fatigue *or* You may walk for miles in this air and not feel fatigued.

But note that voice is sometimes properly changed as between one clause and another, as *Though he suffered constantly, he was never known to complain* and *You should have been rewarded when you found it,* the time relationship as it bears upon the subject deciding the issue.

EXERCISE

Make the following consistent in tense and voice:

1. I hurries away to the street and there I saw the trouble.
2. He replies that he really had no idea of the trouble.
3. You may go at seventy an hour on this road and danger will never be encountered.
4. When I see the fox approaching I ran to the house and grabbed the gun.
5. You place your hand thus; then the brake should have been released.
6. I turn the screw; the lid was then lifted, and the pink powder was seen.
7. We ought to have been thanked, but instead they hardly speak to us.
8. His honors have been well earned, and further ones awaited him.
9. Take the third exercise, and the answer should be put on the board.
10. When he hears the report, he dashed out and asks what it was all about.

134. Keep number and person uniform. The following are wrong:

1. Everyone should try their luck.
2. Take the left-hand road, and in a minute a person can see the bridge.
3. Be sure to take a warm overcoat; they will be necessary in that climate.
4. Two of each is all I want.
5. One of the fellows are ill.

In the first sentence, the plural *their* refers to the singular *everyone;* in the second, the subject of *take* is second person *you* and the subject of *can see* is third person, yet *person* here means *you;* in the third, the singular *overcoat* is referred to by the plural *they;* in the fourth, the plural *two* is subject of the singular *is;* in the fifth, the singular *one* is subject of the plural *are.* The following are correct:

1. Everyone should try his luck.
2. Take the left-hand road and in a minute you will see the bridge.
3. Be sure to take a warm overcoat; you will need it in that climate.
4. Two of each are all I want.
5. One of the fellows is ill.

EXERCISE

Make the following consistent in number and person:

1. A motor has to be oiled frequently to keep their running smooth.
2. All of those cars have to be geared so that it can take steep grades.
3. When one enters the museum you see the priceless Van Gogh immediately on the left.
4. Every serious-minded child should do their best to make the most of your schooling.
5. Nobody wants to see their work ignored, especially when you have spent so much time and effort on them.
6. Are you certain that you have your ticket? Remember they are important when a man is traveling.
7. The farmer in all parts of the eastern states have to put up scarecrows to keep birds from destroying crops.
8. Not one of the women were afraid when she saw the bombers over their head.

9. Just as soon as one is prepared for happiness they find that their capacity for it is limited.
10. All of the soldiers from this community is grimly determined to die rather than submit to defeat.

135. Keep to a logical sequence of time and place. The following are not good:

1. They started down the road at a smart pace, after making themselves comfortable in the car.
2. After I had paid the man and selected what I wanted I went home, first stopping at my sister's.
3. Take one cup of milk, stir in three eggs, and let the mixture boil gently after adding a little flour and flavoring.

The following readings are more consistent because the natural or logical order of events and places is observed:

1. After making themselves comfortable in the car, they started down the road at a smart pace.
2. After I had selected what I wanted and paid the man, I stopped at my sister's and then went home.
3. Take one cup of milk, stir in three eggs, a little flour, and flavoring, and let the mixture boil gently.

There may be occasions when for the sake of emphasis or climax (see page 209) it is desirable to violate this rule, as:

We were on our way with our luggage and our memories and our regrets, having said our last good-by.

The idea that logically comes first here is that of good-by, for good-by naturally precedes being on our way. But reserving good-by till the last gives greater emphasis to the expression. This, however, is an exceptional rather than a regular arrangement.

EXERCISE

Rewrite the following with consistent time and place order:

1. The composition had been well written and carefully outlined.
2. We have had many distinguished presidents, from Roosevelt to Washington.
3. We were finally off to the West after numerous farewells.
4. They came here yesterday after traveling night and day for a month.

5. The valuable ring was finally located after a tedious search.
6. He managed to get the new boots off at last, but not until a good deal of pulling and straining and squirming had been done.
7. That suit is not adapted to this climate. It is very becoming, and all that. I wrote you to bring the thinnest possible wearing apparel.
8. He therefore declined my offer. When I saw him coming, tired and hungry and ill clad as he was, I offered him both comforts and necessities. But he learned that I had at one time been cruel and inconsiderate to one of his people, quite unintentionally and unknowingly.

136. Keep relationships uncontradictory; that is, avoid two negative terms in close modification or connection. The following are bad:

1. I didn't say nothing.
2. He won't come under no conditions.
3. They haven't got no chance hardly.
4. I haven't scarcely begun my work yet.
5. No man couldn't do that no better.
6. We couldn't rarely find him at home.

These are all double or triple negative constructions. Such double negatives as *no* and *not, not* and *nothing, no* and *hardly, not* and *hardly, not* and *rarely, not* and *only, never* and *scarcely* are used in the same constructions, and the expressions thus contradict themselves. They say no when they mean yes, or vice versa, and are probably the worst of inconsistent forms, for they are illiterate. These are correct:

1. I didn't say anything.
2. He won't come under any conditions.
3. They have hardly a chance.
4. I have scarcely begun my work.
5. No man could do that better.
6. We could rarely find him at home.

No, not, none, nothing, used together, make absolute contradictions; *not hardly, not rarely, not scarcely, hardly never* make modified contradictions. All are bad. Avoid them.

EXERCISE

Write the following consistently, that is, uncontradictorily:

1. She doesn't play no better than she did.
2. I scarcely never see them no more.
3. She was so embarrassed she couldn't hardly speak.
4. They hardly never come to see us.
5. We haven't seen none of our friends here.
6. Don't never do a thing like that no more.
7. We haven't scarcely seen nothing of them all the year.
8. They couldn't scarcely see nothing through the fog.
9. I don't never expect to see nothing of him no more.
10. She doesn't never see how nothing can't make no difference.

137. Avoid comparisons or figures of speech that are inappropriate or not easily imagined (see page 42). The following illustrate:

1. Our road is rough, but our sailing must be straight ahead.
2. Fifty per cent of the time he is trying to scale Parnassus.
3. Let's get down to brass tacks and attack the problem at its **very** roots.
4. Madame Curie triumphed in the laboratory as Wellington triumphed at Waterloo.

The first mixes land travel and sea travel; the second mixes the language of commerce with that of poetry; the third mixes hardware and horticulture; the fourth mixes chemistry with military strategy. Each comparison stretches the imagination too far. The mind should be taken easily and consistently from one term of a comparison to another, not abruptly or shockingly as result of uncongenial terms. If you find it difficult to complete a comparison suitably and consistently, give it up and use a straightforward literal statement. Note these improvements of the above:

1. Our road is rough, but our onward march must be straight ahead.
2. Half of the time he is trying to write poetry.
3. Let's attack the problem at its very origin.
4. Madame Curie triumphed in chemistry as Einstein did in physics.

EXERCISE

Rewrite the following comparisons consistently and appropriately:

1. He insists upon paddling his own canoe up to the stars.
2. He beamed with good spirits of which everybody tasted heartily.
3. He said he smelled a rat and thought it ought to be nipped in the bud.
4. He is poised on a wave of business and industrial prosperity.
5. Such chaff as that should be taken with a grain of salt.
6. His flowers of rhetoric stirred up a hornets' nest.
7. He became very successful after being weighed in the scales of failure and found not wanting.
8. It was full steam ahead for Carter as he careered forth in his new car like a knight on a sleek charger.
9. If you could unshackle those culprits from the bonds of their own vicious passions, you would blaze a trail in moral uplift.
10. It seemed to him like the end of the rainbow—like the dawn of a new day—when he entered that office and saw the spick-and-span outfit of the very latest business machinery.

EMPHASIS

Make your sentences emphatic—

138. Repeat words or phrases or entire constructions. Such repetition may be exact; that is, the same word or phrase may be set down two, three, or more times (direct repetition), or an idea may be expressed in different words (indirect repetition), thus:

1. Try and try and try again.
   Strive and struggle and wrestle with the job.
2. In vain; in vain; all, all in vain.
   It's no use; it's futile—hopeless—past retrieving.

The first in each of these pairs is somewhat more emphatic than the second. Now note the effect of deliberate repetition for emphasis in longer passages:

1. Strangers were stared out of countenance by staring white houses, staring white walls, staring white streets, staring tracts of arid road, staring hills from which verdure was burnt away.
2. Blessed are the poor in spirit: for theirs is the kingdom of heaven. Blessed are they that mourn: for they shall be comforted. Blessed are the meek: for they shall inherit the earth.

In these illustrations both repeated word and repeated construction make the emphasis impressive.

EXERCISES

1. Express each of the following ideas more emphatically by means of direct or indirect repetition:

1. The car kept honking all the way down the road.
2. She sat by the window and sewed all day every day.
3. Though it seemed to be unreachable, he finally gained the top.
4. We heard the rain pouring all night on the resonant tin roof.
5. He worked hard all his life but he never really "arrived."
6. The nervous chirping of the crickets prevented our sleeping.
7. They kept playing that tune till I thought I should scream.
8. Suddenly I heard someone knocking at my chamber door.
9. We were becalmed for many days in mid-ocean.
10. He vowed he would never enter her house again.

2. The following illustrate emphasis secured by direct repetition. Rephrase each with indirect repetition:

1. Who is here so base that would be a bondman? If any, speak; for him have I offended. Who is here so rude that would not be a Roman? If any, speak; for him have I offended. Who is here so vile that will not love his country? If any, speak; for him have I offended.
2. Then came rows of houses, with little vane-surmounted masts uprearing themselves from among the scarlet beans. Then ditches. Then pollard willows. Then more ditches. Then unaccountable patches of dirty water, hardly to be descried, for the ships that covered them. Then, the air was perfumed with chips; and all other trades were swallowed up in mast, oar, and block-making, and boat-building. Then, the ground grew marshy and unsettled. Then, there was nothing to be smelt but rum and sugar.

139. Balance words or phrases or longer parts; that is, set two ideas, whether alike or opposite, in parallel constructions. Note, for instance, these balanced sentences:

1. Day unto day uttereth speech, and night unto night showeth knowledge.
2. Reading maketh a full man; conference, a ready man; writing, an exact man.
3. Some ages produce many great men and few great occasions; other times, on the contrary, raise great occasions but few or no great men.

These sentences read smoothly and emphatically because words, phrases, and complete structures in each are balanced; the parts are "teamed up" one with another. Contrast the following wordings, which are awkward and weak:

1. One day speaks to another, and knowledge is shown by one night to another.
2. Reading yields a man much knowledge; readiness or alertness accrue to a man through conference; and practice in writing begets accuracy.
3. There are some ages in which many great men are produced but in which no very great occasions arise; then again there are other times having practically no great men but many important events.

Used in moderation, balanced structure gives dignity, point, and rhythm to expression. Sayings such as *Nothing venture, nothing have* and *Man proposes; God disposes* and *If you would have a friend you must be a friend* have persisted because of the memorable way in which the ideas are balanced. Used to excess, balanced structure may sound artificial and insincere. Use it only when you are sure that you can thus emphasize your expression.

EXERCISE

Form a balanced expression from each of the following:

1. You go by way of the high road; the low route is the one I'll take.
2. I shall take the green car; the blue car will be better for you.
3. If you do anything wrong, suffering will come to you as a result.
4. He possesses a great deal of knowledge, but folly is also a part of his make-up.
5. I have many things to do today: taking Harry to the station, see that the laundry is made ready, and I must arrange my books on the new shelves.
6. He works very inefficiently in the morning when he is rested, and in the afternoon when he is tired he works most inefficiently.
7. Whatever you really are, that is said to be your character; your reputation is what people say about you.
8. Do not try to be the first to try anything new, but at the same time do not fail to adopt the new and the novel before they are accepted by the very last people in the world.
9. Real worth is what distinguishes the man; the fellow, on the other hand, lacks real worth.

10. This boy is always on time; but this is not the merit of either Bob, who is always late, or of Russell, who is usually inconveniently ahead of time.

140. Suspend or postpone the main idea until the end is reached. A sentence in which such delay is arranged is called a periodic sentence because the expression is not complete until the period is reached. The opposite kind of sentence structure, in which an expression is complete at one or more points before the end is reached, is called **loose.** This is a loose sentence:

> He is one of the most celebrated of athletes │ because of his prowess │ on the field │ and his fairness │ in contest.

If a period is placed at any of the points indicated, the part preceding it will be a complete sentence. In periodic construction the sentence reads:

> Because of his prowess on the field and his fairness in contest he is one of the most celebrated of athletes.

In this there is no point of completion before the end; the full meaning is not "unlocked" until *athletes* is reached.

Periodic sentences are emphatic because they create suspense and expectancy. Used to excess, however, they make expression labored and stilted. Loose sentences, too, though rarely emphatic, have an important place in expression. They make it easygoing and intimate, but they may also make it choppy and confusing. It is good practice to mix balanced, periodic, and loose sentences in composition (see page 224).

EXERCISE

Rewrite each of the following loose expressions in periodic form:

1. The fire raged through the heart of the city, over the hills beyond, and straight back into the forest.
2. The community is making great preparations for the increase of employment and for the relief of those who cannot work.
3. The pardon by the governor came over long-distance telephone just as the two culprits had given up in despair.

4. You will burn your shoes if you persist in resting your feet on the fender so close to that blazing fire.
5. You shouldn't attempt to play that overture until you are thoroughly acquainted with its mood and have given hours of practice to it.
6. He has made himself very popular going around among the poor and providing them against cold and hunger.
7. They haven't a kind word for that fellow because he is so headstrong and thus so difficult to train.
8. The game with Excelsior High School was arranged after negotiations with Whitmore Junior College were broken off.
9. It is necessary for a young person to have a good deal of courage if he would resist politely much of the advice doled out by his elders.
10. I saw two cruisers deliberately collide during the war maneuvers off Norfolk, Virginia, one morning last spring.

141. Arrange words, phrases, and clauses of unequal rank in the order of importance, that is, from lesser to greater meaning. Such arrangement is called **climax.** *She is difficult and sullen and impertinent* is more emphatic than *She is impertinent and sullen and difficult* because *impertinent* is the strongest word of the three and is therefore given the position of climax. These are weak:

1. He felt bitter and hurt.
2. You are worse than senseless things; you are blocks and stones.
3. We cannot consecrate, hallow, or dedicate this ground.

These are emphatic because of climactic arrangement.

1. He felt hurt and bitter.
2. You blocks; you stones; you worse than senseless things!
3. We cannot dedicate; we cannot consecrate; we cannot hallow this ground.

The term *periodic* applies to grammatical arrangement. But if periodic structure results in placing the most important or striking idea at the end of an expression, then it builds also for climax.

EXERCISE

Rewrite each of the following so that it will have emphasis as result of climax:

1. I should rather die than be denied my liberty.
2. Like a Colossus doth he bestride the narrow world.

3. We were impressed by the devastation and ruin and waste.
4. He rose rapidly to the top from lowly birth and impoverished youth.
5. He is qualified spiritually, mentally, physically to hold the high position.
6. The flood drowned both the man and the woman, and damaged their home.
7. She was graduated with high honors; she worked hard; she attended regularly.
8. Our old car took us to the very top, though we never thought it could possibly do so.
9. He would die and struggle and endure for her because he loves her so much.
10. I was shocked at the suffering and humiliation and hardship he had been required to undergo as I looked at that picture.

142. Place important words and ideas in emphatic positions. The beginning and the end of an expression are the emphatic points—the starting point and the stopping point. The last is the position of climax and is more emphatic, as a rule, than the first position. Place unimportant or shading words and phrases between the beginning and the end; do not begin or end with them. These are weak:

1. There had never been a tragedy more moving and appalling, however.
2. "If I understand you correctly, murder is your proposition?"
3. He shouted: "Thief! Thief! The police should be called!"

These are emphatic because first and last positions are used for important words or ideas:

1. Never had there been, however, a more moving and appalling tragedy.
2. "Your proposition, if I understand you correctly, is murder?"
3. "Thief! Thief!" he shouted. "Call the police!"

EXERCISE

Rewrite each of the following so that first and last positions are made more emphatic:

1. I will never go to one of your parties again.
2. Then, in the twinkle of an eye, the goal was kicked successfully.
3. We found the long-lost key in the water pipes, to our embarrassment.
4. He said he could take a great many salmon if he had a good guide.

5. At the end of the investigation it was found that the atrocious murder had, however, been committed by the victim's sister, whom nobody had suspected really.
6. After I had with great difficulty and no end of vexation attained the peak, my tragic fate was apparent to me and I plunged abruptly across the canyon, expecting never to see the light of day again.

143. Keep important ideas in independent clauses and less important ones in dependent clauses or in words and phrases. These are weak:

1. He had a motor accident which maimed him for the rest of his life.
2. Though he gave millions to the cause, he appeared to be indifferent to it.
3. The waters reached the first floor of the powerhouse, when the lights went out.

These are emphatic because principal ideas are placed in principal clauses and subordinate ideas in subordinate clauses:

1. He was maimed for the rest of his life because of a motor accident.
2. Though he appeared to be indifferent to the cause, he gave millions to it.
3. When the waters reached the first floor of the powerhouse, the lights went out.

Be especially careful not to place principal ideas in clauses beginning with *which, who, while, when, though,* and *if.*

EXERCISE

Make each of the following more emphatic by placing principal ideas in principal clauses and subordinate ideas in subordinate expressions:

1. The boy ate a great many green apples, which made him sick.
2. When the heavy guns began to fire, the birds flew swiftly away.
3. One minute before, the children had been playing where the awful crash occurred.
4. While he was explaining his uncle's horrible death, he munched away at his precious candy.
5. She had not been among the popular contestants, though she easily won every prize.
6. The alarm of fire made a tremendous noise, though the pupils went quietly about their regular fire drill.
7. Grandmother has had a bad fall off the kitchen steps, which will keep her in bed for at least four weeks.

144. Use strong, direct, simple, pictorial words—specific rather than generic nouns, active rather than passive verbs, forceful and unusual adjectives and adverbs rather than hackneyed ones (see pages 3–5). These are weak:

1. The wall was climbed by him with difficulty.
2. The car made the grade only with the greatest difficulty.
3. I think it's positively wonderful the way that boat docked.

These are more emphatic:

1. He scrambled up the steep wall laboriously.
2. The motor chugged and groaned and strained till the top was won.
3. I was astonished at the ease with which the ship nosed into her slip.

When the present tense is used to relate a past event, it is called the **historical present.** *Napoleon masses his troops on the border* is more emphatic than *Napoleon massed his troops on the border,* though the latter is accurate and the former imaginative.

Do not use the passive voice in such a way as to leave in doubt by whom an act was done. *The signal was heard from afar* is vague. Was heard by whom? Say either *The officers heard the signal from afar* or *The signal was heard by the officers from afar,* the former being preferred.

EXERCISE

Make the following emphatic by means of stronger, more suggestive, and more pictorial words:

1. Just the grandest possible time was had at your party.
2. We think it's marvelous the way you drove up that crooked road.
3. You must try repeatedly before you can hope to be successful.
4. We saw a number of beautiful things as we came down the mountain.
5. The dog revealed his delight in every possible manner imaginable.
6. John knocked at the door as if he meant business.
7. The recommendation that you have written is very much appreciated.
8. On her arrival she was handed a wonderful bouquet, to which she was not indifferent.
9. His appearance was not good; his speech was likewise bad; he was not attractive in any way.
10. She was ridiculously overdressed and was wearing far too many ornaments.

145. Change the construction suddenly or devise a completely new construction. This means particularly that excessive use of connectives, especially of *and* and *but,* may weaken emphasis. These are weak:

1. This was the hottest day we had, and, to make matters worse, all our fans were broken.
2. The truck driver thundered at Mary that amateur drivers had no business on the public highways, and Mary agreed by fainting.
3. Granny was always saying, "Cheer up, honey; don't you fret," and on hearing *cheer* we would join in a chorus with her, much to her annoyance.

These are emphatic:

1. This was the hottest day we had. To make matters worse, all our fans were broken.
2. The truck driver thundered at Mary that amateur drivers had no business on the public highways. Mary agreed—by fainting.
3. "Cheer up, honey; don't you fret." This is what Granny was always saying. On hearing *cheer* we would join in a chorus with her. Did this annoy her!

EXERCISE

Make the following more emphatic by a change of construction or by some sudden turn of expression:

1. That was the worst overturn we ever had, and we hope never to have another like it.
2. He is a strange-looking individual, and I fancy you will agree once you have seen him.
3. Tom grabbed the flag out of my hands shouting, "Down with the traitors!" and he seemed to be taken with some sort of unconscious frenzy.
4. The waters swirled and roared, and washed away all of our earthly possessions, and we were grateful that we were not drowned.
5. The old preacher usually got desired results with the famous lines from Longfellow: "Life is real; life is earnest," but today something went wrong and the congregation made no response at all.
6. There couldn't possibly have been a more awe-inspiring voice, and Janet was visibly terrified, and I felt a little shaky myself, but we took to our heels and were soon out of sight and out of hearing.

146. Omit all unnecessary words, phrases, and clauses (see also page 39). The following sentences show that every part of speech (with the exception of the interjection, which is usually an "extra") may be used superfluously:

1. Give that to the manager man at the window. (noun)
2. The boy he took his book. (pronoun)
3. These two are both alike. (adjective)
4. I have got a new overcoat. (verb)
5. The figures amount up to $524. (adverb)
6. With whom are you going with? (preposition)
7. His arguments were considered as unanswerable. (conjunction)

These should, of course, read:

1. Give that to the manager at the window.
2. The boy took his book.
3. These two are alike.
4. I have a new overcoat.
5. The figures amount to $524.
6. With whom are you going?
7. His arguments were considered unanswerable.

The following violate this rule by way of sheer wordiness (page 39), that is, by the use of words, phrases, and clauses that are not necessary:

1. *Lorna Doone* is the type of book that everybody likes.
2. Permit me to say that the goods have not as yet been delivered.
3. Let me repeat that over again for your benefit.
4. The chancellor made a declaration to the effect that there would be no football this year.
5. We had a perfectly excruciating time at your gorgeous party.
6. Once upon a time I had occasion to serve in the capacity of arbitrator.

These should read:

1. *Lorna Doone* is a good book.
2. The goods have not yet been delivered.
3. Let me repeat.
4. The chancellor has canceled football this year.
5. What a grand party!
6. I once served as arbitrator.

But it should be noted that sometimes emphasis is achieved by the deliberate violation of this rule. Extension or elaboration of a term for the sake of impressing it on the reader has always been a method of achieving emphasis in literature. The following oft-quoted excerpt from Charles Dickens' *The Chimes* illustrates. The enumeration is used to emphasize the merchandising ambition of the little shop.

> Cheese, butter, firewood, soap, pickles, matches, bacon, table-beer, peg-tops, sweetmeats, boys' kites, bird-seed, cold ham, birch brooms, hearthstones, salt, vinegar, blacking, red-herrings, stationery, lard, mushroom-ketchup, staylaces, loaves of bread, shuttlecocks, eggs, and slate-pencils: everything was fish that came to the net of this greedy little shop, and all these articles were in its net.

EXERCISE

Make each of the following more emphatic by omitting unnecessary words:

1. Samuel Worthington is writing the autobiography of his life.
2. The president made a statement saying that better times are coming.
3. He expects to take up work along the lines of financial undertakings.
4. I write to say that up to this time the bedding has not been received.
5. Let me reiterate that once again so that you may clinch it fast in mind.
6. They have abundance and plenty and want for nothing at all.
7. Last Thursday I took advantage of the opportunity to visit the works.
8. According to the leader he says that the boys they ought to behave better.
9. Some of the pupils they expect too much along the lines of school service, such as passes, free lunches, free textbooks, etc.
10. He dropped his pad and his pencil and his eraser.
11. He is of about six years old.
12. Don't fall down; stand up; advance forward.
13. The three had ought to go now, each taking one book apiece.
14. They liked the machine and especially its motor.

UNITY

Make your sentences unified—

147. Keep apart ideas that are clearly unrelated and keep together ideas that are clearly related.

In *The Eskimos are an interesting people and we won the game last Saturday* there are two ideas having no logical connection. They should be expressed in two independent sentences —*The Eskimos are an interesting people. We won the game last Saturday.*

In *The gong rang and we went to dinner* there are two ideas that are so closely related that one idea may be made dependent upon the other by means of subordination, as *When the gong rang we went to dinner* or *On the ringing of the gong we went to dinner.*

But note that each of several related ideas may be sufficiently important to be expressed in an independent sentence; thus:

> We were playing down the field as strongly as we could, when suddenly Johnson, his old lameness recurring, had to yield the ball, and we knew that the game was up.

This contains too many details to be completely unified as a single sentence. It is more unified written as three sentences in close succession:

> We were playing down the field as strongly as we could. Suddenly Johnson's old lameness recurred and he had to yield the ball. We knew then that the game was up.

EXERCISE

Rewrite each of the following so that it is more unified:

1. The boy attends school regularly, and the news is dull today.
2. We were standing not very far away, and Mary had lost her scarf.
3. He had no idea that we were watching, and Russell had a very bad cold.
4. What made him do it we never knew, but just as the train was pulling into the station he leaped up in the air wildly and, to the amazement of everyone, jumped across the tracks.
5. Long, long ago, when he was very young, he had married and, as he thought, settled down, but before he had reached middle life, he met with this terrible accident which left him a cripple but he nevertheless remained the gay and cheerful person he had always been.

148. Condense expression as much as possible without impairing its exact meaning; that is, make one sentence do the work of two or more short ones, provided you do not change the intended meaning. This is best done by subordinating unimportant ideas to phrases or dependent clauses. These expressions are choppy and detached:

1. Every night he hangs his coat on a frame. The frame is fastened to the closet door.
2. The new aerial giant took eighty passengers on its maiden flight. It has eight motors. The flight was made over Washington.
3. There is a large electric sign in Chicago. It is visible for ten miles up Lake Michigan. It is equipped with an elevator.

Here they are condensed and unified:

1. Every night he hangs his coat on a frame fastened to the closet door.
2. The new eight-motor aerial giant took eighty passengers on its maiden flight over Washington.
3. In Chicago there is an electric sign so large that it is equipped with an elevator and can be seen for ten miles up Lake Michigan.

EXERCISE

Unify each of the following groups of sentences by expressing them in one good sentence:

1. Three boys narrowly escaped drowning. Their rowboat sank in the river. They were about two hundred yards from shore.
2. He attempted to turn in front of an approaching bus. The bus was going at fifty miles an hour. He barely escaped serious accident.
3. My chiffonier has six drawers. I keep my handkerchiefs in the top drawer. I keep my socks in the second drawer. I keep my shirts in the third drawer.
4. The thirteenth-century castle was noble and interesting. It was usually built in a difficult position. Its builder took advantage of every inch of ground. He did this to make it safe against attack.
5. I saw him enter the room. I was just leaving. He had a pistol in his hand. He also carried a large club.
6. I had no hose reel. I could not afford one. I devised one from an old bucket. I wound the hose around this to keep it from twisting and knotting.

7. The committee is studying ways to reduce high-school expenses. The principal made this announcement yesterday. He said he was happy to make the announcement. It is also studying ways to establish more scholarships.

149. Distinguish carefully between co-ordinate ideas and subordinate ideas, and place them in corresponding constructions. The following sentence is rambling and stringy; the four ideas expressed co-ordinately and loosely connected by *ands* are not of equal importance:

> I looked up at the sky and I saw an airplane and it was wobbling and it came down with a crash.

Subordinating details and omitting the *ands,* it reads:

> Looking up at the sky I saw a wobbling airplane which came down with a crash, *or* The airplane which I had seen wobbling in the sky came down with a crash.

The latter, with the idea of crashing in the principal clause, is probably the better reading. But if the idea of wobbling and the suspense it created are to be stressed, the first reading is correct. In the same way *Though the attack was merciless, she escaped* and *When she fainted a second time, we were genuinely frightened* are more unified and more emphatic (see page 181) than *The attack was merciless though she escaped* and *She fainted a second time when we were genuinely frightened.*

EXERCISE

Rewrite the following so that excessive use of *and* is avoided or so that subordinate ideas are placed in dependent constructions:

1. The pain began to be unbearable when we called the doctor.
2. You next dip them into the solution and this is very important.
3. While the lion was roaring and crouching we took steady aim.
4. Though she had a bad headache she kept on with her work.
5. As the flood rose and increasingly threatened the sky cleared.
6. His desire to go to the circus was great though the boy overcame it.
7. Though the accident had been most serious, she had remained calm.

8. The rabbit is pretty but useless and he is a pest to farmers and he is good in a stew.
9. I waited on the corner for an hour and he didn't appear and I was disgusted and I went home.
10. They went fishing yesterday and they caught several trout and they were excellent for dinner.

150. Avoid a series of similar constructions—phrases and clauses—one depending upon another in descending order. This construction is sometimes called the endless-chain or the tandem construction or the house-that-Jack-built sequence (see page 160). These lack unity because of endless-chain phrases:

1. You will find it in the bucket in the pantry of the cottage behind the barn.
2. I put it in the right-hand pocket of my old black coat hanging in the closet on the stairs.

These lack unity because of endless-chain clauses:

3. I know a boy who is never ready to do a job that is assigned to him until he asks a great many questions which are calculated to waste time that is valuable.
4. We liked Harris, but he was indifferent to us, and he seemed always to be thinking of his old place, for he had left it, we learned, unwillingly.

This kind of disunity may sometimes be corrected by condensation (page 217), sometimes by breaking an expression into two or more clauses, sometimes by forming compound-complex sentences and separating clauses by semicolons. Note these better readings of the foregoing:

1. You will find it in the bucket in the cottage pantry. The cottage is behind the barn.
2. I put it in the pocket of my old black coat which hangs in the stairs closet.
3. I know a boy who is never ready to do an assigned job without asking a great many questions, thus wasting valuable time.
4. We liked Harris, but he was indifferent to us; he seemed always to be thinking of his old place, which, we learned, he had left unwillingly.

EXERCISE

Rewrite the following endless-chain expressions so that they will be more unified:

1. He suddenly stopped, for he had forgotten something for which he must return.
2. I found this antique in the old shop on the corner of Canal and Rushton streets along the outer edge of the city.
3. Here is the man who wants the painting that we bought while we were visiting the museum that we liked so much.
4. These are the first of the vegetables from the garden in the old field down by the mill.
5. We were puzzled when he first came, but now we understand him, for he has become one of us, for he feels at home now.
6. I never before saw a car that can so easily take a road that is so steep and rough that most drivers avoid it when they go out.
7. This is the horse that won the race that was run on the day that we had our outing that celebrated our anniversary.
8. I admired him, for he had done fine things, for his output amply proved that he stood foremost in a profession that it is difficult to achieve a high standing in.

151. Avoid run-on sentences; that is, avoid running together two or more independent sentences with no punctuation or with only a comma in place of a period. The former is the opposite of the fragmentary expression (see page 190); the latter is sometimes called the comma splice. These are wrong:

1. You come to an intersection at the bottom of the hill you will see the traffic lights.
2. Harrison doesn't look at all well, he has been working day and night for the past three weeks.

These are correct:

1. You come to an intersection at the bottom of the hill. There you will see the traffic lights.
2. Harrison doesn't look well. He has been working day and night for the past three weeks.

Instead of the period a semicolon may sometimes be used to separate run-on expressions. Sometimes one part may be made subordinate. These are correct:

1. Harrison doesn't look well; he has been working day and night for the past three weeks.
2. As a result of his working day and night for the past three weeks, Harrison doesn't look well.

Two or more very short independent clauses may be separated by commas:

1. We called, we shouted, we yelled, we screamed.
2. I came, I saw, I conquered.

But semicolons are also correct in these expressions.

EXERCISE

Rewrite each of the following either as two or more independent sentences or as a single sentence with proper subordination:

1. The second box is different it has a red top and a blue bottom.
2. Billy came in tired and hungry, he had been playing all afternoon.
3. Times have changed now we no longer have to feed the horses.
4. I think we can get the nine o'clock train, if we miss that there is one at ten.
5. On the right you will see a red barn turn there and go straight ahead.
6. The wind blew the rain poured the windows rattled the sky darkened.
7. Don't take all that trouble for Bill he isn't worth it.
8. Nothing could have surprised me more, I sat down and gasped.
9. Alice looks gay and chipper this morning, she has just returned home.
10. That new overcoat of mine is very warm, it came from England, you can't beat good old English wool.

152. Avoid an unnecessary change of subject. These are not good:

1. Ferguson has done the job well, and fine results have been shown.
2. The boy has studied five hours every night but very little progress has been made.

The change of subject in the second member of the sentence requires an unnecessary switch of attention from the subject of the first member. Both sentences are more unified as follows:

1. Ferguson has done the job well and he shows fine results.
2. The boy has studied five hours every night, but he has made very little progress.

Frequently, of course, a change of subject is necessary, as in *The train was late and we were in a hurry,* and it would be a mistake to belabor structure in order to avoid a natural change. But one of the marks of loose and careless expression is unnecessary subject change (see page 200).

EXERCISE

Unify each of the following by rewriting it with the same subject in all the clauses:

1. You had a difficult problem but its solution has been good for you.
2. They laughed at the old codger until he finally was annoyed at them.
3. When you have an accident on the road, knowledge of first aid is valuable.
4. We turned on the lights and the robber was then clearly seen.
5. A task has been set before you and you must do it immediately.
6. John has been employed in Washington, but Denver is his beloved home town.
7. In the first place, your working tools should be assembled; then you go to work.
8. Whenever a difficulty confronts you and whenever you are discouraged as a result, this book may be depended upon to help you.

VARIETY

Make your sentences varied—

153. Avoid unnecessary, awkward, unemphatic repetition of words, such as:

1. Just as we began to be interested in the game, the wind began to blow, then the thunder and lightning began, and then it began to pour.
2. The Birchwood Road, the Turkey Hill Road, and the Red Oak Road are all macadamized roads. The Birchwood Road crosses the Turkey Hill Road at right angles, and the Red Oak Road merges with the Turkey Hill Road just before the intersection of the Birchwood Road and the Turkey Hill Road.
3. While the sheep dog is my favorite among breeds, I must say that sheep dog of yours is the most beautiful sheep dog of all the sheep dogs I have ever seen.

Such monotonous and bad-sounding repetition may be avoided by the use of synonyms or pronouns, or by reconstructing and condensing an expression, thus:

1. Just as we were getting interested in the game, the wind began to blow, thunder and lightning followed, and then it poured.
2. The Birchwood, Turkey Hill, and Red Oak roads are all macadamized. The first two intersect at right angles, and the third merges with the second just before the intersection.
3. The sheep dog is my favorite among breeds, and yours is the most beautiful of all I have ever seen.

EXERCISE

Rewrite the following, avoiding the repetitions:

1. When a worker does his work well, everybody, including other workers, admires him for his work.
2. Up bobbed Mary, her eyes lighting up and her lips puckered up as if she had been greatly cheered up by it all.
3. How to go to get to the museum or whom to go to to inquire how to go, we were at a loss to know.
4. One can never tell when one may be called upon to speak; therefore, one should keep oneself prepared.
5. The pleasant view from the portico pleased them immensely; they also found the hotel pleasing, and when they left they said they would be pleased to come again.
6. The audience definitely took sides with our side, for the applause did not subside until those on the other side began to show embarrassment.
7. Your lessons should be proceeded with with all possible speed, so that you may later proceed with the other procedures with which you are supposed to proceed.

154. Avoid excessive use of words, phrases, and clauses in series, especially hackneyed introductory and connecting words and phrases, as:

1. The great broad meadows were alive with glowing brilliant color as the sun shone brightly and expansively on this gorgeously beautiful spring day.
2. Lying lazily on the couch reading, Billy, having been playing golf all day, suddenly fell asleep, forgetting all the games he lost and dreaming of those he had hoped to win.

3. In the main I think he is very good. As a rule, however, he is better when he plays just for us. But by and large he is undoubtedly a great artist.

Such monotonous phrasing may usually be corrected by the omission of unnecessary words, or by the substitution of one part of speech for another or of one kind of phrase for another, or by the variation of placement, thus:

1. The broad meadows were alive with color as the sun shone brightly on this beautiful spring day.
2. Billy, who had played golf all day, was on the couch reading. Suddenly he fell asleep—forgot all the games he lost and dreamed of those he had hoped to win.
3. He is undoubtedly a great artist, but he is at his best when he plays just for us rather than for the public.

EXERCISE

Rewrite the following, making them more varied and less mechanical in construction:

1. My dear delightful old granddaddy gave me a great big beautiful new car for my birthday.
2. In trying to turn the handle by using his left hand, Harry, not being accustomed to cranking a motor, was seriously hurt.
3. On the whole, I think this is the better arrangement. Moreover, it appeals to our customers. On the other hand, I can see its possible defects. Nevertheless, let's give it a trial.
4. We stole down into the deep, dark, underground dungeon quietly and fearfully and suspiciously, and there he was, crouching and moaning and trembling in a damp, vermin-ridden unhealthful corner.
5. In spring, in summer, in autumn, in winter, the four boys—Bill, Tom, Harry, Carver—indulge their four favorite sports—tennis, basketball, hockey, skating—which they play zestfully, skillfully, congenially, and wholeheartedly.

155. Avoid similarity of construction in successive expressions. This may be done: (*a*) by starting expressions with different words and constructions; (*b*) by intermixing different kinds of sentences—loose, periodic, balanced; simple, compound, complex, compound-complex; declarative, interrogative, imperative, exclamatory; long, short, medium; (c) by changing the placement of phrases and clauses among sentences; (d) by using direct discourse when indirect tends to become monotonous, and vice versa. These constructions are monotonous:

1. He has received a great shock. He had found it almost too much for him. He bore up as well as he could. He had many friends to comfort him. He finally succumbed.
2. While I was waiting, Jameson came in. When he saw me, he approached with extended hand. As he did so, the door opened and Sara stood between us. When he saw her, he turned on his heel and left.
3. I asked him whether he thought there would be a raid. He answered, somewhat gruffly I thought, that he had no way of knowing but that he certainly hoped not.

In the first example the sentences are short and choppy; all are short simple sentences, and all begin with the same word. In the second, there are four complex sentences, each beginning with a dependent clause and ending with an independent clause. In the third, the indirect discourse tends to become mixed and heavy. These readings are better:

1. The great shock had been almost too much for him. He bore up as well as he could but, in spite of comforting friends, he finally succumbed.
2. While I was waiting, Jameson came in. He approached me with extended hand. But just then the door opened and Sara stood between us. Turning on his heel, he left abruptly.
3. I asked him whether he thought there would be a raid. "How should I know!" he answered somewhat gruffly; "I certainly hope not."

EXERCISE

Rewrite the following, making them more varied in construction:

1. We rarely go to that place. We have been invited frequently. We don't care for it very much. We must decline your invitation therefore.
2. The house was old and it was located on a hill. We had lived in it for years and we hated to give it up. It was an easy prey for wind and storm, and we were not surprised at its being destroyed by the hurricane.

3. They inquired what route to take to Springfield. I asked them which Springfield they meant. They said Springfield, Illinois. I replied that Route 4 was their most direct route but that Route 6 was more picturesque and that most tourists preferred the latter therefore.

4. The truck crashed violently into our car. We were naturally shocked by the impact. No one was seriously hurt by the accident. We had had a miraculous escape from death.

5. Inasmuch as we were expected early, we took the nine o'clock train. As the day was cold and rainy, we probably took more luggage, including umbrellas, than necessary. When we arrived at the house, we found that two pieces had been left in the car. While Harry dashed frantically to the station to recover them, Dick did a great deal of telephoning. When the lost luggage finally turned up, we were greatly relieved.

REVIEW EXERCISES[1]

1. The conjunction in each of the following sentences connects parts that are not co-ordinate. Re-express each statement in a good simple sentence.

1. I sat up all night and doing my homework.
2. He gave me his decision and in positive terms.
3. She jumped from the tenth floor and thus causing a sensation.
4. We went to the movies and leaving the dishes unwashed.
5. They have rented the new house and moving in tomorrow.
6. He entered gaily and with his cheeks flushed.
7. They carried the hose straight into the fire and thus showing their courage.
8. This pond has been leased by us and with all rights and privileges.
9. They will have their answer here tonight, and through the services of a telegraph company.
10. He declined my invitation and giving no hint of regrets.

2. The comma in each of the following sentences separates thoughts that should be expressed in a unified simple sentence. Re-express each so that it has one subject and one predicate.

1. The bolt turns down, this unlocks the door.
2. That man is hurt, he has had an accident.
3. You are too easygoing, you lose everything.
4. The house is high and wide, it is made of bricks.
5. The top of the frame is then put on, it is pasted to the corners.

[1] These exercises are intended to cover the sections on grammar (pages 72–147) as well as those preceding.

6. The tractor has made plowing easy, the farmer thinks so.
7. I have only ten dollars, I offer you that.
8. He firmly denied it, he hammered the table with his fist.
9. I was unable to continue, I rested for a time.
10. They refused to help her, they did not explain their attitude.

3. Rewrite the following sentences, placing phrases where they logically belong but keeping each sentence simple:

1. She stood beside the piano wearing blue shorts.
2. Those colors are pleasing to the eye on the bureau.
3. We drove slowly along the road with the top down.
4. I took the bus from the station with a gay heart.
5. Darting into the street, a wrecked car was seen by us going up in smoke.
6. On entering the theater the fire alarm rang.
7. Being very noisy outside I closed the door.
8. Never take these pills without dissolving in water.
9. To lubricate thoroughly the car must be brought in.
10. Arriving just in time, the opening number pleased us.

4. The following sentences are too highly co-ordinated. Reconstruct them, omitting unnecessary conjunctions and making a good simple sentence of each one.

1. I have a new car and it is a Buick.
2. I grew very tired and I went to bed early.
3. Jameson is our chauffeur and he is very skillful.
4. He carried my parcels and he carried my bag also.
5. I was walking in the forest and I looked up into a tree and I saw a spring thrush.
6. He has been very successful in his studies and he is ambitious and he will get on.
7. Harrison is our guide and he knows the trails bv heart and he will take good care of us.
8. The paint is put on in coats or layers and it hardens quickly and it preserves the wood.

5. Rewrite the following awkward sentences more simply and coherently:

1. One, in the effort to win fame and fortune, must not be too aggressive.
2. She was unwilling to ever again so much as try.
3. For one thing at least in case of fire everybody must remain calm.
4. Bill, hearing the news for the first time at dinner, could eat no more.
5. The committee, in view of the serious situation confronting it, was called for special meeting.

6. No one could in that strained atmosphere so much regretted by all possibly be himself.
7. Nothing under the dreadful circumstances before us all could or should have proceeded without serious thought.
8. What in the long run and under such conditions do you consider most expedient?
9. The decision, in view of all the difficulties attending the discussion, is a very satisfactory one.
10. Very satisfactory indeed, in view of all the difficulties attending the discussion, is the decision arrived at.

6. Some of the statements below should be expressed as two or more independent simple sentences; some should be condensed to one simple sentence. Make such revisions as are required, giving reasons for the changes you make.

1. We are going to attend your party Bill has a bad toothache.
2. All along the route I felt in seventh heaven it was very beautiful.
3. Drive slowly take no chances there's plenty of room in the cemeteries.
4. The best route is by the river it is an excellent road it is beautiful.
5. It was a perfect day for an outing everybody enjoyed the happy event.
6. Most people are right-handed there is much to be said for right-hand driving.
7. They caught many fish they used worms for bait they cooked their catch over a fire in the meadow.
8. Never try swimming there it is a deep and dangerous hole the current is very treacherous.
9. A professional packer is recommended Mary goes to school regularly the sun shines bright today.
10. Turn it up on end this releases the snap and this stirs the contents this makes unpacking safe.

7. All of the following simple expressions are defective. Tell why they are defective. Make each one a good simple sentence.

1. Vacationing in the mountains, many sports were indulged in.
2. The habits of woodchucks are different from ground moles.
3. The examination was over. I started to go, I was too ill to move.
4. They have excellent merchandise at Livingstone's.
5. She is very fond of cooking and to mix new drinks.
6. Yours received and in reply would say.
7. He ought to in the interests of everybody present have spoken louder.
8. You lift the ladder ever so little this shifts a weight the door opens.
9. She was taken suddenly very ill and was quite unwell really.

10. They have for several years continuously now resided in our midst.
11. He has with all the energy and initiative at his command controlled the meeting.
12. She stood by the huge chiffonier with a look of utter indifference.
13. On buying a ticket for the affair, the guard told us to stay in line.
14. In that moving picture it showed the horrors of modern warfare.
15. Unaccustomed to eating such rich food, sickness came upon me in the night.

8. Rewrite the following, correcting the faulty use of *because, when, where:*

1. His excuse for trickery is because he is ignorant of the law.
2. A figure of speech is when pictorial comparisons are made.
3. Because you have a great deal of money does not bring you happiness.
4. The radio is where messages and the like come over the air.
5. Good English is when one speaks and writes correctly.
6. The reason I came is because I want to see her.
7. The tolling of the bells is when the service begins.
8. Because he is ill is the best possible reason for his absence.
9. A court trial is where judge and jury decide a wrongdoer's fate.
10. The reason why I wanted that one is because it is like one my mother had.

9. Correct the faulty subordination in the sentences below:

1. Although he was a very sick man, his family appeared indifferent.
2. I was telephoning about the party when the earthquake occurred.
3. We were having a good game when suddenly he threw his racket into the net and ran off the court.
4. Over there by the low hill is the place where the poet was born.
5. As the dam broke and did the damage I was sauntering down the road.
6. I thought he was the man, for he waved the signal vigorously at us.
7. He is a good-looking person, though I wouldn't trust him around the corner.
8. While the mob roared and threatened I was doing my hair.
9. While the storm broke furiously I was paddling my canoe.
10. Inasmuch as the proprietor has died, I shall seek another job.

10. The expressions below contain phrases and clauses that modify in series, that is, one follows the other in modification like the house-that-Jack-built sentence on page 219. Make them better.

1. A person who wants a friend who will be a friend indeed when need arises has a long search to make to find one to suit him.

2. That was the second of the conferences in the office of the new building to which we hope to move when Mr. Olsen returns from Europe, where he has been since early spring.
3. When I leave for California, where I hope to remain with Horace, who is my very best friend, I shall take along all the books of Malvinson, of whose writings I am very fond.
4. Antonio was a friend of Bassanio, who was a friend of Nerissa, who fell in love with Gratiano, who with the other two young men openly annoyed Shylock, who, after all, had right on his side of the argument which arose among them.
5. This will be the last of the games of the college in this city in which it has been located through years of prosperity and through years of depression in business as well as in professional life.

11. Clauses are misplaced in the following sentences. Read the sentences with the clauses where they should be.

1. I passed the cake around to our little party which my sister had made.
2. The woman is both an actress and a writer whom I spoke to just now.
3. There is a sweater in the last box on the shelf that has a brown number on it.
4. He has an opportunity to go to California which was offered by his uncle.
5. He took us to the old chapel in the curious and irregular churchyard where she is to be married tomorrow.
6. The police found jewels in the prisoner's pockets which looked like Mrs. Happerdean's.
7. He very soon confessed that he had struck his wife when he was cross-questioned by the lawyer.
8. We had to drive carefully among the children playing in the streets because we could not turn off.
9. We found it to be a small house having but three rooms when we arrived to inspect it.
10. Please find a good story in some newspaper or magazine which you can recommend for dramatizing.

12. By means of an adjective clause (clauses) make a single complex sentence of each group below:

1. We liked the old house. It had many a quaint old nook and corner.
2. The hall was crowded to the walls. The statesman spoke eloquently.
3. Here is the world-famous shrine. Millions visit it every year.
4. The circus came to town yesterday. It is the delight of every boy.
5. This is one of our greatest parks. It is filled with people every Sunday.

6. That harbor is one of the safest in the world. Ships of all nations are anchored here.

7. People of different races and nationalities live here. They get along peaceably and work together co-operatively.

8. That man will go far in this world. He is now head of the largest business house in Central City. You saw him with me yesterday.

9. The Halls promised to come over tonight after dinner. You will like them. They have been our neighbors for many years.

10. It was ten o'clock. At this hour John was supposed to appear. His appearance was prevented by a sudden and unaccountable illness.

13. By means of an adverbial clause (clauses) make a single complex sentence of each group below:

1. I shall meet you at eleven. Only serious accident will prevent my doing so.

2. The old village is extremely picturesque. Many houses are quite old and dilapidated.

3. They entered my office unannounced and demanded money. I was dictating letters at the time.

4. She dressed. She wore the new chiffon. She dressed at the proper time. She dressed in my sister's room.

5. I sat on the bench for an hour reading the paper. I was awaiting my turn for an interview with the president.

6. She is probably feeling under the weather. She has eaten nothing at all for two days. She may be reducing.

7. I cannot undertake that job now. I am far too busy. I have engagements in many different parts of the country.

8. John has been appointed delegate to the convention to be held in Cleveland. He had not expected the honor to be conferred upon him.

9. The Rotarians are going to hold their outdoor meeting on July 2. Many members objected to the date. Some did not favor the place.

10. The population of that country is rapidly increasing. Its many small islands cannot accommodate its people. It deserves the right to colonize in uncivilized parts.

14. By means of a noun clause (clauses) make a single complex sentence of each group below:

1. Are you going to the show? Tell me.

2. Bill is studying at Oxford. I heard this at the party.

3. He was very nervous and touchy. We observed this yesterday.

4. Bill was very ill today. This is the reason for his absence.

5. They are leaving for a year. I learned this from the newspaper this morning.

231

6. They have at last run down Public Enemy No. 1. This is reported in all of the afternoon papers.
7. Mr. Harrison indignantly denies the reports of his marriage. I read in the *Daily Record* of his indignation.
8. He accomplished the somersault by nosing the plane away from the increasing winds. The official report announced this fact.
9. The new geography announces many interesting facts to the youngsters. It tells of the roundness of the earth. It tells of the rotation and revolution made by the earth.
10. How did you manage to drive the truck so easily? How could you find the building in all this fog? How could you avoid hitting someone in the huge crowd? We should like to know.

15. Reduce each of the following complex sentences to a simple one:

1. We do not know what his name is.
2. They say that it cannot be done.
3. He did easily the work that was assigned.
4. The men who are graduates have made good records.
5. They live in that house that is covered with ivy.
6. The police have found a picture of the girl who is missing.
7. A question that was obviously unfair was asked in the examination.
8. Books the contents of which are informing should be respected.
9. Eyes that sparkle and teeth that shine are invariably attractive.
10. Among the important works of Sinclair Lewis, one of his earliest, which is *Main Street*, still has a circulation that is very large.

16. Substitute a phrase (or phrases) for each dependent clause below:

1. She welcomed him when he arrived.
2. If you can assist, I shall be obliged.
3. He earns little though he works hard.
4. He stayed away three months because he was ill.
5. He went by plane, as he was instructed to do.
6. We shall return when the sun is directly overhead.
7. Although he has driven for forty years, he has never had an accident.
8. He covered the subject thoroughly in the speech which he made before the school.
9. Because we had all seen the play, we did not go to the picture.
10. Practically every mechanical device that is invented helps mankind.
11. He has a fine new craft which he calls *Blue Point* and which is painted a red color.
12. While they were visiting in Japan they picked up some beautiful artificial pearls.
13. As he was sure his daughter would be graduated with honors, he appeared at commencement in his full-dress uniform.

14. Inasmuch as she had failed in all subjects, he did not have the pleasure of seeing her receive a diploma.
15. A factory that has enormous proportions has turned out fewer cars than it ever did before.

17. Make each of the following a good simple or complex sentence by supplying whatever is lacking now:

1. They said his hunger was equal to a wolf.
2. I like Blaney as well as John.
3. Sunlight penetrates the fabric almost as well as glass.
4. When still a boy, Chicago became my home.
5. While out of the office, my telephone rang.
6. Here is a man who is trained in every phase of the radio.
7. Do you recall in the picture at which we had such a pleasant evening?
8. It was the custom when company came with whom we were not intimately acquainted.
9. There was a young woman who, ambitious and good-looking and excellently trained in business.
10. As far as my being dissatisfied, all I can say is to whoever may be interested.

18. The following sentences contain "squinters," that is, dependent parts so placed that they may modify more than one word. Rewrite each, making the squinting construction perfectly clear.

1. He who complains much of the time has really nothing to complain of.
2. Playing charades in many ways quickens the intelligence.
3. When she received that good mark much to her own surprise she wept.
4. We assured him when next he saw it he would take it for a new car.
5. The boys promised if we made awards they would participate in the events.
6. Certain persons I know will be shocked to hear this bit of news.
7. When the dam broke for the first time in its history the river became dangerous.
8. When I had that tooth drawn much to my disappointment the root broke off.
9. When the train stopped for a moment I thought it was threatened with danger just ahead.
10. They promised when the hour struck they would have the bridge wide open.

19. Rewrite each of the following so that better use is made of emphatic positions in the sentence:

1. It is wonderful to view Niagara when it is covered with ice in the winter.
2. He has taken pains to say that he will never again be a party to such a movement.
3. The dear old lady screamed: "Assistance, please! Murder is being committed! Do come, somebody!" at the top of her voice.
4. If you will please pardon this intrusion upon your privacy, I should like to say that fire has broken out in your beautiful home on the green.
5. In the first place, however, I must be permitted to say that our favorite candidate has been defeated in spite of all our efforts in his behalf.
6. There happened in our village yesterday the most terrible, the most horrible, the most appalling atrocity ever recorded in the place since it was settled by the Puritan fathers.
7. Notwithstanding your objections, I must say that the legislation is imperative if we are ever again to have reasonable observance of law and order in this community.
8. After driving for hours on bad roads we were completely off the track and going in exactly the opposite direction to which we had intended to go when we started.
9. It was some time before the doctors were able to report on the outcome of the operation, and she sat there in a stupor, muttering to herself and wringing her hands, as you have often doubtless seen anxious and dejected people do.
10. Whoever it was who said: "Love will find a way," should have added "in the moonlight," or at least so I think after observing some of my friends and acquaintances.

20. The following sentences are awkward and lacking in euphony as result of unnecessary repetition. Rewrite them, retaining only so much of the repetition as may be necessary to preserve emphasis.

1. The one who attempts to make one's own way in this world will find first one thing and then another to thwart one and thus cause one almost infinite delay and vexation in reaching one's one and only goal in life.
2. When we got to the top of the hill, we got a beautiful view of the valley and got our eyes filled with unspeakable beauty such as is to be got only on those rare occasions when one has got a chance to "get away from it all" and visit the great beauty spots that Nature has got in store for us.

3. He outwitted us on every point on our way out, and while we were out there sitting out on the lawn he outlined his plans for outdoing the competitors we had come out to meet and to outplay if we possibly could.

4. Place it there, please, at the place where the statue was formerly placed, and if that placement is not satisfactory after a few days we shall ring up your place and ask you to come out to our place to re-place it for us.

5. To whom to give the prize to to celebrate the anniversary, they are puzzled to decide, inasmuch as there are two to whom it might very well be awarded, not to mention a third one too who comes almost as close to meeting requirements as the other two.

6. We aim to please, and by that aim we aim also to keep our firm strictly to the aims of those who founded it a hundred years ago—aims the observance of which have given us the standing that we enjoy today and than which there can be no higher aims.

21. The following sentences are awkward and unwieldy for the reason that ideas are not properly balanced. Rewrite them in good balanced form.

1. In dear old New England the scenery, especially in the spring and fall, is exciting, and in the winter too if you happen to like snow and ice.

2. In college he was serious and studious and always plodding away to attain high standing, but gaiety to the point of fickleness marks his conduct when he is on vacation.

3. She spent the summer on a dude ranch and reported that she had a glorious time, much better, indeed, than she had last summer when she went to Mexico with her parents.

4. I like that car better than mine because it has automatic gears which mine hasn't and also because of its easily adjustable top (you just push a button!) and mine doesn't have this either.

5. Try as he would, he seemed always to be a marked man, for hard luck was his lot and almost the end of him until one day a huge fortune by way of a land inheritance fell to him, to his utter bewilderment.

6. It doesn't so much matter what people say about you, for people will talk, you know, but what you think and are able truthfully to say about yourself is indicative of an invaluable gift of self-evaluation which nobody can possibly take away from you.

7. It has been said, and I think very truthfully, that whatever you sow shall be reaped by you, and whether the harvest be good or bad depends altogether upon what you sow and how conscientiously you sow.

22. Rewrite each of the following sentences in periodic form:

1. Someone struck him over the head as he entered the room.
2. We overcame our enemies magnificently after we had decided upon our strategy.
3. I'd die rather than live under a tyrant whose only thought and effort were to enslave me.
4. He became a hero as result of a stunt which might have been performed by a thousand other persons.
5. He won all the honors they had to give because he worked day and night, never missed a session, and invariably made way for others.
6. Say what you mean if you want to establish for yourself a reputation for directness and frankness and courage.
7. He stood condemned, for he had broken the law more than once, had defied authority, and had shown nothing but disrespect for the established rights of others.
8. "I shall drown; no one will save me!" cried the terror-stricken woman who had jumped into the canal with the intention of committing suicide.
9. He became a martyr to the cause after long years of struggle to overcome obstacles and after every possible personal sacrifice in the fight against ignorance.
10. He stood alone and unchallenged that dreadful night, everybody within sound of his voice being deservedly intimidated by the cold facts of misery and injustice as he had so eloquently poured them forth.

23. Substitute as many specific terms as you can for each italicized term below, in order to make the picture more detailed and elaborate:

1. They were startled at the *unusual things* they saw.
2. The tramp had a very *alarming attitude* as he spoke.
3. The furnishings of the old castle had a *grotesque appearance.*
4. *Everything in the world sold here*, was the slogan of the little shop.
5. He devotes Saturday afternoons to doing his *thousand and one little chores.*
6. He had a *strange assortment of knickknacks* on his overfilled desk.
7. The old place of which we were once so fond was now *seriously run down.*
8. Never had I seen a more *dilapidated old barn* than this one by the creek.
9. The old arbor supported an *entanglement of vines* that had become twisted and knotted.
10. At its height the party gave the impression of *unutterable confusion* because of the *babel of chatter.*

24. The following sentences are confused in ideas or pictures or comparisons. Rewrite them so that the figures are consistent:

1. He ran the race like a bird in its flight.
2. She made her entrance with the grace of a deer and the dignity of a mountain.
3. He stood on the threshold of his career prepared to face the tides of life with the courage of a lion.
4. Her smile seemed to light up her whole being like an incandescent lamp, and it spread a furrow of good cheer to all who basked beneath its beneficent warmth.
5. Let my words, young gentlemen, be as a lamp to your hearts, a sword to your feet, and an everlasting fountain of guidance as you fare forth from this institution today to blaze the voyage of life.
6. He has emerged from the storm-tossed seas of failure and despair upon a prairie of unparalleled vistas of opportunity, and the new outlooks have made his heart beat in unison with the rhythm of the spheres.
7. Bridle your passions, young man, curb your ambitions within reasonable latitudes and longitudes, and launch into the path of life with the humility of a Napoleon and the fortitude of a Gibraltar.
8. We are again financially on the rocks, but it is a comfort to remember that the sea is never so rough that it cannot be mastered by keeping our hands firmly on the wheel and our eyes continuously on the road.

25. The following excerpt is taken from Charles Dickens' *A Tale of Two Cities*. As it stands it is neither in strictly direct discourse nor in strictly indirect discourse, but, rather, in implied reportorial form. Write it first in direct discourse, then in indirect discourse. (See page 265.)

Had he ever been a spy himself? No, he scorned the base insinuation. What did he live upon? His property. Where was his property? He didn't precisely remember where it was. What was it? No business of anybody's. Had he inherited it? Yes, he had. From whom? Distant relation. Very distant? Rather. Ever been in prison? Certainly not. Never in a debtor's prison? Didn't see what that had to do with it. Never in a debtor's prison?—Come, once again. Never? Yes. How many times? Two or three times. Not five or six? Perhaps. Of what profession? Gentleman. Ever been kicked? Might have been. Frequently? No. Ever kicked down stairs? Decidedly not; once received a kick on the top of a staircase, and fell down stairs of his own accord. Kicked on that occasion for cheating at dice? Something to that effect was said by the intoxicated liar who committed the assault, but it was not true. Swear it was not true? Positively. Ever live by cheating at play? Never.

Ever live by play? Not more than other gentlemen do. Ever borrow money of the prisoner? Yes. Ever pay him? No. Was not this intimacy with the prisoner, in reality a very slight one, forced upon the prisoner in coaches, inns, and packets? No. Sure he saw the prisoner with these lists? Certain. Knew no more about the lists? No. Had not procured them himself, for instance? No. Expect to get anything by this evidence? No. Not in regular government pay and employment, to lay traps? Oh, dear, no. Or to do anything? Oh, dear, no. Swear that? Over and over again. No motives but motives of sheer patriotism? None whatever.

26. The following sentences are incoherent because of defective pronominal reference. Make them better.

1. He said to his chief that he thought he ought to go to the funeral.
2. Once you have made your debut, it is no certainty you will be a social success.
3. There is a saying to the effect that everybody gets what they deserve in this life.
4. We heard a strange noise on the right side of the house which seemed to say something to us.
5. This is Howard Anson's book who has just returned from college.
6. We think the new wing is very beautiful and which is large enough to accommodate all the specimens.
7. The bells have been ringing all morning, which has made it impossible for anyone to concentrate on their work.
8. I have always been very fond of the company of actors, which profession I shall try to become a member of.
9. They say in this newspaper that our neighborhood should not spend the money they do on schools.
10. When he said to him that he thought he was talking wildly, you should have seen the anger flare in his eyes.
11. In this book it says that the old maple on the Kellogg road near the village that has afforded me shade on many a hot day, it was the tree under which Washington once rested.
12. The children have been out all morning in their pony cart which is their favorite animal.

27. The following sentences are incoherent because of dangling and squinting constructions. Make them better.

1. When choosing a dress for graduation, it should be something you can wear later.
2. All of us suddenly began to feel quite ill, caused doubtless by something we had eaten.

3. Entering the room from the east entrance a large oil painting of Washington is seen on the right.

4. He means conscientiously to help her with her music, and she tries faithfully to practice, but both are inclined continuously to dawdle.

5. If clear and cool, the trout will be seen veering suddenly to the surface, and then striking down again with unbelievable speed to evade the tricks of the angler.

6. While going down with that man this morning he told me the most amazing tale about that scandalous theater affair, apparently being involved in it.

7. In discussing merit as evinced on the job, much may be said for the youngster who is not necessarily brilliant but who keeps hammering away with all his might working for the best interests of the firm.

8. After the cream and the sugar are thoroughly mixed, a little flour is put into the mixture, being careful not to make it too thick.

9. After blowing my horn and waiting a long time, a man suddenly appeared at the front door asking me whether I wanted to see someone or was just toying with the gadgets on the car.

10. While taking a bath yesterday, the soap suddenly flew out of my hands, and I jumped to get it with all my might falling against the chair.

PUNCTUATION AND MISCELLANEOUS TECHNIQUES

THE PERIOD

156. The **period** is used—

1. At the end of a declarative sentence, as *He will be here at twelve.*

2. At the end of an imperative sentence, as *Come at twelve.* But if either a declarative or an imperative sentence is exclaimed or spoken with a rising inflection, it may be followed by the exclamation point or the question mark respectively, thus:

> You must never, never do that again!
> Please try to come at twelve?

3. At the end of a whole number to set off a decimal, as $4211.71. It is increasingly the custom in business letters to place a period after a whole number indicating dollars, as *We have this day credited $151. to your account.* This prevents the addition of dollars without an erasure.

4. At the end of a unit abbreviation or after each member of an abbreviation consisting of two or more parts, as *acct., Mr., C.P.A., Ph.D.*

Modern usage tends to omit the period after an abbreviation, as *Mr Baxter, Dr Wilson, Col Tompkins.* Be consistent: either use the period for all abbreviations or omit it for all abbreviations.

Do not mistake such words as *en, et, per, pro, via* for abbreviations. They are independent words adopted from other languages, not abbreviations.

In general, abbreviations are to be avoided; but if it is necessary, in order to save space, to shorten words like *account, association, Brooklyn, manufacturing,* either the period or the apostrophe is correct. Do not use both.

Right: acc't, acct.; ass'n, assn.; m'f'g, mfg.
Wrong: acc't., ass'n., m'f'g.

Terms in which the apostrophe is used to indicate shortening are, strictly speaking, contractions rather than abbreviations.

5. After numbers and letters used for notation in outlines (see page 296). But the open form is being increasingly used. Omit the period after Roman numerals, as *Book IV is the longest*. No period is used after a letter which is used in place of a name or after a letter which is used as a symbol, as:

> Madam X retained her mystery.
> Let *A* represent the amount lost.

Do not use a period after a phrase or a clause, thus making it stand alone. Phrases and clauses are fragments only and cannot be separated from their sentence relationships by means of periods (see page 190).

Wrong: Having had a good game. We enjoyed our dinner.
Wrong: When I saw Thompson enter. I was astonished.
Right: Having had a good game, we enjoyed our dinner.
Right: When I saw Thompson enter, I was astonished.

But words and phrases having obvious relationship and standing for complete expressions may be followed by a period or other final mark, as:

> Are you going? No.
> I am going. Really?
> Are you going to Europe? Never again.

Do not use a period after the salutation or the complimentary close of a letter. *Dear Sir.* and *Yours sincerely.* are wrong.

EXERCISES

1. Supply periods as required in the following:

   1. I am going to the store
   2. Place the book where you found it
   3. My dear child, be careful
   4. He has $182 in his pocket
   5. Here comes Horace Green, Esq, of N Y
   6. This is Mr Forest L Priestly
   7. Introduce me to Dr Havemeyer
   8. Danger Don't turn right

2. Use the period correctly in the following:

1. We went via. the Pennsylvania route.
2. Traveling southward. We ran into warm weather.
3. Dear Mr. Brown. Enclosed acc't. is what you asked for.
4. As it began to rain. They decided to start early.
5. Very truly yours. Mabel Martinson.
6. Let line *B* cross line *C* at this point.
7. Mrs. So-and-So. lives in S't. Louis.
8. Suppose Mr. B. has $30 to invest.
9. He discussed the question pro. and con. very skillfully.
10. I read Book II. of that long novel while I was en. route.

THE INTERROGATION POINT

157. The **interrogation point,** or **question mark,** is used—

1. After a direct question, as:

Will you come to my party?
She asked, "Will you come to my party?"

But do not capitalize the first word of an indirect question or use the question mark after it. *She asked Whether I would come to her party?* is wrong. Indirect questions are usually followed by a period, as *She asked whether I would come to her party.* (See page 265.)

When a direct question ends within a sentence, no other mark but the question mark is required after it. In *"Will you come to my party?," she asked,* the comma after the question mark is unnecessary.

A polite request put in interrogative form may be followed by a period, as *Will you please close the window.*

Similarly (see page 240), a declarative sentence or an imperative sentence may by voice inflection require a question mark after it, as:

I should like to see your new watch? (May I see your new watch?)
Show me your new watch? (rising inflection)

2. After a word or expression (place name or date) to indicate uncertainty, usually in parentheses, as *Shakespeare was born on April 23(?), 1564.*

3. After each unit in a series of questions embodied in the same expression, as *Where are the smokestacks? the skyscrapers? the steeples? the watchtowers? the obelisks? the statues?* Note that each item begins with a small letter. This is somewhat better form than *Where are the smokestacks, the skyscrapers, the steeples, the watchtowers, the obelisks, the statues?* But both are correct.

Do not use the question mark to indicate irony or an uncomplimentary expression. *The genius(?) then rose and addressed us* and *The well-dressed(?) dowager swept into the room,* and similar usages are in bad taste.

THE EXCLAMATION POINT

158. The **exclamation point** is used—

1. After words, phrases, and longer expressions to denote strong emotion, as:

> Behold!
> How dare you!
> Not on your life!

2. After a word or other expression to show astonishment, surprise, or irony, as:

> He left her twenty million(!) and the castle.

If you use the exclamation point too frequently, you will weaken rather than emphasize your expression.

Do not use the exclamation after all interjections. If an interjection is exclaimed, it should be followed by the exclamation point, as *Hark! I think I hear them.* But if what follows an interjection is emotional or exclamatory, the interjection is followed by a comma and the exclamation point is placed at the end of the expression, as *Alas, he is dead!* (See page 146.)

159

PUNCTUATION

EXERCISE

Supply the interrogation and exclamation points in the following:

1. Will you please take me to the train
2. John asked, "Will you please take me to the train"
3. What have you done with the scissors with the workbasket with the thimble
4. What in the world are you doing there
5. Nonsense that paper was prepared by me
6. And do you now put on your best attire
7. Don't ever do a thing like that again
8. He asked where have you been what have you been doing when did you come
9. They inquired "What course shall we follow from here"
10. Will you please let me have that rewritten theme before noon

THE COMMA

159. The **comma** is used—

1. To set off co-ordinate words, phrases, and clauses in a series. If the last two members in a series are connected by a conjunction, the comma should be used before the conjunction. Observe the following:

> Never, never, never say die.
> Harry, Bill, and I are going.
> In April, in May, and in June it was very rainy.
> If you do not care to come, if you prefer another date, if you think the effort futile, please speak frankly.
> The thunder roared, the lightning flashed, the rain poured, but he slept soundly through all.

Since the comma takes the place of a conjunction, no comma is necessary when the conjunction is expressed, as *Harry and Bill and I are going.*

Terms of a series grouped by means of conjunctions are separated by commas, as:

> They walked up and down, back and forth, in and out.
> Men and women, boys and girls are all astir.

244

Sometimes in such a grouping the conjunction is used to connect the different groups as well as the members of a group. The comma is thus required to clarify to both ear and eye, as follows:

> They walked up and down, and back and forth, and in and out.

Sometimes, again, groups are listed among single terms, as:

> We sell lumber, coal and firewood, seeds, cement, fertilizer, and farm machinery.

In such expressions as *beautiful new car, clever young surveyor, unhappy old man* no comma is required, for the noun and the adjective immediately preceding it are so closely related as to constitute a single expression; that is, *new* modifies *car,* and *beautiful* modifies *new car; young* modifies *surveyor,* and *clever* modifies *young surveyor; old* modifies *man,* and *unhappy* modifies *old man.* It is not idiomatic to say *beautiful and new car, clever and young surveyor, unhappy and old man,* though these expressions may be quite correct under certain circumstances.

2. To set off nonrestrictive phrases and clauses. Nonrestrictive here means not essential. A phrase or a clause not strictly essential to the sentence is called nonrestrictive; it may complement a principal clause, but its omission would not change the meaning of the principal clause. In other words, it may be regarded as parenthetical.

In *That old house facing the shore road is for sale,* the phrase *facing the shore road* is restrictive because it tells which house is meant, and without the phrase the meaning would not be clear. This phrase must therefore not be set off by commas. But in *Jack Smith, swimming with all his might, rescued the children,* the phrase *swimming with all his might* is nonrestrictive because without it the sentence is complete. The phrase merely gives additional information and is therefore set off by commas.

In *My old car, which has served me well, is still good for five thousand miles,* the clause *which has served me well* is not essential to the sentence; because it is nonrestrictive it is set off by commas. Now note *A car that is still good for five thousand miles has substantial value.* Here the clause *that is still good for five thousand miles* is essential to the meaning; it is restrictive and is not set off by commas.

If, in such expression as *That brook running closely along the highway is very crooked,* there is likelihood that *highway* may be taken as subject of *is crooked,* a comma may be used after *highway* or the entire restrictive phrase may be set off by commas.

3. To set off parenthetical words, phrases, and clauses when they cause hesitation or stoppage in reading or other vocal inflection, as:

> He will go, *therefore,* when his job is done.
> This road is, *as a rule,* closed to the public.
> The candidate is, *I believe,* ready for examination.
> *In the main,* this is a policy that is usually workable.

The most commonly used expressions thus set off are:

after all	however	in the main	on the other hand
also	I believe	indeed	perhaps
as a rule	I'm sure	it is said	then
at least	I repeat	moreover	therefore
by the way	I said	nevertheless	to tell the truth
consequently	I think	now	well
for example	in fact	of course	why

But when such expressions are built into the construction as modifiers, they are not set off by commas; thus, in *He is likewise going, She is indeed clever, Perhaps she is afraid,* the words *likewise, indeed, perhaps* are adverbs modifying the respective verbs. And in very short sentences in which the single words above listed cause no interruption, commas are not necessary, as *He is therefore ready, They are nevertheless silent, He is indeed the man.* Note the difference between *He did it well, however, and will take the prize* and *However well he did it, he was doomed to failure.*

And so forth, and so on, etc. are always preceded by a comma. They are likewise followed by a comma if they occur before the end of a sentence, as *I have desks, chairs, tables, and so forth, for sale.*

Now, then, well, why, at the beginning of a sentence, are usually set off by a comma. Such use is likely to be conversational.

4. To set off appositive or explanatory constructions, as:

> We are going to Catalina, the island off the southwest coast of California, to spend the winter.
> I want you to meet my brother-in-law, Charles Bronson.

This rule covers titles, degrees, or other explanatory details following a name, as:

> Jerry Brown, Esquire, has been elected.
> Harrison Carlton, D.D., and Thomas Everett, Mayor of Evansville, will address us.

An appositive phrase beginning with *or* or *known as* or *well-known,* is similarly set off by commas, as:

> The hack, or horse-drawn carriage, is now almost extinct.
> Adamson, the widely known author, has written another book.

When, however, the explanatory term is actually a part of the major term without which the sense would be incomplete, no comma is required, as *I myself, Richard the Lionhearted, the poet Tennyson, the year 1940, the liner Normandie.* In such expressions as *the adjective beautiful and the slang term hooey,* the word in apposition is really restrictive. It is customary to set it apart by underscoring for italics. No comma should be used.

5. After an introductory phrase or clause that is nonrestrictive and somewhat long, as:

> Entering by the north gate, we saved both time and distance.
> If you care to do so, meet me at the desk at twelve.

Short introductory participial phrases are sometimes restrictive and require no comma, as:

> Coming early we got good seats. (We got good seats because we came early.)
> Driving slowly he made the grade easily. (He made the grade easily by driving slowly.)

As the rule implies, introductory clauses that are restrictive do not require the comma, but it is often used. Both of these are correct:

> If you wish to be kind you will do it.
> If you wish to be kind, you will do it.

6. To set off clauses beginning with *and, but, or, nor, for, so, yet, while, though,* in compound sentences, as:

> This car had been taken without permission, and the "borrower" was therefore responsible for the damage.
> He gave up his position willingly, but no one had expected him to do so.

If in long or involved compound sentences and in compound-complex sentences no connectives are used between the independent clauses, the semicolon (see page 254) must be used to separate them, as:

> When I reached the station after my race with death, they were anxiously awaiting me; there was not the slightest evidence, however, that any one of them had so much as turned a hand to help.
> (This may also be written as two sentences, the second sentence beginning with *There.*)

The so-called **comma blunder,** or **comma error,** occurs when such a sentence is punctuated with a comma instead of a semicolon between the main parts, as:

> When I reached the station, after my race with death, they were anxiously awaiting me, there was not the slightest evidence, however, that any of them had so much as turned a hand to help.

This kind of mistake is also known as the **comma fault** and the **comma splice.** The term **comma sentence** is used to denote the use of too many commas in a sentence by which meaning may be confused rather than clarified, as:

> He stood, while Cedric, the Saxon, spoke.
> The big, red car, running at top speed, proved, that mere miles are negligible.

The first of these needs no commas at all. The second, written with open punctuation, •needs none; written with close punctuation, it needs the commas after *car* and *speed*.

7. To set off clauses beginning with *as, for, since* when they explain or illustrate what has preceded, as:

> He worked day and night, for he wanted that prize.
> I am not going to the party, since my lame knee prevents my dancing.

8. To set off terms used in direct address, as:

> John, please sit there.
> Ask her, Harry, whether she is coming.

9. To set off independent or absolute constructions, as:

> The shower coming just at noon, lunch had to be postponed.
> Commencement will be held earlier than usual, the world convention requiring the campus and buildings.

10. To set off contrasted expressions introduced, as a rule, by *not* or *but,* as:

> I came not to send peace, but a sword.
> Please hand me the red ink, not the black.
> He went to school, not to study, but to play football.

11. To set off any word, phrase, or clause that might easily be run in with a following one and thus be the cause of misreading and misunderstanding if the comma were not used after it (see 2 above), as:

> Without, the snow fell steadily and silently.
> Inside, the room glowed warm and bright.
> The day before, John had been initiated.

12. To set off short informal quotations, as:

> "You are quite right," he answered.
> He asked, "When shall I expect you?"

Before a formal statement or a long quotation the colon is used (see page 258).

13. To set off parts in an address or a date line that do not pertain to the same kinds of place or time, as:

20 Hampshire Street, Philadelphia, Pennsylvania.
Friday, October 10, 1945.

The comma is also used in formally written-out expressions as *He arrived at Tampa, in Florida, on Washington's Birthday, in 1845.*

14. In numerical expressions containing more than four digits, as *12,672; 106,708.* In straight matter, numbers containing only four digits require no comma, as *He has $1234 in the bank.* But in tabulations of numbers consisting of four and of five or more digits, the comma is used with numbers having four digits in order that the digits may be aligned vertically.

15. After the salutation in friendly or informal letters (unless the open style of punctuation is used), as:

Dear Bill,
Dear Friend,

16. After the complimentary close in both friendly and business letters (unless the open style of punctuation is used), as:

Faithfully yours,
Yours very truly,

17. After interjections and other exclamatory terms, as:

Alas, he never came!
Oh, you startled me!
Really now, this is too much!
My word, this is a terrible accident!

18. After responses, as:

Certainly, I shall be glad to go.
No, that is the wrong way.
Yes, I shall deliver it.

19. After such words as *first, second, third,* in serial notation, as:

Give me, first, liberty; second, equality; third, fraternity.

20. After a subject when its predicate is understood, as *May likes tennis; Bill, golf.*

Do not use a comma to separate a subject from its predicate, as in *John, threw the ball* for *John threw the ball.*

Do not use a comma, in writing figures, to separate hours from minutes or dollars from cents, as in *7,30* for *7.30* or *7:30;* or *$25,50* for *$25.50.*

Do not use a comma to separate an adjective from its noun or an adverb from its verb, as in *a beautiful, scene* for *a beautiful scene;* or in *a cleverly, performed trick* for *a cleverly performed trick.*

Do not use a comma after a verb to introduce a series, as in *He had studied, geometry, geography, drawing, and Latin* for *He had studied geometry, geography, drawing, and Latin.*

Do not use a comma after a preposition to separate it from its object, as in *He is going to tell us of, his travels in Africa* for *He is going to tell us of his travels in Africa.*

Do not use a comma after *to* in an infinitive to separate it from the verb that should immediately follow, as in *I want you to, study hard* for *I want you to study hard.*

Do not use a comma for a period between independent sentences, or for a semicolon between clauses that are remotely related. In *Down he came with a bang, we were all aghast at the tragedy* a period should be used in place of the comma. In *I like this kind of sweater, it is the double-weave breast* a semicolon, not a comma, is required.

EXERCISES

1. Supply commas in the following sentences as directed under Rules 1–3:

   1. John James and Howard occupied the three seats assigned to them.
   2. John James and Howard are friends collaborators and—twins.
   3. Dry weather or wet warm or cold sleet or mud he goes every day.
   4. That old coat of his which he bought in London years ago has been lost.
   5. The girl who shares my locker won four sets in rapid succession.

6. This rule which you have just made will in the main tend to discourage us.

7. North Carolina pine which is sold so largely in all parts of the country is I think best for telephone poles.

8. He could paint a house hang pictures repair blinds solder and repair gas fittings and electrical fixtures lay carpets and sharpen knives.

9. The young man who wins is the young man who drives straight ahead no matter what obstacles there are to be overcome.

10. James Brown who last week was promoted from assistant buyer to buyer is I'm sure you'll agree a young man who never permits trivial happenings to annoy him.

2. Supply commas in the following sentences as directed under Rules 4–7:

1. Hoping that you will make it a point to come to see me immediately on your return to town I am yours faithfully Alice.

2. Though he was tired and spent by the terrible experience he had had he nevertheless bore up cheerfully.

3. Alice Kane Mary's sister was determined to win her teacher's favor yet she couldn't tell exactly what tactics to adopt.

4. Harrison Rayson the boy sitting there at the left is the one who should apply for the job since he surpassed everyone else in that special field.

5. While there can be no doubt that positions are available there is every doubt about his being able to get the sort of work he wants.

6. You will probably think my story as I tell it to you is colored with personal enthusiasm but I can assure you it is the whole truth.

7. When I arrived at the station in the new car Jenkins the new chauffeur calmly announced his intention to take the down train.

8. The young surveyor Russell Sanford shows zeal and skill and industry but he has much to learn in manipulating human relationships.

9. Entering as he did from the left of the hall at so late an hour he was quite naturally bewildered and confused by it all.

10. Try as he would he was able neither to extricate his limbs nor to call for help though he was able to move slightly and to breathe normally.

3. Supply commas in the following sentences as directed under Rules 8–12:

1. As I was remarking the boy is beyond control.

2. Whatever you do my dear man will be all right with me.

3. We decided to remain another night the storm making roads impassable.

4. "No" he replied "we will never do that but this course is acceptable."

THE COMMA **159**

5. After all is said and done I am not only satisfied but pleased.
6. The evening before the catastrophe had made us all the worse for wear.
7. Believe it or not the train was ahead of time not late.
8. The offices being closed we visited the museum until two o'clock.
9. "Never" he roared "will I abandon this policy ladies and gentlemen no matter who taunts 'Coward' or who sneers 'Quitter.' "
10. What's more to the point we have decided kind friends to make you remain here with us not for a day or for two days but until your habitations are repaired and again fit for occupancy.

4. Supply commas in the following sentences as directed under Rules 13–20:

1. Mr. Albert Seabury 139 West 72 Street New York City.
2. Dear Mr. Seabury I am faithfully yours Harrison Wentworth.
3. Bill played three games; Harry six; Russell nine.
4. Certainly I shall go with you to the station that ramshackle old box.
5. Afterward I thought it over and felt better.
6. She received $31429 by the will.
7. Why I never thought of such a thing!
8. Besides this field for tillage was set aside for the purpose.
9. Yes besides this field for tillage there was also set aside a barn.
10. Mr. James Henderson Central Hanover Bank and Trust Company Fifth Avenue at Sixtieth Street, New York City Attention Mr. Brown Saxton Trust Department Second floor.

5. The comma is incorrectly used or omitted in the following sentences. Write the sentences correctly and give reasons for your changes.

1. Mary, came early and stayed, late.
2. She was very extravagantly, dressed.
3. While I waited I read about that dreadful murder.
4. I want to learn to dance well and to sing beautifully.
5. She brought us apples and oranges and pears and nectarines.
6. I received my check for $12,25 at closing time—5,30.
7. I think he is faithful and studious and industrious.
8. Our Thursday night meetings are held in Holden Hall 327 Waver Street at eight p. m.
9 That letter was written in 1,939 by C. V. Anderson while he was traveling through China Japan Hawaii and California.
10. Never never never let me hear you say such a thing again about your good friend John.

THE SEMICOLON

160. The **semicolon** is used—

1. To separate co-ordinate clauses in a compound sentence or a compound-complex sentence, provided they are not closely or immediately related and are not connected by conjunctions, as:

> He did not go to the city yesterday; he went to the fair instead.
>
> The common belief that a sentence is wrong if it ends with a preposition is itself wrong; such sentences, you will find, abound in good literature.
>
> John excels in the classroom; Bill leads on the field; Sam shines in his father's workshop; Harry is an expert chauffeur; but not one of these fellows can be called an all-round chap.

If such clauses are very short, the comma may be used, as *I came, I saw, I conquered.* If the relationship between clauses is remote, they may be written as independent sentences, as:

> He came earlier than expected. John arrived immediately afterward.

It would not be incorrect to use a semicolon after *expected.*

2. To separate phrases and clauses that within their own construction require the use of the comma, as:

> Having lived for many years in Khartoum, Egypt; having traveled and resided in many other Eastern countries, especially those bordering on the Indian Ocean; having now returned to Tucson, Arizona, to spend his remaining days, the interesting old gentleman is writing his memoirs.
>
> As Caesar loved me, I weep for him; as he was fortunate, I rejoice at it; as he was valiant, I honour him; but as he was ambitious, I slew him.

In the first example a comma is used to separate the main clause from the last phrase in the series. In the second example both semicolon and conjunction are used before the last complex member. This is an exception to Rule 1 above, but is correct when clauses are detached and when the clauses themselves contain commas.

3. To separate words, phrases, and clauses that might otherwise run together and convey vague or absurd meanings, as:

> If I were a millionaire I would have horses, motors, yachts, palaces, and estates; and the whole world should minister to my pleasures.

In this example the semicolon after *estates* establishes the values of the preceding *and* and the following one, the former being the connective in the series, the latter connecting the two clauses. In other words, it clarifies relationships. Note that in comparatively short serial expressions the semicolon is similarly used to indicate a different kind of classification from that indicated by the comma:

> The flower of Illinois is the wood violet; of Indiana, the tulip tree blossom; of Michigan, the apple blossom; of Ohio, the scarlet carnation; of Wisconsin, the violet.

4. To separate an independent clause from a following clause beginning with:

accordingly	finally	moreover	still
also	hence	nevertheless	then
besides	however	otherwise	therefore
consequently	likewise	so	thus

Note the following:

> John knew that he should have gone; besides, he had intended to do so up to the last minute.
> I am not in favor of the proposition; still, I think it may bring about certain improvements if it is passed.
> They were aware of the danger ahead of them; nevertheless, they forged onward unafraid and undaunted.

Note that in the sentence *He refused point-blank; so we went without him* there is more of a break before *so* than in *She was ill, so she canceled her appointment*. In the latter example the comma is a sufficient point before *so*. It is sufficient also before the other terms above listed when they occur in short expressions, as:

> He was hungry, therefore we fed him. (and we therefore)
> He was feeling ill, still he came (but still he)

5. Before such terms as the following when they introduce illustrations or explanations expressed in clauses or in long phrases (see page 258):

as	for example	namely	that is
as follows	for instance	such as	to illustrate

This sentence is correct:

> The good knot must have three qualities; namely, rapidity with which it can be tied, ability to hold fast when tied, readiness with which it can be undone.

In short expressions with no other punctuation these terms may be set off by the comma, as:

> There is one person who will not go, namely, John.
> Some verbs are most irregular in their parts, such as *be, go, see.*

Do not use the semicolon after the salutation or the complimentary close in a letter. *Dear Sir;* and *Very truly yours;* are wrong.

Do not use the semicolon directly before a listing. *I bought these articles; paper, ink, erasers, pencils* is wrong. A colon or a dash should be used after *articles.*

Do not use the semicolon before a direct quotation. *He said; "I am happy"* is wrong. The comma is correct after *said.*

EXERCISE

The following sentences require semicolons. Insert them at the proper places.

1. We rang and rang no one answered.
2. Her eyes glared she turned deathly pale then she fell.
3. He won money, fame, position and friends envied him, relatives pestered him.
4. You should put on your overcoat the day is bitter cold.
5. My father is not here, sir he went to the city this morning.
6. Go where you please stay as long as you please get what you please but please leave me alone.
7. I cannot understand why he came I do not see why he remains consequently I am at a loss to see why I should be civil to him.

8. What he says may be true however I cannot believe it until I hear it from a more authoritative source.

9. Our employes' club is an organization for the promotion of social life it is in no sense an organization for agitation or missionary purposes.

10. The articles that indicate either membership or rank in our club are for sale only to members that is to say our pin, our badge, and our ring may be bought by no one outside the club.

11. Whether you are in earnest I know not whether your friends take you seriously I cannot tell whether you are responsible for your acts I shall make no effort to discover but so much is certain: I shall never trust you again.

12. Cassius well knew what would be the effect of an attack on the forces of Mark Antony and Octavius Caesar yet he had agreed that on the following day the attack should be made at Philippi.

13. Whatever you may do when the time comes wherever you may go with whomever you may associate in however many ways you again disgrace yourself, have the courtesy at least to pay me the respect you owe me.

14. When the king of the country was young, he was constantly at war with his neighbors when old age overcame him and his warlike spirits had died, he was greatly concerned because his hostile neighbors would not let him live in peace and quiet.

15. On a certain day he went to look at his palace and the woman riding ahead, who was the first to enter the gate, turned and hailed him as the new king of a new country.

THE COLON

161. The **colon** is used—

1. Before a list or illustration or explanation, as:

> There are three boys in the room: John, Harry, and Bill.
> The operation is performed in this way: Take a string a yard long; cut it into four equal lengths; cross them; knot them at the cross point.
> The situation was just this: He was too tired to go; he didn't care to go; and, what is more to the point, he wasn't invited.

The first word following the colon is preferably capitalized when it begins a complete, independent sentence, especially if the statement is formal.

If such terms as *namely, as follows, following, for example* stand before the list or illustration or explanation, and on the same line, they may be preceded by a comma and followed by a colon, as:

> There are three boys in the room, as follows: John, Harry, and Bill.

2. Before a final clause indicating a sudden change in thought or adding a climax to what precedes, as:

> Kill him if you will; slay him; torture him: his name will live and shine long after all of you are forgotten.

3. Before a formal statement or quotation, as:

> The poet Lowell wrote: "Who gives himself with his alms feeds three—himself, his hungering neighbor, and me."

Before a short or informal statement in ordinary dialogue the comma is correct.

4. After the salutation in a business letter, unless the letter style follows completely open punctuation (see page 323), as:

> Dear Sir: Dear Mr. Hamilton: Gentlemen:

5. Between figures denoting different kinds of time, and between different kinds of place and other names, as:

> Matthew 12:6–12.
> They leave at 10:30.
> New York: The Macmillan Company

The period is frequently used, however, for the separation of figures, and the dash for the separation of names. Do not use either a colon or a period when a symbol makes sufficient separation of terms. Write *89° 27′ 31″*, not *89° : 27′ : 31″*.

6. After the word *Resolved* in the statement of questions for debate, as:

> *Resolved:* That learning by thinking is more important than learning by doing.

Do not use a colon before such terms as *namely, as follows, thus, for example. The letter* c *has two distinct sounds: thus, soft and hard* is wrong. It should be written either *The letter* c *has two distinct sounds; thus, soft and hard* or *The letter* c *has two distinct sounds, thus: soft and hard.*

Do not use a colon before a serial object or an attribute complement. *I ate: apples, pears, peaches, and bananas* is wrong, as is also *He is, the man.* No punctuation is required after *ate* and *is.*

EXERCISE

Supply the colon as required in the following:

1. He has served our nation in the following countries China, Japan, Australia, Africa.
2. Tennyson long ago wrote the memorable line "More things are wrought by prayer than this world dreams of."
3. I could believe you but for this very important exception The boy was here at the time you say it was done.
4. This is the unanswerable question If Mars is indeed inhabited, what kind of creatures inhabit it?
5. All I can say for him is this He has never yet failed us in his duty, no matter how difficult of performance.
6. The following articles can be made and sold to advantage for the fair sofa pillows, needlework, candy, blouses, sweaters.
7. My employer says that I am doing the work extremely well in Thompson's absence this is why Thompson has been told to take another week off.
8. Winter recreations are by no means scarce in good old Canada skating, skiing, sliding, tobogganing, snowshoeing, sleighing, curling, sugaring-off, and feeding winter birds.
9. He concluded his speech with the following appropriate quotation from Shakespeare "How far that little candle throws his beams! So shines a good deed in a naughty world."
10. Baron Rothschild's Rules of Business were as follows carefully examine every detail of your business, be prompt in everything, take time to consider but decide positively, dare to go forward, bear trouble patiently, be brave in the struggle of life, maintain your integrity as a sacred thing, never tell business lies, make no useless acquaintances, never appear something more than you are, pay your debts promptly, shun strong liquor, employ your time well, do not reckon upon chance, be polite to everybody, never be discouraged—then work hard and you will be certain to succeed.

THE DASH

162. The dash is used—

1. To change or break off an expression abruptly, as:

Yes—no—let me see. Perhaps I shall after all.
Lady Derringdo then entered—one vast area of gewgaws.

2. To mark off appositive or explanatory or parenthetical matter, as:

These cities—Brussels, Paris, Lisbon—are in Western Europe.
We were waiting—Jane and I—for the uptown bus.

In strict usage the dash in this construction should mark off matter that is less intimate to the sentence than the comma would indicate, and more intimate to it than the parentheses would indicate. But consistency under this rule is impossible of achievement.

3. To point to a concluding expression that is a summary or an afterthought, or a list concluding a statement, as:

Books, movies, museums—these were his life.
He knows me better than I know myself—indeed, he is my Boswell.
He had everything—brains, character, good looks, wealth, and all the rest.

4. To denote omission of letters or words or figures, as:

Th——s.
Hip, hip, hurrah, ——, ——!
19—.

The first may be written *Th***s* or *Th...s;* the last *19...* Dots, dashes, or asterisks so used are called **ellipsis.**

Do not substitute a dash for a period at the end of a sentence. The following is wrong:

I am going skating tomorrow—

Do not use a dash after a comma or a colon or a semicolon. The following are wrong:

Dear Sir:— and Dear Joe,—

Do not make a dash so short that it may be mistaken for a hyphen. These are correct:

He is true-blue.
What you say is true—blue is my favorite color.

Technically the dash is a little more than twice as long as the hyphen. For a dash strike two hyphens on the typewriter — —.

EXERCISE

Supply the dash and other punctuation as required in the following:

1. This that no the other one is my choice.
2. We did this Bill and I by the midnight oil.
3. Mary Sally and Terese these were the girls finally selected.
4. If you meet him he may be at the game give him my best wishes.
5. I worked at that problem very late in fact all night long.
6. Billy Young remember him has just taken high honors.
7. That old cedar torn old tree that it is must come down.
8. Our old sheepdog Blunder Boy we call him has almost human instincts.
9. Blanken oh what a golfer gave us a fine exhibition yesterday.
10. Take some cream take some eggs take some fresh tomatoes take some seasoning mix them all together and heat them that's how to make tasty tomato gravy.

PARENTHESES

163. Parentheses are used—

1. To enclose matter that explains or comments upon the thought expressed but is not part of the structure of a sentence or a paragraph; that is, an aside or a foreign element, as:

Please bring that book (the one I gave you yesterday).
I shall ask him to take me in his car. (He certainly must have a car.)

When the matter within the parentheses may easily be given grammatical connection, final punctuation is placed outside the parenthesis; when it is completely independent, final punctuation is placed inside. But when a parenthetical expression does not occur at the end of a sentence, such intermediate marks as comma, semicolon, and colon follow the parenthesis, as:

> If he comes early (and I am sure he will do so), we shall have time for the game.
> Never cross in that direction again (unless you are quite out of your mind); many accidents have occurred here as result of taking the wrong direction.
> A few such terms are here given (sufficient to illustrate this important rule): fanning, manning, planning, tanning.

2. To enclose letters and figures used to mark off or classify divisions in written matter, as (*a*), (*1*).

> His two ambitions are (*a*) to go to college and (*b*) to study music.
> Our government has three branches: (1) the legislative, (2) the executive, (3) the judiciary.

In such notation the parenthesis is not followed by any punctuation.

3. Figures and symbols used in parentheses to verify words should follow rather than precede the words, as:

> There are twelve (12) men on the job today, *not* There are (12) twelve men.
> They are paid five dollars ($5.) a day *or* They are paid five (5) dollars a day, *not* They are paid ($5.) five dollars.

Do not use parentheses to excess. Too many unnecessary expressions make your writing incoherent and confusing.

Do not enclose in parentheses matter you wish to omit. Such matter should be crossed out.

BRACKETS

164. Brackets are used—

1. To enclose matter that is even more remotely related to the meaning of an expression than parenthetical matter is; for instance, such words as *applause, cheers, disorder* in a report of a meeting, as:

> The speaker continued: "I am astonished at this report." [*Laughter and applause.*]

2. To enclose your own words inserted in quoted matter, as:

"In that novel [Katrina] the author spoke of the prim and proper dress of the period [the Victorian era] as if the churches were to blame for it."

3. To insert unquoted matter in a quotation, as:

George wrote: "I am leaving you [he meant his mother] forever and so ask this favor."

EXERCISE

Insert parentheses and brackets as required in the following:

1. The tellers report that 101 one hundred and one votes were cast.
2. Enclosed you will find three dollars $3. for which please send me six 6 ties. See attached card.
3. The man warned us and results now reveal that he was right not to attempt that highest peak the Zermatt.
4. "I inform you here and now that no member of this organization will ever force my resignation." Hisses and catcalls.
5. It was in the retreat from Moscow that the Little Corporal Napoleon Bonaparte first felt the bitterness of defeat.
6. "With that car," said the salesman, "you will have comfort, service, and pleasure assured." (Insert name of car.)
7. His excuses are *a* illness, *b* absence, *c* misunderstanding, *d* general indifference. The last covers all!

THE APOSTROPHE

165. The **apostrophe** is used—

1. To denote the possessive case. To form the possessive singular add *'s* to the nominative form of a noun, as *dog's, John's, sister-in-law's.*

When the nominative ends with *s,* add *'s* to the full word or name, as *boss's, Burns's, Jones's.* If a word of two or more syllables ends with *s* or with some other hissing sound, and is not accented on the last syllable, the possessive singular may be formed by adding either *'s* or the apostrophe alone; thus, *Dickens' novels, conscience' sake* are correct. Names of one syllable hav-

ing such endings are sometimes included in this rule, as *Jones'
car* and *Burns' poems.*

To form the possessive plural of a noun, write first its plural
form. If this ends in *s,* add the apostrophe only; if it does not
end in *s,* add *'s;* thus, *girl, girls, girls'; man, men, men's; sister-in-law, sisters-in-law, sisters-in-law's; ox, oxen, oxen's.*

2. To denote omitted letters in words and omitted figures in
numbers, as *isn't, don't, o'clock, we'll; '76* (for *1776*). Be careful
to place the apostrophe at the place where the omission occurs;
do'nt and *is'nt* are incorrect (see page 285).

3. To form the plural of individual letters, figures, and symbols, as *a's, 2's, &'s. Four 8s* and *four 8's* are correct. The apostrophe is preferred, however, and it is imperative in cases where
its omission would deceive the eye, as *as* for *a's* and *is* for *i's.*
But the pluralization of words by means of *'s,* though still sometimes seen, is passing out of use; thus, *buts* and *ands* and *don'ts*
are preferable to *but's* and *and's* and *don't's.*

4. The possessives of compound proper names are formed as
follows: When joint possession is indicated, *'s* is added to the
last name only; when separate or individual possession is indicated, *'s* is added to each name. *Brown and Logan's store* means
a store owned jointly by Brown and Logan. *Brown's and Logan's
stores* means two stores, one owned by Brown and one by Logan.
Brown and Logan's stores means the stores in a chain system
owned by Brown and Logan (see page 84).

Do not use the apostrophe in the possessive forms of personal, relative, and interrogative pronouns. *Its, his, hers, theirs,
ours, yours, whose* are correct. *It's* means *it is; who's* means *who
is;* the apostrophe standing in each instance for the omitted *i.*

Do not form the plural of proper names by adding *'s. The
Joneses are coming to dinner* is correct (see page 79).

EXERCISE

Insert the apostrophe or the apostrophe and *s* as required in the following:

1. We have just had two weeks vacation.
2. Is that Thomas suit on the hook?

3. Theyre coming up the hill and its slippery.
4. Dont forget to dot your *i*s and cross your *t*s.
5. Theyll all go together if it doesnt rain.
6. Were going in Mr. Perkins car because its larger.
7. The Smiths home is more luxurious than the Jones.
8. Womens dresses are sometimes more expensive than mens suits.
9. Hell never finish talking about the stock-market crash of 29.
10. The editor-in-chiefs work is far more important than yours.
11. Turner and James store didnt close till ten oclock last night.
12. Turner and James stores everywhere are excellent.
13. Turners and James stores follow completely different policies.
14. Keats poems have had their effect upon Marys character.

QUOTATION MARKS

166. Quotation marks are used—

1. To enclose direct quotations, as:

They shouted, "Hurry or we shall drown!"
"I shall go," he retorted, "when I am ready."

But do not enclose indirect statements or questions in quotation marks. *He retorted that he would go when he was ready* is correct. In *He retorted "that he would go when he was ready"* the quotation marks are incorrect. In *He said yes and she said no* the words *yes* and *no* are indirect statements and therefore should not be enclosed in quotation marks and should not be capitalized.

Indirect questions, like indirect statements, should not be enclosed in quotation marks. They should not begin with a capital and should end with a period, not with a question mark, as *He asked what time it was.* For a direct question, *He asked, "What time is it?"* is the correct form.

Direct quotations are called **direct discourse;** indirect quotations, **indirect discourse.** For expert handling of direct and indirect questions and answers by three different methods see Dickens' *A Tale of Two Cities,* Book II, Chapter III. One of these methods is reproduced on pages 237–238.

When such terms as *he said, she declared, they replied* are used at the beginning, at the end, or in the middle of informal direct quotations, they are usually set off by commas, as in the above examples; but the construction and the sense sometimes call for a period or a semicolon. After such an expression in the middle of a sentence use the punctuation mark which would be correct if the quotation were not interrupted:

> "Please omit that," said the instructor. "It is quite unnecessary. ("Please omit that. It is quite unnecessary.")
> "You had better take this route," said the guide; "it is by all odds the safest." ("You had better take this route; it is by all odds the safest.")

The second part of such broken quotations does not begin with a capital letter unless it begins a new sentence.

Note also that the first word of the introductory term is not capitalized even when it follows the question mark or the exclamation point, as:

> "Where are you going?" he inquired.
> "What a mess!" she complained.

The period and the comma precede the closing quotation marks, as:

> "Please let me see that," said Tom.
> Bill replied, "Not until I have finished with it."

The semicolon and the colon follow the closing quotation marks, as:

> Then, flushing, he replied, "That, sir, I will never do"; and, turning, he left the room.
> Here is your previous "must-have list": [here a series of words or items].

These placements of period, comma, semicolon, and colon have been established by printers and have become printing conventions. They are by no means always a logical arrangement.

The question mark and the exclamation point are always placed logically. If they pertain to the quotation only, they must be placed inside the closing quotation marks; if they pertain to the entire expression, including the introductory term, they must be placed outside the closing quotation marks. Observe:

> She said, "Are you coming along?" (The question begins with *Are*.)
> Did she say, "Please pass the butter"? (The question begins with *Did*.)

A quotation within a quotation is set off by single quotation marks, as:

> "Just at that moment," he continued, "I was shocked to hear the cry of 'Murder! Murder!' "
> "It is appropriate at this time," thundered the orator, "to quote Patrick Henry: 'Millions for defense but not one cent for tribute.' "

2. To set off titles of stories, chapters, essays, lectures, poems, and articles when these appear in association with broader and more general titles, as:

> I have just read "Catch Three" in *The Saturday Evening Post*.
> The third chapter of Tom Harrison's *Energy and Thought* is entitled "Happy Combinations."

Titles of books and periodicals are preferably italicized (see page 294).

3. To set off quoted paragraphs. If only one paragraph is quoted, quotation marks belong immediately before and immediately after it. If two or more paragraphs are quoted successively, opening quotation marks are placed at the beginning of each paragraph and closing quotation marks at the end of the last paragraph only.

In a continuous conversation the remarks of each speaker should be in a separate paragraph and should be enclosed in quotation marks.

> "Are you going?" he asked.
> "I think not," she replied.
> "But why?" he persisted.
> "For many reasons," she answered.

4. To set off special words, technical terms, slang, nicknames, as:

> They have nicknamed him "Butch."
> The new boy is really a "brick."

This use of quotation marks is not invariable. Words to which special attention is called are usually italicized; nicknames that are well established and slang that is commonly known require no quotation marks. The following are correct:

Al Smith, *not* "Al" Smith
Doug Fairbanks, *not* "Doug" Fairbanks
I want no tomfoolery here, *not* I want no "tomfoolery" here.

Do not use quotation marks to enclose the title of a theme or other kind of writing you may do.

Do not use quotation marks to set off expressions that you may think clever, humorous, or ironic. This includes big or show-off words, coined expressions, advertising words, well-known quotations that are fitted into expression. The quotation marks in the following sentences should be omitted:

The "temperate" Mr. Blank then "rolled in."
I always insist that "a word to the wise is sufficient."
Remember that "it's smart to be thrifty."

Do not overuse quotation marks. No other mark of punctuation is so confusing to the eye or so distracting to the mind as these little inverted commas used to excess.

EXERCISES

1. Punctuate and capitalize the following correctly:

1. Brown said my boy is going to college please wish him well.
2. How strange exclaimed Julia I never saw that before.
3. This sir is strictly my business said he do not presume.
4. He asked what is the meaning of the words might and main.
5. Please arrange to be present she writes if you can't let me know.
6. Is this your theme asked the teacher if so then I shall examine it.
7. Should not the ruler regard the voice of the people the statesman asked.
8. I do not understand you said he what in the world do you mean.
9. Why all this trouble queried John I'm sure I'm rather tired of it all.
10. Don't tell the old gentleman please he implored or he'll think me really a weak sister.

11. What do you understand by to him that hath shall be given and from him that hath not shall be taken even the little that he seemeth to have.

12. It reads as follows extra values by the people for the people are added to a product already superlatively fine.

   Particularly is the brisk and spirited character of its supremely smooth quiet performance of notable interest.

   You will make no mistake in buying one of these now and if you do depend upon it your family will fall at your feet.

2. Convert the following indirect expressions into direct discourse and explain the required changes in punctuation:

1. She asked me where I was going.
2. They inquired what I was doing.
3. He asked me how my father was.
4. He said that they were all well.
5. He replied that I was wrong.
6. The Good Book says that you must love your neighbors.
7. The teacher advises us to read over everything we write before handing it in.
8. We are commanded to be kind.
9. They thought that the end had come.
10. We exclaimed that we thought the situation disgraceful.
11. She quickly inquired what I meant.
12. They told me that they expected to leave tomorrow.
13. The magistrate ordered him to hand over his pistol and his knife.
14. He was told to try again and to be a little more patient about the job.
15. She explained the pattern to me and said I could easily make the dress.
16. Mary said to Alice that she was expected home by ten o'clock, but that her mother had said that she might be a little late if she found it hard to get away.
17. After he had felicitated us most graciously upon our graduation, he added that he thought he had never in his life seen a more beautiful group of young men and young women.
18. The Wedding Guest, one of three on their way to a wedding, asked the Ancient Mariner, with his long gray beard and glittering eye, wherefore he stopped him.
19. Barbara said that they might strike her old gray head, if they felt they had to, but that they must spare her country's flag.
20. He wanted to know what the meaning of all this was, what we had in our minds, and why we couldn't behave like human beings—and he said he wanted to know right away, too.

3. Convert the following direct expressions into indirect discourse and explain the required changes in punctuation:

1. "Come quick," she called, "and see the parade."
2. "Know thyself," said Chilo.
3. "When shall we three meet again?" asked one witch of another.
4. "Oh?" said she, "there's a snake."
5. "Thou shalt not kill," is the sixth Commandment.
6. "Love truth but pardon error," said Voltaire.
7. "Spare the rod and spoil the child," says an old maxim.
8. "What shall I do?" she asked.
9. "Do? Why, run with all your might," quickly answered her little brother.
10. Says the proverb, "Train up a child in the way he should go, and when he is old he will not depart from it."
11. "Where did you put my slippers, Martha?" asked William.
12. "Have you ever served as an airplane pilot?" asked the inspector. "Well, sir, not exactly," replied the candidate, "but I've known a great many pilots."
13. The vision answered: "The names of those who love the Lord are being written here." "And is mine one?" asked Abou. "Nay, not so," replied the vision.
14. "It may be," said Senator Johnson, "that my opponents are right in their point of view, but I must now refer them to that great statesman who said, 'The right is never decided until the vote is taken.' "
15. "Will you join me for luncheon?" asked he politely. "Why, certainly," she replied. "Delighted," said he. "Thanks," said she, "but remember, it's to be no tablecloth spread under a tree. I'll join you at a real restaurant where there are music and dancing."
16. "How appropriate to our times," said the orator, "are those immortal words of Cassius to Brutus regarding Caesar: 'Why, man, he doth bestride the narrow world like a Colossus, and we petty men walk under his huge legs, and peep about to find ourselves dishonourable graves.' "

THE HYPHEN

167. There are three kinds of compound terms; namely, those written solid, like *henceforth* and *switchboard;* those written as two separate words, like *income tax* and *parcel post;* those written with a hyphen, like *mother-in-law* and *so-called.* These three classes of terms constitute probably the most troublesome element in technical English and are responsible for numerous inconsistencies. The dictionaries must be consulted frequently in regard to them, but even the dictionaries themselves are in disagreement about them in many instances. Generally speaking, the hyphen should be avoided if possible by writing compound expressions either as solid words or as two separate words. There are some situations, however, in which it is a valuable aid to the eye because it shows directly the relationship in meaning of the elements joined by it. The spellings below are based on Webster's *New International Dictionary*, but the *Standard Dictionary* should be consulted by the student for interesting comparisons.

168. Use the hyphen—

1. At the end of a line to show that a word is divided.

2. Between words denoting numerals from 21 to 99, as *forty-one;* but *one hundred two* or *one hundred and two.*

3. Between the numerator and the denominator of a fraction used as a modifier, as *a two-thirds part, three-quarters empty.* When the fraction is a noun no hyphen is required, as *I have sent one half of my books* and *I have read two thirds of the story.*

4. Between two similar vowels when they belong in different syllables, as *re-enlist, co-ordinate, semi-independent;* and to prevent three *l*'s from coming together, as *shell-like.*

5. Between a prefix and a verb when the meaning is different from that of the solid word. Compare the meanings of *re-cover* and *recover, re-form* and *reform.* Note also the differences in accent.

6. Between a prefix and a proper adjective, as *anti-Japanese; pro-British.*

7. Between two or more words which form a single modifier, as *ten-room house, never-to-be-forgotten day, hand-to-mouth existence, happy-go-lucky boy.*

8. Between the parts of a compound noun one of whose elements is in the possessive case, as *cat's-eye, dog's-ear, bachelor's-button.*

9. In compounds consisting of a noun and a prepositional phrase, as *brother-in-law, Jack-in-the-pulpit, mother-of-pearl.*

10. Between two co-ordinate nouns when *and* is understood, as *author-editor, owner-operator.*

11. Between a noun and an adjective combined as a modifier, as *iron-gray, lemon-yellow, ankle-deep, world-wide, stone-cold, germ-free, rust-proof.* In these condensed expressions the conjunction *as* or a preposition is understood.

12. Between two adjectives when the first modifies the second to give a meaning different from that of the adjectives used co-ordinately, as in *white-hot metal, blue-black feathers.*

13. Between a verb and a preposition and between a verb and an adverb combined to form a noun, as *go-between, lean-to.* When such compounds have become familiar to the eye they are often written solid, as *lookout, hookup.*

14. Between different parts of speech combined to form a new meaning, as *to water-cool, the make-believe, merry-go-round, old-timer.*

15. Between an adjective and a past participle used as a single modifier, as *good-humored, old-fashioned, deep-seated, quick-witted.*

16. Between a verbal and an adverb combined to form a noun, as *the summing-up, the putting-off, the coming-together, the wasting-away.*

17. When two or three words are individually combined with another word as a modifier, as *two-, three-, and four-story houses.*

18. In compounds with the following prefixes or combining forms:

cross—cross-question. But usage is not consistent.
ex (meaning formerly)—ex-governor.
great (denoting family relationships)—great-aunt, great-grandfather; *but* greatcoat, great seal.
half—half-hour, half-wit. There is considerable inconsistency.
ill—ill-advised, ill-tempered.
self (in the reflexive sense)—self-reliant, self-seeking; *but* selfsame, selfhood.
vice—vice-presidency, vice-consul. Usage varies.

well—well-informed, well-known. Use the hyphen only when the modifier *precedes* the noun, as *He stated well-known facts*. In *The facts were well known* and *The facts, already well known, were broadcast* **no** hyphen should be used with *well known*.

19. In compounds with *elect* or *general* as the second element, as:

elect—bride-elect
general—governor-general

169. Do not use a hyphen—

1. Between two proper adjectives, as *Latin American policy, French Canadian settlement, New Hampshire resort*.

2. Between foreign words combined as modifiers, as *bona fide sale, laissez faire attitude, a priori reasoning, 2 per cent discount*.

3. Between chemical terms used as adjectives, as *carbon monoxide poisoning*.

4. Between an adverb and the word it modifies, as in *an easily adjusted claim, a purely imaginary situation*. Do not use a hyphen with the adverbs *ever* and *never*, as in *an ever decreasing supply*.

170. A compound term should be written as a **solid word** when its meaning is different from that of the component parts used individually and when the accent is on the first syllable. Compare both meanings and accents in the following: *bluebird, blue bird; cattail, cat tail; whitecap, white cap; eyesore, eye sore*.

But if the solid word would look awkward or unfamiliar to the eye, write the compound term as two separate words. Compare the following:

bookkeeper	blood poisoning
horsepower	book learning
pocketbook	candle power
rattlesnake	mother wit
seafaring	subject matter

Because there is considerable variance in this matter, be sure you have at least one dictionary as authority.

171. Write as solid words—

1. Compound pronouns, as *myself, whoever, someone, everyone, anybody.*

2. Points of the compass, as *northeast;* but *north-northeast.*

3. Common expressions such as:

altogether	everywhere	nowhere	tomorrow
anywhere	indoors	outdoors	tonight
downtown	midnight	today	upstairs

4. Compounds with the following prefixes or combining forms:

after—afterthought, aftertaste
ante—antedate, anteroom
anti—antisocial, antiwar
by—bygone, bylaw
circum—circumscribe, circumlocution
co—coeducation; *but* co-operate, because two *o*'s come together.
contra—contradistinction, contraindicate
counter—counterclockwise, counterbalance
cross—crosspiece, crossbreed. But there is considerable inconsistency.
de—derail, dethrone
down—downstairs, downhearted, downfall
extra—extracurricular, extrabold
fore—forearm, foregone, forerunner
hyper—hypersensitive, hypercritical
in—inborn, inattention
inter—interstate, interchangeable, interrelate
intra—intramural, intrastate
life—lifeboat, lifeblood
master—masterpiece, mastersingers. There is inconsistency in usage.
mis—misinterpret, misspell
news—newsboy, newspaper, newsstand (*Webster*), news-stand (*Standard*)
non—nonsectarian, nonneutral
off—offhand, offspring
out—outnumber, outspoken, outbuilding
over—overindulge, oversea, overshoe
post (meaning after)—postgraduate, postwar
pre—preview, preconceive
re—reconsider, reimburse, retrial; *but* re-enter, because two *e*'s come together.
semi—semiconscious, semiannual
sub—subhead, subnormal

sun—sunshine, sunburn, sunshade, *but* (as yet) sun lamp
super—superhuman, superimpose
thorough—thoroughgoing, thoroughfare
trans—transplant, transship
ultra—ultramodern, ultraviolet
un—unconcerned, unimaginative
under—undercurrent, undersecretary, underfed
up—upbringing, upkeep

5. Compounds with the following suffixes or combining forms:

fold—twofold; *but* fifteen fold, because a solid word would be hard
   to read.
ful—tablespoonful, spoonful
hood—adulthood, womanhood
less—fatherless, hopeless
like—warlike, businesslike
proof—waterproof, foolproof
self—yourself, itself
ward—backward, afterward

172. Write as two separate words:

1. Compounds containing the following:

fellow—fellow man, fellow being
master—master mason, master artist. Consult the dictionary for exceptions.
world—world power, world war

2. Such terms as:

all right	in spite of	some day
et cetera	per cent	some place

EXERCISE

The sentences below contain terms some of which should be hyphened,
some written solid, some written as separate words. Rewrite them first
without consulting the dictionary or the text above; then check by the
dictionary or the text.

1. I need thirty two inches of all wool cloth.
2. The longed for party was attended by three fourths of the students.
3. The new high school teacher is standing on the court house steps.
4. The president elect had him appointed ambassador at large.

5. Here are fifty one five dollar bills that were taken in the hold up.
6. My son in law is running a one man business on a pay as you go plan.
7. He had a grim never say die expression on his face at the wind up of the fight.
8. Yes, rubber is a non conductor but this new fangled material is not.
9. The ladies in waiting were richly gowned, but the whole ceremony was quite un American.
10. The boy who works in the green house is a twelve dollar a week office helper, and he pays the rent for his mother who lives in the green house on the hill.

CAPITALIZATION

173. Capitals are used—

1. For proper nouns—names of:

Deity—God; Jehovah
Persons—Thomas Jefferson
Places—Detroit
Months—December
Holidays—Christmas
Days of the week—Sunday
Religions—Christianity; Roman Catholic
Races—Negro
Creeds—Apostles' Creed
Periods—Victorian; Renaissance
Historical events—Civil War
Documents—Constitution of the United States
Political parties—Republican Party
Organizations—Salvation Army
Institutions—Johns Hopkins University
Government departments—The Supreme Court
Buildings—Lincoln Memorial
Books of the Bible—Acts of the Apostles
Versions of the Bible—Authorized Version

Common nouns such as *church, club, college, company, county, lake, park, railroad, river, school, street,* when linked with proper nouns to denote location or organization, are capitalized, as *Tony Club, Grinnell College, Sears Company, Bucks County.* You write *John is going to high school* and *John is going to Manwaring High School; The river is very wide here* and *The*

Missouri River is very wide here. In some publications the final term in such combinations is written with a small letter, as *York county* and *Central park,* but this is not the better usage. When such final term is plural, however, it should always be written with a small letter, as *Central and Prospect parks, Blaine and Hoover high schools, Colorado and Missouri rivers.* This rule is not always observed.

The names of the seasons are capitalized only when they are used figuratively, as *When Summer smiles,* but *This has been a mild winter.*

Names used to indicate broad, well-known divisions of territory are capitalized, as *He lives in the West* and *We have visited the Southwest* and *The Northwest Territory was rapidly developed.*

In capitalized titles and headings only the most important members of a hyphened expression—usually the noun members —are capitalized, as *British-ruled Peoples, Twentieth-Century Limited, Forty-second Street, Mother-in-Law's Visit.*

The French articles *la, le, de, du* in proper names are not capitalized when preceded by Christian names; they should be capitalized when not so preceded; thus *Jean la Tour, the Du Bois* residence. The German *von* is never capitalized; the Dutch *van* usually is; thus, *Baron von Schulenberg, Jon Van Sicklen.*

2. For proper adjectives, as *Indian relics, British goods, French taste.*

But some adjectives that were once proper or that are derived from proper names have become common and are thus not capitalized in general usage, as *india rubber, china ware, oriental character, satanic attitude, godly purpose, pasteurized milk, utopian plan, gypsy habits, titanic strength* (see page 74).

3. For words that begin sentences and lines of poetry, as:

Let me not to the marriage of true minds
Admit impediments.

Much modernistic or free verse ignores the second part of this rule, lines beginning not with capitals but with small letters.

This rule applies to the first word in a quoted sentence, as:

They shouted, "We are going to the party."

But if only part of a sentence is quoted after its first word, the quotation does not begin with a capital, as:

He said that the announcement made neither "good sense nor bad nonsense."

4. For words and abbreviations indicating parts, sections, or groupings in books, outlines, and papers, as *Act I, Scene 2* and *Part VI, Paragraph 4* and *Vol. III, Chap.* 2. Or major sections may be capitalized and minor ones written with small letters, as *Act I, scene ii.* Usage varies widely in this regard.

5. For words that begin points in an outline, as:

I. Results of the training
   A. Better health
   B. Greater mental alertness

Major points may, however, begin with capitals, and minor ones with small letters. Minor points that read consecutively from major ones begin with small letters, as:

I. This is neither plausible nor desirable, for
   A. it interferes with speed, and
   B. it entails danger

6. For the first word in the salutation and in the complimentary close of a letter. No other word in the complimentary close should be capitalized, but in a two-word salutation both words are capitalized; in a three- or four-word (or longer) salutation the first and last words are always capitalized, as are titles and other important words, but adjectives are not, thus:

Dear Sir: Dear Colonel Mapleson:
My dear Jane,   My dear Major Robble:
Dear Dr. Nelson: My Dear,
Dear little teeny-weeny Mine,   John Dear,
                    Very truly yours,
                    Sincerely your friend,

7. For the first and all other important words in titles of books and themes, as:

The Reign of Terror
A Merry Picnic in the Woods
If the Devil a Prince Would Be

8. For nouns that are personified, as:

When fickle Fortune turns her back
Now kindly Nature becks and nods.

9. For abbreviations of proper names and for abbreviated titles before and after names (though *Jr.* and *Sr.* may also be written with small letters), as *Pa., Robt., The Brand Co., Mr., Mrs., Dr., Esq.*

10. For the personal pronoun *I* and the interjection *O*.

Do not capitalize the names of school subjects, such as *biology, history, mathematics.* These are common nouns. But *English* is always a proper noun or proper adjective and must be capitalized.

Do not use capitals for the sake of emphasis. Their excessive use for this purpose may weaken rather than strengthen, and also beget the habit of mistaking common for proper nouns.

EXERCISE

Supply capital letters as required in the following:

1. i read *marmion* and liked it better than *the courtship of miles standish.*
2. they traveled to southern california on the crack sunset limited.
3. the second part of the motto "live and let live" is ignored by dictators.
4. "it is always like this," he cried, "i'm tired of it, i tell you."
5. mr. harrison le fevre will address the y.m.c.a. tonight at nine.
6. thomas r. wainright, esq., 815 west forty-second street, new york city.
7. the bill of rights is found in the first ten amendments to our constitution.
8. the subject of his essay is *the english-speaking peoples and their neighbors.*
9. the catholic priest was the first man on the job when it came to saving the burning jewish synagogue.

10. the g.a.r. had headquarters in washington, d.c., and branch offices in almost every state in the union.

11. he said something about " 'tis nobler in the mind to suffer" but bobby lamontage kept tickling me and i couldn't hear clearly.

12. harold bronson, our ex-president, advocates increased membership fees for the trainers' club but most pupils of edison high school are opposed to the increase.

REVIEW EXERCISES

1. Indicate how many nouns of the third person there are in each of the following sentences:

1. Mary, Elizabeth, and Lawrence came yesterday.
2. Mary, Elizabeth and Lawrence came yesterday.
3. Mary Elizabeth and Lawrence came yesterday.
4. Mary Elizabeth Lawrence came yesterday.
5. To Mary, Elizabeth, Lawrence came yesterday.
6. To Mary Elizabeth, Lawrence came yesterday.
7. To Mary Elizabeth Lawrence came a letter yesterday.

2. Punctuate each of the following sentences in two ways to convey two different meanings:

1. Helen said Mary you are mistaken
2. To Mary Conrad be all the glory
3. Dana the small boy cried I will go
4. May I go to the beach Louise asked Mabel
5. Mother whispered take Betty Leonard and Mabel to the park
6. The teacher replied Herbert Frank and George Hudson were absent
7. What do you think
   Here for no gold you'll find
   Victuals and drink

3. Punctuate such of the following sentences as require punctuation:

1. Mary admired Tennyson but Edith hated him
2. Mary admired Tennyson Edith hated him
3. Mary who was particularly interested in beauty of expression admired Tennyson while Edith who cared very little for beauty of any kind hated him
4. Bess swept and dusted the room
5. Bess swept the room and Mary dusted it
6. Bess swept the room before Mary dusted it
7. Bess swept Mary dusted

8. While Bess swept Mary dusted
9. Mary and Bess swept the room
10. Mary and Bess swept and dusted the room
11. Mary swept dusted and put the room in order while Mary sewed
12. Mary sewed mended and cooked while Bess put the room in order and swept and dusted

4. Supply punctuation, capitalization, and hyphenation as required in each of the following sentences:

1. base ball tennis and soccer require accuracy and skill
2. in english history we studied the magna charta and the bill of rights
3. have you seen sherwoods play there shall be no night
4. oh mother cried esther i received a in french and in arithmetic
5. last summer i read the biographies of the following madame curie queen victoria and helen keller
6. Mary went to south america mother to florida and aunt jane to the rockies
7. poland was invaded by germany in september 1939
8. boulder dam is in the black canyon of the colorado river in nevada
9. franklin delano roosevelt was the first president of the united states to be elected for a third term
10. we read about the crusades in *ivanhoe* by sir walter scott
11. we enjoy reading four poets millay frost robinson and sandburg
12. we enjoy reading millay frost robinson and sandburg
13. we enjoy reading four poets namely millay frost robinson and sandburg
14. have you any plan for the work if so what is it
15. have you any plan for the work if so state what it is
16. tell us whether you have any plan for the work and if so what it is
17. he asked whether we have any plan for the work and if so what it is
18. oh we exclaimed what shall we do where shall we go
19. all men who had been imprisoned for ten hours or more died
20. may asked do you know the author of these two quotations the child is father of the man and a thing of beauty is a joy for ever
21. stevenson in el dorado says an aspiration is a joy for ever a possession as solid as a landed estate a fortune which we can never exhaust and which gives us year by year a revenue of pleasurable activity to have many of these is to be spiritually rich

5. Tell, with reasons for your opinion, which of the following sentences are correctly punctuated, which incorrectly:

1. Will you please hand me the blotter.
2. She asked why I did the work?
3. "Where are you going," inquired the child?

4. "Have you read *Evangeline?*" asked the librarian.
5. "I have never read *Evangeline*, Mrs. Brown," I replied.
6. Solon was a lawgiver; Socrates, a philosopher, and Demosthenes, an orator.
7. Hannibal the great Carthaginian leader was finally defeated by the Romans.
8. The players then made their appearance—on their heads, the wreaths of glory; in their hands, their country's flag; around their waists, the bands of victory—marching to the martial air.
9. Then said he, "You must set the furrow straight and narrow, hold the plow firmly by the hand and keep the eyes steadily ahead as far as you can see."
10. How strange yet how appropriate the word *capricious* (which really means behaving like a goat) seems when applied to the behavior of a lively boy!

6. Rewrite each of the following, spacing the words properly, supplying the correct punctuation and capitalization, and making some words more important than others if the meaning seems to demand such differentiation:

1. letsgoovertojims
2. whosinthatoffice
3. thekittenslostitscollar
4. whoswhoandwhatswhat
5. scissorsispluralmolassessingular
6. wigwamisderivedfromindianherculeanfromgreekandteafromchinese
7. distinguishbetweenalacarteandtabledhoteandbetweenenglishandbritish
8. manyfirmshavetradenamessuggestedbymythologyforexample venushairnetsajaxtiresphenixinsurance
9. aboutmaybeusedforeverysenseofaroundbutnotviceversaarounddoes notmeannearlythereforearoundahundredisincorrectforaboutahundred

7. The following sentences contain quotations, some direct and some indirect. Those that contain direct quotations, express in the indirect form; those that contain indirect quotations, express in the direct form.

1. Finally he asked, "And what did you do then?"
2. "Oh, Mary," declared Helen in a cross tone, "I don't want to go to bed!"
3. He referred to the proverb that tells us that where there is no vision the people perish.
4. Mary said to Jean that she supposed that she would enter college in the fall.
5. "Catherine," asked Elizabeth, "what was it you meant when you said, 'You should have read the letter more carefully'?"

6. Paul asked Henry whether he believed in the proverb: "Faithful are the wounds of a friend."

7. Mr. Riley told Mr. Tulliver that there was no greater advantage he could give Tom than a good education.

8. When the teacher asked: "Who wrote *In Memoriam?*" the pupil hesitatingly replied: "I think Tennyson wrote the poem."

9. The father of John Scott told me that he began to save money when he was a mere child in kilts.

10. The speaker said that the adage: "Haste makes waste" is in particular need of observance and enforcement in large cities.

11. In one of his famous letters Lord Chesterfield writes: "A vulgar ordinary way of thinking, acting, or speaking implies a low education and a habit of low company."

12. George Saintsbury said: "The art of letter writing is a sort of mosaic or macedoine of nearly all departments of the general art of literature."

13. When the prosecuting attorney asked: "What did you do next with the $25,000 check?" the witness replied: "I remember distinctly handing it over to somebody, but I forget to whom."

8. Write the following lines of poetry in correct poetical form:

1. stand the grounds your own my braves will ye give it up to slaves

2. ill fares the land to hastening ills a prey where wealth accumulates and men decay

3. his life was gentle and the elements so mixed in him that nature might stand up and say to all the world this was a man

4. then conquer we must for our cause it is just and this be our motto in god is our trust

5. thou too sail on o ship of state sail on o union strong and great humanity with all its fears with all the hopes of future years is hanging breathless on thy fate

9. Capitalize, punctuate, and arrange the following letter parts correctly:

1. 301 lenox avenue new york city january 25 1942

2. 14 travers avenue los angeles california may 2 1942

3. william a douglas brockton mass dear sir

4. samuel evans company 3744 rokeby avenue pasadena california gentlemen

5. andrew f harte and sons 525 market street philadelphia penna dear sirs

6. very truly yours harold kunser secretary hk vr

7. cordially yours thomas r green for the marvin safe company inc trg cc tni

8. very truly yours walter baker and company limited per c m groots jr cmg hvb

9. yours very truly mason and hamlin company j d mclean manager trenton branch mcl ss

10. yours sincerely the american multigraph sales company l w jared general sales manager lwj 671

10. Write each of the following statements in correct form:

1. i was paid $11 125 by mr jay coe on march 11 1942

2. 53 yds of ribbon @ ten cts per yard come to five $s and 30 cents

3. the club has 1871 members and has eleven thousand eight hundred sixty five dollars in its treas

4. if 30 men work for you at three $ eighty seven cts per day what is their total wage at end of a 5 day wk

11. Explain the placement of the last two marks of punctuation in each of the following:

1. What is meant by "taxation without representation"?

2. He asked, "What is the meaning of taxation without representation?"

3. He asked, "What is the meaning of 'taxation without representation'?"

4. She was much disturbed when he said to her, "You must apply to your conduct the good old rule: 'It's never too late to mend.' "

5. As she wrote the troublesome little word wrongly for the tenth time, she wailed, "Ugh, that bothersome 'each'!"

ABBREVIATIONS

174. Abbreviations are used—

1. For the sake of brevity, economy, or convenience in technical and business statements, in tabulations, in footnotes, in listings, statistics, and stock quotations, as:

% *for* per cent	pp. *for* pages
acc't *for* account	recd. *for* received
acct. *for* account	Va. *for* Virginia

Strictly speaking, the first of these is a sign; the second, a contraction; the remaining ones are abbreviations. Do not use both the period and the apostrophe in writing the same term. Use *advt.* as the abbreviation of *advertisement,* and *adv't* as the contraction. The form *adv't.* is wrong (see page 240). A fractional abbreviation is one in which a diagonal line is used between two letters, as *b/l* for *bill of lading* and *l/c* for *letter of credit.* Letters in abbreviations follow the general rules of capitalization. Proper nouns, nouns in titles, and names are abbreviated by means of capitals; common nouns and lesser parts of speech, by small letters.

2. In compliance with accepted forms in letters and documents. Such abbreviations as *Mr., Mrs., Messrs., Dr., St.* (Saint) before names are so generally used that they would appear strange if written out. Similarly, *D.D., Ph.D., D.D.S., Esq., Sr., Jr.,* and numerous other abbreviations are used after names; *a.m.* and *p.m.,* denoting forenoon and afternoon; *B.C.* and *A.D.,* with numbers representing years; *no.* and *#,* before numbers.

Do not use *a.m.* and *p.m.* without preceding figures (or words). Say *They came in the forenoon* or *in the morning* or *before lunch,* not *They came in the a.m.* Say *They arrived at ten o'clock at night* or *at 10 p.m.,* not *They arrived in the late p.m.*

In ordinary, or "straight," writing it is better to spell out most titles and degrees (with the above exceptions); all names of persons and places; and the words *street* (not *st.*), *avenue* (not *ave.*), *for example* (not *e.g.*), *namely* (not *viz.*), *and* (not *&*), *that is* (not *i.e.*), *professor* (not *prof.*), *all right* (not *o.k.*), *and so forth* (not *etc.*).

3. Do not use *and* before *etc.* The full term is *et cetera*— Latin for and other things; *et* means and.

4. Do not use *&* in the name of a company unless it appears on the letterhead of the firm. In answering a business letter look to see whether you should address *Brandt and Charlton* or *Brandt & Charlton.*

5. Do not use *Mr., Mrs.,* or *Dr.,* or any other abbreviated title unless the name of a person follows.

6. Short monosyllables, dissyllables, and trisyllables are customarily written out rather than abbreviated. The following should always be written out: *March, April, May, June, July, Alaska, Guam, Hawaii, Idaho, Iowa, Maine, Ohio, Samoa, Texas, Utah.*

A period is usually placed at the end of an abbreviation as well as at the end of each individual part in a compound abbreviation. But governmental abbreviations are increasingly used without periods, as are many geographical ones. Present usage is inconsistent, if not confused, in this respect. Justify your use or omission of the period by consulting the dictionary. The following list of commonly used abbreviations is based mainly on that found in Webster's *New International Dictionary*.

COMMON ABBREVIATIONS

AAA—Agricultural Adjustment Administration
A.B.—Bachelor of Arts
A.D. (*Anno Domini*)—in the year of our Lord
ad lib. (*ad libitum*)—at pleasure
ad val. (*ad valorem*)—according to value
A.E.F.—American Expeditionary Forces
A.F.of L.—American Federation of Labor
A1—first class
Ala.—Alabama
A.L.A.—American Library Association
A.M., a.m. (*ante meridiem*)—before noon
A.M.—Master of Arts
anon.—anonymous
A.P., AP, Æ—Associated Press
Ariz.—Arizona
Ark.—Arkansas
assn.—association
asst.—assistant

att.—attention
atty.—attorney
A.V.—Authorized Version (of Bible)
Av., Ave.—Avenue
A.W.O.L.—absent without leave
B.A.—Bachelor of Arts
Bart.—Baronet
bbl.—barrel
B.C.—Before Christ
B.C.E.—Bachelor of Civil Engineering; Bachelor of Chemical Engineering
B.D.—Bachelor of Divinity
B.E., B/E, b.e.—bill of exchange
B.L.—Bachelor of Laws
B.P.O.E.—Benevolent and Protective Order of Elks
B.S.—Bachelor of Science
B.T.U., Btu—British thermal unit
B.W.I.—British West Indies
c., ca. (*circa*)—about
C.—Centigrade
Calif.—California
capt.—captain
CCC—Civilian Conservation Corps

cc., c.c.—cubic centimeters

C.E.—Church of England, Civil Engineer

cent.—centigrade

cf. (*confer*)—compare, consult

C.F.I., c.f.i.—cost, freight, insurance

C.I.O.—Congress of Industrial Organizations

C.I.F., c.i.f.—cost, insurance, freight

cm.—centimeter

c/o—care of

c.o.d.—cash on delivery

Col.—Colonel

Colo.—Colorado

comdr.—commander

Cong.—Congress

Conn.—Connecticut

Comr.—Commissioner

corp.—corporal, corporation

C.P.A.—Certified Public Accountant

C.S.—Christian Science, Civil Service

CST—Central Standard Time

cwt.—hundredweight

C.Z.—Canal Zone

d. (*denarius*)—pence

D—five hundred

D.A.R.—Daughters of the American Revolution

D.C.—District of Columbia

D.D.—Doctor of Divinity

D.D.S.—Doctor of Dental Surgery

Del.—Delaware

dist.—district

D. Litt.—Doctor of Literature or Letters

do.—ditto, the same

Dr.—Doctor

dr.—debtor

D.Sc.—Doctor of Science

D.S.C.—Distinguished Service Cross

D.S.M.—Distinguished Service Medal

D.S.O.—Distinguished Service Order

D.V. (*Deo volente*)—God willing

EDT—Eastern Daylight Time

E.E.—Electrical Engineer

e.g. (*exempli gratia*)—for example

8vo—octavo

enc., encl.—enclosed

ENE—east-northeast

ESE—east-southeast

Esq., Esqr.—esquire

EST—Eastern Standard Time

et al. (*et alii, aliae*)—and others

et seq. (*et sequentes, sequentia*)—and following, what follows

F.—Fahrenheit

f.—following (page)

Fahr.—Fahrenheit

F.&A.M.—Free and Accepted Masons

FBI—Federal Bureau of Investigation

ff.—following (pages)

FHA—Federal Housing Administration

Fla.—Florida

f.o.b.—free on board

4to—quarto

FSA—Farm Security Administration

ft.-lb.—foot-pound

FTC—Federal Trade Commission

Ga.—Georgia

G.A.R.—Grand Army of the Republic

Gen.—General

G.H.Q.—General Headquarters

gm.—gram

G.O.P.—Grand Old Party

Gov., gov.—Governor

gr.—grain, gram, gross

hdqrs.—headquarters

H.E.—His Excellency
hhd.—hogshead
H.I.H.—His or Her Imperial Highness
H.I.M.—His or Her Imperial Majesty
H.M.—His or Her Majesty
H.M.S.—His or Her Majesty's Ship or Service
HOLC—Home Owners' Loan Corporation
h.p.—horse power
H.R.—House of Representatives
H.R.H.—His or Her Royal Highness
ib., ibid. (*ibidem*)—in the same place
ICC—Interstate Commerce Commission
id. (*idem*)—the same
i.e. (*id est*)—that is
IHS, I.H.S. (*Jesus Hominum Salvator*)—Jesus, Saviour of Men
Ill.—Illinois
inc.—incorporated
incl.—inclusive, inclosure
Ind.—Indiana
I.N.R.I. (*Jesus Nazarenus, Rex Judaeorum*)—Jesus of Nazareth, King of the Jews
Inst.—institute, institution
inst. (instant)—in the present month
I.O.O.F.—Independent Order of Odd Fellows
IOU—I owe you
I.Q.—intelligence quotient
ital.—italics
I.W.W.—Industrial Workers of the World
J.D.—Doctor of Laws
J.P.—Justice of the Peace
Jr., jr., jun.—junior
Kans.—Kansas

K.B.—Knight of the Bath
K.C.—Knights of Columbus
K.C.B.—Knight Commander of the Bath
K.C.M.G.—Knight Commander of the Order of St. Michael and St. George
K.C.V.O.—Knight Commander of the Victorian Order
kg.—kilogram
K.G.—Knight of the Garter
km.—kilometer
K. of C.—Knights of Columbus
K. of P.—Knights of Pythias
Ky.—Kentucky
£, L., l.—pound sterling
La.—Louisiana
lat.—latitude
l.c.—lower case, or small letter
Lieut., Lt.—lieutenant
Lit.D.—Doctor of Literature
LL.B.—Bachelor of Laws
LL.D.—Doctor of Laws
loc. cit. (*loco citato*)—in the place cited
lon., long.—longitude
ltd.—limited
M—one thousand
m. (*meridies*)—noon
M., M—Monsieur
M.A.—Master of Arts
Maj.—major
Mass.—Massachusetts
M.C.—Member of Congress
Md.—Maryland
M.D.—Medical Doctor
M.E.—Methodist Episcopal, Mechanical or Mining Engineer
Messrs., Messrs—Gentlemen
mfd., mfg., mfr.— manufactured, manufacturing, manufacturer
Mgr.—Monsignor, manager
Mich.—Michigan

min.—minute
Minn.—Minnesota
Miss.—Mississippi
Mlle., Mlle—Mademoiselle
mm.—millimeter(s)
MM., MM—Messieurs
Mme., Mme—Madame
Mo.—Missouri
Mont.—Montana
M.P.—Member of Parliament, Military Police
mph., m.p.h.—miles per hour
MS., ms.—manuscript
Msgr.—Monsignor
Mt., mt.—mount, mountain
N.B., n.b. (*nota bene*)—note well
N.C.—North Carolina
N.Dak.—North Dakota
NE, N.E., ne.—northeast
N.E.A.—National Education Association
Nebr.—Nebraska
Nev.—Nevada
N.G.—National Guard
N.H.—New Hampshire
N.J.—New Jersey
N.Lat.—north latitude
NLRB—National Labor Relations Board
N.Mex.—New Mexico
NNE—north-northeast
NNW—north-northwest
No.—north
No., no. (*numero*)—number
N.S.—New Style (calendar), Nova Scotia
N.T.—New Testament
N.Y.—New York
NYA—National Youth Administration
N.Y.C.—New York City
ob. (*obit*)—died
O.K., OK—correct, satisfactory
Okla.—Oklahoma

OPM—Office of Production Management
op. cit. (*opere citato*)—in the work cited
Oreg., Ore.—Oregon
O.S.—Old Style (calendar)
O.T.—Old Testament
oz.—ounce
Pa.—Pennsylvania
par.—paragraph, parallel
P.E.—Protestant Episcopal
Penna.—Pennsylvania
pfd.—preferred
Ph.B.—Bachelor of Philosophy
Ph.D.—Doctor of Philosophy
Ph.G.—Graduate in Pharmacy
P.I.—Philippine Islands
pk.—peck
P.M.—postmaster
P.M., p.m. (*post meridiem*)—afternoon
P.O., p.o.—post office, postal order
P.P., p.p.—parcel post
P.R.—Puerto Rico
pro tem (*pro tempore*)—for the time
prox. (*proximo*)—next month
P.S., p.s.(*post scriptum*)—postscript; P.SS.—postscripts
pseud.—pseudonym
PST—Pacific Standard Time
pt.—pint, point
P.T.A.—Parent-Teachers' Association
Pvt.—Private
q.e.d. (*quod erat demonstrandum*)—which was to be proved
Q.M.C., QMC—Quartermaster Corps
qr.—quarter, quire
qt.—quart
q.v. (*quod vide*)—which see
R.A.—Regular Army, Royal Academy
R.A.F.—Royal Air Force

R.C.—Roman Catholic
Rev.—Reverend
RFC—Reconstruction Finance Corporation
R.F.D.—Rural Free Delivery
R.I.—Rhode Island
R.I.P. (*requiescat in pace*)—Rest in peace
R.N.—registered nurse, Royal Navy
ROTC—Reserve Officers' Training Corps
r.p.m.—revolutions per minute
R.P.O.—Railway Post Office
R.R.—railroad
R.S.V.P. (*Répondez s'il vous plaît*)—please reply
R.V.—Revised Version (of Bible)
Ry.—railway
S.A.R.—Sons of the American Revolution
sc., scil. (*scilicet*)—to wit, namely
S.C.—South Carolina
S.Dak.—South Dakota
SE, S.E., s.e.—southeast
SEC—Securities and Exchange Commission
sec.—second, secretary
Sen.—Senator
seq., seqq. (*sequentia*)—next, following
Sgt., serg., sergt.—sergeant
sh., s.—shilling
S.J.—Society of Jesus
S.Lat.—South Latitude
So.—south
S O S—suspend other servce (wireless distress call at sea), "save our ship"
S.P.C.A.—Society for the Prevention of Cruelty to Animals
S.P.C.C.—Society for the Prevention of Cruelty to Children
sp.gr.—specific gravity
Sr., sr.—senior

SRO—standing room only
S.S., SS—steamship (before name)
SSE—south-southeast
SSW—south-southwest
St.—Saint, Strait, Street
S.W., SW, s.w.—southwest
Tenn.—Tennessee
T.H.—Territory of Hawaii
TNT, T.N.T.—trinitrotoluene, trinitrotoluol
TVA—Tennessee Valley Authority
12mo.—duodecimo
u.c.—upper case, capital letters
ult., ulto. (*ultimo*)—last month
U.P.—United Press
U.S.—United States
U.S.A.—United States of America
U.S.N.—United States Navy
U.S.N.G.—United States National Guard
U.S.S.—United States Ship or Steamer
U.S.S.R., USSR—Union of Soviet Socialist Republics
Va.—Virginia
viz. (*videlicet*)—namely, to wit
V.P.—Vice-President
vs., v. (*versus*)—against, opposed
Vt.—Vermont
Wash.—Washington
W.C.T.U.—Women's Christian Temperance Union
Wis.—Wisconsin
WNW—west-northwest
WPA—Work Projects Administration
WSW—west-southwest
W.Va.—West Virginia
Wyo.—Wyoming
X.D., x.d., x.div.—ex-dividend
Y.M.C.A.—Young Men's Christian Association

Y.M.H.A.—Young Men's Hebrew
Association
Y.P.S.C.E.—Young People's
Society of Christian Endeavor

Y.W.C.A.—Young Women's
Christian Association
Y.W.H.A.—Young Women's
Hebrew Association

EXERCISE

Write the following expressions correctly:

1. I'll be there early in the p.m.
2. Pres. T. Roosevelt was a memorable character.
3. He brought us food, clothing, & so on.
4. Oh to be in Eng. now that Apr.'s there!
5. The Mister and the Missis arrived too late.
6. Both the Dr. and the Col. were on time.
7. Does he live on a st. or an ave.?
8. Quite a no. refused to go, inc. both of us.
9. Dear S'r, I am Respy. yrs.
10. Up in Bangor, Me., I saw Thos., Saml., Jno., and etc.

NUMBERS

175. Numbers may be expressed either in words or in figures. In so-called straight composition they should generally be written out; in commercial paper they should be expressed by figures.

176. Write as words—

1. Numbers which can be expressed in one or two words, as *twenty-one years old.*

2. Numbers below 100 when they appear singly.

3. Round numbers, as *five hundred, twelve hundred* (not *one thousand two hundred*).

4. Amounts of money smaller than one dollar, as *sixty-five cents.*

5. Numbers of centuries and decades, as *the nineties of the nineteenth century.*

177. Use figures for—

1. Numbers larger than 100, as *143* and *3157*.

2. Dates, as *April 18, 1775* (not *April 18th, 1775*). Do not use *d, nd, rd, st,* or *th* after numbers of any kind.

3. House numbers as *129 Lenox Avenue*. But you may spell out the street numbers, as *35 East Twenty-fifth Street*. On an envelope 35 East 25 Street is the style increasingly used.

4. Divisions of a written work or of a document, such as page, chapter, article, section, canto, or stanza numbers, as *Chapter 3, page 86;* for volume, part, and chapter numbers Roman numerals are often preferred, as *Volume II, Part I, Chapter III.*

5. Sums of money larger than one dollar, as $12.49, $143. Do not write *$143.00* or *.55* except in tabulations.

6. Time when it is expressed with a. m. and p. m. as *12:15* p. m. But *at twelve-fifteen* is correct.

7. Per cent, as *12 per cent.*

178. Numbers appearing close together, regardless of their size, should be in the same style, preferably in figures, as:

> There were 181 applicants, only 27 of whom were high-school graduates, in spite of the fact that the 347 circulars we mailed stated that only graduates would be eligible.

179. Never use figures at the beginning of a sentence. *Nineteen hundred thirty-nine was the first year of World War II* is correct. To avoid spelling out an awkward number reconstruct the sentence so that the number will not come at the beginning.

180. Do not use consecutively figures of two distinct categories, as *I received $1428.21 4 times a year* for *I received $1428.21 four times a year.* In the date line of a letter a comma prevents figures' running together, as *July 4, 1776.*

EXERCISE

Write the following correctly:

1. At 12 o'clock I received 7 letters.

2. She bought 1 morning paper, 2 afternoon papers, and 3 magazines.

3. The 3rd on the right is holding 8 balloons in 1 hand.

4. I paid $.50 for it, and only yesterday it was marked $1.00.

5. 1913 was the year of his birth; he now resides at one thousand three hundred forty-seven Euclid Avenue.

6. We have three hundred girls in the school, all of whom assemble daily at 9.45 for prayers.

7. On the 13th page you will find the reference to section seven hundred and eighty-one in the 2nd book of the encyclopedia.

8. The land brought one thousand one hundred sixteen dollars an acre, the price for the 20 acres totaling twenty-two thousand three hundred twenty dollars.

9. At eight o'clock Thursday evening—February eighteenth 1945—I am invited to preside at a dinner given for the nine hundred ninety-one employes from the 30 shops of the firm.

10. My traveling expenses were as follows: fifty dollars for carfare; $12.00 for food; $.10 daily for reading matter (absence of 6 days makes this total $.60); general incidental expenses five dollars and twenty-nine cents. The total is sixty-seven dollars and eighty-nine cents.

ITALICS

181. Italic, in printing, is the name for slanting type. Italics are used for emphasis and other purposes (see below). In hand-written and typewritten matter such purposes are served by underscoring.

182. Italics are used—

1. To distinguish titles of books, periodicals, newspapers, manuscripts, and the like, as:

A Tale of Two Cities by Charles Dickens
The New York Times
The Saturday Evening Post

The article is capitalized when it is a part of the title. Observation supplies the only rule in this connection. Note:

New York Herald Tribune and *The New York Times*
The Saturday Review of Literature and *Time*

2. To distinguish foreign terms not yet accepted as English, as:

> He has always been the *persona non grata* in the field.
> She has *savoir-faire*.

It is better to use in English writing and speaking only such foreign terms as are generally familiar or such as have no exact equivalent in English.

3. To distinguish the names of ships, as:

> The *Normandie* sails tonight.

4. To distinguish a word spoken of as a word, and thus removed from context, as:

> This *and* belongs where that *but* is.

Quotation marks are sometimes used instead of italics.

5. To emphasize a word or an expression, as:

> Please come *promptly*.

If italics are overused, emphasis will not be achieved.

OUTLINING

183. Outlining

1. List all the points you can think of (or find by means of research) when you plan or outline a composition. Then assort them so that you have major, or important, points and minor points belonging to each major one.

2. Write the major points far enough apart to accommodate the minor points belonging under each. Order the major points by means of roman numerals; the minor ones by means of capital letters; thus:

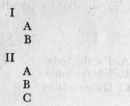

```
I
   A
   B
II
   A
   B
   C
```

The following shows notation for additional degrees of minor points:

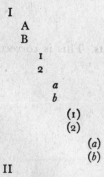

```
I
   A
   B
      1
      2
         a
         b
            (1)
            (2)
               (a)
               (b)
II
```

Here are represented five descending degrees of subordinating topics. Rarely are more required. Indent as here indicated; topics of equal value must start from the same margin.

Each notation symbol (unless parenthetical) may be followed by a period, and the statement following it should be likewise punctuated. But periods may be omitted after these symbols and after the statements that follow them.

3. Use hanging or blocked **margining** for all points that run to more than one line. These are right:

I. The story of intercollegiate football falls into four clearly marked divisions.
I. The story of intercollegiate football falls into four clearly marked divisions.

This is less desirable:

I. The story of intercollegiate football falls into four clearly marked divisions.

4. Aim to express co-ordinate points in similar or parallel form, as:

I. Recreation is important
  A. Bodily
  B. Mentally   *or*
  C. Socially

A. For the body
B. For the mind
C. For sociability

This is not good:

I. Recreation is important
  A. Body
  B. For the mind
  C. It is also important socially.

5. Do not confuse major and minor points. This is correct:

I. Characteristics of the hero
  A. Courage
  B. Unselfishness
  C. Alertness
  D. Endurance

This is wrong:

I. Characteristics of the hero
  A. Courage
  B. Unselfishness
  C. Alertness
II. The hero must also have ability to endure.

6. Do not include so many points in an outline that one repeats or overlaps another. If, in the above, fearlessness and self-sacrifice were added, the one would repeat courage, and the other unselfishness.

7. Do not use the term *and so forth* or *etc.* in an outline. The purpose of outlining is to indicate definitely what is to be spoken or written about, but *and so forth* is always vague. Similarly such words as *effects, results, outcome,* especially at the end of an outline, are to be avoided; as a rule, they are not sufficiently specific to be of value in a point-by-point statement of what constitutes a table of contents. And an outline is similar to a table of contents.

184. **A running outline** is one in which words and phrases are run end to end, line by line, dashes and different type faces being used to denote relative importance of points; thus:

Marks—high—low—medium — *their importance*—class standing—promotion — honors — *their unimportance* — high-mark failures — low-mark successes—*marks and money*—neither an ideal standard—just something to go by—both may be made to work well.

185. **A topical outline** is one in which points are set down in columns. In expository and descriptive outlines the points are preferably expressed by nouns and phrases, thus:

   I. Marks
     A. High marks
     B. Low marks
     C. Medium marks

  II. Importance of marks
     A. Class standing
     B. Grade promotions
     C. Various honors

 III. Unimportance of marks
     A. High-mark failures
     B. Low-mark successes

 IV. Marks and money
     A. Not ideal
     B. Mere guides or approximates
     C. Both workable

186. A sentence outline is one in which points are set down in complete sentences. This style of outlining is used primarily in expository and narrative composition, thus:

   I. Marks or class ratings are essential in the educational process.
     A. High marks establish scholarship standards.
     B. Low marks invite analyses and adjustments.
     C. Medium marks may or may not denote "the wholesome average."

   II. Marks are important.
     A. They key individual and class-group standing.
     B. They decide progress and promotion.
     C. They are the basis of most honor awards.

   III. Marks may be quite unimportant as prophecy.
     A. Many high-standing students fail in later life.
     B. Many low-standing students succeed in later life.

   IV. Marks are to the educational process very much what money is to the economic process.
     A. Neither is a completely satisfactory medium.
     B. Each is a guide or an approximate to an ideal.
     C. Both may be made to work in the vast majority of cases.

Note that in a narrative outline the sentence form yields progress and action provided the verbs are well selected, thus:

   I. He ran madly for the train.
     A. He tripped and fell.
     B. He scrambled up with difficulty.

   II. He dashed up to the ticket window.
     A. He elbowed into line.
     B. He dropped his change.

   III. He jumped the last car of the wrong train.

Any part of speech may be used as the initial term in stating points provided the statements are kept consistent with one another, thus:

    I. Running madly   I. Out of the house
    II. Dashing wildly   II. Down to the station
   III. Jumping blindly   III. On the wrong train

187. A **run-in outline** is one in which major points read in consecutive construction with minor points, and perhaps minor points with minor points. This form of outline is used chiefly in the briefing of arguments; thus:

> I. This policy has proved unfair to the community as well as to labor, for
>   A. men have been thrown out of work, and
>   B. families have thus been obliged to modify buying habits.

In this type of outline the first word in dependent points is preferably not capitalized.

188. A descriptive outline, as a rule, falls naturally into *point of view, general view, detailed view, the "framed picture"* or *total impression.* But do not use these terms unless the picture is logically divisible into such parts. On the other hand, exposition and argument fall naturally into the three main divisions of *introduction, discussion* or *development,* and *conclusion.* But they do not always do so, and it is a mistake to think that every outline must follow such cut-and-dried partitioning. Often no point of view is required or possible in writing a description; introductory and conclusive details may be superfluous in exposition and argument.

EXERCISES

1. Under the general title *Four Roads to Culture* assemble the following mixed points in topical outline form: books, architecture, reading, concerts, statesmen, radio, art, friends, opera, painting, papers, writers, sculpture, lecturers, orchestras, other notables, theater, teachers, magazines, other documents, conversation, music.

2. Criticize the following outline on *Home Economics as a Vocation.* Then rewrite it consistently.

> I. Introduction
>   A It has great promise.
>   1. Now in infancy
>   2. It is important to home and to community

II. Discussion

    A It is peculiarly a woman's field

    B Various fields into which it leads

        1. One may teach it.

        2. Research

        3. It has social-service values.

        4. Leads to business

        (*a*) Restaurants, cafeterias, etc.

        (*b*) Dietetics is more and more important.

        (*c*) Advisers.

        (*d*) Clothing, publications, and the like.

III. Growing importance

    A In business

    B It is taught in all vocational schools and colleges.

    C Qualifications

        1. Knowledge of home life

        2. You must have training and apprenticeship.

IV Conclusion

    A What are the financial rewards?

        1. They are comparable to others open to women.

        2. Better than ordinary business occupations, such as stenography, store service, etc.

PARAGRAPHING

189. A paragraph is a group of sentences pertaining to a single phase of thought. Paragraphs are divisions and subdivisions of a whole composition and are related to the composition much as the clauses in a compound or a complex sentence are related to the whole sentence.

If, for instance, an explanation is to be written on *Trimming a Hat,* the following partitioning, or paragraphing, of the subject will probably be helpful to both writer and reader:

1. Gathering materials
2. Arranging and pinning materials to frame
3. Sewing and finishing hat

Likewise, the subject *Engine Coughing* may be advantageously divided into paragraphs as follows:

1. Sounds of engine "coughing"
2. Causes of engine "coughing"
3. How to stop it immediately
4. How to prevent it in the future

190. A paragraph is usually indicated to the eye by means of the indention of the first line. Sometimes, especially in business composition, paragraphs are not indented but are separated by spacing. This style is known as **blocked.** Again, the first line of a paragraph may be extended to the left of the remaining lines. This style of paragraphing is called **extended** or **hanging.** Most of the paragraphs in this book are indented; on page 237 some paragraphs are blocked; others are extended.

191. The **length** of a paragraph is determined by the thought. However, paragraphs should be neither too short nor too long. A series of short paragraphs makes a composition seem choppy and careless; a series of long ones makes it ponderous and tiresome. Often several short paragraphs may be reconstructed into one good long paragraph, and an overlong paragraph may be divided into two or more satisfactory short paragraphs.

1. The units of direct, or conversational, discourse are always written in separate paragraphs, regardless of their length, thus:

> "Were you present at the meeting?" asked the attorney.
> "Yes," replied the witness.
> "Did you vote?"
> "No."
> "Why not?"
> The witness refused to answer.

2. Short paragraphs are effective in creating a quick, vigorous impression. They make for emphasis when they appear among long paragraphs or at the end of a composition. Observe the following:

> Now she would have nothing to do with any of them. They had treated her too badly, and she could never forget, no matter how hard she tried or how wrong she knew it to be to harbor bad feeling. Those terrible days of her apprenticeship—how vividly they all came back to her now! The awful insults she had been obliged to endure—how she still felt them! No, sir! She would do her job as well as she could—as well as it could be done. After that—she was a stranger to the shop and to everybody in it.
> That's how Frances was.

3. The short paragraphs of the Bible, like those of codes and credos, have an individuality and a memorableness that long paragraphs can rarely have.

4. In business correspondence short paragraphs are preferred because they are easy to read and are terse in style.

192. The **average paragraph** consists of from eight to twelve sentences or of about two hundred fifty words. The length may be controlled by planning the distribution of the material. Note the following specifications for a paragraph dealing with an incident:

> *First sentence*—Explain what the incident is (connected with fire, flood, storm, runaway, motor crash?).
> *Second and third sentences*—Explain its cause.

Next four or five sentences—Elaborate details of the incident, such as persons involved, casualties, feeling aroused, arrests, and the like.

Last two or three sentences—Tell what the consequences of the incident have been (investigations, revision of regulations, re-licensing, insurance adjustments, check-up of personnel, reorganization of company).

193. The subject of a paragraph is usually found in a sentence at or near the beginning. This sentence is called the **topic sentence.** If the subject is expressed in the form of a conclusion or summary at the end, the sentence is called a **summary sentence.** Some paragraphs have both a topic and a summary sentence; others have neither, the topic being obvious from the content.

194. A paragraph with either a topic or a summary sentence is **formal**; a paragraph without such sentences is **informal.**

In the following formal paragraph the first sentence is the topic sentence:

> The person of this illustrious old gentleman was formed and proportioned, as though it had been moulded by the hands of some cunning Dutch statuary, as a model of majesty and lordly grandeur. He was exactly five feet six inches in height, and six feet five inches in circumference. His head was a perfect sphere, and of such stupendous dimensions, that dame Nature, with all her sex's ingenuity, would have been puzzled to construct a neck capable of supporting it; wherefore she wisely declined the attempt, and settled it firmly on the top of his backbone, just between the shoulders. His body was oblong and particularly capacious at bottom; which was wisely ordered by Providence, seeing that he was a man of sedentary habits, and very averse to the idle labor of walking. His legs were short, but sturdy in proportion to the weight they had to sustain; so that when erect he had not a little the appearance of a beer-barrel on skids. His face, that infallible index of the mind, presented a vast expanse, unfurrowed by any of those lines and angles which disfigure the human countenance with what is termed expression. Two small grey eyes twinkled feebly in the midst, like two stars of lesser magnitude in a hazy firmament; and his full-fed cheeks, which seemed to have taken toll of everything that went into his mouth, were curiously mottled and streaked with dusky red, like a spitzenberg apple.
>
> Washington Irving, *Wouter van Twiller*

In the following paragraph the topic, though not expressed, is easily derived from the content: *The Make-up of Our Present English Language.* *inductive*

> At court, and in the castles of the great nobles, where the pomp and state of a court were emulated, Norman-French was the only language employed; in courts of law the pleadings and judgements were delivered in the same tongue. In short, French was the language of honour, of chivalry, and even of justice; while the far more manly and expressive Anglo-Saxon was abandoned to the use of rustics and hinds, who knew no other. Still, however, the necessary intercourse between the lords of the soil and those oppressed inferior beings by whom that soil was cultivated occasioned the gradual formation of a dialect compounded betwixt the French and the Anglo-Saxon, in which they could render themselves mutually intelligible to each other; and from this necessity arose by degrees the structure of our present English language, in which the speech of the victors and the vanquished have been so happily blended together, and which has since been so richly improved by importations from the classical languages, and from those spoken by the southern nations of Europe.
>
> Walter Scott, *Ivanhoe*

In the formal paragraph below, the last sentence is the summary sentence:

> The tremendous sea itself, when I could find sufficient pause to look at it, in the agitation of the blinding wind, the flying stones and sand, and the awful noise, confounded me. As the high watery walls came rolling in, and, at their highest, tumbled into surf, they looked as if the least would engulf the town. As the receding wave swept back with a hoarse roar, it seemed to scoop out deep caves in the beach, as if its purpose were to undermine the earth. When some white-headed billows thundered on, and dashed themselves to pieces before they reached the land, every fragment of the late whole seemed possessed by the full might of its wrath, rushing to be gathered to the composition of another monster. Undulating hills were changed to valleys, undulating valleys (with a solitary storm-bird sometimes skimming through them) were lifted up to hills; masses of water shivered and shook the beach with a booming sound; every shape tumultuously rolled on, as soon as made, to change its shape and place, and beat another shape and place

away; the ideal shore on the horizon, with its towers and buildings, rose and fell; the clouds flew fast and thick; I seemed to see a rending and upheaving of all nature.

Charles Dickens, *David Copperfield*

195. Just as there may be a topic sentence to introduce a paragraph and a summary sentence to conclude it, so there may be a **topic paragraph** or a **summary paragraph,** or both, to a whole composition. Such paragraphs are usually short. A topic paragraph may set forth the divisions and subdivisions in the treatment of a subject, the purpose in writing, the event that occasioned the writing, and the like. A summary paragraph may enumerate the points covered or the propositions proved or the effects of a course advocated. Where the dots appear below, between the topic paragraph and the summary paragraph, there are probably four paragraphs omitted, one for each of the four reasons: more than four in case any of the reasons cannot be adequately treated in a single paragraph, fewer than four in case two or more of the reasons are so closely related as to permit of treatment in a single paragraph.

> Among the many reasons why every high-school graduate should know how to drive a car, the four explained below are urged by the authorities as paramount.
>
> .   .   .   .
>
> Certainly there can be no successful refutation of this reasoning. The sooner it is made the basis of legislative enactment, the safer will both pedestrian and vehicular traffic be made on our streets and highways.

196. A good paragraph must have **unity.** This is achieved by sticking to the subject, which may be announced in a topic sentence. A student should not feel that he must write a topic sentence for each paragraph. Such practice might make his style mechanical or stilted. But he must remember to keep clearly in mind what his subject is and must hold to that subject throughout the paragraph. If the content of a paragraph cannot be reduced to a few covering words, the paragraph lacks unity. Note in the paragraph from *David Copperfield* on page

304 how every sentence pertains to and drives home the single idea of the *confusion of the sea*—"the awful noise confounded me" . . . "a rending and upheaving of all nature." There is not a sentence in the paragraph that does not enforce this idea.

197. A paragraph must also have **coherence.** This is achieved by arranging the sentences in logical order, by placing the words so that the thought relationships in succeeding sentences are close and obvious, by making pronominal reference natural and unmistakable, and by using accurate connectives for transition. Observe the following connecting words and phrases:

> *Additive:* again, also, and, and then, besides, finally, further, furthermore, in addition, in like manner, likewise, moreover, too, secondly, thirdly, fourthly
>
> *Comparative:* in like manner, in the same way, likewise, similarly, at the same time
>
> *Consequential:* accordingly, after all, as a consequence, as a result, at last, consequently, finally, hence, in conclusion, in fine, later, so, therefore, thereafter, thereupon, thus
>
> *Contrasting:* but, conversely, however, nevertheless, notwithstanding, on the contrary, on the one hand, on the other hand, rather, still, whereas, yet
>
> *Illustrative:* for example, for instance, in this way, namely, that is, to illustrate, thus
>
> *Repetitive:* as has been said, in fact, indeed, in fine, in other words, to recapitulate, to repeat

Now note how the italicized words in the following paragraph seal and ease connections, carrying the thought along from one sentence and clause to another without shock or abruptness. These "smoothing" transition terms are in the main pronouns and conjunctions, but other parts of speech may occasionally serve the same purpose.

> *As you know*, the trade of Europe from the West Coast of America around the Horn is carried by large sailing vessels (the passage being too long for steamships without coaling stations). One day America starts in earnest to cut the Panama Canal. *Forthwith* the provident British Shipowner begins to get quit of *these* sailing vessels: noble three- and four-masters, almost all Clyde-built. He sells *them* to Italian firms. Why to Italian firms? *Because* these ships have considerable draught and are built of iron. *Their* draught

unfits them for general coasting trade; *they* could not begin to navigate the Baltic, for instance. *Now* Italy has deep-water harbours. *But* the Genoese firms (I am told) buy *these* ships for the second reason, that they are of iron; *because* while the Italian Government lays a crippling duty on ordinary iron, broken-up ship-iron may enter free. *So*, after a coastwise voyage or two, it pays to rip *their* plates out, pass them under the rollers, and re-issue them for new iron; *and thus* for a few months these beautiful things that used to wing it home, five months without sighting land, and anchor under my garden, eke out a new brief traffic until the last of them shall be towed to the breaker's yard. *Even* in such unnoticed ways grew, thrived, passed, died, the commercial glories of Venice, Spain, Holland.

Sir Arthur T. Quiller-Couch, *The Commerce of Thought*[1]

198. Besides unity and coherence a paragraph should have **emphasis**. As in sentences, the emphatic positions are the beginning and the end. The most important points should therefore appear in the first one or two sentences and in the last one or two sentences. The sentences should be apportioned according to the importance of the elements of the thought. Other means of obtaining emphasis are judicious repetition (page 205), the occasional inversion or transposition of sentence parts (page 224), variation in the openings of sentences and paragraphs (page 224), and use of varied sentence constructions (page 224).

199. Competent writers do not, of course, follow any cut-and-dried pattern in developing a paragraph thought. Rather, they "turn their paragraphs" with an ease and facility bred of long and arduous practice. Good paragraphing comes as natural to them as correct fingering comes to an expert pianist. Students, however, will best attain unity, coherence, and emphasis in their paragraphs by following a particular method. There are several methods of **developing a paragraph**:

1. By details, as in the passage from *Wouter van Twiller* on page 303. This is the deductive method, beginning with a general statement which is proved by following details.

2. By details leading to a conclusion, as illustrated by the

---

[1] From *Studies in Literature*, by Arthur Quiller-Couch. Courtesy of G. P. Putnam's Sons.

passage from *Ivanhoe* on page 304. This is the inductive method, beginning with the particular and leading to the general.

3. By illustrative incident, as in the selection from *David Copperfield* on page 304.

4. By contrast, as in the following passage:

> The human species, according to the best theory I can form of it, is composed of two distinct races, *the men who borrow* and *the men who lend*. To these two original diversities may be reduced all those impertinent classifications of Gothic and Celtic tribes, white men, black men, red men. All the dwellers upon earth, "Parthians, and Medes, and Elamites," flock hither, and do naturally fall in with one or other of these primary distinctions. The infinite superiority of the former, which I choose to designate as the *great race*, is discernible in their figure, port, and a certain instinctive sovereignty. The latter are born degraded. "He shall serve his brethren." There is something in the air of one of this cast, lean and suspicious; contrasting with the open, trusting, generous manner of the other.
>
> Charles Lamb, *The Two Races of Men*

5. By comparison, as in this selection:

> Mountains are to the rest of the body of the earth what violent muscular action is to the body of man. The muscles and tendons of its anatomy are, in the mountain, brought out with fierce and convulsive energy, full of expression, passion, and strength; the plains and the lower hills are the repose and the effortless motion of the frame, when its muscles lie dormant and concealed beneath the lines of its beauty, yet ruling those lines in their every undulation. This, then, is the first grand principle of the truth of the earth. The spirit of the hills is action; that of the lowlands, repose; and between these there is to be found every variety of motion and of rest; from the inactive plain, sleeping like the firmament, with cities for stars, to the fiery peaks, which, with heaving bosoms and exulting limbs, with the clouds drifting like hair from their bright foreheads, lift up their Titan hands to Heaven, saying, "I live forever!"
>
> John Ruskin, *Modern Painters*

6. By oratorical devices of exclamation and interrogation, as here:

> It is vain, sir, to extenuate the matter. Gentlemen may cry Peace, Peace—but there is no peace. The war is actually begun!

The next gale that sweeps from the north will bring to our ears the clash of resounding arms! Our brethren are already in the field! Why stand we here idle? What is it that gentlemen wish? What would they have? Is life so dear, or peace so sweet, as to be purchased at the price of chains and slavery? Forbid it, Almighty God! I know not what course others may take; but as for me, give me liberty or give me death!

Patrick Henry, *Speech in the Virginia Convention*, March 23, 1775

7. By repetition, as in the following:

Throughout the long day Fritz experienced over and over again his embarrassment—his befuddlement—not only in trying to speak our unbelievable language but in "trying to hear" it as well. He heard Jameson say, for instance, that a *tip* on the market had netted a good two-thousand-dollar profit that very day. Afterward, his host said that he would *tip* the waiter, and they would go. And just as they were rising to do so, Harris knocked over a goblet and spilled some wine on the cloth, apologizing with the remark that he had no idea that the table would *tip* so easily. On the way home, someone said that So-and-so's business was in the *red;* someone else expressed the regret that his son had turned *red;* and another spoke of *red* roses in a florist's window. The word *green* repeated the experience, for dear old Fritz. Brown said he had to hurry back to the office because he had taken on a *green* hand and his old employes were *green* with jealousy toward him. But he promised to meet Jameson on the putting-*green* next Saturday. Again, there was a remark about a sixth *inning* and a Sunday *outing*, and Fritz wondered whether the two words could be antonyms. Brown strained his eyes forward and asked who it was that he saw in the *offing*, and Fritz immediately began to wonder about *onning*. He was very much confused and bewildered about it all—this strange English tongue with its puzzling contradictions and incomprehensible diction.

8. By enumerating effects, as in the following:

Travel by ———— coaches and when your journey's done you'll have the delightful feeling of "no regrets." You will not "enjoy" a single moment of discomfort, for our streamlined, intercity coaches provide every modern convenience for the traveler. What's even more important, you will always feel safe—the latest improved safety devices make our vehicles just about accident-proof. Too, you will always have the satisfaction of being on time; ———— coaches are notable for punctuality—they start on time and they ARRIVE on time. You will also like the stop-off privileges, the round-trip privileges, the special multi-trip commuting privileges offered by ——— coaches, for with all their schedule precision these services are to a high degree go-as-you-please services. Again, you will be just as clean when you arrive at your destination as you were when you started—just as clean as you would be at the end of a train trip of equal distance—cleaner perhaps. The reason why: A new dust-proof ventilating system has recently been installed in all coaches. And most important of all—consider ——— coach travel in relation to your pocketbook: For short trips as well as long ones, these coaches are cheaper and *cheaper* and CHEAPER than any other means of conveyance between two geographical points—not excepting, of course, your own private car.

It will be observed that more than one method of development may be used in a single paragraph provided no violation of logic and coherence results. The above paragraph by Scott (page 304), for instance, combines contrast with details. The paragraph by Ruskin brings many details to bear upon the comparison made. The paragraph about Fritz's difficulties with English repeats his troublesome experiences at the same time that it illustrates them. But nothing is lost in the way of unity, emphasis, or coherence in these paragraphs for the reason that the mixture of method leads logically and naturally to the central idea involved in each instance.

There are still other methods of paragraph development, but those above explained and illustrated are sufficient to emphasize the fact that students should have some "policy" in framing a paragraph, that they should not go about it in a random or hit-or-miss manner. They show clearly that paragraphing is not merely a matter of an occasional indention here and there on a page but is really a reflection of thought organization—a system of thought division which breaks up a subject into small, easily digested parts.

EXERCISES

1. The sentences in the following paragraph are out of order. Rearrange them so that the paragraph will have unity, coherence, and emphasis.

These plants, now protected by the water, are just peeping forth. Nature loses not a moment, takes no vacation. How they improve their time! One thing I may depend on, there has been no idling with the flowers. One cowslip, though it shows the yellow, is not fairly out but will be by tomorrow. Not a moment of sunshine is lost. I should not be surprised to find that they drew in their heads on a frosty night. They advance as steadily as a clock.

2. Rewrite the following, paragraphing each unit of conversation and using quotation marks correctly (some changes in phraseology will be necessary):

What was I going to do about it, he asked. Well, I said that I had not made up my mind yet but that I would find a way out. Then he queried, didn't I think I had been a little too leisurely in attending to such a serious matter. I said, no one had even hinted to me that the matter was so serious as he was apparently trying to make out. In that case, he said, I think the duty of the court is to bring you to a rational consideration of daily affairs by imprisoning you until you can think your way out. More than one innocent person has thought himself out of prison, I replied, and I assure you that I shall do so.

3. Compose paragraphs based upon the following suggestions:

1. You are sick in bed, telling the doctor how you feel.
2. You are explaining to your parents why you prefer one subject to another.
3. You are urging a friend to join you in a trip, repeating in various ways its joys and benefits.
4. You are picturing the magnificent physique of an athlete you admire, comparing his muscular reactions to those of some machine.
5. You are enumerating to a group of friends all the little incidents in a certain game that prevented your making a better showing for yourself.

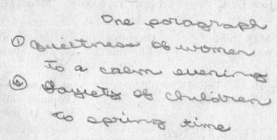

LETTER WRITING

200. **Letter writing,** that is, good letter writing, makes exacting demands. Not only must the content of the letter itself—the body—be impressive and challenging, if the letter is to carry any weight, but it must be framed in accordance with precise conventions so that the total letter-picture may subtly aid and abet the message.

The paragraphs that follow explain most of the meticulous points in letter mechanics. The letters on pages 314–317 illustrate most of them. Everything said in the preceding sections of this book applies to the composition of the body of a letter as well as to composition in general. Remember, however, that the letter is the most highly personalized form of composition. Your letter is *you*. Someone has said that, if you can write a good letter, the world is yours—for the writing.

201. The **heading** written by hand or typewritten on plain stationery is usually in either of these styles:

<table>
<tr><td>200 Bearworth Avenue
Cleveland, Ohio
October 20, 0000</td><td>18 Morgan Place
New York, New York
May 28, 0000</td></tr>
</table>

1. On printed letterheads the **date line** may be written in **various** ways, as:

<table>
<tr><td>June Eighth
0000</td><td>February 18, 0000</td><td>March 24, 0000.</td></tr>
<tr><td>May Third
00   00</td><td>December
Eleventh
0000</td><td>0000
June
Third</td></tr>
<tr><td>425 Hotspur Drive, Kent, Ohio
January Third 0000</td><td>101 Blaine Street
Columbus Ohio
March 31   0000</td></tr>
</table>

January Third 0000
425 Hotspur Drive, Kent, Ohio

2. In case the printed letterhead lists two or more addresses, it may be necessary to indicate the address of a branch office above the date, as:

BORNER INVESTMENT SERVICES

New York   Chicago   Denver   San Francisco

891 Market Street
Denver, Colorado
April 4, 0000

---

3. Full address and date lines are usually placed near the upper right-hand corner of the letter sheet. On plain paper, they are generally placed about an inch and a half from the top and indented about three quarters of an inch from the right. On a sheet with a letterhead, they are usually placed an inch or less below the last line of printing, depending upon the size of the letterhead. Often, however, in both business and friendly letters such lines are centered.

4. Do not place the date line between two place lines, as:

114 Fifth Avenue
June 12, 0000
New York, New York

This is an incoherent mixture of place and time.

5. Do not use place and time **abbreviations** in letter writing. They are discourteous short cuts. Besides, *st, th, nd, rd, d* set close up to figures may make them illegible or confusing. Omit also *prox., inst., ult.,* and the place forms *No.* and # before street numbers and delivery routes.

6. Do not write **dates** by figures alone. Write *April 12, 1945,* not *4/12/45.* In European countries the latter would stand *12/4/45;* that is, the order is day, month, year, rather than month, day, year as it is in the United States. This difference

I. Block Form

1. Heading

Blaine, Greyston, and Witherspoon

WHOLESALE DISTRIBUTORS

18 Cass Street

DETROIT · MICHIGAN

September 29, 0000

2. Inside address or superscription

The Harrison Company
25 Decatur Street
Des Moines, Iowa

3. Salutation

Gentlemen

The business letter consists of seven parts, as numbered on the margin of this page.

The heading contains the name of the firm from which the letter comes, its location, and the date on which the letter is written. The inside address contains the name of the person or firm addressed, with exact location.

4. Body

Then follow the salutation, the body, the complimentary close, the signature, and the annotations.

On a sheet of paper not bearing a printed letterhead, the address of the writer is placed above the date line.

This letter is written in block form with open punctuation. The contents of the various parts are single-spaced, and double spacing separates one part from another and one paragraph from another in the body. There is usually a wider space between the date line and the inside address than elsewhere.

Very truly yours

Winthrop Greyston

5. Complimentary close

6. Signature

Winthrop Greyston

7. Annotations

WG/CC

314

II. Diagonal Form

ALUMINUM PRODUCTS CORPORATION
230 Market Street
SAN FRANCISCO

BRANCHES
New York
Chicago
London

CABLE ADDRESS
APCO
Telephone:
Market 3-4400

January 28, 0000.

Mr. George Granville,
123 Langton Avenue,
Denver, Colorado.

Dear Mr. Granville:

This business letter is written in indented, or diagonal, style, with complete punctuation. The diagonal margining in such set-up as this should be kept at the same angle in all places where indentions are necessary.

The first paragraph in a letter of this kind is preferably started on the diagonal angle of the inside address, and paragraphs following the first should start at the same point.

But the first paragraph may start on a margin with the first word in the date line or on a margin with the final mark of punctuation in the salutation line.

When the surname is used in the salutation of a business letter, it implies that former cordial relations have been enjoyed between the two parties to the letter. Dear Sir is a correct salutation in most business letters addressed as this one is, but it is more formal and implies a less personal relationship.

Very truly yours,

Bronson Winthrop

Bronson Winthrop
Manager

BW/v

III. Modified Form

BROWN, HOLLIDAY, AND COMPANY
INSURANCE OF EVERY KIND

28 STATE STREET

CHICAGO

TELEPHONE STATE 7-5555

DIRECTORS

WILLIAM FORSTER
WINTHROP BROWNE
STANLEY REISMAN
HUMPHREY ELLIS

HOWARD DOE, PRESIDENT
JAMES KAYE, SECRETARY

October Tenth
00   00

Hart, Coe, and Company
1773 Broadway
New York, New York

Dear Sirs:

Many business firms use this combination form
of letter. The formal parts are blocked, and open
in punctuation, with the exception of the salutation and the complimentary close. The paragraphing
in the body is indented.

This modified form represents a kind of compromise between the old diagonal set-up, which was
once used exclusively, and the modern form illustrated on page 314. Some firms today omit all
terminal punctuation, even at the ends of paragraphs, unless the last sentence in the paragraph is
interrogative or exclamatory. But this may be a
somewhat too radical departure—yet.

While the salutation in this letter is correct,
Gentlemen has come to be the preferred form in all
letters bearing company inside addresses.

Yours very truly,

James R. Trainor

James R. Trainor
Vice President

JRT/12

316

IV. Friendly Letter

324 East Macon Street,
Atlanta, Georgia,
April 24, 0000.

Dear Alice,

    I could just as well put the above inside address in the lower left-hand corner of this letter, a space or two below my signature. And I could write this letter in strictly blocked form with open punctuation. But the indented form with complete punctuation is a little more intimate and homey in a letter written to a friend.

    The comma after the salutation in this letter is a part of its intimacy and friendliness. A colon there would make my greeting to you chilly, if not downright cold. As a matter of fact, your address ought to be placed somewhere in this letter. But it would be much too formal and businesslike to place it above the salutation. Since I have placed my own address above, I think I shall place yours in the lower left-hand corner below the signature.

    Of course, both addresses are rarely included in a friendly letter. But the writer's full name and address should always be, so that the addressee may know exactly how and where to address a reply. Then, too, it happens occasionally that a letter gets separated from its envelope—sneaks diabolically into a wrong envelope or slips out of its own. If there's no address at all in the letter, it may be hopelessly lost; whereas if there is at least one address in it, it can be salvaged through the postmaster or some other kindly person.

    And please don't let anyone make you believe that it's wrong to open the body of a letter with I. It's perfectly all right to do so. But don't begin every sentence and every paragraph with I, for though you may be correct grammatically, you may get yourself misjudged personally.

Faithfully yours,
Frances Hallowell
(Miss) Frances Hallowell

Miss Alice Granniss
    Wyncote,
      Ohio.

in custom has occasionally caused confusion and embarrassment to international concerns.

Street numbers and dates (with the exception of the year) may correctly be written out when the words substituted are short and simple; thus, *May Fifth* is permissible in business as well as in friendly letters, and *122 Seventh Avenue* is preferable to *122 7 Avenue* for the reason that in the latter *122* and *7* may get themselves read as *1227*. The year is never written out except in formal notes (see page 336). It is sometimes ruled that numeric names of streets, as well as dates of the month, should not be written out unless they are monosyllabic, or that all such names and dates up to and including *ten* may be written out. But convenience and appearance are the better guides here. The words *seventh* and *eleventh* are preferable to *7* and *11* if they fit into letter make-up easily and gracefully. Indeed, such forms as *April Twenty-second* and *November Thirtieth* are frequent today in letters of all kinds. Note carefully the capitalization and the hyphenation:

2774 Twenty-second Avenue   December Thirty-first 0000

No comma is required before the year when the day of the month is written out.

202. The **inside address, or superscription,** in business letters should be placed a few spaces below the heading or the date line, on the left-hand margin. The first line of the inside address really establishes the left-hand margin for the letter. In friendly and official letters the inside address should be placed in the lower left-hand part of the letter sheet, a few spaces below the signature, beginning on the left-hand margin.

1. Marginal adjustments and measurements must always be based upon the length of the letter. Left-hand margining should be somewhat wider than right-hand, and bottom margining wider than top. An extremely short letter should be proportionately placed on the letter sheet, not huddled toward an "exit" at any corner. The relation of the letter proper to the letter sheet is very much the same as that of the framed print

to the mat. The address used on the envelope should be an exact copy of that used in the letter.

2. It is a mark of courtesy to get the name of the individual or of the firm you address exactly right. This you can usually prove by referring to letters received or to booklets or advertisements. If you write *Howard Upton* for *Howard Opton,* you may offend. Small error though it is, the letter *U* is some distance away from *O* in alphabetic filing. Accuracy in regard to such details is revealing of mental habits and even of character. Be sure that you know, before you write the inside address, whether the person addressed is manager or secretary or auditor, whether the publisher addressed is *Macmillan Co.* or *The Macmillan Company,* whether the brokerage firm is *Smith Wallington & Co.* or *Smith, Wallington, and Company,* or *Smith Wallington & Co., Inc.* Of course, inaccurately addressed letters may reach their destinations, thanks to our postal service, but this is no excuse for carelessness.

3. Do not use the word *city* or *town* alone in local addresses, as:

> Mr. Horace Wentworth
> 456 Cannon Avenue
> City

The letter so addressed may easily wander out of the locality; then *city* will mean any city.

203. An **official title** may properly be given in the address. Sometimes it may be so long as to require an additional line, as:

> Mr. Horace Wentworth, President
> The Boston Hardware Company
> 1443 Summer Street
> Boston, Massachusetts

204. Titles that most commonly precede names in addresses are *Dr., Hon., Messrs., Miss, Mr., Mrs., Rev., Prof.* All of these but Miss are abbreviations and are followed by a period. In strictly open-letter form, however, many firms now omit periods after abbreviations, and the practice is apparently growing, widely supported as it is by such governmental forms as FBI, FHA, NYA, WPA, and the rest. The title *Esq.* (Esquire) follows the personal name. *Mr.* should not be used before a name that is followed by *Esq.* Other abbreviations of titles that follow names are such as denote professional degrees and honors— *M.D., D.D.S., A.M., Ph.D., LL.D., D.C.S., F.R.H.S., C.P.A., L.H.D., Lit.D.* The abbreviation used after a name should not duplicate in meaning that used before it. This is the reason for not using both *Mr.* and *Esq.* with a name. Both are, in general usage, equivalent to *gentleman,* the latter being used in England much as *Mr.* is used in the United States. *Prof. Harrison Tweed, A.B., A.M.* is wrong for the reason that titles indicated before and after the name denote the same kind of academic status. But *Prof. Harrison Tweed, M.D.* tells two *different* things about Harrison Tweed—he is a professor and he is also a medical doctor.

1. Titles before names should not be abbreviated unless the entire name is given; thus, *Gen. Howard P. Suffern* and *General Suffern* are correct, but *Gen. Suffern* is incorrect. The use of *The* or *Very* or *His* or *Right* before a title gives it a more formal or a "higher" significance, as *The Honorable Thomas Danburn, His Honor The Mayor, The Right Reverend Bishop Hopkins, The Very Reverend Dean of Stottlesbury* (see page 334).

2. The title *Messrs.* (abbreviation of French *Messieurs*) is used in addressing two or more men who represent a legal or other professional group or partnership. It is not used in addressing business organizations even when they are represented by personal names. Do not write *Messrs. The Standard Oil Company of New Jersey* or *Messrs. R. H. Macy and Company.* Do not use the singular form *Mr.* before a firm name that stands for a business establishment, as *Mr. Marshall Field* and *Mr. John Wanamaker.* But *Messrs. Davidson and Hollingsworth, Attorneys-at-Law,* and *Messrs. Grimm and Stone, Certified Public Accountants,* are correct. Do not write *Messers.* or *Mess.* for *Messrs.*

3. *Miss* is used in addressing a single woman, *Mrs.* in address-

ing a married woman. The words *Misses* and *Mesdames* are used in addressing two or more women, the former for unmarried women, the latter (plural of *Madam*) for either married or unmarried women. These plural forms may be preceded by *The,* as:

The Misses Townsend
Misses Clara and Alice Browning .
The Misses Fay and Flora Brown
Mesdames Horton and Craig

205. The so-called **attention notice** has come to be regarded as a part of the inside address of a business letter. It may be made an actual part of it, as:

Messrs. Jones and Thompson
1200 Wabash Avenue
Chicago, Illinois

Attention of Mr. Arthur Jones

Gentlemen:

It may be placed on a line with the salutation several spaces to the right, as:

Gentlemen: *Attention of Mr. Arthur Jones*

It may be placed in the lower left-hand corner of the envelope. In all placements it is preferably underlined.

206. In business letters, block or diagonal, the **salutation** is written below the inside address, beginning on the left-hand margin. There should be double spacing between the last line of the inside address and the salutation. In official letters and in friendly letters carrying the inside address at the end, the salutation belongs two spaces below the last line of the heading, beginning, as in the business letter, on the left-hand margin. It should, as a rule, stand on a line by itself, but the attention

notice may share the same line (page 321). The following salutations are listed in order of decreasing formality:

Men		*Women*	
Sir:	Sirs:	Madam:	Mesdames
My dear Sir:	My dear Sirs:	My dear Madam:	My dear Mesdames
Dear Sir:	Dear Sirs:	Dear Madam:	(*or* Ladies):
My dear Mr. Coe:	Gentlemen:	My dear Mrs. Coe:	Dear Mesdames
Dear Mr. Coe:		Dear Mrs. Coe:	(*or* Ladies):
Dear Coe:		My dear Alice,	Ladies:
My dear Tom,		Dear Alice,	
Dear Tom,			

1. *Madam* is used in saluting either a married or an unmarried woman. In saluting more than one woman *Mesdames* is
used, but *Ladies* is supplanting *Mesdames*. *Sir* and *Sirs* are now
used mainly in official letters. The *My dear* form is passing.
Note that *dear* is not capitalized in this form of salutation. If
the writer of a business letter is personally acquainted with
an addressee or has had agreeable relationships with him, he may
correctly use one of the surname salutations.

2. Do not use *Dear Miss, Dear Mister, Dear Friend, Friend
John, Dear Messrs., Dear Mrs., My dear Col., D'r Sr, Gents,*
or other familiar or clipped forms as salutations. Do not use
the addressee's name alone as a salutation.

3. *Gentlemen* has come to be the preferred salutation to follow company inside addresses. It is correct when the company
name is that of a man and when it is that of a man and a woman,
as:

John Wanamaker
Broadway at Tenth Street
New York, New York

Gentlemen:

James B. Harrigan, Inc.,
345 Market Street,
San Francisco,
California.

Gentlemen:

Jay Coe and Ida Blaine
Printers and Publishers
1445 Stanton Street
Washington, D. C.

Gentlemen

but

The Misses Comiston
Gowns and Bonnets
130 West 57 Street
New York, New York

Ladies

4. In informal business letters and in friendly letters the salutation should be followed by a comma unless, of course, open punctuation is used throughout. In official and business letters it should be followed by a colon. Never use after the salutation a dash, or a colon and a dash, or a comma and a dash.

5. **Compound salutations** such as *Dear Sir and Madam* or *Dear Sir or Madam, Sirs and Mesdames, Ladies and Gentlemen* are labored and should be avoided. In an impersonal organization gender is of no importance.

6. The salutation in a business letter is not influenced by the attention notice. It belongs "in spirit" to the firm addressed, not to the individual to whose attention it may be especially directed, thus:

Right	*Wrong*
The Robertson Company 118 Grand Avenue Des Moines, Iowa	The Robertson Company 118 Grand Avenue Des Moines, Iowa
Attention of Mr. Robert Day	*Attention of Mr. Robert Day*
Gentlemen:	Dear Mr. Day:

207. The **body of a letter** should begin two spaces below the salutation and at the left-hand margin in block style. The first line may, however, be indented, as explained on page 315.

1. The writer of a business letter should judge in advance about how much space his letter will occupy so that the letter-picture may be made attractive and harmonious and so that the placement of the content on the sheet may be kept proportionate (page 315). Paragraphs should be short; and if the block style is used, they should be separated by double or triple spacing. If the indented style is used, no such spacing is necessary, but many firms prefer the spacing between paragraphs in all forms of letter set-up. If two or more items, such as prices or catalog numbers or measurements, require mention, they should be clearly set in tabulated form. Such form or diagram clarifies and prevents mistakes, and it also improves the letter-picture.

2. If a letter requires more than one sheet, plain sheets with-

out letterhead may follow the first one with letterhead. These should be properly numbered. In addition, these extra sheets should carry at the top annotations to indicate subject matter, addressee, date, and perhaps other details. A second sheet should never be used unless at least a short paragraph makes it necessary. Do not use a second sheet for complimentary close, signature, and annotations only.

208. The **complimentary close** should be placed two spaces below the last line of the body and should begin about the middle of the page (see pages 314-317). It makes for harmony in the letter-picture if it is begun on the margin with the date line, but this arrangement is not always possible without throwing the letter-picture out of focus.

1. The following complimentary closes are listed in order of decreasing formality:

1. Obediently yours,	10. Sincerely yours,
2. Yours obediently,	11. Yours sincerely,
3. Respectfully yours,	12. Sincerely,
4. Yours respectfully,	13. Cordially yours,
5. Respectfully submitted,	14. Yours cordially,
6. Very truly yours,	15. Cordially,
7. Yours very truly,	16. Faithfully yours,
8. Very sincerely yours,	17. Yours faithfully,
9. Yours very sincerely,	18. Faithfully,

2. The short forms *Truly, Truly yours, Yours truly* are not recommended. The first five forms above are appropriate in official letters; the next ten, in business letters; the last three, in intimate letters and in letters written in support of some person or cause; all but the first seven may correctly be used in friendly letters. The placement of the pronoun *yours,* whether first or last, is unimportant; and among those ten designated as business-letter closes there is not much difference as to degree of formality. The latter ones in this group may, however, be used in cases of long-standing relationships. It is sometimes ruled that a single-word complimentary close should never be used in a business letter.

3. Do not use *Y'rs, Res'y, Respectively* (for *Respectfully*), or any such flippancies as *Yours for more pep* and *Yours somewhat,* as complimentary closes. Do not use *and oblige* as part of a complimentary close. And do not link with a complimentary close such expressions as *I am, Believe me, I beg to remain. Hoping to receive a favorable reply,* sometimes called the "participial getaway," is not only unnecessary but frequently ungrammatical, as the initial participle is often left dangling (page 173).

4. Only the first word of the complimentary close is capitalized. The complimentary close is followed by a comma unless open punctuation has been used throughout the letter.

209. The **signature** follows the complimentary close, beginning on the same margin in block style, two or three spaces to the right of it in diagonal style. It should be followed by the typewritten name of the writer in both formal and informal letters. This is especially important when a signature is difficult to read. Below the typewritten name should be typed the writer's title in the firm, as *Vice-President, Secretary, Manager.* A signature should not be preceded by such titles as *Mr., Prof., Dr.,* nor followed by such academic letters as *A.M., D.D., Ph.D.* A signature with a single initial before the surname is not good. As the signature is the most responsible part of a letter, it should represent an established legal usage. *Harrison Boonton Smith* and *Harrison B. Smith* are good; *H. B. Smith* is acceptable; *H. Smith* is not good.

1. A married woman should sign her full name (which may include her maiden name) and immediately before it should write *(Mrs.).* If she wishes to be addressed by her married name, she should place on a separate line her full married name, thus:

(Mrs.) Angela Dow Robbins   *or*   Angela Dow Robbins
                                         (Mrs. Robert R. Robbins)

2. An unmarried woman should place *Miss* in parentheses before her signature. If a feminine name is signed without the parenthetical *Mrs.* or *Miss,* it is permissible to assume *Miss* and to use this in making reply. It is similarly permissible to assume that such a signature as *H. B. Smith* or *H. Smith* is that of a

man unless the content of the letter shows that the writer is a woman, but the recipient should not be made to guess.

3. The signature must always be written by hand. Such rubber-stamp forms as *Dictated but not signed, Dictated but not read,* should never be used in business letters.

210. At the left-hand margin below the signature data it is customary in business letters to carry the **initials** of the person responsible for a letter and of the person who types it. *RR/CF* means that the letter was dictated, perhaps, by Robert Robbins and was typed by Clara Foster; *RR/F, R/f, R...F,* are variations of the same kind of note. Sometimes the typist is indicated by a number, as *RR/12.* The initials are sometimes run vertically on the left-hand margin opposite the complimentary close and the signature, thus forming a kind of coverage, as:

O	Very truly yours,
B	
W	
c	Ogden B. Whitehouse
r	Managing Editor

211. Annotations such as *Two enclosures, Catalog enclosed, Statement attached* are placed at the end of a letter for the convenience and protection of the firm from which the letter is sent. Annotations for the benefit of the receiving firm, as *In replying please refer to D R 14223; Dictated June 18, 0000, mailed June 20, 0000; Re Batten Brothers' order,* are placed at the beginning of the business letter, preferably several spaces above the inside address at the left-hand margin. The *Re* or *In re* note is sometimes placed above the salutation or on the salutation line, but this placement is not recommended. *Re* is not an abbreviation and is not followed by a period.

Some firms use this form at the top of the letter sheet:

From ....
To ....
Subject ....
Dictated...................
Mailed ....

This constitutes a record for both houses concerned in the correspondence. On pages after the first, if a letter is long, this abridgment may be run across the top:

From....... To....... Subject....... Dictated....... Mailed.......

the fill-ins being shortened—initials in the first three spaces and
numbers only in the last two.

212. Of the numerous *Don'ts* that might justifiably be stated
in regard to the troublesome subject of letter writing, the following half dozen are among the most important, if not, indeed,
the most important.

1. Don't use hackneyed expressions in letters, such as *kind
order, beg to state, valued patronage, contents noted, as per,
permit us to advise, regretting the delay, enclosed please find,
would say.*

2. Don't use clipped or stenographic forms, such as *Yours rec'd*
for *Your letter is received; Enclose check for ten dollars* for *I
enclose a check for ten dollars; Mr. Harold Thoms, mgr First
National B'k* for *Mr. Harold Thoms, manager of the First
National Bank.*

3. Don't call a letter an "esteemed favor" or a "communication" or a "unit of exchange in correspondence."

4. Don't abbreviate. The names of cities and states should
be written out. *N.Y. City* for *New York City* is incorrect, as are
Phila. for *Philadelphia, Chi.* for *Chicago, Clev.* for *Cleveland.*

5. Don't mix pronominal sequence in a letter, as in *We are
happy to hear from you, but the company is at a loss to understand your reference to Amalgamated Copper '45. I have just
received a statement,* etc. Here *We* is first plural, *company* is
third singular, and *I* is first singular. This is a more unified and
coherent equivalent—*Thank you for your letter. We are at a
loss to understand your reference to Amalgamated Copper '45
but we have just received a letter,* etc.

6. Don't be afraid to use the first-person pronouns *I* and *we*

in a letter of any kind. But do not overuse them in letters or in any other type of expression. It is not incorrect to begin a letter with either of these pronouns. It is not the best form to begin every sentence or even every paragraph with *I* or *we*.

213. To fit the large commercial envelope (about 10 inches by 4½ inches) the paper should be folded up from the bottom slightly less than one third its length and then folded down from the top slightly more than one third its length. This makes two horizontal creases with the top edge of the paper extending slightly. This extension permits the thumb to catch it easily in opening the letter.

For the small commercial envelope (about 6½ inches by 3½ inches), the paper should be folded up from the bottom slightly less than one half its length, and then turned in first from the right, then from the left, to give two vertical creases. The top fold should be slightly wider than the other so that it may extend over and be caught by the thumb in unfolding.

214. Envelopes should always be addressed clearly. The style should follow that used in the letter—block or diagonal, open or close punctuation. The first line in the address should be placed at the optical center of the envelope, for immediacy of reading grasp. If typewritten, the items should be double-spaced to facilitate reading; but if the address consists of four or more lines, single spacing prevents a sprawling effect. In the upper left-hand corner the exact name and address of the sender should be placed. This is called the **return address**. Some business houses prefer its placement on the seal flap, giving nothing on the face of the envelope but the address.

Such envelope annotations as *c/o Halloran, R.F.D. 10,* and *Department C* may be placed in the lower left-hand corner. They are preferably so placed in case, woven in with the address proper, they make it crowded or unduly long. Examples of good envelope addresses are given on page 331.

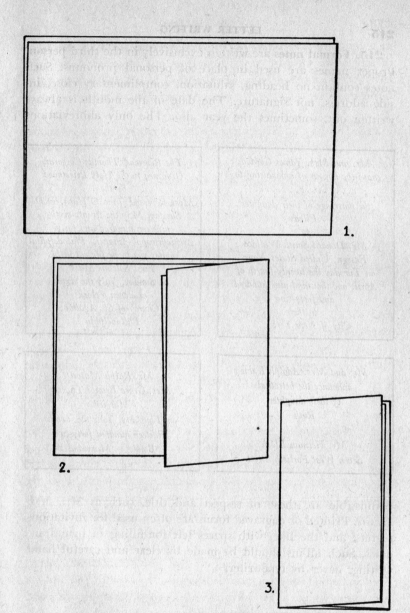

1.

2.

3.

Letter folds for small commercial envelope

215. Formal notes are written exclusively in the third person. Proper names are used in place of personal pronouns. Such notes contain no heading, salutation, complimentary close, inside address, nor signature. The date of the month is always written out, sometimes the year also. The only abbreviations

---

Mr. and Mrs. James Gordon
have the honour of announcing to
. . . .
the marriage of their daughter
Ellen
to
Mr. Donald Smith Wallace
Ensign, United States Navy
on Tuesday the twenty-fourth of
April, one thousand nine hundred
and forty-two
in the
City of New York

The Reverend Thomas Corcoran
Ordained to the Holy Priesthood
by the
Most Reverend John O'Hara, D.D.
Sunday, May the twenty-sixth
nineteen hundred and forty
Archiepiscopal Chapel, Philadelphia
invites you to be present at his
First Solemn Mass
on Sunday, July the sixth
at eleven o'clock
Church of St. Agatha
Philadelphia

Mr. and Mrs. Adolph Kahn
announce the betrothal
of their daughter
Ruth
to
Mr. Herman Bloch
Seven West Fortieth Street

Mr. Ralph Mason
Mrs. Grace Brown Thorne
Married
on Thursday, June the Tenth
Nineteen hundred forty-two
Bowie   Maryland

---

permissible are those of respect and title, such as *Mr., Mrs., Messrs.* Printed or engraved forms are often used for invitations, regrets, and the like, with spaces left for filling in names and dates. Such fill-ins should be made by clear and careful handwriting, never by typewriter.

```
HORNER AND BLAINE
  356 State Street
  Chicago, Illinois

                                                        ┌──────────┐
                                                        │          │
                                                        │   STAMP  │
                                                        │          │
                                                        └──────────┘

                    The Brailsford Company

                    842 Eleventh Avenue

                    New York

                    New York

Adjustments
```

```
      After five days return to
WORTHINGTON HASBROUCK,
      25 North Broad Street,
        Philadelphia, Pa.                               ┌──────────┐
                                                        │          │
                                                        │   STAMP  │
                                                        │          │
                                                        └──────────┘

                    Mr. Horace Wigglesworth,
                    18 High Rock Terrace,
                      San Francisco,
                        California.




C/O Mr. Thomas Coe.
```

```
CAMP GREEN,
  Rutland,
  Vermont.
                                                        ┌──────────┐
                                                        │          │
                                                        │   STAMP  │
                                                        │          │
                                                        └──────────┘

                    Mrs. Johnson Hillman,

                    "Maple Dale,"

                    Marblehead,

                    Massachusetts.
```

FORMS OF ADDRESS

In addressing dignitaries of church and state it is desirable to follow certain prescribed forms that have become accepted in letter-writing practice. But these forms are more or less fluid and varied, and in some instances they change just as style in dress changes. In general, correct form in addressing and saluting persons holding special or distinguished positions means polite form. Almost any polite form in writing to a military or a cabinet official, for instance, must be considered correct. The forms given below are representative of present-day usage in correspondence, and there is really not nearly so much difference among those listed in a given case as is generally supposed. For more detailed listings of correspondence forms such as these the student should consult special books on letter writing [*] and the supplementary matter in the leading dictionaries. The tabulation below follows the practice and style of the best stationers and engravers in the country.

Office	Address Title	Salutation[†]	Complimentary Close[†]
The President of the United States	The President The President of the United States His Excellency, The President of the United States (The name is not necessary after this title.)	Sir: Mr. President: To the President: Dear Mr. President: Dear President _____:	Very respectfully, Respectfully, Sincerely yours,
The Vice-President	The Vice-President The Honorable The Vice-President of the United States The Honorable _____, Vice-President of the United States	Sir: Mr. Vice-President: To the Vice-President: My dear Mr. Vice-President: Dear Vice-President _____:	Very respectfully, Respectfully, Very truly yours, Sincerely yours,
Speaker of the House	The Honorable The Speaker of the House of Representatives The Speaker of the House of Representatives The Honorable _____, Speaker of the House of Representatives	Sir: Mr. Speaker: To the Speaker of the House of Representatives: My dear Mr. Speaker: Dear Mr. Speaker: My dear Mr. _____: Dear Mr. _____:	Respectfully yours, Very truly yours, Sincerely yours, Cordially yours,
Members of the Supreme Court	The Chief Justice (no name) Chief Justice of the United States Supreme Court Chief Justice _____ of the United States Supreme Court (Other members are addressed as "Associate Justice" with the foregoing variations.)	Sir: Mr. Chief Justice: To the Chief Justice of the Supreme Court of the United States: To _____, Associate Justice of the Supreme Court of the United States: Mr. Justice _____: Your Honor: My dear Mr. Justice: My dear Justice _____:	Respectfully yours, Very truly yours, Sincerely yours,

[*] See Opdycke's *Take a Letter Please*, published by Funk & Wagnalls Company.

[†] Arranged in decreasing formality. The complimentary close in a foreign letter is usually much more formal than it is in an American letter. In a letter to a cardinal or archbishop or bishop, it may take the form of *I have the honor to remain your most humble and obedient servant* or *Believe me, Your Excellency* (or *Reverend Sir*), *Your ever faithful and respectful servant*. While *Respectfully yours* is regarded as inappropriate in business and friendly letters because it savors of subservience, it is nevertheless correct in formal official letters, especially in those that make suggestions or ask favors or express gratitude or congratulation.

332

Office	Address Title	Salutation	Complimentary Close
Cabinet Officer	The Honorable The Secretary of State The Honorable _____, Secretary of War The Assistant Secretary of the Navy	Sir: Mr. Secretary: To the Secretary of _____: Dear Sir: My dear Mr. Secretary: Dear Mr. Secretary: (An assistant secretary must never be addressed or greeted as Secretary or Mr. Secretary, but the other forms may be used for an assistant secretary as well as for the secretary.)	Respectfully yours, Very truly yours, Sincerely yours, Cordially yours,
Senator	Honorable _____ The Honorable _____ Honorable _____, United States Senate Senator _____, The United States Senate	Sir: Dear Sir: My dear Mr. Senator: My dear Senator: Dear Senator: Dear Senator _____:	Respectfully yours, Very truly yours, Sincerely yours, Cordially yours,
Representative (Congressman)	Honorable _____ The Honorable _____ Honorable _____, United States House of Representatives Representative _____, House of Representatives	Sir: Dear Sir: My dear Representative: Dear Representative _____:	Respectfully yours, Very truly yours, Sincerely yours, Cordially yours,
Ambassador	His Excellency the American Ambassador to Great Britain His Excellency the British Ambassador to the United States His Excellency _____, Ambassador of the Japanese Empire	Sir: Excellency: Your Excellency: My dear Mr. Ambassador:	Very respectfully, Very truly yours, Sincerely yours,
Consul	The American Consul at _____ The British Consul at _____ The Honorable _____, American Consul at _____	Sir: Dear Sir: My dear Consul: Dear Consul _____:	Respectfully yours, Very truly yours, Sincerely yours, Cordially yours,
Governor	His Excellency the Governor of _____ The Honorable _____, Governor of _____	Sir: To the Governor: Dear Sir: My dear Governor _____: Dear Governor _____:	Respectfully yours, Very truly yours, Sincerely yours, Cordially yours,

Office	Address Title	Salutation	Complimentary Close
Mayor	The Honorable _____, Mayor of the City of _____ The Mayor of the City of _____	Sir: To the Mayor of _____: Dear Sir: My dear Mr. Mayor: Dear Mr. Mayor: My dear Mayor: Dear Mayor _____:	Respectfully yours, Very truly yours, Sincerely yours, Cordially yours,
The Pope	His Holiness Pope _____	Your Holiness: Most Holy Father:	Obediently yours, Faithfully yours, Respectfully yours,
Cardinal	His Eminence _____	Your Eminence: My Lord Cardinal: (Foreign)	Faithfully yours, Your faithful and obedient servant
Archbishop	Most Reverend _____	Your Excellency:	Faithfully yours, Respectfully yours,
Bishop	Most Reverend _____ The Right Reverend _____	Your Excellency: (Catholic) My Lord Bishop: (Anglican) Right Reverend Sir: Right Reverend and Dear Sir: My dear Bishop _____: Dear Bishop:	Faithfully and respectfully yours, Respectfully yours, Sincerely yours,
Monsignor	The Right Reverend Monsignor _____	Right Reverend and dear Monsignor:	Yours faithfully and respectfully,
Priest	Very Reverend _____	Dear Reverend Father:	Respectfully yours, Sincerely yours,
Superior of a Sister Order	Mother _____, Mother General Mother _____, Superior General Sister _____, Superior	Dear Mother General: Dear Mother Superior: Dear Sister Superior,	Faithfully yours, Respectfully yours, Sincerely yours,
Nun	Sister _____	Dear Sister _____:	Respectfully yours, Sincerely yours,
Monk	Brother _____	Dear Brother _____:	Sincerely yours, Cordially yours,
Dean (church)	Very Reverend _____ The Reverend Dr.* _____ The Very Reverend the Dean of _____	Very Reverend Sir: Sir: Dear Dean:	Respectfully yours, Very truly yours, Sincerely yours,
Rabbi	Rabbi _____ The Reverend _____ The Reverend Dr. _____:	Reverend Sir: My dear Rabbi _____: My dear Mr. (or Dr.) _____:	Respectfully yours, Very truly yours, Sincerely yours,
Clergyman	The Reverend _____ The Reverend Dr. _____	Reverend Sir: My dear Sir: My dear Mr. (or Dr.) _____:	Respectfully yours, Very truly yours, Sincerely yours,

* A related title may always be added.

Office	Address Title	Salutation	Complimentary Close
General	General (full name) Commanding Officer Army of the United States or United States Army	Sir: My dear Sir: Dear Sir: My dear General _____: Dear General _____: (The last two are informal.)	Respectfully yours, Very truly yours, Sincerely yours, Cordially yours,
Lieutenant General Major General Brigadier General	Follow the above forms with the exception of those for informal salutations. Use *My dear General James* or *Dear General James:*, not *My dear Brigadier General James:* or *Dear Lieutenant General Atwater:*		
Colonel	Colonel Jay Turner, U. S. A.	My dear Sir: Dear Sir: My dear Colonel Turner: Dear Colonel Turner:	Respectfully yours, Very truly yours, Sincerely, yours, Cordially yours,
Lieutenant	Mr. Howard Sewall, Lieutenant, U. S. A.	Dear Sir: My dear Mr. Sewall: Dear Mr. Sewall:	Respectfully yours, Very truly yours, Sincerely yours, Cordially yours,
Admiral	The Admiral of the Navy of the United States or Admiral (full name) Commanding United States Navy	Sir: My dear Sir: Dear Sir: My dear Admiral _____: Dear Admiral _____: (The last two are informal.)	Respectfully yours, Very truly yours, Sincerely yours, Cordially yours,
Captain	Captain H. B. Cary, U. S. N.	My dear Sir: Dear Sir: My dear Captain Cary: Dear Captain Cary:	Very truly yours, Sincerely yours, Cordially yours,

The initials U. S. A. (United States Army) and U. S. N. (United States Navy) are omitted in addressing retired officers. Salutations for officers below the rank of captain should not contain any indication of rank or title but should be stated as *Sir:* or *Mr.* only— *Dear Sir:* or *My dear Mr. _____:* or *Dear Mr. _____* In both army and navy, official correspondence among officers themselves follows a more or less rigid formula, ceremonial openings and closings being omitted as a rule.

EXERCISES

1. "Unravel" the following business letter parts; that is, capitalize and punctuate them correctly, and arrange them as they should be on the letter sheet. Indicate the body of the letter by a horizontal line.

> very truly yours april tenth oooo fifth avenue at eighteenth street harrison p wheeler new york city the turner-baldwin company hpw...rr chief of staff topeka gentlemen manufacturers of uniforms kansas united states army corps new jersey eighth division national guard fort dix

2. Write a letter of application in answer to the advertisement below. Enclose names and addresses of three persons who are able to recommend you in three different ways, one for character, one for general intelligence, and one for the special qualities called for by the advertisement.

> Wanted: Young man or woman as private secretary to president of a large wholesale merchandising company. Excellent opportunity for one seeking a position of trust and responsibility and desiring permanent relationship with established firm. Explain fully education and experience to date and enclose three authoritative references. X3456 *Times*.

3. Write a letter to a mail-order house or to the mail-order department of a department store in which you order at least six articles, some in quantity. Build into your letter a diagram containing five or more vertical divisions—catalog number or letter, name of article, quantity ordered, prices each, total price. Total the whole amount of purchase, and enclose payment by check or money order.

4. Write the following friendly letters:

1. To a friend congratulating him upon his birthday.
2. To your father or your mother from the school you attend.
3. To a former teacher telling him about your new job.
4. To a girl (or boy) asking her (or him) to go to a party with you.
5. To a neighbor asking permission to swim in his creek.
6. To an old schoolmate inviting him (or her) to a reunion.
7. To a friend inviting him (or her) to spend the week-end with you.
8. To your brother in reply to his letter asking for help.
9. To a sports competitor to whom you lost the game yesterday.
10. To a friend with whom you spent a very pleasant week-end.

USING THE LIBRARY

216. Most libraries—large and small, public and private—are now organized on the basis of the *Decimal Classification and Relativ Index* devised by Melvil Dewey. By this system all knowledge is classified into ten divisions, and all printed matter is grouped and numbered as follows:

0	General works	5	Pure science
1	Filosofy	6	Useful arts
2	Religion	7	Fine arts
3	Sociology	8	Literature
4	Filology	9	History

These ten major divisions are expanded by the **decimal system,** as illustrated below, and each of these subdivisions may be still further expanded. The decimal notation makes it possible to expand the listing or cataloging of works to keep up with the progress of human knowledge. Observe, for instance, the following expansion of a part of number 590.[1]

590 Zoology

590.1 Philosofy, classification   .2 Compends   .3 Dictionaries. .4 Essays, lectures, etc.   .5 Periodicals   .6 Societies   .7 Study and teaching, zoologic gardens, aquaria, museums   .8 Collectiv works .9 History

591 Physiologic zoology

.1	**Physiology**
.11	Circulation
.12	Respiration
.121	Nature
.122	Dermal
.123	Aquivascular

[1] This, the above ten divisions, and pages 338–339 are reprinted from *Decimal Classification and Relativ Index* by Melvil Dewey, by permission of the copyright holders, Lake Placid Club Education Foundation, Lake Placid Club, New York. The spelling of the original is retained.

.125	Branchial
.126	Tracheal
.127	Pulmonary
.129	Exhalation of aqueous vapor
.13	Nutrition
.131	Acquisition of food
.132	Digestion of food
.133	Assimilation of food
.134	Growth
.135	Development
.136	Repair of waste
.137	Production of organic material
.138	Conditions of nutritiv activity
.139	Longevity, vitality
.14	Secretion and excretion

DEWEY DECIMAL CLASSIFICATION

000 General works
Prolegomena

010 Bibliografy
020 Library economy
030 General cyclopedias
040 General collected essays
050 General periodicals
060 General societies Museums
070 Journalism Newspapers
080 Polygrafy Special libraries
090 Book rarities

100 Filosofy
110 Metaphysics
120 Other metaphysical topics
130 Physiologic, abnormal and differential psychology Metapsychology
140 Filosofic sistems and doctrins
150 Psychology
160 Logic Dialectics
170 Ethics
180 Ancient and Oriental filosofers
190 Modern filosofers

200 Religion
210 National theology
220 Bible
230 Doctrinal Dogmatics Theology
240 Devotional Practical
250 Homiletic Pastoral Parochial
260 Church: institutions and work
270 General hist. of the church
280 Christian churches and sects
290 Nonchristian religions

300 Social sciences Sociology
310 Statistics
320 Political science
330 Economics Political economy
340 Law
350 Administration
360 Welfare and social associations and institutions
370 Education
380 Commerce Communication
390 Customs Costumes Folklore

400	Filology		700	Fine arts Recreation
410	Comparativ		710	Landscape gardening
420	English Anglo-Saxon		720	Architecture
430	German and other Teutonic		730	Sculpture
440	French Provençal		740	Drawing Decoration **Design**
450	Italian Rumanian		750	Painting
460	Spanish Portuguese		760	Engraving
470	Latin and other Italic		770	Fotografy
480	Greek and other Hellenic		780	Music
490	Other languages		790	Amusements

500	Pure science		800	Literature
510	Mathematics		810	American
520	Astronomy		820	English Anglo-Saxon
530	Physics		830	German and other Teutonic
540	Chemistry		840	French Provençal
550	Geology		850	Italian Rumanian
560	Paleontology		860	Spanish Portuguese
570	Biology Anthropology		870	Latin and other Italic
580	Botany		880	Greek and other Hellenic
590	Zoology		890	Other literatures

600	Useful arts		900	History	
610	Medicin		910		Geografy Travels
620	Engineering		920		Biografy
630	Agriculture		930		Ancient history
640	Home economics		940		Europe
650	Communication Business		950	Modern	Asia
660	Chemic technology		960		Africa
670	Manufactures		970		North America
680	Mechanic trades		980		South America
690	Bilding		990		Oceania and polar regions

217. The printed matter in a library is **cataloged** in a stack of drawers containing hundreds of 5 inch by 3 inch cards called **index cards.** Each card bears as a minimum finding guide a Dewey Decimal notation, the name of an author, and the title of his work. To get a book you copy these on a slip of paper provided by the library set up as shown at the top of page 340. Your name and address are required to show your good faith as a book borrower. The call number is, of course, the Dewey classification number.

Author........................	Call Number
Title.........................	
Your name.....................	
Your address..................	

218. There are four different kinds of cards in the average library catalog. An **author card** is one on which the author's name comes first. A **title card** is one on which the title comes first. A **subject card** is one on which the subject is given together with certain details regarding its treatment. An **analytic card** is an extension of either an author or a title card; it may give the table of contents, the general aim of the work, the field covered, and like details. The analytic card is used most frequently in connection with collections, such as essays, stories, poems, short biographies. Subject cards and analytic cards are necessary because book titles are sometimes misleading or offer no immediate clue to finding what is wanted. Examples of the four types are presented on the opposite page.

1. The two principal types of cards are the author card and the title card. Some analysis is almost always carried on even the simplest of such cards. Usage varies among different libraries as to how much. The date of copyright (or publication), the name of publisher, the number of pages (sometimes of chapters also), the name of illustrator, the number of plates and maps, the size of book (8vo, 12mo) are among the items most commonly listed by abbreviation on a library card. Note these items on the cards above reproduced.

2. Note also that on the second card above there is no call number listed, but rather the call letters *BT*, meaning *Biography Thoreau*. Similarly, **reference books** are usually cataloged under *R*, actual numbers being unnecessary inasmuch as all such books and other publications are to be found on open shelves

```
Canby, Henry Seidel
   The age of confidence; life
in the nineties; illustrated by
Albert Kruse.     New York:
Farrar & Rinehart, Inc.  c1934
260p        front pl.
```

```
        THOREAU,  HENRY  DAVID
BT  Canby, Henry Seidel
      Thoreau.            Houghton 1939.
    xx, 509p.  il.
      An interpretative study of the life,
    personality, and work of the famous Amer-
    ican recluse,naturalist,and writer of the
    nineteenth century.
```

```
           UNITED   STATES——HISTORY
973B       British—American discords and con-
           cords; a record of three centuries;
           compiled by The History Circle.
           New York:G.P.Putnam's Sons,1918.
           85p       fac.map        12°
           Bibliography p71-85
```

```
428.3    Opdycke,John Baker
           Don't say it;a cyclopedia of
         English use and abuse.Funk 1939.
         850p.
         The purpose of the book is to correct
         errors and to remove uncertainty about
         the spelling,pronunciation,use,and
         meaning of about twenty thousand
         terms the average literate person may
         read and use in daily life.

         1 English language—idiom,corrections,
         errors.    2 English language—pronun-
         ciation.
```

in the reference department. Such details as date of publication and name of publisher are unimportant, as far as library cataloging is concerned, on cards for standard fiction. The novels of Eliot, Thackeray, Dumas, and Zola, for instance, are reissued by different publishers at different times, and even small libraries are likely to have more than one copy of a work by an author in this category. One card may thus represent all copies, and that card may be written in the simplest possible form, as:

Author card	*Title card*
Dickens, Charles	Barnaby Rudge.
Barnaby Rudge.	Dickens, Charles
	Barnaby Rudge.

3. It is not uncommon, indeed, for so-called standard fiction to be placed on the open shelves of a library as works of reference are. They are arranged alphabetically by author and are usually found by this alphabetic arrangement. But both reference books and standard novels are cataloged in the library records (see pages 338, 339), and as a rule the decimal numbers will be found clearly marked in them. Sometimes both numbers

and letters may be used in cataloging them, as $\dfrac{R}{920}\Big/ W$ (*Who's Who*

in America, the R standing for Reference and the W for the first word in the title).

219. A knowledge of library cataloging in general, and of library cards in particular, is most important for the student who is required to compile a bibliography in connection, say, with a speech or a debate. A **bibliography** is more than a mere list of books on a given subject; it is an explanation of all the literature bearing upon that subject. Building a bibliography is sometimes called "surrounding a subject." Start, if you wish, with the encyclopedia article on the subject and run down all the library references given at the end of it. Or start with subject cards in the library that suggest themselves as containing sources of information. Both of these starting points will contain cross references that will enable you to cover most, if not all, of the different phases of your treatment. The general divisions and subdivisions in the classification of knowledge (pages 338–339) that suggest relationship to your subject will yield invaluable aid in making your bibliographical data complete.

A bibliography may be made on regular library cards or on sheets of paper. In final form all entries should be precisely alphabetized. Accompanying every book and article listed should be the author's name, surname first, as fully stated as sources permit, together with the date of birth, and the date of death if the author is not living. Exact titles should be given. In listing books the bibliographer should give the date and place of publication (date of copyright, if different), and the name of the publisher. In listing periodical articles he should give all of these things if possible, though the name of the publisher may not be important; the week or month and year of issue are important, together with the pages covered by the article.

220. Note in the above-reproduced cards that **abbreviations** are used for the sake of economizing space. *Pages,* for instance, is noted by *p, copyright* by *c,* and only the main part of a double or longer publishing name is given. The articles *a* and *the* are often omitted in titles for the reason that they do not in themselves suggest relationship to subject matter. Shakespeare's *The Two Gentlemen of Verona* is cataloged as *Two Gentlemen of Verona* and Dickens' *A Tale of Two Cities* as *Tale of Two Cities,* whereas in other usage these titles should be given exactly. The arrangement of cards in the card-catalog drawers follows this rule of omitting *a* and *the.*

221. In **alphabetizing,** abbreviations are treated as they would be if the terms they stand for were spelled in full, as are figures used as titles; namely, *Sahara, St. Joan, Saks,* and *18th century, eighteenth hole.* The apostrophe is generally disregarded in library alphabetizing; thus, *Girl Scouts Inc., girls' work, girl's* *zest* and *Who goes, Who'd go, Who's going* and *D'antucci, D'Marcuti, L'Fevre, O'Rourke*. Such surname prefixes as *Da, De, La, Le, Van, von* (capital or small letter) follow strict alphabetical order in library cards, as they do in the telephone book. But given-name prefixes are not used unless, of course, they constitute an important part of a title as in *Mr. Emmanuel* and *Dr. Jekyll and Mr. Hyde*. In case the same word represents person, place, subject, title, the library card follows this order:

Hamilton, Alexander (author)
Hamilton, Alexander (title)
Hamilton (Bermuda)
Hamilton (New York)
Hamilton (New Zealand)
Hamilton, secretary of the treasury

Given names of historical, literary, or religious importance precede the same names used as surnames:

Louis, St.
Louis XV
Louis XVI
Louis, Robert P.
Pius VII
Pius, William Vincent

222. The **reference room,** or **reference division,** of the library is probably the most generally used. Its shelves are open. The contents of practically all books in the reference division are alphabetically arranged. There are six main kinds of books in the reference department:

1. *General dictionaries*

Webster's New International Dictionary of the English Language
The New Standard Dictionary of the English Language
The Oxford English Dictionary

The first two are now carried in all libraries. The third is to be found complete in only large libraries, but an abridgment of it called *The Concise Oxford Dictionary* is found practically everywhere and is widely used. Abridgments of the first two—*Collegiate, Practical, Desk, High School,* and still other editions—are likewise to be found in most libraries.

2. *Encyclopedias*

   The Encyclopaedia Britannica
   The Encyclopedia Americana
   The New International Encyclopedia
   The Catholic Encyclopedia
   The Jewish Encyclopedia

3. *Biographical dictionaries*

   Dictionary of National Biography
   Dictionary of American Biography
   Congressional Directory
   Who's Who in America

4. *Almanacs, yearbooks, directories*

   The World Almanac (almanacs of other large newspapers)
   New Standard Encyclopedia Year Book
   Dun and Bradstreet's Directory (financial)
   American Jewish Year Book
   Official Catholic Directory
   Statesman's Year Book

5. *Guides and indexes to periodical and other literature*

   The Readers' Guide to Periodical Literature
   The Cumulative Book Index
   The United States Catalog
   Mudge's Guide to Reference Books
   The Publishers' Weekly

   These are of particular value to research workers and are not always to be consulted at the library without speaking to the librarian in charge. Most periodical publications, including news papers, issue annual or semiannual summaries of certain departments, and these belong under this general heading.

6. *Collections, anthologies, manuals, word books, and the like*

   Crabb's *English Synonyms* (many others)
   Bartlett's *Familiar Quotations* (many others)
   Roget's *Thesaurus of English Words and Phrases*
   Style Manual of the United States Government Printing Office
   Manual of Style of the University of Chicago Press
   Bullfinch's *The Age of Fable*
   Fowler's *Modern English Usage*
   Opdycke's *Get It Right* and *Don't Say It*
   Stevenson's *Home Book of Verse*
   Vizetelly's *Essentials of English Speech and Literature*

The foregoing are representative titles under each classification. Many others could be added, as you will learn by browsing around in the always interesting reference room of your library.

EXERCISES

1. Write author and title catalog cards for each one of your school textbooks.

2. Write an analytic card for some collection of stories or essays or poems that you have at home or at school. Include the table of contents.

3. Make a bibliography of some subject in which you are interested Consult first of all the encyclopedia. Follow this by looking up the library cards for the authorities listed at the end of the article. Look up related headings in the decimal index on pages 338–339, and insert related titles alphabetically from library cards.

4. Look up the following in the card catalog of your library, write a title card for each, and arrange all the cards alphabetically: Zuyder Zee, Leo XIII, Da Vinci, The House of the Seven Gables, Mr. Higginbotham's Catastrophe, Edgar Allan Poe, La Plata, St. John, The Last Supper, Laporte, Van Dyck, von Weber.

REPORTS

223. A report is a well-planned, systematic presentation of facts about some action or enterprise or situation or document (literary or other).

1. The purpose of a report is to give information in compact form for some special reason to some particular individual or group of individuals. The accumulated information is sometimes called **findings.**

2. A report may, in addition to findings, make **recommendations** drawn from the findings. These are usually placed at the end, but they may be transposed to the beginning so that interested readers may see at very first glance what course of action is recommended.

3. A report is based upon experience, experiment, investigation, observation, reading, statistics, study. Every field of activity depends from time to time upon reports made on one phase or another of its practice and development. Reports that are made at regularly stated times are called **periodic reports;** those made for some special reason between these times are called **interim reports.** Business, industry, education, literature (books), sports, library service are the fields in which school and college students are most frequently required to make reports.

4. The general qualities of a good report are the same as those of any other kind of good composition—coherence, compactness, completeness, consistency, emphasis, unity, variety. The special qualities are adaptation, arrangement, and proportion.

5. **Adaptation.** A report made on some public subject for the general reader should be formal in presentation; it should not contain technical terms. A report made on some special subject to individuals who are in the main acquainted with it may be less formal and may, of course, contain terms technical to the subject. A confidential report made to one person or to a group of persons may be informal and even intimate, and it may be

written in regular letter form. In other words, the writer's point of departure in composing his report should be the knowledge already held by the person or persons for whom it is intended.

6. **Arrangement.** Inasmuch as a report is written for special readers, interest may be taken for granted to a large degree. But the facts with which it deals should be presented in the best manner possible for quick and easy grasp. A good outline is imperative, the numbered and lettered headings of which should be run through the report (1) centered above sections or (2) written on the margin or (3) blocked into the written matter (see page 352). In a long report the outline should be adapted as a table of contents so that any part may be referred to quickly and easily. A long report usually has an appendix in which tables and diagrams may be presented, and letters and other papers accumulated in research are arranged in some definite order. Recommendations, however brief, should be separately paragraphed and numbered. Usually they are placed at the end, where they naturally belong; sometimes they are stated at the beginning (see page 347); sometimes they are run through as section or paragraph headings. Most reports open with a line indicating to whom they are made (see page 351). This is usually, but not always, followed by *Dear Sir* or *Dear Sirs* or *Ladies* or *Gentlemen* or *Ladies and Gentlemen* or *Dear Madam*. An intimate, informal report may be addressed to an individual, as *Dear Mr. Brown* or *Dear Miss Peabody*. The complimentary close is always *Respectfully submitted.*

7. **Proportion.** The circumstances or conditions that have made a report necessary or desirable should be stated at the outset, and these should be used as the deciding factor as to how much space is to be devoted to major and minor headings in the outline. Requirements, special or limited, placed upon the writer of a report, should also be indicated at the beginning. Findings should be given *as facts.* In long and elaborate reports these may be accompanied by diagrams, pictures, maps, tables, and the like, or such graphic accompaniments may be placed in the appendix (see above) and carefully keyed. Unimportant

details should be omitted. The major headings of the outline should be carefully held to, and nothing should be mentioned in the report proper that is not indicated in the outline. Recommendations should be kept at a minimum, but each one should cover a particular section or particular sections in the copy. They should be stated uniformly and in order of importance. They are usually prefaced by *It is recommended* or *We recommend,* or *The above findings justify the following recommendations.*

8. The tone of a report should be direct and businesslike. Wordiness and extravagance of expression are very objectionable in a report. Bias or prejudice must, of course, be avoided; even all inclination to evince enthusiasm or to urge acceptance of a recommendation must be firmly resisted. If you have been assigned, for instance, to report on the desirability of a certain piece of land as a sports field, these expressions:

> The proposed field runs for five hundred miles along the river.
> It is recommended that this tract be purchased as a sports field.

are to be preferred to these:

> The proposed field saunters for five hundred wonderful yards along the enchanting Nolachucky River.
> We cannot too highly recommend the purchase of this magnificent area for the training and recreation of our promising American youth.

The latter style of writing is out of place in a report of any kind. The former unemotional, hard-fact style is appropriate because it is pointed and economical.

9. Following is an example of outline for a brief report:

REPORT OF COMMITTEE APPOINTED BY THE BOARD OF TRUSTEES OF HENDERSON ACADEMY TO EXAMINE INTO THE DESIRABILITY AND THE POSSIBILITY OF DISPOSING OF THE PRESENT SPORTS FIELD AND ACQUIRING A NEW ONE

Introduction
I. Circumstances leading to this report
  A. Present field widely condemned
    1. By student body
    2. By teachers

3. By old "grads" and other visitors
4. By athletes and athletic clubs
5. By townspeople, especially shop owners
  B. Joint committee of teachers and students appealed to Board of Trustees
  C. The Trustees requested a formal detailed report on the present field and on proposals for a new one

II. The present field
  A. School has outgrown it
  B. Insufficient accommodations
    1. For spectators
    2. For players
    3. For summer rental
    4. For motor parking
  C. No longer easily accessible
  D. Approaches on all sides hampered by traffic
    1. Two railway crossings
    2. Dangerous turn-ins
  E. Profitable sale now possible
    1. Expansion of Sobel Construction Company on adjacent plots
    2. Readiness of officers to make cash offer

III. The proposed tract
  A. Location
    1. Between Nelson Parkway and Nolachucky River, east and west
    2. Between 43 Boulevard and 55 Avenue, north and south
    3. On main routes through town
    4. Easy access to campus
  B. Size and shape
    1. Almost perfect square, approximately 2500 feet on each side
    2. Ample room for diamond, gridiron, courts, pool, track
    3. Ample parking space within and on all sides for approximately one thousand cars
  C. Terrain
    1. Central part—a perfect level
    2. Lower end low and swampy—may be drained advantageously
    3. Upper end knolly—may be graded or used for required buildings
  D. Sale now imperative in order to settle estate

IV. Results of proposed disposal of old field and acquisition of
    new one
  A. Increased revenues
    1. Attendance
    2. Rentals
  B. Opportunity for increased student participation in all
     forms of sport
  C. Increased advertising values for the academy
  D. Increased business for town—coming and going traffic
     must pass through

 V. On the basis of the above findings your committee recom-
    mends
  A. That old field be sold within next six months
  B. That new field be acquired at once
  C. That the small mortgage necessary to pay for the new
     field over and above the selling price of the old be
     allowed to the general sports organization of the
     academy
  D. That a committee of the Board of Trustees be appointed
     to proceed with these negotiations at once, lest the
     present buying and selling opportunities lapse
  Conclusion

The introductory matter of such a report might well read:

To the Board of Trustees of Henderson Academy
West Heifersville
Tennessee

LADIES AND GENTLEMEN:
  Compliant with your instructions of December 2, 0000, when
you appointed the undersigned a committee of three to look into
the desirability and the possibility of disposing of the present
sports field of Henderson Academy and of acquiring a new one,
the members of your committee supply you the information below,
and follow it with definite recommendations, as requested. They
have made a thorough examination of all the problems entailed,
and they attach at the end of this report all letters, estimates, statistics, surveys, and other papers involved in compiling this report.
Should any questions arise in regard to any of the issues raised,
they stand ready upon call to explain or investigate further.

A typical paragraph (II **E** 1 and 2) in the report:

> On the north, east, and west sides of the present field the Sobel Construction Company has during the past five years erected
> PROFITABLE
> SALE NOW
> POSSIBLE
> model apartment houses with quadrangle gardens, detached buildings, garage conveniences, and other modern arrangements. The Company desires to extend its worthy enterprise and is desirous of acquiring the field for this purpose. The President of the Company has signified his willingness (see exhibit E in appendix) to discuss the purchase with the Board of Trustees, preferably before April 1, 0000.

The heading may be centered at the top of the paragraph, or it may stand independently on the margin without indention.

The conclusion might well read:

> It is the belief of your committee that this report was requested by the Board of Trustees of Henderson Academy at a most opportune time. The old field may now be sold; the proposed new field may now be bought. It is likewise the belief of your committee that action, if taken at all, should be taken now, so that the new field may be made partly, if not entirely, ready for fall athletic events.

> Respectfully submitted

> HORACE SILL, *Chairman*
> JAMES BLANDERSON
> THOMAS WINTERFELDT

February 17, 0000.

REPORTS ON READING

224. The so-called **book report** (**book review** is the better term) may take many different forms. Below is one good form. It is necessarily general inasmuch as it is designed to serve for any type of book.

I. Summary of Theme or Story

Express no opinion as to whether you consider the work good, bad, or indifferent; but summarize the contents, including argument or **plot**, scene, period, background,

```
┌─────────────────────────────────────────────────────┐
│                 MY READING RECORD                     │
│                                                       │
│ Title_____      │
│                                                       │
│ Literary type or classification_____   │
│                                                       │
│ Author_____      │
│                                                       │
│ Publisher_____Date of publication____ │
│                                                       │
│ Edition_____      │
│                                                       │
│ Reason for reading the book_____  │
│                                                       │
│ _____        │
│                                                       │
│ Date begun_____Date finished_____  │
└─────────────────────────────────────────────────────┘
```

atmosphere, character cast, quality and appropriateness of illustrations (if any), and other outstanding features. In conclusion, show whether or not the subject matter is applicable to present-day problems and experiences. It is by no means to be assumed that *all* the points indicated under this heading and the headings that follow are to be discussed in connection with a single piece of literature. They are rather to be considered according as the content of poem, play, story, sketch, essay, or other type of work offers opportunity.

II. Estimates

Tell what this piece of literature has done for you. Have you learned anything about history, geography, science, human character, politics, and so forth? Did it make you think and imagine? Was there anything in it by way of either knowledge or imagination that surprised you? Compare the book with other books in the same field by the same author and by other authors. If possible, tell what estimate has been placed upon it by prominent critics.

III. **Excerpts and References**

Quote from the work to show: (1) what the author's opinions are on certain subjects, (2) what general, lasting opinions are to be found in the book. The latter should, if possible, be epigrams. Make specific references to page, chapter, paragraph, or line.

IV. **Composition Qualities**

List a few words, with meanings, that you have learned from this book. Quote a few sentences that you can prove are especially well written. List any lapses of word usage or sentence construction that you have noticed.

V. **Emotional Qualities**

Explain what made you feel like crying or fighting or laughing or daydreaming. Explain what impressed you as being unlikely or unbelievable, in very good taste or in very bad taste, as especially strong and vivid or weak and vague.

VI. **Additional Remarks**

NAME ....DATE...................
        Last   **First**

INDEX

References are to the folios at the foot of the page.

a, an, 109

Abbreviations, 284–91; to be avoided, 240; capitalization of, 279; common, list of, 286–91; in formal notes, 330; fractional, 285; in letters, 313, 319–20, 327; in library catalog, 343; not to be divided, 65; period with, 240; of titles, 285

ability, capacity, 16

Absolute constructions, 156, 249

Abstract word, 4

Academic degrees, 247; in addresses, 320

Accents, dictionary, 50; word division according to, 64

accept, except, 17

Active voice, 116, 129; conjugation, 121–24

Address, envelope, 292, 319, 328, 331; return, 328

Address, forms of: for business organizations, 285, 320; degrees with, 320; for married woman, 320–21; for military and naval officers, 335; for more than one woman, 322; for officials of church and state, 332–34; for report, 348; for single woman, 320; titles with, 319–20

Adjective clauses, 158–59

Adjective phrases, 155, 156

Adjective pronouns, 103

Adjectives, 108–12; absolute, 111; abstract, 108; articles, 109; attributive, 108; cardinal, 108; comparison of, 110–12; compound, 271, 272; concrete, 108; demonstrative, 108; derived from proper nouns, 277; descriptive, 108; ending in *ly,* 136; extravagant, 112; limiting, 108; numeral, 108; objective, 109; ordinal,

108; participial, 108; predicate, 108 pronominal, 108; proper, 277; substantive, 108

Admiral, forms of address for, 335   -

admission, admittance, 17

Adverbial clauses, 159

Adverbial conjunction, 143

Adverbial objective, 87

Adverbial phrases, 155, 156

Adverbs, 135–37; absolute, 136; comparison of, 136; conjunctive, 143; extravagant, 136; hyphen not to be used with, 273; not to be used with linking verb, 108

advice, advise, 17

affect, effect, 17

after, 27

aggravate, exasperate, 17

ain't, 27

all, compounds of, 17, 59

all ready, already, 17

all right, 27

all-round, 27

all the, 27

all together, altogether, 17

all ways, always, 17

allusion, delusion, illusion, 17

Almanacs, 345

almost, most, 24

Alphabetizing, 343

already, all ready, 17

alternative, choice, 17

altogether, all together, 17

always, 17

a. m., 285, 292

Ambassador, forms of address for, 333

Ambiguity: incompleteness causes, 195; in elliptical clauses, 174–75; in parallel expressions, 180; of pronominal

355

INDEX

INDEX

conscience, conscious, 19

Consistency, 166, 197–205

Consonants, in word divisions, 64

Construction, 73, 147; absolute, 156, 249; balanced, 206–7; choppy, 160; dangling, 173–74; fragments, 99, 156–57, 159, 190; loose, 208; parallel, 177–81, 197–98, 206; periodic, 208; split, 171–72; squinting, 172; stenographic, 327; stringy, 160, 218; variety, 224–25

Consul, forms of address for, 333

consul, council, counsel, 19

contact, 28

contemptible, contemptuous, 19

continual, continuous, 19

Contractions, 284. *See also* Abbreviations

Co-ordinate conjunctions, 142, 143, 160

Co-ordination, faulty, 160

Copulative (linking) verb, 116; followed by adjective, 108

Correlative conjunctions, 143–44, 179

could of, 31

council, counsel, consul, 19

couple, 28

Courtesy construction, 91

credible, creditable, credulous, 20

criticism, 29

Curate, Catholic, form of address for, 334

cute, 36

Dangling constructions; elliptical clauses, 174; phrases, 173–74

Dash, 260–61

data, 29

Date line, in letters, 250, 292, 312–13, 318

Dates, style for writing, 292

Dative. *See* Indirect object

David Copperfield, extract from, 304–5, 308

deal of, many, 29

Dean (church), forms of address for, 334

Declarative sentence, 150

Declension, 73

Deductive method of paragraph development, 307

Definitions, 185

Degrees, academic: in address, 320; punctuation of, 247

Degrees of comparison. *See* Comparison

delusion, allusion, illusion, 17

Demonstrative adjective, 108

Demonstrative pronouns, 102

Denotation, 5

Dependent (subordinate) clauses, 157–61

Description, outline for, 297, 299

desert, dessert, 20

Determination, expressed by *will* and *shall,* 127

Development of paragraph, 307–10; by comparison, 308; by contrast, 308; by deductive method, 307; by enumeration of effects, 309; by inductive method, 308; by oratorical devices, 308; by repetition, 309

device, devise, 20

Dewey Decimal System, 337–39

Diagonal style in letters, 315, 317

Dialect, 1

Dialogue: paragraphing of, 302; punctuation of, 267; quotation marks for, 267

Dickens, Charles, quoted, 237–38, 304–5

Diction, 1

Dictional Demons, 16–27

Dictionaries, 2–3; abridged, 3; biographical, 345; general, 344

different, 29

Digraph, 50, 65

Diphthong, 50

Direct discourse, 265–66

Directories, 345

discomfit, discomfort, 20

discover, invent, 20

disremember, 29

Dissyllable, 50

dive, past tense of, 29

Division of words, 63–65; according to accent, 64; of compound terms, 64; of consonants, single and double, 64; digraphs, 65; hyphened terms, 64; *le* ending, 65; one- and two-letter, 65; after prefixes, 64; of short words, 65;

INDEX

for instance, punctuation with, 256

Foreign nouns, plurals of, 78

Foreign terms: articles, 277; compound, 273; italicized, 294; pompous, 37

Formal notes, 330

formally, formerly, 21

Fractions, 271

Fragments, sentence (period fault), 241; clauses, 99, 159, 190; phrases, 156–57, 190

Friendly letter, 317, 323

full, compounds with, 59

funny, 30

further, farther, 21

Future tense, 127; present tense used for, 127

Gender, 76–77

Generals, military, forms of address for, 335

Generic word, 3

genial, congenial, 19

Gerund, 131; possessive case with, 85, 94

get, loose usage of, 30

gorgeous, 36

gotten, 30

Governor, forms of address for, 333

grand, 36

guarantee, guaranty, 21

h, indefinite article before word beginning with, 109

Habitual action, expressed by *would,* 128

Hackneyed terms, 39, 327

had of, 31

had ought, 30

hang, 21

Hanging indention: in outlines, 296; paragraph, 301

happen, transpire, 26

he, in place of *one,* 91

Heading of letter, 312, 314

healthful, healthy, wholesome, 21

Henry, Patrick, quoted, 308–9

his, general reference of, 91

Historical present, 127, 199, 212

home, 30

Homonyms, 12–15; list of, 13–15

honest, honorable, 21

House-that-Jack-built (endless-chain, tandem) construction, 160, 219

human, humane, 22

hygienic, sanitary, 22

Hyphen, 270–73; between adjective and participle, 272; to avoid ambiguity, 271; when one adjective modifies another, 272; in compound modifiers, 271; in compounds containing a possessive, 271; in compounds containing a verb and a preposition or an adverb, 272; in compound of noun and prepositional phrase, 272; with co-ordinate nouns, 272; with *elect* and *general,* 273; in fractions, 271; to form new term, 272; after individual modifiers of same word, 272; in noun formed from verbal and adverb, 272; in noun-adjective modifier, 272; in numerals, 271; with certain prefixes and combining forms, 272–73; between prefix and proper adjective, 271; to separate similar vowels, 271

I in letters, 327; position of, in series, 91

Idiom, 42

Idiomatic usage, 1

ie and *ei* (spelling), 57

illusion, allusion, delusion, 17

immanent, imminent, eminent, 20

immigration, emigration, 20

Imperative mode, 130

Imperative sentence, 150

Imperfect tense. *See* Past tense

Impersonal subject, 151

Impersonal verb, 116

imply, infer, 22

import, importance, 22

Impropriety, 16, 42

in, superfluous, 30

in back of, 30

in re, 326

Inclosures in letters, 326

Incomplete predication, verb of, 116

Incompleteness, permissible, 190

Indefinite pronouns, 102–4

Indefinite reference, 167–68

INDEX

INDEX

Proper nouns, 74; abbreviations of, 285; capitalization of, 74, 276; compound, plural of, 264; plural, 79; possessive, 84, 263, 264; used as common nouns, 74

propose, purpose, 25

proposition, person, 25

proven, 33

provided, providing, 25

Provincialism, 45

Punctuation: close, in letters, 315, 317; of direct discourse, 265–67; of indirect discourse, 265; open, in letters, 314, 315, 316, 319–20; of outlines, 296; with parentheses, 261; placement of, with quotation marks, 266; of salutations, 258, 323. *See also* individual marks, as Comma, Period, Semicolon, etc.

purpose, propose, 25

Quadrisyllable, 50

quantity, amount, number, 17

Questions: indirect, 265; *shall* and *will* in, 127

Question mark. *See* Interrogation point

quiet, quite, 25

Quiller-Couch, Sir Arthur T., quoted, 306–7

quite, 33

quite, quiet, 25

quite a few, quite a little, quite some, 33

Quotation marks, 265–68; for consecutive paragraphs, 267; for direct discourse, 265–67; in place of italics, 294; for literary titles, 267; for nicknames, 267; when not used, 268; with other punctuation, 266; single, 267; for slang, 267; for technical terms, 267

Quotations (discourse): capitalization of, 278; direct, 265–67; formal, 258; indirect, 265; informal, 249, 258; interpolations, 263; interrupted, 266; paragraphing of, 302; quotation within, 267; *shall* and *will* in, 128; unquoted matter within, 263. *See also* Quotation marks

Rabbi, forms of address for, 334

raise, rise, 25

rarely, 33

re, 326

real, 33

reason . . . because, 183

receipt, recipe, 25

Redundancy, 39

Reference pronominal, 166–70; broad, 167; divided, 169; indefinite, 167; weak, 168. *See also* Antecedent

Reference books: cataloging of, 340, 342; list of, 344–45

Reflexive pronouns, 90–91

regardless, 33

relations, relatives, 25

Relative adverbs, 143

Relative clauses, 99, 158, 245–46

Relative pronouns, 96–99; compound, 96, 97; co-ordinate conjunctions with, 99; omission of, 98; placement of, 98. *See also* Antecedent; Reference, pronominal

remainder, rest, 18; *number of,* 103

Repetition: for emphasis, 205; of introductory and connecting words, 223; unnecessary, 222

Reports, 347–54; adaptation, 347; address, 348; appendix, 348; arrangement, 347; book, 352–54; complimentary close, 348; conclusion, 352; findings, 347, 348; interim, 347; introduction, 351; outline, 348, 349–51; paragraph, typical, 352; periodic, 347; proportion, 348; recommendations, 347, 348, 349; salutation, 348

Representative, United States, forms of address for, 333

reputation, character, 19

Resolved, punctuation with, 258

respectfully, respectively, 26

rest, remainder, 18; *number of,* 103

Restrictive clauses, 99, 158, 245, 248

Restrictive phrases, 245, 247

Retained object, 87, 129

Return address. 328

right, 33

rise, raise, 25

INDEX

Roman numerals, no punctuation after, 241
Root (spelling), 50
Run-in outline, 299
Run-on sentence, 220
Running outline, 297
Ruskin, John, quoted, 308

Salutations: in business letters, 321–23; capitalization, 278; compound, 323; for military and naval officers, 335; for officials of church and state, 332–34; punctuation, 241, 250, 258; in report, 348, 351; for women, 322, 323
same, 33, 97
sanitary, hygienic, 22
say, 34
Scott, Walter, quoted, 304
Seasons, personified, 277
Second sheet of business letter, 323
see, 34
seldom, 34
Semicolon, 254–56; before clauses beginning with conjunctive adverbs, 255; in compound sentences, 220, 248, 254; in compound-complex sentences, 248, 254; in constructions containing comma, 255; not to be followed by dash, 260; position of, in relation to quotation marks, 266
Senator, United States, forms of address for, 333
Sentence fragments (period fault), 241; clause, 99, 159, 190; phrase, 99, 156–57, 190
Sentence outline, 298
Sentences: analysis, 161–62; complex, 157, 159; compound, 157, 159; declarative, 150; exclamatory, 150; fragments, 99, 156–57, 159, 190; imperative, 150; interrogative, 150; loose, 208; periodic, 208; run-on, 220; simple, 150–54; summary, 303; topic, 303
Sequence of time and place, 202
Sequence of tenses, 128
series, 34
Series, punctuation of, 244, 255

set, sit, 26
shall and *will:* in future tense, 127; in indirect questions, 128; in questions, 127
Ships, italic for names of, 294
should, 128
should of, 31
Shultz-Gerhard, quoted, 149
sight of, 34
Sign of the infinitive, 130
Signature, 325–26; legal, 325; of married woman, 325; titles with, 325
Sister Superior, forms of address for, 334
sit, set, 26
size, 34
Slang, 37, 267–68
so (adverb), 34
so (conjunction), punctuation with, 255
so . . . as, for negative comparison, 28
so . . . as (correlatives), 144, 193
so . . . that, 144
sold, 34
Solid words, 273–75
some, 34
some place, 27
somebody, 103
somewhere, 27
sort of, 30
Speaker of the House, forms of address for, 332
species, 34
Specific words, 3
Spelling, 49–63; accents, 50; compound words, 270–75; definitions, 50; *ei* and *ie*, 57; errors due to mispronunciation, 61; final consonant, 53–56; final *e*, 50–52; final *y*, 57; homonyms, 12–15; hyphened words, 271–73; prefixes, 59; solid words, 274–75; suffixes, 59–61; troublesome words, list of, 61–63
Split constructions, 171
Split infinitive, 171–72
Squinting construction, 172
State officials, forms of address for, 332–34
stationary, stationery, 26
statue, stature, statute, 26
Stem (spelling), 50